ATLANTIS

THE ANTEDILUVIAN WORLD

by Ignatius Donnelly

With a New Introduction by
E. F. BLEILER

DOVER PUBLICATIONS, INC.
NEW YORK

This Dover edition, first published in 1976, is an
unabridged and unaltered republication of the
work originally published by Harper & Brothers,
New York, in 1882. E. F. Bleiler has written a
new Introduction and supplied notes especially for
the Dover edition.

International Standard Book Number: 0-486-23371-5
Library of Congress Catalog Card Number: 76-24138

Manufactured in the United States of America
Dover Publications, Inc.
180 Varick Street
New York, N. Y. 10014

IGNATIUS DONNELLY AND ATLANTIS

THE men who make the great myths remain nameless, for the most part, unless they happen to be religious leaders. And for the most part mythopoets are fortunate if they create a single viable myth. Ignatius Donnelly, American politician, scholar and author, however, had the remarkable distinction of having created three of the golden myths of our day, myths that have gained tens of thousands of adherents, have permeated the thought and culture of later years, and have even stimulated their own rebuttal and disappearance.

These three myths are the concept of Atlantis as the mother of all civilization, the demonstration by mathematical means that Bacon wrote Shakespeare's plays and embodied a cipher message in them, and the explanation of geological features by cataclysms from the sky. Each of these myths is demonstrably false, yet each has reached far into the life and literature of the world. Each may have done some small harm, but each has also brought much pleasure to certain readers.

The historical Ignatius Donnelly (1831–1901) was not the man one might have expected to create scientific dreams. He was a land speculator in Minnesota, a gentleman farmer, and a medium-time politician who operated in and out of the various parties of his day. Sometimes he was a Republican, less often a Democrat, much more frequently a Populist of one sort or another. His affiliation was dependent on a very elaborate interplay between opportunism and principle.

Ignatius Donnelly was born in Philadelphia of Irish stock.

His father was an almost penniless immigrant who worked his way through medical school, while Ignatius's mother conducted a pawnshop to keep husband and growing family in necessities. Not long after receiving his licence, however, Donnelly Sr. caught yellow fever from one of his patients and died, leaving the family in very poor circumstances. This early poverty undoubtedly conditioned many of Ignatius Donnelly's ideas about money and security.

By the 1850's Ignatius Donnelly had become a Philadelphia lawyer, first training in a prestigious law office, then hanging out his own shingle. He found it impossible to make a living, however, and after working for a time settling immigrants westward, in 1857 he and his wife moved to Minnesota to take advantage of the frontier land boom. He became a partner in the development of Nininger City, which was about fifteen miles south of St. Paul. In Nininger City, which was a moderately savory speculation, the modus operandi was obtaining cheap land, subdividing it by means of imaginary streets, selling suckers lots covered with glowing predictions, pressuring railways and state governments for development—and profiteering. Donnelly worked hard at this, even to shilling through the railroad cars filled with would-be pioneers, pointing out the rosy future for Nininger City. For a time Donnelly thought himself a millionaire, but the land boom collapsed, and he was fortunate to evade the bankruptcy fate that met most of his fellows in land sharking.

A natural outgrowth of city founding was political activity, and in a short time Donnelly had drifted into local politics, where he remained for the rest of his life. He started his career as a Radical Republican, but his allegiance over the next fifty years shifted through just about every available range of state-level politics. It would be pointless to list the variations.

Donnelly's political life graphed two humps. His earlier life shows a strange balancing between self-aggrandizement and conscience, a series of controversies and compromises among expediency, desire for profit (which never came) and principles (which did exist). He claimed his loyalty lay with these principles and was above party or individuals; his opponents claimed it lay with his own interests. On the external level he backed some progressive legislation, fought on behalf of the emancipated Negroes and unpopular battle against race prejudice, and took on the corruption of the Indian Agency in Washington. Yet he also took bribes from the railroads, sold information to profiteers, and made deals in the areas he was supposed to be cleansing. He was recognized as an outstanding parliamentarian and as one of the finest florid orators of the day.

Something must have happened during the middle period of Donnelly's life, though, some gradual change, for in his later years a very different Ignatius Donnelly was to be met with in Minnesota. This was an Ignatius Donnelly who quite consciously allied himself with small Populist groups that he knew had no chance of winning; a man who, as state senator, did his best to break the milling, mining, lumbering and railroad monopolies, and devoted his life to improving the lot of the "common man." From an agile performer on the political trampoline, he had become a universally respected statesman.

Donnelly was lieutenant governor of Minnesota for two terms during the Civil War period; congressman from Minnesota for several terms in the 1860's and 1870's; and state senator in Minnesota at scattered intervals up until very late in his life. His politics became national in 1900 when he was vice-presidential candidate for the Mid-Road People's Party, a Middle Western splinter group with strong socialist leanings. He died of a stroke on New Year's Day, 1901.

In person Ignatius Donnelly was short, fat, red-headed—in appearance very similar to George McManus's Jiggs. (His political enemies called him Ignis fatuus.) Ebullient, witty, hardworking, gifted with remarkable powers of self-conviction, cheerful despite repeated misfortune on all levels of life, he never quite reached the apple that the gods (or the larger political bosses) kept dangling before him.

This Ignatius Donnelly, the historical Ignatius Donnelly, is practically forgotten today except by historians of the State of Minnesota or of splinter political parties of the late nineteenth century. The Ignatius Donnelly that is remembered today was the author of three novels that were popular and socially influential and three historical fantasies. How this second Donnelly matches the politician is a matter for speculation.

What enthusiasm led a hardworking opportunistic idealist to take the minor idea of Atlantis, which had been lying about idly since the Renaissance, spend years of research in a dozen areas of science, and reintroduce Atlantis as a major scientific myth? What led him into the even larger, even more thankless task of performing intricate calculations for years, to extract mathematically a trivial message he thought was enciphered in Shakespeare's plays?

We do not know. His mental processes are not known. Perhaps they can be deduced from the 90-odd boxes of letters, notes and diaries in the collection of the Minnesota Historical Society in St. Paul. All we can do is comment on the activities of Donnelly, the energetic, erratic, learned, misdirected cultural force.

Let us consider Donnelly's three novels first. Today they are almost forgotten, but during the 1890's they circulated by the hundreds of thousands among left-oriented workers and farmers, who read them avidly. Much the most important of these novels was *Caesar's Column* (1889), which sold more than a quarter of a million copies throughout activist circles just before the turn of the century. A negative utopia, set in New York in the 1980's, it pictured a world where great families and monopolies own everything and viciously exploit the downtrodden public. The plot of the novel is based on the experiences of an outsider, a colonist from Kenya, who lives through the revolution that overthrows the bosses and shatters the corrupt civilization.

Donnelly's other two novels are less important. *Doctor Huguet* (1891) strikes out against race prejudice. A white doctor and a Negro criminal exchange bodies by unexplained supernatural means, and both suffer. Donnelly's intention was good, but today many of the details would be regarded as offensive. *The Golden Bottle* (1892) is a political allegory advocating abandonment of metal standards. Donnelly's solution for all economic ills was controlled issuance of scrip to restrain the over-wealthy and the usurious.

All three novels are political in the larger sense, fantastic in idea and in treatment, and somewhat amateurish. Like so many of the offshoots of nineteenth-century socialist thought they contain germs of totalitarianism as well as elements of libertarianism and anarchism. In them one can find either strain of development.

Much more important, ultimately, than even the very widely read *Caesar's Column* were Donnelly's three fantasies of history.

Atlantis: The Antediluvian World was the first of these. Written during his spare time in Minnesota, it was published by Harper's in 1882, and went through twenty-three printings by 1890. It was well received critically, on the whole, and was treated with respect, if at times with serious disagreement. Donnelly, the overall feeling went, was not a crank, but he was wrong.

To anticipate what I shall mention in more detail below, *Atlantis: The Antediluvian World* became the "standard" account of Atlantis, and set the pattern for all later work in this area. It was probably the most influential pseudo-scientific work of the later nineteenth century.

The second myth created by Ignatius Donnelly was less successful financially, critically and historically. This was the theory embodied in *Ragnarok: The Age of Fire and Gravel* (1883). Donnelly, basing his arguments on geology and comparative mythology, explained certain earth features

by catastrophic interference from outside the earth. He proposed that a great comet had sailed close to the earth,
created various upheavals, dumped loads of gravel and stone
on earth (whence what we now call glacial till and tillite),
and gave rise to oceans of myth and folklore.

Ragnarok: The Age of Fire and Gravel, however, did not
succeed. Its imagination was too great and its argument too
weak. It was ridiculed by scientists and after a time ignored
by laymen, who quite reasonably did not care where till
came from and looked askance at "scientific" explanations
of the Bible. It remained for the twentieth century to become
excited over newer but similar strains of extraterrestrial
catastrophism offered by Hoerbiger, Bellamy and, most
important of all, Velikovsky.

Donnelly's third flight was *The Great Cryptogram: Francis
Bacon's Cipher in the So-Called Shakespeare Plays* (1887),
his contribution to the Bacon-Shakespeare delusion. Before
Donnelly's book there had been a few books and articles
proposing Francis Bacon as the author of the Shakespearean
plays, but everything that went before Donnelly and everything that came later was trivial compared to Donnelly's
contribution. A gigantic volume that embodied an incredible
amount of detailed work, *The Great Cryptogram* first surveyed the biography and cultural settings of Shakespeare and
Bacon, carefully analyzing parallelisms of thought and language between the plays and Bacon's acknowledged writings.
The second and more important part of the book used mathematical tabulations to extract from the plays a hidden history
that Bacon did not care to record elsewhere.

Donnelly worked out his cryptogram by starting with the
words "Bacon" and "St. Albans" in the First Folio text of
the *Henry* plays. He believed he saw number relationships
between the numerical word position of such elements on
the printed page and such matters as italics and brackets.
Eventually, after immense arithmetical labor, using "constants" which were really convenience numbers that enabled
him to find the next word that would make sense, Donnelly

extracted a few pages of innocuous court scandal. But, as has been demonstrated many times since, using similar techniques one can extract messages from almost any passage of text.

The Great Cryptogram was received with great excitement. Many scholars, including a mathematical referee, were bowled over by Donnelly's arithmetic, and its other arguments were taken seriously by many people who should have known better. *The Great Cryptogram* also aroused popular interest, since the late nineteenth century was one of the high points of Shakespeare-idolatry, and Donnelly found that he had a good source of income from debating with unbelievers and lecturing to believers. In later years such lectures in the United States and England became his main source of income.

During the very last years of Donnelly's life his historical tripos fell somewhat into disrepute. Atlantis, as more was learned about archeology and geology, melted away; and the Baconian cipher was overshadowed for the zealous by even more elaborate disentanglements. For more thoughtful readers the flaws in Donnelly's work became exposed with *The Cipher in the Plays and on the Tombstone* (1899), Donnelly's last work in this field. Here Donnelly analyzed Shakespeare's tombstone in Stratford-on-Avon, and incidentally revealed that Bacon had written not only Marlowe's and Ben Jonson's plays but also *The Pilgrim's Progress* and *Don Quixote*. This was enough to sink any reader's confidence.

II

Atlantis: The Antediluvian World, today, has no scientific relevance except in some of its smaller, incidental details. It is best seen as an unwitting act of fiction or as a prolonged poetic trope. In terms of archeology and anthropology the civilization of Atlantis is an un-necessity, and in terms of geology the submergence of Atlantis is as likely to have happened as Noah's flood.

In its own day, however, Donnelly's work was not as

rickety as it is today, and Donnelly has suffered much unjust criticism from a vantage point of seventy-five years and more later. Donnelly was not a lunatic nor an occultist, and much of what was wrong with *Atlantis: The Antediluvian World* was what was wrong with the state of knowledge in his day, both in facts and in scientific method.

Let us ignore Donnelly's deplorable rhetoric and rhapsody, which belong more to a debating society than to a work that pretends to be scientific, and examine his major ideas and areas of research in terms of their own historical milieu as well as our own.

(1) *Plato's Atlantis.* Donnelly assumed that Plato's account was meant to be taken literally, and that beyond the Greek text stood a matching historical reality.

No sane modern scholar, in all probability, would accept Donnelly's double thesis, but it should also be pointed out that there is no agreement about Plato's account: why Plato wrote it, what sources he may have used, and how it should be interpreted.

Summarizing the more reasonable modern interpretations of Plato's narratives in the *Timaeus* and *Critias* would lead us too far astray, but it might be valuable to see the range of opinion against which Donnelly can be matched today.

The strongest, most generally accepted interpretation of the Platonic Atlantis, today and in Donnelly's day, has been that Plato created Atlantis as a philosophical myth, and that it is pure imagination embellished suitably to create verisimilitude. A variant of this theory interprets the struggle between Atlantis and the Athens of 9600 B.C. as a parallel to and perhaps an allegory of the struggle between Persia and Greece, Orient and Occident.

Several other strong modern theories regard Plato's Atlantis as a reworking and elaboration of bits and shreds of local traditions, history, mythical patterns and travellers' tales, to which Plato supplied a form. The most important of these interpretations equates Atlantis with a garbled memory of the Minoan culture of Crete. A further refinement identifies the historical volcanic destruction of the island of Thera, around 1500 B.C., with both the destruction of Minoan culture and the folk memories that evolved into Atlantis. For scholars holding these theories Plato's text is far removed from historical reality and very little of Plato's Atlantis remains.

Still another significant modern theory removes the onus from Greece, and taking Plato's text literally, identifies Atlantis as a collection of dragomans' tales from Egypt, picked up and further misunderstood by Greek tourists. According to this theory, Plato was simply reporting what he had heard.

Thus it can be seen that there is no agreement what Plato's Atlantis signified, and it does not seem likely that there ever will be agreement.

(2) *Catastrophic continental subsidence.* Ignatius Donnelly did not distinguish between local disasters, which were well enough recorded in his day, and the destruction of a continent. It is one thing to sink a few square miles of Lisbon or Iceland, another to drown perhaps a million square miles overnight.

Yet in Donnelly's day geology was an infant science, and his position, though extreme, was not outside the range of acceptance. Eighteenth and nineteenth-century geology sheltered many theories of violent earth action, and the concept of cataclysm was still current during Donnelly's lifetime. It was a commonplace of historical geology to speak of cataclysmic events, often involving continental submergences, as demarcating the major geological periods. Indeed, well into the twentieth century one can find reputable geologists writing of land bridges that might break or sink in relatively brief periods. Where Donnelly differed was in time; he believed that the gods worked very fast. In general we may say that Donnelly was an extremist within a not yet discarded scientific set. He was wrong, but not discreditably.

The second geological prop for Donnelly's Atlantis was the discovery of sea-bottom geography by the famous Challenger oceanographic expedition. The Atlantic sea-bottom, it was revealed, was not a flat plain, but a surface that concealed long, puzzling submarine ridges and mountains. Odd rocks, too, were to be found near the site of Plato's Atlantis. Donnelly interpreted these phenomena as evidences for Atlantis, an interpretation which was wrong. But his contemporaries and their successors, up until a few years ago, did not know how to explain these ridges, and much conventional geology and zoology was based on supercontinents and land bridges that had become submerged. Donnelly cites, for example, the hypothetical continent of Lemuria (invented to explain the erratic distribution of lemurs in the Old World), which was not discarded until a generation or so ago. Among the authorities whom Donnelly cites frequently and properly, it will be observed, are Lyell and Darwin.

(3) *The Atlantean colonies in the New World and anthropology.* Surprisingly enough, in his facts, Donnelly was pretty much abreast of the American archeology of his day; it was just that so little was known. It is difficult for us to remember that when Donnelly wrote, practically nothing was known of pre-Columbian cultures in the United States beyond a few artifacts looted from mounds and shellheaps. Everything came after Donnelly's publication date: the ethnographic surveys published by the Bureau of American Ethnology and the universities, the excavations in the Southwest, the isolation of the various Mississippi and Woodland cultures—all this came one generation, two generations, almost three generations after Donnelly's work.

In Middle and South America, too, Donnelly was reasonably up to date. He knew as much about the Aztecs and Incas as was available—excavations had not yet been undertaken. Almost nothing was known about the Maya: only a few illustrations of stelae and ruins in travellers' accounts, the Landa "alphabet," and LePlongeon's fantastic interpretations of minor discoveries in Yucatan. A decade after Donnelly's book appeared, the first serious studies of Maya hieroglyphs began with Seler and Bowditch; excavation waited much longer.

Much the same holds true for Donnelly's Old World archeology. The rough division of the stone and metal ages had been worked out in Scandinavia, where they had some relevance. Donnelly assumed that this classification was universally valid and extremely important, a belief which the professional archeologists and historians of his day shared. Donnelly knew about Swiss lake dwellings. His comments about the lack of archeology in Egypt before the age of the pyramid builders were valid as fact in his day, no matter how far his interpretation went astray. The pre-dynastic cultures of Egypt were not really known until the 1920's.

As far as anthropology proper goes, here, too, Donnelly knew and utilized the important English-language books, Tylor's *Primitive Culture,* and the works of Brinton and Lubbock. It might not be too strong to say that beyond Tylor and Lubbock there really was nothing else in English worth reading at this time.

(4) *Linguistic material.* Donnelly quoted with approval older sources that tried to show linguistic relationships by tabulating words that looked somewhat alike from one language to another. This was a generally accepted method in the early and middle nineteenth century, and it is still conditionally valid although dangerous, since it does not allow for loan words or chance. Today, a linguistic anthropologist prefers to work with grammatical material even more than with vocabularies derived by sophisticated means; yet, all else failing (as a reader in Bureau of American Ethnology Reports of a few years back will see), vocabulary comparisons are still used. The difference is that a modern specialist studying, say, vocabularies from two South American tribes resident a few score miles apart has a reasonable basis for relationship. Ignatius Donnelly, writing of Welsh and Man-

dans, 5,000 miles apart, 1,000 years apart, did not—if Atlantis is subtracted.

Grimm's Law and Werner's Law were still novelties, although generally accepted, and there was still a thrill inherent in the Indo-European family of languages, but Donnelly, if he had used German sources, could have done much better with his linguistic material. The same criticism should be made of Donnelly's work in classical scholarship and comparative religions, two arteries in his work. Donnelly suffered badly by relying on English-language sources. I do not know if he could read German, but if he had been aware of the penetrating work that was being done on classical culture by men like Mommsen and Bachofen, his comments on classical religion might have moved beyond the level of Bulfinch's *Mythology*.

If we turn to the larger presuppositions within Donnelly's working method, we can see that here, too, he was not far astray for his time. In fact, occasionally he is quite valid.

Donnelly was essentially an arch-geneticist in the study of cultures. He assumed that similarities between one culture and another indicated common descent or, less important to him, borrowing. If, for example, the North American Indians had occasional copper axes of a certain shape and this same shape was also to be found in Danish axes, Donnelly assumed that there had to be a relationship between the two cultures. A modern archeologist might conclude (from the axes shown) that the process of hammering out cold metal tended to create certain shapes. Donnelly explained likenesses between crude incised pottery from various parts of the world as evidences of common descent. A modern anthropologist might notice a band of such pottery across Siberia, through North America into New England, and wonder about the spread of an idea or technique.

Even today, however, the question of resemblances between pre-Columbian artifacts, customs, institutions, myths, economic plants, and so on, and those of the Old World is far from being settled. Donnelly assumed connections, while

Americanists on the whole have considered the higher American civilizations as independent. Yet this is not a one-sided matter, and there are many reputable anthropologists who accept connections, on individual points, between Old and New World. They would accept, for instance, genetic relationships between the very early Valdivia pottery of Ecuador and the prehistoric pottery of Japan; the spread of the banana (plantain) to the Americas before Columbus, botanical relationships between Old World and New World cottons, the diffusion of the sweet potato across the Pacific from South America in prehistoric times, relationships between ancient Oriental and ancient Mexican calendrical systems, close resemblances between board games in India and Middle America, Buddhist iconography on Mexican monuments, and much else. Donnelly, strangely enough, called attention to many of these points almost a hundred years ago, and in Part III of his book raised many questions that might have been extremely fruitful. There was nothing wrong with his making the comparisons he made, and he should not be censured for pointing out resemblances. It was just that he offered for everything a one-word answer, Atlantis.

A second conceptual frame, strongly present in nineteenth-century thought, put Donnelly into difficulties in both Atlantis and Elizabethan England. These were the notions of folkloristic syncretism and philosophical monism, which permeated many places where they did not belong. At this time a strong thrust existed toward Systems and Supersystems that would encompass everything in their folds. Schelling, Hegel, Spencer, Marx, all tried to create pyramids that worked up toward unities and down toward multiplicity. In folklore and comparative religion, which were sister fields to Donnelly's researches, the same concepts occasionally held. If one uncovered a mass of Finnish songs, one strung them together into a *Kalevala*, whether they belonged together or not. One worked out an elaborate pedigree and an enormous master form that encompassed all variants. Like the great scholars Max Mueller and James Frazer one could interpret the world's mysteries in terms of sun worship or sacred kings.

This concept of structural monism caused much mischief in Donnelly's work, since it pushed him into syncretisms far beyond his data. He sought one source and one answer, instead of a multitude of sources and answers. In his studies of Renaissance literature this consistency and rigidity drove him into assigning the works of Marlowe, Jonson, Cervantes (in English), and Bunyan to a single source, since they shared common traits of language. This was just as logical as assigning Shakespeare to Bacon. Unfortunately, Donnelly never recognized the implications of reading his equation backwards.

A third epistemological factor in Donnelly's work has often been criticized. Donnelly worked in a circle: he found his answer first, then looked about for supporting data. I am not sure, however, that I would wholly agree with the criticism here. As Lord Keynes has shown, in his essay on Isaac Newton, Newton followed exactly the same method. He "intuited" the principle of gravity, then looked about for evidence to support it. Where Newton differed from Donnelly was in inherent checks that balanced his venturing, perhaps some sort of preestablished harmony that Donnelly lacked. Newton stopped when he discovered that the motion of the moon did not fit his theory. But he held his mind, and when new data of the moon's motion were published, reexamined his theory and discovered that he was right. Donnelly lacked such a bridling.

Donnelly worked with facts and theories that on the whole were not discreditable or discredited in his day; he used methodologies that were in vogue and are sometimes still valid; he pointed out many paradoxes and anomalies and raised many questions that deserved answers—but emerged with a whole that was wrong. When he observed the likenesses between the pyramids of ancient Mexico and those of

Egypt, when he noticed that the Maya *Popul Vuh* contained themes parallel to European folklore, by asking the right questions and leaving the questions open for later research, he might have accomplished much. Instead, he inserted as an explanation an easy middle term: Atlantis. He thereby violated two of the old philosophical saws: *ne ignotum per ignotius* and *essentia non sunt multiplicanda praeter necessitatem.*

If one creates models to explain phenomena, one should be prepared to discard them if they do not work. Donnelly's Atlantis (if the obvious loose ends and flapping tags are cut off) had a certain low degree of fit within the knowledge of 1880. By 1890 it had far less, and by 1900 it had none at all. But Donnelly, despite his truly impressive learning and industry, did not have an open mind and missed the chance to play Zeus and sink Atlantis once again.

III

WHY should Dover Publications reprint a book that cannot be taken seriously, a book that is admittedly wrong in all its major conclusions, and can never be rehabilitated?

The answer is a strange aside of Western cultural history. Donnelly's *Atlantis: The Antediluvian World* is a remarkable tour de force. His enthusiasm vivified what might have been embalmed in a cabinet, and turned it into a book vital for certain temperaments. Donnelly created a vision of a golden past, of soaring adventurers spreading civilization around the world, of Edens that once existed, were let perish—and should be a lesson to all of us. Strangely enough there is a moral in Donnelly's Atlantis, just as there was in Plato's: power corrupts.

More than this—Donnelly's *Atlantis: The Antediluvian World* has served as a catapult book. Itself unworthy, it has led many young readers into, first, wonder and question, then disillusionment, then into serious science. Like the

Mars books of Edgar Rice Burroughs it has been an unwitting culture bearer. I, personally, do not regard Burroughs
very highly, yet it is true, as Ray Bradbury has pointed out,
that an astonishing number of today's physicists, mathematicians and engineers cut their wisdom teeth on Burroughs and moved on. It has been much the same with
Ignatius Donnelly's book. It stimulated an interest that finally
found fruition in serious work.

Even more—Donnelly's *Atlantis: The Antediluvian World*
has served as the source for many other books in one of the
steadiest streams of diffusion in literature. Scores, perhaps
hundreds, of works of fiction stand in his debt, and a strong
strain in modern science-fiction would not be understood
without recourse to Donnelly. Donnelly may not have been
the Balboa he thought himself, but he was the John Mande-
ville of his day.

New York, 1976   E. F. BLEILER

FURTHER READING

Martin Ridge. *Ignatius Donnelly, The Portrait of a Politician.* Chicago, 1962. A very full account of Donnelly's
political career, which avoids the bowdlerization of
earlier biographical accounts.

William F. Friedman and Elizebeth S. Friedman. *The Shakespearean Ciphers Examined.* New York, 1958. The great
American cryptographer analyzes Donnelly's Baconian
work in detail.

L. Sprague de Camp. *Lost Continents. The Atlantis Theme
in History, Science, and Literature.* New York, 1970.
A thorough, scholarly debunking account.

Henry M. Eichner. *Atlantean Chronicles.* Alhambra, California, 1971. Not on the same level as de Camp's work,
but useful for many summaries of modern science-fiction
dealing with Atlantis.

CONTENTS.

PART I.

THE HISTORY OF ATLANTIS.

Chap.   Page

I. The Purpose of the Book 1

II. Plato's History of Atlantis 5

III. The Probabilities of Plato's Story 22

IV. Was such a Catastrophe Possible? 31

V. The Testimony of the Sea 46

VI. The Testimony of the Flora and Fauna 54

PART II.

THE DELUGE.

I. The Destruction of Atlantis described in the Deluge
Legends 65

II. The Deluge of the Bible 68

III. The Deluge of the Chaldeans 75

IV. The Deluge Legends of other Nations 85

V. The Deluge Legends of America 98

VI. Some Consideration of the Deluge Legends 119

PART III.

THE CIVILIZATION OF THE OLD WORLD AND NEW COMPARED.

I. Civilization an Inheritance 129

II. The Identity of the Civilizations of the Old World and
the New 136

III. American Evidences of Intercourse with Europe or Atlantis 165

Chap.   Page

  IV. Corroborating Circumstances 171
   V. The Question of Complexion 183
  VI. Genesis contains a History of Atlantis 198
 VII. The Origin of our Alphabet 214
VIII. The Bronze Age in Europe. 237
  IX. Artificial Deformation of the Skull 268

PART IV.

*THE MYTHOLOGIES OF THE OLD WORLD A RECOLLECTION OF
ATLANTIS.*

   I. Traditions of Atlantis 276
  II. The Kings of Atlantis become the Gods of the Greeks . 283
 III. The Gods of the Phœnicians also Kings of Atlantis . . 308
  IV. The God Odin, Woden, or Wotan 313
   V. The Pyramid, the Cross, and the Garden of Eden . . . 317
  VI. Gold and Silver the Sacred Metals of Atlantis. . . . 343

PART V.

THE COLONIES OF ATLANTIS.

   I. The Central American and Mexican Colonies 348
  II. The Egyptian Colony. 358
 III. The Colonies of the Mississippi Valley 370
  IV. The Iberian Colonies of Atlantis 387
   V. The Peruvian Colony 390
  VI. The African Colonies 404
 VII. The Irish Colonies from Atlantis 408
VIII. The Oldest Son of Noah 423
  IX. The Antiquity of some of our Great Inventions . . . 440
   X. The Aryan Colonies from Atlantis. 456
  XI. Atlantis Reconstructed 472

ATLANTIS:

THE ANTEDILUVIAN WORLD.

PART I.

THE HISTORY OF ATLANTIS.

Chapter I.

THE PURPOSE OF THE BOOK.

This book is an attempt to demonstrate several distinct and novel propositions. These are:

1. That there once existed in the Atlantic Ocean, opposite the mouth of the Mediterranean Sea, a large island, which was the remnant of an Atlantic continent, and known to the ancient world as Atlantis.

2. That the description of this island given by Plato is not, as has been long supposed, fable, but veritable history.

3. That Atlantis was the region where man first rose from a state of barbarism to civilization.

4. That it became, in the course of ages, a populous and mighty nation, from whose overflowings the shores of the Gulf of Mexico, the Mississippi River, the Amazon, the Pacific coast of South America, the Mediterranean, the west coast of Europe and Africa, the Baltic, the Black Sea, and the Caspian were populated by civilized nations.

5. That it was the true Antediluvian world; the Garden of Eden; the Gardens of the Hesperides; the Elysian Fields;

1

the Gardens of Alcinous; the Mesomphalos; the Olympos; the Asgard of the traditions of the ancient nations; representing a universal memory of a great land, where early mankind dwelt for ages in peace and happiness.

6. That the gods and goddesses of the ancient Greeks, the Phœnicians, the Hindoos, and the Scandinavians were simply the kings, queens, and heroes of Atlantis; and the acts attributed to them in mythology are a confused recollection of real historical events.

7. That the mythology of Egypt and Peru represented the original religion of Atlantis, which was sun-worship.

8. That the oldest colony formed by the Atlanteans was probably in Egypt, whose civilization was a reproduction of that of the Atlantic island.

9. That the implements of the "Bronze Age" of Europe were derived from Atlantis. The Atlanteans were also the first manufacturers of iron.

10. That the Phœnician alphabet, parent of all the European alphabets, was derived from an Atlantis alphabet, which was also conveyed from Atlantis to the Mayas of Central America.

11. That Atlantis was the original seat of the Aryan or Indo-European family of nations, as well as of the Semitic peoples, and possibly also of the Turanian races.

12. That Atlantis perished in a terrible convulsion of nature, in which the whole island sunk into the ocean, with nearly all its inhabitants.

13. That a few persons escaped in ships and on rafts, and carried to the nations east and west the tidings of the appalling catastrophe, which has survived to our own time in the Flood and Deluge legends of the different nations of the old and new worlds.

If these propositions can be proved, they will solve many problems which now perplex mankind; they will confirm in many respects the statements in the opening chapters of Genesis; they will widen the area of human history; they will explain the remarkable resemblances which exist between the ancient civilizations found upon the opposite shores of the Atlantic Ocean, in the old and new worlds; and they will aid us to rehabilitate the fathers of our civilization, our blood, and our fundamental ideas—the men who lived, loved, and labored ages before the Aryans descended upon India, or the Phœnician had settled in Syria, or the Goth had reached the shores of the Baltic.

The fact that the story of Atlantis was for thousands of years regarded as a fable proves nothing. There is an unbelief which grows out of ignorance, as well as a scepticism which is born of intelligence. The people nearest to the past are not always those who are best informed concerning the past.

For a thousand years it was believed that the legends of the buried cities of Pompeii and Herculaneum were myths: they were spoken of as "the fabulous cities." For a thousand years the educated world did not credit the accounts given by Herodotus of the wonders of the ancient civilizations of the Nile and of Chaldea. He was called "the father of liars." Even Plutarch sneered at him. Now, in the language of Frederick Schlegel, "the deeper and more comprehensive the researches of the moderns have been, the more their regard and esteem for Herodotus has increased." Buckle says, "His minute information about Egypt and Asia Minor is admitted by all geographers."

There was a time when the expedition sent out by Pharaoh Necho to circumnavigate Africa was doubted, because the explorers stated that after they had progressed a certain distance the sun was north of them; this circumstance, which then aroused suspicion, now proves to us that the Egyptian navigators had really passed the equator, and anticipated by 2100 years Vasquez de Gama in his discovery of the Cape of Good Hope.

If I succeed in demonstrating the truth of the somewhat startling propositions with which I commenced this chapter, it will only be by bringing to bear upon the question of Atlantis a thousand converging lines of light from a multitude of researches made by scholars in different fields of modern thought. Further investigations and discoveries will, I trust, confirm the correctness of the conclusions at which I have arrived.

> *" The world has made such comet-like advance*
> *Lately on science, we may almost hope,*
> *Before we die of sheer decay, to learn*
> *Something about our infancy ; when lived*
> *That great, original, broad-eyed, sunken race,*
> *Whose knowledge, like the sea-sustaining rocks,*
> *Hath formed the base of this world's fluctuous lore."*
>   FESTUS.

Chapter II.

PLATO'S HISTORY OF ATLANTIS.

PLATO has preserved for us the history of Atlantis. If our views are correct, it is one of the most valuable records which have come down to us from antiquity.

Plato lived 400 years before the birth of Christ. His ancestor, Solon, was the great law-giver of Athens 600 years before the Christian era. Solon visited Egypt. Plutarch says, "Solon attempted in verse a large description, or rather fabulous account of the Atlantic Island, which he had learned from the wise men of Sais, and which particularly concerned the Athenians; but by reason of his age, not want of leisure (as Plato would have it), he was apprehensive the work would be too much for him, and therefore did not go through with it. These verses are a proof that business was not the hinderance:

> " 'I grow in learning as I grow in age.'

And again:

> " ' Wine, wit, and beauty still their charms bestow,
> Light all the shades of life, and cheer us as we go.'

"Plato, ambitious to cultivate and adorn the subject of the Atlantic Island, as a delightful spot in some fair field unoccupied, to which also he had some claim by reason of his being related to Solon, laid out magnificent courts and enclosures, and erected a grand entrance to it, such as no other story, fable, or poem ever had. But, as he began it late, he ended his life before the work, so that the more the reader is delighted with

the part that is written, the more regret he has to find it unfinished."

There can be no question that Solon visited Egypt. The
causes of his departure from Athens, for a period of ten years,
are fully explained by Plutarch. He dwelt, he tells us,

"On the Canopian shore, by Nile's deep mouth."

There he conversed upon points of philosophy and history
with the most learned of the Egyptian priests. He was a man
of extraordinary force and penetration of mind, as his laws and
his sayings, which have been preserved to us, testify. There is
no improbability in the statement that he commenced in verse
a history and description of Atlantis, which he left unfinished
at his death; and it requires no great stretch of the imagination to believe that this manuscript reached the hands of his
successor and descendant, Plato; a scholar, thinker, and historian like himself, and, like himself, one of the profoundest
minds of the ancient world. The Egyptian priest had said to
Solon, "You have no antiquity of history, and no history of
antiquity;" and Solon doubtless realized fully the vast importance of a record which carried human history back, not only
thousands of years before the era of Greek civilization, but
many thousands of years before even the establishment of the
kingdom of Egypt; and he was anxious to preserve for his
half-civilized countrymen this inestimable record of the past.

We know of no better way to commence a book about Atlantis than by giving in full the record preserved by Plato.
It is as follows:

Critias. Then listen, Socrates, to a strange tale, which is,
however, certainly true, as Solon, who was the wisest of the
seven sages, declared. He was a relative and great friend of
my great-grandfather, Dropidas, as he himself says in several of
his poems; and Dropidas told Critias, my grandfather, who remembered, and told us, that there were of old great and marvellous actions of the Athenians, which have passed into ob-
livion through time and the destruction of the human race—

and one in particular, which was the greatest of them all, the recital of which will be a suitable testimony of our gratitude to you. . . .

Socrates. Very good; and what is this ancient famous action of which Critias spoke, not as a mere legend, but as a veritable action of the Athenian State, which Solon recounted?

Critias. I will tell an old-world story which I heard from an aged man; for Critias was, as he said, at that time nearly ninety years of age, and I was about ten years of age. Now the day was that day of the Apaturia which is called the registration of youth; at which, according to custom, our parents gave prizes for recitations, and the poems of several poets were recited by us boys, and many of us sung the poems of Solon, which were new at the time. One of our tribe, either because this was his real opinion, or because he thought that he would please Critias, said that, in his judgment, Solon was not only the wisest of men but the noblest of poets. The old man, I well remember, brightened up at this, and said, smiling : " Yes, Amynander, if Solon had only, like other poets, made poetry the business of his life, and had completed the tale which he brought with him from Egypt, and had not been compelled, by reason of the factions and troubles which he found stirring in this country when he came home, to attend to other matters, in my opinion he would have been as famous as Homer, or Hesiod, or any poet."

"And what was that poem about, Critias?" said the person who addressed him.

"About the greatest action which the Athenians ever did, and which ought to have been most famous, but which, through the lapse of time and the destruction of the actors, has not come down to us."

"Tell us," said the other, "the whole story, and how and from whom Solon heard this veritable tradition."

He replied : "At the head of the Egyptian Delta, where the river Nile divides, there is a certain district which is called the district of Sais, and the great city of the district is also called Sais, and is the city from which Amasis the king was sprung. And the citizens have a deity who is their foundress : she is called in the Egyptian tongue Neith, which is asserted by them to be the same whom the Hellenes called Athene. Now, the citizens of this city are great lovers of the Athenians, and say that they are in some way related to them. Thither came Solon, who was received by them with great honor; and he asked the priests, who were most skilful in such matters, about antiquity, and made the discovery that neither he nor any other Hellene knew anything worth mentioning about the times of old. On one occasion, when he was drawing them on to speak of antiquity, he began to tell about the most ancient things in our part of the world — about Phoroneus, who is called 'the first,' and about Niobe; and, after the Deluge, to tell of the lives of Deucalion and Pyrrha; and he traced the genealogy of their descendants, and attempted to reckon how many years old were the events of which he was speaking, and to give the dates. Thereupon, one of the priests, who was of very great age, said, 'O Solon, Solon, you Hellenes are but children, and there is never an old man who is an Hellene.' Solon, hearing this, said, 'What do you mean?' 'I mean to say,' he replied, 'that in mind you are all young; there is no old opinion handed down among you by ancient tradition, nor any science which is hoary with age. And I will tell you the reason of this: there have been, and there will be again, many destructions of mankind arising out of many causes. There is a story which even you have preserved, that once upon a time Phaëthon, the son of Helios, having yoked the steeds in his father's chariot, because he was not able to drive them in the path of his father, burnt up all that was upon the earth, and was himself destroyed by a thunder-bolt. Now, this has the form of a myth, but really signifies a declination of the bodies moving around the earth and in the heavens, and a great conflagration of things upon the earth recurring at long intervals of time: when this happens, those who live upon the mountains and in dry and lofty places are more liable to destruction than those who dwell by rivers or on the sea-shore; and from this calamity the Nile, who is our never-failing savior, saves and delivers us. When, on the other hand, the gods purge the earth with a deluge of water, among you herdsmen and shepherds on the mountains are the survivors, whereas those of you who live in cities are carried by the rivers into the sea; but in this country neither at that time nor at any other does the water come from above on the fields, having always a tendency to come up from below, for which reason the things preserved here are said to be the oldest. The fact is, that wherever the extremity of winter frost or of summer sun does not prevent, the human race is always increasing at times, and at other times diminishing in numbers. And whatever happened either in your country or in ours, or in any other region of which we are informed—if any action which is noble or great, or in any other way remarkable has taken place, all that has been written down of old, and is preserved in our temples; whereas you and other nations are just being provided with letters and the other things which States require; and then, at the usual period, the stream from heaven descends like a pestilence, and leaves only those of you who are destitute of letters and education; and thus you have to begin all over again as children, and know nothing of what happened in ancient times, either among us or among yourselves. As for those genealogies of yours which you have recounted to us, Solon, they are no better than the tales of children; for, in the first place, you remember one deluge only, whereas there were many of them; and, in the next place, you do not know that there dwelt in your land the fairest and noblest race of men which ever lived, of whom you and your whole city are but a seed or remnant. And this was unknown to you, because for many generations the survivors of that destruction died and made no sign. For there was a time, Solon, before that great deluge of all, when the city which now is Athens was first in war, and was pre-eminent for the excellence of her laws, and is said to have performed the noblest deeds, and to have had the fairest constitution of any of which tradition tells, under the face of heaven.' Solon marvelled at this, and earnestly requested the priest to inform him exactly and in order about these former citizens. 'You are welcome to hear about them, Solon,' said the priest, 'both for your own sake and for that of the city; and, above all, for the sake of the goddess who is the common patron and protector and educator of both our cities. She founded your city a thousand years before ours, receiving from the Earth and Hephæstus the seed of your race, and then she founded ours, the constitution of which is set down in our sacred registers as 8000 years old. As touching the citizens of 9000 years ago, I will briefly inform you of their laws and of the noblest of their actions; and the exact particulars of the whole we will hereafter go through at our leisure in the sacred registers themselves. If you compare these very laws with your own, you will find that many of ours are the counterpart of yours, as they were in the olden time. In the first place, there is the caste of priests, which is separated from all the others; next there are the artificers, who exercise their several crafts by themselves, and without admixture of any other; and also there is the class of shepherds and that of hunters, as well as that of husbandmen; and you will observe, too, that the warriors in Egypt are separated from all the other classes, and are commanded by the law only to engage in war; moreover, the weapons with which they are equipped are shields and spears, and this the goddess taught first among you, and then in Asiatic countries, and we among the Asiatics first adopted.

" 'Then, as to wisdom, do you observe what care the law took from the very first, searching out and comprehending the whole order of things down to prophecy and medicine (the latter with a view to health); and out of these divine elements drawing what was needful for human life, and adding every sort of knowledge which was connected with them. All this order and arrangement the goddess first imparted to you when establishing your city; and she chose the spot of earth in which you were born, because she saw that the happy temperament of the seasons in that land would produce the wisest of men. Wherefore the goddess, who was a lover both of war and of wisdom, selected, and first of all settled that spot which was the most likely to produce men likest herself. And there you dwelt, having such laws as these and still better ones, and excelled all mankind in all virtue, as became the children and disciples of the gods. Many great and wonderful deeds are recorded of your State in our histories; but one of them exceeds all the rest in greatness and valor; for these histories tell of a mighty power which was aggressing wantonly against the whole of Europe and Asia, and to which your city put an end. This power came forth out of the Atlantic Ocean, for in those days the Atlantic was navigable; and there was an island situated in front of the straits which you call the Columns of Heracles: the island was larger than Libya and Asia put together, and was the way to other islands, and from the islands you might pass through the whole of the opposite continent which surrounded the true ocean; for this sea which is within the Straits of Heracles is only a harbor, having a narrow entrance, but that other is a real sea, and the surrounding land may be most truly called a continent. Now, in the island of Atlantis there was a great and wonderful empire, which had rule over the whole island and several others, as well as over parts of the continent; and, besides these, they subjected the parts of Libya within the Columns of Heracles as far as Egypt, and of Europe as far as Tyrrhenia. The vast power thus gathered into one, endeavored to subdue at one blow our country and yours, and the whole of the land which was within the straits; and then, Solon, your country shone forth, in the excellence of her virtue and strength, among all mankind; for she was the first in courage and military skill, and was the leader of the Hellenes. And when the rest fell off from her, being compelled to stand alone, after having undergone the very extremity of danger, she defeated and triumphed over the invaders, and preserved from slavery those who were not yet subjected, and freely liberated all the others who dwelt within the limits of Heracles. But afterward there occurred violent earthquakes and floods, and in a single day and night of rain all your warlike men in a body sunk into the earth, and the island of Atlantis in like manner disappeared, and was sunk beneath the sea. And that is the reason why the sea in those parts is impassable and impenetrable, because there is such a quantity of shallow mud in the way; and this was caused by the subsidence of the island.' (" Plato's Dialogues," ii., 517, *Timæus.*) . . .

"But in addition to the gods whom you have mentioned, I would specially invoke Mnemosyne; for all the important part of what I have to tell is dependent on her favor, and if I can recollect and recite enough of what was said by the priests, and brought hither by Solon, I doubt not that I shall satisfy the requirements of this theatre. To that task, then, I will at once address myself.

"Let me begin by observing, first of all, that nine thousand was the sum of years which had elapsed since the war which was said to have taken place between all those who dwelt outside the Pillars of Heracles and those who dwelt within them: this war I am now to describe. Of the combatants on the one side the city of Athens was reported to have been the ruler, and to have directed the contest; the combatants on the other side were led by the kings of the islands of Atlantis, which, as I was saying, once had an extent greater than that of Libya and Asia; and, when afterward sunk by an earthquake, became an impassable barrier of mud to voyagers sailing from hence to the ocean.   The progress of the history will unfold the various tribes of barbarians and Hellenes which then existed, as they successively appear on the scene; but I must begin by describing, first of all, the Athenians as they were in that day, and their enemies who fought with them; and I shall have to tell of the power and form of government of both of them.   Let us give the precedence to Athens. . . .

"Many great deluges have taken place during the nine thousand years, for that is the number of years which have elapsed since the time of which I am speaking; and in all the ages and changes of things there has never been any settlement of the earth flowing down from the mountains, as in other places, which is worth speaking of; it has always been carried round in a circle, and disappeared in the depths below.   The consequence is that, in comparison of what then was, there are remaining in small islets only the bones of the wasted body, as they may be called, all the richer and softer parts of the soil having fallen away, and the mere skeleton of the country being left. . . .

"And next, if I have not forgotten what I heard when I was a child, I will impart to you the character and origin of their adversaries; for friends should not keep their stories to themselves, but have them in common.   Yet, before proceeding farther in the narrative, I ought to warn you that you must not be surprised if you should hear Hellenic names given to foreigners.   I will tell you the reason of this: Solon, who was intending to use the tale for his poem, made an investigation into the meaning of the names, and found that the early Egyptians, in writing them down, had translated them into their own language, and he recovered the meaning of the several names and retranslated them, and copied them out again in our language. My great-grandfather, Dropidas, had the original writing, which is still in my possession, and was carefully studied by me when I was a child.   Therefore, if you hear names such as are used in this country, you must not be surprised, for I have told you the reason of them.

"The tale, which was of great length, began as follows: I have before remarked, in speaking of the allotments of the gods, that they distributed the whole earth into portions differing in extent, and made themselves temples and sacrifices. And Poseidon, receiving for his lot the island of Atlantis, begat children by a mortal woman, and settled them in a part of the island which I will proceed to describe. On the side toward the sea, and in the centre of the whole island, there was a plain which is said to have been the fairest of all plains, and very fertile. Near the plain again, and also in the centre of the island, at a distance of about fifty stadia, there was a mountain, not very high on any side. In this mountain there dwelt one of the earth-born primeval men of that country, whose name was Evenor, and he had a wife named Leucippe, and they had an only daughter, who was named Cleito. The maiden was growing up to womanhood when her father and mother died; Poseidon fell in love with her, and had intercourse with her; and, breaking the ground, enclosed the hill in which she dwelt all round, making alternate zones of sea and land, larger and smaller, encircling one another; there were two of land and three of water, which he turned as with a lathe out of the centre of the island, equidistant every way, so that no man could get to the island, for ships and voyages were not yet heard of. He himself, as he was a god, found no difficulty in making special arrangements for the centre island, bringing two streams of water under the earth, which he caused to ascend as springs, one of warm water and the other of cold, and making every variety of food to spring up abundantly in the earth. He also begat and brought up five pairs of male children, dividing the island of Atlantis into ten portions: he gave to the first-born of the eldest pair his mother's dwelling and the surrounding allotment, which was the largest and best, and made him king over the rest; the others he made princes, and gave them rule over many men and a large territory. And he named them all: the eldest, who was king, he named Atlas, and from him the whole island and the ocean received the name of Atlantic. To his twin-brother, who was born after him, and obtained as his lot the extremity of the island toward the Pillars of Heracles, as far as the country which is still called the region of Gades in that part of the world, he gave the name which in the Hellenic language is Eumelus, in the language of the country which is named after him, Gadeirus. Of the second pair of twins, he called one Ampheres and the other Evæmon. To the third pair of twins he gave the name Mneseus to the elder, and Autochthon to the one who followed him. Of the fourth pair of twins he called the elder Elasippus and the younger Mestor. And of the fifth pair he gave to the elder the name of Azaes, and to the younger Diaprepes. All these and their descendants were the inhabitants and rulers of divers islands in the open sea; and also, as has been already said, they held sway in the other direction over the country within the Pillars as far as Egypt and Tyrrhenia. Now Atlas had a numerous and honorable family, and his eldest branch always retained the kingdom, which the eldest son handed on to his eldest for many generations; and they had such an amount of wealth as was never before possessed by kings and potentates, and is not likely ever to be again, and they were furnished with everything which they could have, both in city and country. For, because of the greatness of their empire, many things were brought to them from foreign countries, and the island itself provided much of what was required by them for the uses of life. In the first place, they dug out of the earth whatever was to be found there, mineral as well as metal, and that which is now only a name, and was then something more than a name—orichalcum—was dug out of the earth in many parts of the island, and, with the exception of gold, was esteemed the most precious of metals among the men of those days. There was an abundance of wood for carpenters' work, and sufficient maintenance for tame and wild animals. Moreover, there were a great number of elephants in the island, and there was provision for animals of every kind, both for those which live in lakes and marshes and rivers, and also for those which live in mountains and on plains, and therefore for the animal which is the largest and most voracious of them. Also, whatever fragrant things there are in the earth, whether roots, or herbage, or woods, or distilling drops of flowers or fruits, grew and thrived in that land; and again, the cultivated fruit of the earth, both the dry edible fruit and other species of food, which we call by the general name of legumes, and the fruits having a hard rind, affording drinks, and meats, and ointments, and good store of chestnuts and the like, which may be used to play with, and are fruits which spoil with keeping—and the pleasant kinds of dessert which console us after dinner, when we are full and tired of eating—all these that sacred island lying beneath the sun brought forth fair and wondrous in infinite abundance. All these things they received from the earth, and they employed themselves in constructing their temples, and palaces, and harbors, and docks; and they arranged the whole country in the following manner: First of all they bridged over the zones of sea which surrounded the ancient metropolis, and made a passage into and out of the royal palace; and then they began to build the palace in the habitation of the god and of their ancestors. This they continued to ornament in successive generations, every king surpassing the one who came before him to the utmost of his power, until they made the building a marvel to behold for size and for beauty. And, beginning from the sea, they dug a canal three hundred feet in width and one hundred feet in depth, and fifty stadia in length, which they carried through to the outermost zone, making a passage from the sea up to this, which became a harbor, and leaving an opening sufficient to enable the largest vessels to find ingress. Moreover, they divided the zones of land which parted the zones of sea, constructing bridges of such a width as would leave a passage for a single trireme to pass out of one into another, and roofed them over; and there was a way underneath for the ships, for the banks of the zones were raised considerably above the water. Now the largest of the zones into which a passage was cut from the sea was three stadia in breadth, and the zone of land which came next of equal breadth; but the next two, as well the zone of water as of land, were two stadia, and the one which surrounded the central island was a stadium only in width. The island in which the palace was situated had a diameter of five stadia. This, and the zones and the bridge, which was the sixth part of a stadium in width, they surrounded by a stone wall, on either side placing towers, and gates on the bridges where the sea passed in. The stone which was used in the work they quarried from underneath the centre island and from underneath the zones, on the outer as well as the inner side. One kind of stone was white, another black, and a third red; and, as they quarried, they at the same time hollowed out docks double within, having roofs formed out of the native rock. Some of their buildings were simple, but in others they put together different stones, which they intermingled for the sake of ornament, to be a natural source of delight. The entire circuit of the wall which went round the outermost one they covered with a coating of brass, and the circuit of the next wall they coated with tin, and the third, which encompassed the citadel, flashed with the red light of orichalcum. The palaces in the interior of the citadel were constructed in this wise: In the centre was a holy temple dedicated to Cleito and Poseidon, which remained inaccessible, and was surrounded by an enclosure of gold; this was the spot in which they originally begat the race of the ten princes, and thither they annually brought the fruits of the earth in their season from all the ten portions, and performed sacrifices to each of them. Here, too, was Poseidon's own temple, of a stadium in length and half a stadium in width, and of a proportionate height, having a sort of barbaric splendor. All the outside of the temple, with the exception of the pinnacles, they covered with silver, and the pinnacles with gold. In the interior of the temple the roof was of ivory, adorned everywhere with gold and silver and orichalcum; all the other parts of the walls and pillars and floor they lined with orichalcum. In the temple they placed statues of gold: there was the god himself standing in a chariot—the charioteer of six winged horses—and of such a size that he touched the roof of the building with his head; around him there were a hundred Nereids riding on dolphins, for such was thought to be the number of them in that day. There were also in the interior of the temple other images which had been dedicated by private individuals. And around the temple on the outside were placed statues of gold of all the ten kings and of their wives; and there were many other great offerings, both of kings and of private individuals, coming both from the city itself and the foreign cities over which they held sway. There was an altar, too, which in size and workmanship corresponded to the rest of the work, and there were palaces in like manner which answered to the greatness of the kingdom and the glory of the temple.

"In the next place, they used fountains both of cold and hot springs; these were very abundant, and both kinds wonderfully adapted to use by reason of the sweetness and excellence of their waters. They constructed buildings about them, and planted suitable trees; also cisterns, some open to the heaven, others which they roofed over, to be used in winter as warm baths: there were the king's baths, and the baths of private persons, which were kept apart; also separate baths for women, and others again for horses and cattle, and to them they gave as much adornment as was suitable for them. The water which

ran off they carried, some to the grove of Poseidon, where were
growing all manner of trees of wonderful height and beauty,
owing to the excellence of the soil; the remainder was conveyed by aqueducts which passed over the bridges to the outer
circles: and there were many temples built and dedicated to
many gods; also gardens and places of exercise, some for men,
and some set apart for horses, in both of the two islands formed by the zones; and in the centre of the larger of the two
there was a race-course of a stadium in width, and in length
allowed to extend all round the island, for horses to race in.
Also there were guard-houses at intervals for the body-guard,
the more trusted of whom had their duties appointed to them
in the lesser zone, which was nearer the Acropolis; while the
most trusted of all had houses given them within the citadel,
and about the persons of the kings.   The docks were full of
triremes and naval stores, and all things were quite ready for
use.   Enough of the plan of the royal palace.   Crossing the
outer harbors, which were three in number, you would come to
a wall which began at the sea and went all round: this was
everywhere distant fifty stadia from the largest zone and harbor, and enclosed the whole, meeting at the mouth of the channel toward the sea.   The entire area was densely crowded with
habitations; and the canal and the largest of the harbors were
full of vessels and merchants coming from all parts, who, from
their numbers, kept up a multitudinous sound of human voices
and din of all sorts night and day.   I have repeated his descriptions of the city and the parts about the ancient palace
nearly as he gave them, and now I must endeavor to describe
the nature and arrangement of the rest of the country.   The
whole country was described as being very lofty and precipitous on the side of the sea, but the country immediately about
and surrounding the city was a level plain, itself surrounded
by mountains which descended toward the sea; it was smooth
and even, but of an oblong shape, extending in one direction
three thousand stadia, and going up the country from the sea
through the centre of the island two thousand stadia; the
whole region of the island lies toward the south, and is sheltered from the north.   The surrounding mountains he celebrated
for their number and size and beauty, in which they exceeded
all that are now to be seen anywhere; having in them also
many wealthy inhabited villages, and rivers and lakes, and

meadows supplying food enough for every animal, wild or tame, and wood of various sorts, abundant for every kind of work. I will now describe the plain, which had been cultivated during many ages by many generations of kings. It was rectangular, and for the most part straight and oblong; and what it wanted of the straight line followed the line of the circular ditch. The depth and width and length of this ditch were incredible, and gave the impression that such a work, in addition to so many other works, could hardly have been wrought by the hand of man. But I must say what I have heard. It was excavated to the depth of a hundred feet, and its breadth was a stadium everywhere; it was carried round the whole of the plain, and was ten thousand stadia in length. It received the streams which came down from the mountains, and winding round the plain, and touching the city at various points, was there let off into the sea. From above, likewise, straight canals of a hundred feet in width were cut in the plain, and again let off into the ditch, toward the sea; these canals were at intervals of a hundred stadia, and by them they brought down the wood from the mountains to the city, and conveyed the fruits of the earth in ships, cutting transverse passages from one canal into another, and to the city. Twice in the year they gathered the fruits of the earth—in winter having the benefit of the rains, and in summer introducing the water of the canals. As to the population, each of the lots in the plain had an appointed chief of men who were fit for military service, and the size of the lot was to be a square of ten stadia each way, and the total number of all the lots was sixty thousand.

"And of the inhabitants of the mountains and of the rest of the country there was also a vast multitude having leaders, to whom they were assigned according to their dwellings and villages. The leader was required to furnish for the war the sixth portion of a war-chariot, so as to make up a total of ten thousand chariots; also two horses and riders upon them, and a light chariot without a seat, accompanied by a fighting man on foot carrying a small shield, and having a charioteer mounted to guide the horses; also, he was bound to furnish two heavy-armed men, two archers, two slingers, three stone-shooters, and three javelin men, who were skirmishers, and four sailors to make up a complement of twelve hundred ships. Such was the order of war in the royal city—that of the other nine

governments was different in each of them, and would be wea-
risome to narrate. As to offices and honors, the following was
the arrangement from the first: Each of the ten kings, in his
own division and in his own city, had the absolute control of
the citizens, and in many cases of the laws, punishing and slay-
ing whomsoever he would.

"Now the relations of their governments to one another
were regulated by the injunctions of Poseidon as the law had
handed them down. These were inscribed by the first men on
a column of orichalcum, which was situated in the middle of
the island, at the temple of Poseidon, whither the people were
gathered together every fifth and sixth years alternately, thus
giving equal honor to the odd and to the even number. And
when they were gathered together they consulted about public
affairs, and inquired if any one had transgressed in anything,
and passed judgment on him accordingly—and before they
passed judgment they gave their pledges to one another in
this wise: There were bulls who had the range of the temple
of Poseidon; and the ten who were left alone in the temple,
after they had offered prayers to the gods that they might
take the sacrifices which were acceptable to them, hunted the
bulls without weapons, but with staves and nooses; and the
bull which they caught they led up to the column; the victim
was then struck on the head by them, and slain over the sacred
inscription. Now on the column, besides the law, there was
inscribed an oath invoking mighty curses on the disobedient.
When, therefore, after offering sacrifice according to their customs, they had burnt the limbs of the bull, they mingled a cup
and cast in a clot of blood for each of them; the rest of the
victim they took to the fire, after having made a purification
of the column all round. Then they drew from the cup in
golden vessels, and, pouring a libation on the fire, they swore
that they would judge according to the laws on the column,
and would punish any one who had previously transgressed,
and that for the future they would not, if they could help,
transgress any of the inscriptions, and would not command or
obey any ruler who commanded them to act otherwise than
according to the laws of their father Poseidon. This was the
prayer which each of them offered up for himself and for his
family, at the same time drinking, and dedicating the vessel
in the temple of the god; and, after spending some necessary

time at supper, when darkness came on and the fire about the sacrifice was cool, all of them put on most beautiful azure robes, and, sitting on the ground at night near the embers of the sacrifices on which they had sworn, and extinguishing all the fire about the temple, they received and gave judgment, if any of them had any accusation to bring against any one; and, when they had given judgment, at daybreak they wrote down their sentences on a golden tablet, and deposited them as memorials with their robes. There were many special laws which the several kings had inscribed about the temples, but the most important was the following: That they were not to take up arms against one another, and they were all to come to the rescue if any one in any city attempted to overthrow the royal house. Like their ancestors, they were to deliberate in common about war and other matters, giving the supremacy to the family of Atlas; and the king was not to have the power of life and death over any of his kinsmen, unless he had the assent of the majority of the ten kings.

"Such was the vast power which the god settled in the lost island of Atlantis; and this he afterward directed against our land on the following pretext, as traditions tell: For many generations, as long as the divine nature lasted in them, they were obedient to the laws, and well-affectioned toward the gods, who were their kinsmen; for they possessed true and in every way great spirits, practising gentleness and wisdom in the various chances of life, and in their intercourse with one another. They despised everything but virtue, not caring for their present state of life, and thinking lightly on the possession of gold and other property, which seemed only a burden to them; neither were they intoxicated by luxury; nor did wealth deprive them of their self-control; but they were sober, and saw clearly that all these goods are increased by virtuous friendship with one another, and that by excessive zeal for them, and honor of them, the good of them is lost, and friendship perishes with them.

"By such reflections, and by the continuance in them of a divine nature, all that which we have described waxed and increased in them; but when this divine portion began to fade away in them, and became diluted too often, and with too much of the mortal admixture, and the human nature got the upper-hand, then, they being unable to bear their fortune, became unseemly, and to him who had an eye to see, they began to appear base, and had lost the fairest of their precious gifts; but to those who had no eye to see the true happiness, they still appeared glorious and blessed at the very time when they were filled with unrighteous avarice and power. Zeus, the god of gods, who rules with law, and is able to see into such things, perceiving that an honorable race was in a most wretched state, and wanting to inflict punishment on them, that they might be chastened and improved, collected all the gods into his most holy habitation, which, being placed in the centre of the world, sees all things that partake of generation. And when he had called them together he spake as follows:"

[Here Plato's story abruptly ends.]

Chapter III.

THE PROBABILITIES OF PLATO'S STORY.

There is nothing improbable in this narrative, so far as it describes a great, rich, cultured, and educated people. Almost every part of Plato's story can be paralleled by descriptions of the people of Egypt or Peru; in fact, in some respects Plato's account of Atlantis falls short of Herodotus's description of the grandeur of Egypt, or Prescott's picture of the wealth and civilization of Peru. For instance, Prescott, in his "Conquest of Peru" (vol. i., p. 95), says:

"The most renowned of the Peruvian temples, the pride of the capital and the wonder of the empire, was at Cuzco, where, under the munificence of successive sovereigns, it had become so enriched that it received the name of *Coricancha*, or 'the Place of Gold.' . . . The interior of the temple was literally a mine of gold. On the western wall was emblazoned a representation of the Deity, consisting of a human countenance looking forth from amid innumerable rays of light, which emanated from it in every direction, in the same manner as the sun is often personified with us. The figure was engraved on a massive plate of gold, of enormous dimensions, thickly powdered with emeralds and precious stones. . . . The walls and ceilings were everywhere incrusted with golden ornaments; every part of the interior of the temple glowed with burnished plates and studs of the precious metal; the cornices were of the same material."

There are in Plato's narrative no marvels; no myths; no tales of gods, gorgons, hobgoblins, or giants. It is a plain and reasonable history of a people who built temples, ships, and canals; who lived by agriculture and commerce; who, in pursuit of trade, reached out to all the countries around them. The early history of most nations begins with gods and demons, while here we have nothing of the kind; we see an immigrant enter the country, marry one of the native women, and settle down; in time a great nation grows up around him. It reminds one of the information given by the Egyptian priests to Herodotus. "During the space of eleven thousand three hundred and forty years they assert," says Herodotus, "that no divinity has appeared in human shape, . . . they absolutely denied the possibility of a human being's descent from a god." If Plato had sought to draw from his imagination a wonderful and pleasing story, we should not have had so plain and reasonable a narrative. He would have given us a history like the legends of Greek mythology, full of the adventures of gods and goddesses, nymphs, fauns, and satyrs.

Neither is there any evidence on the face of this history that Plato sought to convey in it a moral or political lesson, 'n the guise of a fable, as did Bacon in the " New Atlantis," and More in the "Kingdom of Nowhere." There is no ideal republic delineated here. It is a straightforward, reasonable history of a people ruled over by their kings, living and progressing as other nations have lived and progressed since their day.

Plato says that in Atlantis there was "a great and wonderful empire," which "aggressed wantonly against the whole of Europe and Asia," thus testifying to the extent of its dominion. It not only subjugated Africa as far as Egypt, and Europe as far as Italy, but it ruled " as well *over parts of the continent*," to wit, "the opposite continent" of America, "which surrounded the true ocean." Those parts of America over which it ruled were, as we will show hereafter, Central America, Peru, and the Valley of the Mississippi, occupied by the "Mound Builders."

Moreover, he tells us that "this vast power was gathered into one;" that is to say, from Egypt to Peru it was one consolidated empire. We will see hereafter that the legends of the Hindoos as to Deva Nahusha distinctly refer to this vast empire, which covered the whole of the known world.

Another corroboration of the truth of Plato's narrative is found in the fact that upon the Azores black lava rocks, and rocks red and white in color, are now found. He says they built with white, red, and black stone. Sir C. Wyville Thomson describes a narrow neck of land between Fayal and Monte da Guia, called "Monte Queimada" (the burnt mountain), as follows: "It is formed partly of stratified tufa of a dark chocolate color, and partly of lumps of *black* lava, porous, and each with a large cavity in the centre, which must have been ejected as volcanic bombs in a glorious display of fireworks at some period beyond the records of Acorean history, but late in the geological annals of the island" ("Voyage of the Challenger," vol. ii., p. 24). He also describes immense walls of black volcanic rock in the island.

The plain of Atlantis, Plato tells us, "had been cultivated during many ages by many generations of kings." If, as we believe, agriculture, the domestication of the horse, ox, sheep, goat, and hog, and the discovery or development of wheat, oats, rye, and barley originated in this region, then this language of Plato in reference to "the many ages, and the successive generations of kings," accords with the great periods of time which were necessary to bring man from a savage to a civilized condition.

In the great ditch surrounding the whole land like a circle, and into which streams flowed down from the mountains, we probably see the original of the four rivers of Paradise, and the emblem of the cross surrounded by a circle, which, as we will show hereafter, was, from the earliest pre-Christian ages, accepted as the emblem of the Garden of Eden.

We know that Plato did not invent the name of Poseidon, for the worship of Poseidon was universal in the earliest ages of Europe; "Poseidon-worship seems to have been a peculiarity of all the colonies previous to the time of Sidon" ("Prehistoric Nations," p. 148.) This worship " was carried to Spain, and to Northern Africa, but most abundantly to Italy, to many of the islands, and to the regions around the Ægean Sea; also to Thrace." (*Ibid.*, p. 155.)

Poseidon, or Neptune, is represented in Greek mythology as a sea-god; but he is figured as standing in a war-chariot drawn by horses. The association of the horse (a land animal) with a sea-god is inexplicable, except with the light given by Plato. Poseidon was a sea-god because he ruled over a great land in the sea, and was the national god of a maritime people; he is associated with horses, because in Atlantis the horse was first domesticated; and, as Plato shows, the Atlanteans had great race-courses for the development of speed in horses; and Poseidon is represented as standing in a war-chariot, because doubtless wheeled vehicles were first invented by the same people who tamed the horse; and they transmitted these war-chariots to their descendants from Egypt to Britain. We know that horses were the favorite objects chosen for sacrifice to Poseidon by the nations of antiquity within the Historical Period; they were killed, and cast into the sea from high precipices. The religious horse-feasts of the pagan Scandinavians were a survival of this Poseidon-worship, which once prevailed along all the coasts of Europe; they continued until the conversion of the people to Christianity, and were then suppressed by the Church with great difficulty.

We find in Plato's narrative the names of some of the Phœnician deities among the kings of Atlantis. Where did the Greek, Plato, get these names if the story is a fable?

Does Plato, in speaking of "the fruits having a hard rind, affording drinks and meats and ointments," refer to the cocoa-nut?

Again: Plato tells us that Atlantis abounded in both cold and hot springs. How did he come to hit upon the hot springs if he was drawing a picture from his imagination? It is a singular confirmation of his story that hot springs abound in the Azores, which are the surviving fragments of Atlantis; and an experience wider than that possessed by Plato has taught scientific men that hot springs are a common feature of regions subject to volcanic convulsions.

Plato tells us, "The whole country was very lofty and precipitous on the side of the sea, but the country immediately about and surrounding the city was a level plain, itself surrounded by mountains which descended toward the sea." One has but to look at the profile of the "Dolphin's Ridge," as revealed by the deep-sea soundings of the *Challenger*, given as the frontispiece to this volume, to see that this is a faithful description of that precipitous elevation. "The surrounding mountains," which sheltered the plain from the north, are represented in the present towering peaks of the Azores.

Plato tells us that the destruction of Atlantis filled the sea with mud, and interfered with navigation. For thousands of years the ancients believed the Atlantic Ocean to be "a muddy, shallow, dark, and misty sea, *Mare tenebrosum.*" ("Cosmos," vol. ii., p. 151.)

The three-pronged sceptre or trident of Poseidon reappears constantly in ancient history. We find it in the hands of Hindoo gods, and at the base of all the religious beliefs of antiquity.

"Among the numerals the *sacred three* has ever been considered the mark of perfection, and was therefore exclusively ascribed to the Supreme Deity, or to its earthly representative —a king, emperor, or any sovereign. For this reason triple emblems of various shapes are found on the belts, neckties, or any encircling fixture, as can be seen on the works of ancient art in Yucatan, Guatemala, Chiapas, Mexico, etc., whenever the object has reference to divine supremacy." (Dr. Arthur Schott, "Smith. Rep.," 1869, p. 391.)

We are reminded of the "tiara," and the "triple round of sovereignty."

In the same manner the ten kingdoms of Atlantis are perpetuated in all the ancient traditions.

" In the number given by the Bible for the Antediluvian patriarchs we have the first instance of a striking agreement with the traditions of various nations. Ten are mentioned in the Book of Genesis. Other nations, to whatever epoch they carry back their ancestors, whether before or after the Deluge, whether the mythical or historical character prevail, they are constant to this sacred number ten, which some have vainly attempted to connect with the speculations of later religious philosophers on the mystical value of numbers. In Chaldea, Berosus enumerates ten Antediluvian kings whose fabulous reign extended to thousands of years. The legends of the Iranian race commence with the reign of ten Peisdadien (Poseidon?) kings, 'men of the ancient law, who lived on pure Homa (water of life)' (nectar?), 'and who preserved their sanctity.' In India we meet with the nine Brahmadikas, who, with Brahma, their founder, make ten, and who are called the Ten Petris, or Fathers. The Chinese count ten emperors, partakers of the divine nature, before the dawn of historical times. The Germans believed in the ten ancestors of Odin, and the Arabs in the ten mythical kings of the Adites." (Lenormant and Chevallier, "Anc. Hist. of the East," vol. i., p. 13.)

The story of Plato finds confirmation from other sources.

An extract preserved in Proclus, taken from a work now lost, which is quoted by Boeckh in his commentary on Plato, mentions islands in the exterior sea, beyond the Pillars of Hercules, and says it was known that in one of these islands " the inhabitants preserved from their ancestors a remembrance of Atlantis, an extremely large island, which for a long time held dominion over all the islands of the Atlantic Ocean."

Ælian, in his "Varia Historia" (book iii., chap. xviii.), tells us that Theopompus (400 B.C.) related the particulars of an interview between Midas, King of Phrygia, and Silenus, in which Silenus reported the existence of a great continent beyond the Atlantic, "larger than Asia, Europe, and Libya together." He stated that a race of men called Meropes dwelt there, and had extensive cities. They were persuaded that their country alone was a continent. Out of curiosity some of them crossed the ocean and visited the Hyperboreans.

"The Gauls possessed traditions upon the subject of Atlantis which were collected by the Roman historian Timagenes, who lived in the first century before Christ. He represents that three distinct people dwelt in Gaul: 1. The indigenous population, which I suppose to be Mongoloids, who had long dwelt in Europe; 2. The invaders from a distant island, which I understand to be Atlantis; 3. The Aryan Gauls." ("Preadamites," p. 380.)

Marcellus, in a work on the Ethiopians, speaks of seven islands lying in the Atlantic Ocean—probably the Canaries—and the inhabitants of these islands, he says, preserve the memory of a much greater island, Atlantis, "which had for a long time exercised dominion over the smaller ones." (Didot Müller, "Fragmenta Historicorum Græcorum," vol. iv., p. 443.)

Diodorus Siculus relates that the Phœnicians discovered "a large island in the Atlantic Ocean, beyond the Pillars of Hercules, several days' sail from the coast of Africa. This island abounded in all manner of riches. The soil was exceedingly fertile; the scenery was diversified by rivers, mountains, and forests. It was the custom of the inhabitants to retire during the summer to magnificent country-houses, which stood in the midst of beautiful gardens. Fish and game were found in great abundance; the climate was delicious, and the trees bore fruit at all seasons of the year." Homer, Plutarch, and other ancient writers mention islands situated in the Atlantic, "several thousand stadia from the Pillars of Hercules." Silenus tells Midas that there was another continent besides Europe, Asia, and Africa—"a country where gold and silver are so plentiful that they are esteemed no more than we esteem iron." St. Clement, in his Epistle to the Corinthians, says that there were other worlds beyond the ocean.

Attention may here be called to the extraordinary number of instances in which allusion is made in the Old Testament to the "islands of the sea," especially in Isaiah and Ezekiel. What had an inland people, like the Jews, to do with seas and islands? Did these references grow out of vague traditions linking their race with "islands in the sea?"

The Orphic Argonaut sings of the division of the ancient Lyktonia into separate islands. He says, "When the dark-haired Poseidon, in anger with Father Kronion, struck Lyktonia with the golden trident."

Plato states that the Egyptians told Solon that the destruction of Atlantis occurred 9000 years before that date, to wit, about 9600 years before the Christian era. This looks like an extraordinarily long period of time, but it must be remembered that geologists claim that the remains of man found in the caves of Europe date back 500,000 years; and the fossil Calaveras skull was found deep under the base of Table Mountain, California, the whole mountain having been formed since the man to whom it belonged lived and died. †

"M. Oppert read an essay at the Brussels Congress to show, from the astronomical observations of the Egyptians and Assyrians, that 11,542 years before our era man existed on the earth at such a stage of civilization as to be able to take note of astronomical phenomena, and to calculate with considerable accuracy the length of the year. The Egyptians, says he, calculated by cycles of 1460 years—zodiacal cycles, as they were called. Their year consisted of 365 days, which caused them to lose one day in every four solar years, and, consequently, they would attain their original starting-point again only after 1460 years (365 × 4). Therefore, the zodiacal cycle ending in the year 139 of our era commenced in the year 1322 b.c. On the other hand, the Assyrian cycle was 1805 years, or 22,325 lunations. An Assyrian cycle began 712 b.c. The Chaldeans state that between the Deluge and their first historic dynasty there was a period of 39,180 years. Now, what means this number? It stands for 12 Egyptian zodiacal cycles *plus* 12 Assyrian lunar cycles.

$$\left. \begin{array}{l} 12 \times 1460 = 17,520 \\ 12 \times 1805 = 21,660 \end{array} \right\} = 39,180.$$

"These two modes of calculating time are in agreement with each other, and were known simultaneously to one peo-

† The Calaveras skull was a hoax.—E.F.B.

ple, the Chaldeans.   Let us now build up the series of both cycles, starting from our era, and the result will be as follows:

Zodiacal Cycle.	Lunar Cycle.
1,460	1,805
1,322	712
2,782	2,517
4,242	4,322
5,702	6,127
7,162	7,932
8,622	9,737
10,082	11,542
11,542	

"At the year 11,542 B.C. the two cycles came together, and consequently they had on that year their common origin in one and the same astronomical observation." †

That observation was probably made in Atlantis.

The wide divergence of languages which is found to exist among the Atlanteans at the beginning of the Historical Period implies a vast lapse of time.   The fact that the nations of the Old World remembered so little of Atlantis, except the colossal fact of its sudden and overwhelming destruction, would also seem to remove that event into a remote past.

Herodotus tells us that he learned from the Egyptians that Hercules was one of their most ancient deities, and that he was one of the twelve produced from the eight gods, 17,000 years before the reign of Amasis.

In short, I fail to see why this story of Plato, told as history, derived from the Egyptians, a people who, it is known, preserved most ancient records, and who were able to trace their existence back to a vast antiquity, should have been contemptuously set aside as a fable by Greeks, Romans, and the modern world.   It can only be because our predecessors, with their limited knowledge of the geological history of the world, did not believe it possible that any large part of the earth's surface could have been thus suddenly swallowed up by the sea.

Let us then first address ourselves to that question.

† Donnelly overlooks the fact that arithmetical series will coincide.—E.F.B.

Chapter IV.

WAS SUCH A CATASTROPHE POSSIBLE?

ALL that is needed to answer this question is to briefly refer to some of the facts revealed by the study of geology.

In the first place, the earth's surface is a record of successive risings and fallings of the land. The accompanying picture represents a section of the anthracite coal-measures of Pennsylvania. Each of the coal deposits here shown, indicated by the black lines, was created when the land had risen sufficiently above the sea to maintain vegetation; each of the strata of rock, many of them hundreds of feet in thickness, was deposited under water. Here we have twenty - three different changes of the level of the land during the formation of 2000 feet of rock and coal; and these changes took place over vast areas, embracing thousands of square miles.

All the continents which now exist were, it is well understood, once under water, and the rocks of which they are composed were deposited beneath the water; more than this, most of the rocks so deposited were the detritus or washings of other continents, which then stood

COAL-MEASURES OF PENN-
SYLVANIA.

where the oceans now roll, and whose mountains and plains were ground down by the action of volcanoes and earthquakes, and frost, ice, wind, and rain, and washed into the sea, to form the rocks upon which the nations now dwell; so that we have changed the conditions of land and water: that which is now continent was once sea, and that which is now sea was formerly continent. There can be no question that the Australian Archipelago is simply the mountain-tops of a drowned continent, which once reached from India to South America. Science has gone so far as to even give it a name; it is called "Lemuria," and here, it is claimed, the human race originated. An examination of the geological formation of our Atlantic States proves beyond a doubt, from the manner in which the sedimentary rocks, the sand, gravel, and mud—aggregating a thickness of 45,000 feet—are deposited, that they came from the north and east. "They represent the detritus of pre-existing lands, the washings of rain, rivers, coast-currents, and other agencies of erosion; and since the areas supplying the waste could scarcely have been of less extent than the new strata it formed, it is reasonably inferred that land masses of continental magnitude must have occupied the region now covered by the North Atlantic before America began to be, and onward at least through the palæozoic ages of American history. The proof of this fact is that the great strata of rocks are thicker the nearer we approach their source in the east: the maximum thickness of the palæozoic rocks of the Appalachian formation is 25,000 to 35,000 feet in Pennsylvania and Virginia, while their minimum thickness in Illinois and Missouri is from 3000 to 4000 feet; the rougher and grosser-textured rocks predominate in the east, while the farther west we go the finer the deposits were of which the rocks are composed; the finer materials were carried farther west by the water." ("New Amer. Cyclop.," art. *Coal.*)

The history of the growth of the European Continent, as recounted by Professor Geikie, gives an instructive illustration

DESTRUCTION OF POMPEII.

of the relations of geology to geography. The earliest European land, he says, appears to have existed in the north and north-west, comprising Scandinavia, Finland, and the north-west of the British area, and to have extended thence through boreal and arctic latitudes into North America. Of the height and mass of this primeval land some idea may be formed by considering the enormous bulk of the material derived from its disintegration. In the Silurian formations of the British Islands alone there is a mass of rock, worn from the land, which would form a mountain-chain extending from Marseilles to the North Cape (1800 miles), with a mean breadth of over thirty-three miles, and an average height of 16,000 feet.

As the great continent which stood where the Atlantic Ocean now is wore away, the continents of America and Europe were formed; and there seems to have been from remote times a continuous rising, still going on, of the new lands, and a sinking of the old ones. Within five thousand years, or since the age of the "polished stone," the shores of Sweden, Denmark, and Norway have risen from 200 to 600 feet.

Professor Winchell says ("The Preadamites," p. 437):

"We are in the midst of great changes, and are scarcely conscious of it. We have seen worlds in flames, and have felt a comet strike the earth. We have seen the whole coast of South America lifted up bodily ten or fifteen feet and let down again in an hour. We have seen the Andes sink 220 feet in seventy years. . . . Vast transpositions have taken place in the coast-line of China. The ancient capital, located, in all probability, in an accessible position near the centre of the empire, has now become nearly surrounded by water, and its site is on the peninsula of Corea. . . . There was a time when the rocky barriers of the Thracian Bosphorus gave way and the Black Sea subsided. It had covered a vast area in the north and east. Now this area became drained, and was known as the ancient Lectonia: it is now the prairie region of Russia, and the granary of Europe."

There is ample geological evidence that at one time the entire area of Great Britain was *submerged to the depth of at least seventeen hundred feet.* Over the face of the submerged land was strewn thick beds of sand, gravel, and clay, termed by geologists "the Northern Drift." The British Islands rose again from the sea, bearing these water-deposits on their bosom. What is now Sicily once lay deep beneath the sea: it subsequently rose 3000 feet above the sea-level. The Desert of Sahara was once under water, and its now burning sands are a deposit of the sea.

Geologically speaking, the submergence of Atlantis, within the historical period, was simply the last of a number of vast changes, by which the continent which once occupied the greater part of the Atlantic had gradually sunk under the ocean, while the new lands were rising on both sides of it.

We come now to the second question, Is it possible that Atlantis could have been suddenly destroyed by such a convulsion of nature as is described by Plato ? The ancients regarded this part of his story as a fable. With the wider knowledge which scientific research has afforded the modern world, we can affirm that such an event is not only possible, but that the history of even the last two centuries has furnished us with striking parallels for it. We now possess the record of numerous islands lifted above the waters, and others sunk beneath the waves, accompanied by storms and earthquakes similar to those which marked the destruction of Atlantis.

In 1783 Iceland was visited by convulsions more tremendous than any recorded in the modern annals of that country. About a month previous to the eruption on the main-land a submarine volcano burst forth in the sea, at a distance of thirty miles from the shore. It ejected so much pumice that the sea was covered with it for a distance of 150 miles, and ships were considerably impeded in their course. A new island was thrown up, consisting of high cliffs, which was claimed by his Danish Majesty, and named "Nyöe," or the New Island; but before a year had elapsed it sunk beneath the sea, leaving a reef of rocks thirty fathoms under water.

The earthquake of 1783 in Iceland destroyed 9000 people out of a population of 50,000; twenty villages were consumed by fire or inundated by water, and a mass of lava thrown out "greater than the bulk of Mont Blanc."

On the 8th of October, 1822, a great earthquake occurred on the island of Java, near the mountain of Galung Gung. "A loud explosion was heard, the earth shook, and immense columns of hot water and boiling mud, mixed with burning brimstone, ashes, and lapilli, of the size of nuts, were projected from the mountain like a water-spout, with such prodigious violence that large quantities fell beyond the river Tandoi, which is forty miles distant. . . . The first eruption lasted

nearly five hours; and on the following days the rain fell in
torrents, and the rivers, densely charged with mud, deluged
the country far and wide. At the end of four days (October
12th), a second eruption occurred, more violent than the first,
in which hot water and mud were again vomited, and great
blocks of basalt were thrown to the distance of seven miles
from the volcano. There was at the same time a violent earthquake, the face of the mountain was utterly changed, its summits broken down, and one side, which had been covered with
trees, became an enormous gulf in the form of a semicircle.
Over 4000 persons were killed and 114 villages destroyed."
(Lyell's "Principles of Geology," p. 430.)

In 1831 a new island was born in the Mediterranean, near
the coast of Sicily. It was called Graham's Island. It came
up with an earthquake, and "a water-spout sixty feet high and
eight hundred yards in circumference rising from the sea." In
about a month the island was two hundred feet high and three
miles in circumference; it soon, however, sunk beneath the sea.

The Canary Islands were probably a part of the original
empire of Atlantis. On the 1st of September, 1730, the earth
split open near Yaira, in the island of Lancerota. In one night
a considerable hill of ejected matter was thrown up; in a few
days another vent opened and gave out a lava stream which
overran several villages. It flowed at first rapidly, like water,
but became afterward heavy and slow, like honey. On the
11th of September more lava flowed out, covering up a village,
and precipitating itself with a horrible roar into the sea. Dead
fish floated on the waters in indescribable multitudes, or were
thrown dying on the shore; the cattle throughout the country
dropped lifeless to the ground, suffocated by putrid vapors,
which condensed and fell down in drops. These manifestations were accompanied by a storm such as the people of the
country had never known before. These dreadful commotions
lasted for *five years*. The lavas thrown out covered *one-third
of the whole island of Lancerota.*

The Gulf of Santorin, in the Grecian Archipelago, has been for two thousand years a scene of active volcanic operations. Pliny informs us that in the year 186 B.C. the island of "Old Kaimeni," or the Sacred Isle, was lifted up from the sea; and in A.D. 19 the island of "Thia" (the Divine) made its appearance. In A.D. 1573 another island was created, called "the small sunburnt island." In 1848 a volcanic convulsion of three months' duration created a great shoal; an earthquake

CALABRIAN PEASANTS INGULFED BY CREVASSES (1783).

destroyed many houses in Thera, and the sulphur and hydrogen issuing from the sea killed 50 persons and 1000 domestic animals. A recent examination of these islands shows that the whole mass of Santorin *has sunk, since its projection from the sea, over* 1200 *feet.*

The fort and village of Sindree, on the eastern arm of the Indus, above Luckput, was submerged in 1819 by an earthquake, together *with a tract of country* 2000 *square miles in extent.*

"In 1828 Sir A. Burnes went in a boat to the ruins of Sindree, where a single remaining tower was seen in the midst of a wide expanse of sea. The tops of the ruined walls still rose two or three feet above the level of the water; and, standing on one of these, he could behold nothing in the horizon but water, except in one direction, where a blue streak of land to the north indicated the Ullah Bund. This scene," says Lyell ("Principles of Geology," p. 462), "presents to the imagination a lively picture of the revolutions now in progress on the earth—a waste of waters where a few years before all was land, and the only land visible consisting of ground uplifted by a recent earthquake."

We give from Lyell's great work the following curious pictures of the appearance of the Fort of Sindree before and after the inundation.

In April, 1815, one of the most frightful eruptions recorded in history occurred in the province of Tomboro, in the island of Sumbawa, about two hundred miles from the eastern extremity of Java. It lasted from April 5th to July of that year; but was most violent on the 11th and 12th of July. The sound of the explosions was heard for nearly one thousand miles. *Out of a population of* 12,000, *in the province of Tombora, only twenty-six individuals escaped.* "Violent whirlwinds carried up men, horses, and cattle into the air, tore up the largest trees by the roots, and covered the whole sea with floating timber." (Raffles's "History of Java," vol. i., p. 28.) *The ashes darkened the air;* "the floating cinders to the westward of Sumatra formed, on the 12th of April, a mass two feet thick and several miles in extent, *through which ships with difficulty forced their way.*" The darkness in daytime was more profound than the blackest night. "The town called Tomboro, on the west side of Sumbawa, was overflowed by the sea, which encroached upon the shore, *so that the water remained*

FORT OF SINDREE, ON THE EASTERN BRANCH OF THE INDUS, BEFORE IT WAS
SUBMERGED BY THE EARTHQUAKE OF 1819.

VIEW OF THE FORT OF SINDREE FROM THE WEST IN MARCH, 1838.

*permanently eighteen feet deep in places where there was land
before.* The area covered by the convulsion was 1000 English miles in circumference. "*In the island of Amboyna, in
the same month and year, the ground opened, threw out water,*

and then closed again." (Raffles's "History of Java," vol. i., p. 25.)

But it is at that point of the European coast nearest to the site of Atlantis at Lisbon that the most tremendous earthquake of modern times has occurred. On the 1st of November, 1775, a sound of thunder was heard underground, and immediately afterward a violent shock threw down the greater part of the city. *In six minutes* 60,000 *persons perished.* A great concourse of people had collected for safety upon a new quay, built entirely of marble; but suddenly it sunk down with all the people on it, and not one of the dead bodies ever floated to the surface. A great number of small boats and vessels anchored near it, and, full of people, were swallowed up as in a whirlpool. No fragments of these wrecks ever rose again to the surface; the water where the quay went down is now 600 feet deep. The area covered by this earthquake was very great. Humboldt says that a portion of *the earth's surface, four times as great as the size of Europe, was simultaneously shaken.* It extended from the Baltic to the West Indies, and from Canada to Algiers. At eight leagues from Morocco the ground opened and swallowed a village of 10,000 inhabitants, and closed again over them.

It is very probable that the centre of the convulsion was in the bed of the Atlantic, at or near the buried island of Atlantis, and that it was a successor of the great earth throe which, thousands of years before, had brought destruction upon that land.

Ireland also lies near the axis of this great volcanic area, reaching from the Canaries to Iceland, and it has been many times in the past the seat of disturbance. The ancient annals contain numerous accounts of eruptions, preceded by volcanic action. In 1490, at the Ox Mountains, Sligo, one occurred by which one hundred persons and numbers of cattle were destroyed; and a volcanic eruption in May, 1788, on the hill of Knocklade, Antrim, poured a stream of lava sixty yards wide for thir-

ERUPTION OF VESUVIUS IN 1737.

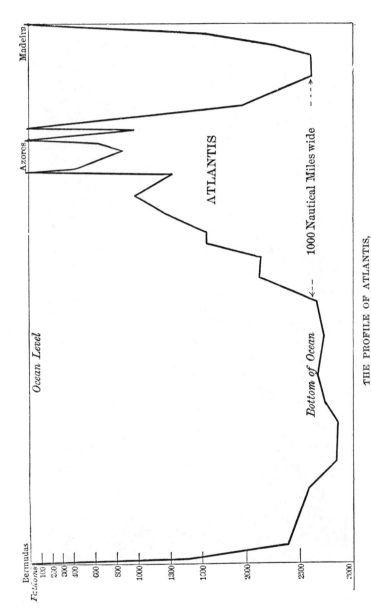

THE PROFILE OF ATLANTIS,

As revealed by the deep-sea soundings of H. M. ship "Challenger," and the U. S. ship "Dolphin."

ty-nine hours, and destroyed the village of Ballyowen and all the inhabitants, save a man and his wife and two children. ("Amer. Cyclop.," art. *Ireland.*)

While we find Lisbon and Ireland, east of Atlantis, subjected to these great earthquake shocks, the West India Islands, west of the same centre, have been repeatedly visited in a similar manner. In 1692 Jamaica suffered from a violent earthquake. The earth opened, and great quantities of water were cast out; many people were swallowed up in these rents; the earth caught some of them by the middle and squeezed them to death; the heads of others only appeared above-ground. A tract of land near the town of Port Royal, about a thousand acres in extent, sunk down in less than one minute, and the sea immediately rolled in.

The Azore Islands are undoubtedly the peaks of the mountains of Atlantis. They are even yet the centre of great volcanic activity. They have suffered severely from eruptions and earthquakes. In 1808 a volcano rose suddenly in San Jorge to the height of 3500 feet, and burnt for six days, desolating the entire island. In 1811 a volcano rose from the sea, near San Miguel, creating an island 300 feet high, which was named Sambrina, but which soon sunk beneath the sea. Similar volcanic eruptions occurred in the Azores in 1691 and 1720.

Along a great line, a mighty fracture in the surface of the globe, stretching north and south through the Atlantic, we find a continuous series of active or extinct volcanoes. In Iceland we have Ocrafa, Hecla, and Rauda Kamba; another in Pico, in the Azores; the peak of Teneriffe; Fogo, in one of the Cape de Verde Islands: while of extinct volcanoes we have several in Iceland, and two in Madeira; while Fernando de Noronha, the island of Ascension, St. Helena, and Tristan d'Acunha are all of volcanic origin. ("Cosmos," vol. v., p. 331.)

The following singular passage we quote entire from Lyell's "Principles of Geology," p. 436:

"In the *Nautical Magazine* for 1835, p. 642, and for 1838, p. 361, and in the *Comptes Rendus*, April, 1838, accounts are given of a series of volcanic phenomena, earthquakes, troubled water, floating scoria, and columns of smoke, which have been observed at intervals since the middle of the last century, in a space of open sea between longitudes 20° and 22° W., about half a degree south of the equator. These facts, says Mr. Darwin, seem to show that an island or archipelago is in process of formation in the middle of the Atlantic. A line joining St. Helena and Ascension would, if prolonged, intersect this slowly nascent focus of volcanic action. Should land be eventually formed here, it will not be the first that has been produced by igneous action in this ocean since it was inhabited by the existing species of testacea. At Porto Praya, in St. Jago, one of the Azores, a horizontal, calcareous stratum occurs, containing shells of recent marine species, covered by a great sheet of basalt eighty feet thick. It would be difficult to estimate too highly the commercial and political importance which a group of islands might acquire if, in the next two or three thousand years, they should rise in mid-ocean between St. Helena and Ascension."

These facts would seem to show that the great fires which destroyed Atlantis are still smouldering in the depths of the ocean; that the vast oscillations which carried Plato's continent beneath the sea may again bring it, with all its buried treasures, to the light; and that even the wild imagination of Jules Verne, when he described Captain Nemo, in his diving-armor, looking down upon the temples and towers of the lost island, lit by the fires of submarine volcanoes, had some groundwork of possibility to build upon.

But who will say, in the presence of all the facts here enumerated, that the submergence of Atlantis, in some great world-shaking cataclysm, is either impossible or improbable? As will be shown hereafter, when we come to discuss the Flood legends, every particular which has come down to us of the destruction of Atlantis has been duplicated in some of the accounts just given.

We conclude, therefore: 1. That it is proven beyond question, by geological evidence, that vast masses of land once existed in the region where Atlantis is located by Plato, and that therefore such an island must have existed; 2. That there is nothing improbable or impossible in the statement that it was destroyed suddenly by an earthquake " in one dreadful night and day."

Chapter V.

THE TESTIMONY OF THE SEA.

Suppose we were to find in mid-Atlantic, in front of the Mediterranean, in the neighborhood of the Azores, the remains of an immense island, sunk beneath the sea—one thousand miles in width, and two or three thousand miles long—would it not go far to confirm the statement of Plato that, "beyond the strait where you place the Pillars of Hercules, there was an island larger than Asia (Minor) and Libya combined," called Atlantis? And suppose we found that the Azores were the mountain peaks of this drowned island, and were torn and rent by tremendous volcanic convulsions; while around them, descending into the sea, were found great strata of lava; and the whole face of the sunken land was covered for thousands of miles with volcanic débris, would we not be obliged to confess that these facts furnished strong corroborative proofs of the truth of Plato's statement, that "in one day and one fatal night there came mighty earthquakes and inundations which ingulfed that mighty people? Atlantis disappeared beneath the sea; and then that sea became inaccessible on account of the quantity of mud which the ingulfed island left in its place."

And all these things recent investigation has proved conclusively. Deep-sea soundings have been made by ships of different nations; the United States ship *Dolphin*, the German frigate *Gazelle*, and the British ships *Hydra*, *Porcupine*, and *Challenger* have mapped out the bottom of the Atlantic, and the result is the revelation of a great elevation, reaching from a point on the coast of the British Islands southwardly to the coast of South America, at Cape Orange, thence south-east-

MAP OF ATLANTIS, WITH ITS ISLANDS AND CONNECTING RIDGES, FROM DEEP-SEA SOUNDINGS.

wardly to the coast of Africa, and thence southwardly to Tristan d'Acunha. I give one map showing the profile of this eleva- tion in the frontispiece, and another map, showing the outlines of the submerged land, on page 47. It rises about 9000 feet above the great Atlantic depths around it, and in the Azores, St. Paul's Rocks, Ascension, and Tristan d'Acunha it reaches the surface of the ocean.

Evidence that this elevation was once dry land is found in the fact that "the inequalities, the mountains and valleys of its surface, could never have been produced in accordance with any laws for the deposition of sediment, nor by submarine ele- vation; but, on the contrary, must have been carved by agen- cies *acting above the water level*." (*Scientific American*, July 28th, 1877.)

Mr. J. Starke Gardner, the eminent English geologist, is of the opinion that in the Eocene Period a great extension of land existed to the west of Cornwall. Referring to the loca- tion of the "Dolphin" and "Challenger" ridges, he asserts that "a great tract of land formerly existed where the sea now is, and that Cornwall, the Scilly and Channel Islands, Ireland and Brittany, are the remains of its highest summits." (*Popular Science Review*, July, 1878.)

Here, then, we have the backbone of the ancient continent which once occupied the whole of the Atlantic Ocean, and from whose washings Europe and America were constructed; the deepest parts of the ocean, 3500 fathoms deep, represent those portions which sunk first, to wit, the plains to the east and west of the central mountain range; some of the loftiest peaks of this range—the Azores, St. Paul's, Ascension, Tristan d'Acunha—are still above the ocean level; while the great body of Atlantis lies a few hundred fathoms beneath the sea. In these "connecting ridges" we see the pathway which once extended between the New World and the Old, and by means of which the plants and animals of one continent travelled to the other; and by the same avenues black men found their

way, as we will show hereafter, from Africa to America, and
red men from America to Africa.

And, as I have shown, the same great law which gradually
depressed the Atlantic continent, and raised the lands east
and west of it, is still at work: the coast of Greenland, which
may be regarded as the northern extremity of the Atlantic
continent, is still sinking "so rapidly that ancient buildings
on low rock-islands are now submerged, and the Greenlander
has learned by experience never to build near the water's edge."
("North Amer. of Antiq.," p. 504.)   The same subsidence is
going on along the shore of South Carolina and Georgia, while
the north of Europe and the Atlantic coast of South America
are rising rapidly.   Along the latter raised beaches, 1180 miles
long and from 100 to 1300 feet high, have been traced.

When these connecting ridges extended from America to
Europe and Africa, they shut off the flow of the tropical waters of the ocean to the north; there was then no "Gulf
Stream;" the land-locked ocean that laved the shores of Northern Europe was then intensely cold; and the result was the
Glacial Period.   When the barriers of Atlantis sunk sufficiently to permit the natural expansion of the heated water
of the tropics to the north, the ice and snow which covered
Europe gradually disappeared; the Gulf Stream flowed around
Atlantis, and it still retains the circular motion first imparted
to it by the presence of that island.

The officers of the *Challenger* found the entire ridge of Atlantis covered with volcanic deposits; these are the subsided
mud which, as Plato tells us, rendered the sea impassable after
the destruction of the island.

It does not follow that, at the time Atlantis was finally ingulfed, the ridges connecting it with America and Africa rose
above the water-level; these may have gradually subsided into
the sea, or have gone down in cataclysms such as are described
in the Central American books.   The Atlantis of Plato may
have been confined to the "Dolphin Ridge" of our map.

ANCIENT ISLANDS BETWEEN ATLANTIS AND THE MEDITERRANEAN, FROM DEEP-SEA
SOUNDINGS.

The United States sloop *Gettysburg* has also made some remarkable discoveries in a neighboring field. I quote from John James Wild (in *Nature*, March 1st, 1877, p. 377):

"The recently announced discovery by Commander Gorringe, of the United States sloop *Gettysburg*, of a bank of soundings bearing N. 85° W., and distant 130 miles from Cape St. Vincent, during the last voyage of the vessel across the Atlantic, taken in connection with previous soundings obtained in the same region of the North Atlantic, suggests the probable existence of a submarine ridge or plateau connecting the island of Madeira with the coast of Portugal, and the probable subaerial connection in prehistoric times of that island with the south-western extremity of Europe." . . . "These soundings reveal the existence of a channel of an average depth of from 2000 to 3000 fathoms, extending in a northeasterly direction from its entrance between Madeira and the Canary Islands toward Cape St. Vincent. . . . Commander Gorringe, when about 150 miles from the Strait of Gibraltar, found that the soundings decreased from 2700 fathoms to 1600 fathoms in the distance of a few miles. The subsequent soundings (five miles apart) gave 900, 500, 400, and 100 fathoms; and eventually a depth of 32 fathoms was obtained, in which the vessel anchored. The bottom was found to consist of live pink coral, and the position of the bank in lat. 36° 29' N., long. 11° 33' W."

The map on page 51 shows the position of these elevations. They must have been originally islands;—stepping-stones, as it were, between Atlantis and the coast of Europe.

Sir C. Wyville Thomson found that the specimens of the fauna of the coast of Brazil, brought up in his dredging-machine, are similar to those of the western coast of Southern Europe. This is accounted for by the connecting ridges reaching from Europe to South America.

A member of the *Challenger* staff, in a lecture delivered in London, soon after the termination of the expedition, gave it as his opinion that the great submarine plateau is the remains of "the lost Atlantis."

Chapter VI.

THE TESTIMONY OF THE FLORA AND FAUNA.

Proofs are abundant that there must have been at one time uninterrupted land communication between Europe and America. In the words of a writer upon this subject,

"When the animals and plants of the Old and New World are compared, one cannot but be struck with their identity; all or nearly all belong to the same genera, while many, even of the species, are common to both continents. This is most important in its bearing on our theory, as indicating that they radiated from a common centre *after the Glacial Period.* . . . The hairy mammoth, woolly-haired rhinoceros, the Irish elk, the musk-ox, the reindeer, the glutton, the lemming, etc., more or less accompanied this flora, and their remains are always found in the post-glacial deposits of Europe as low down as the South of France. In the New World beds of the same age contain similar remains, indicating that they came from a common centre, and were spread out over both continents alike." (*Westminster Review*, January, 1872, p. 19.)

Recent discoveries in the fossil beds of the Bad Lands of Nebraska prove that the horse originated in America. Professor Marsh, of Yale College, has identified the several preceding forms from which it was developed, rising, in the course of ages, from a creature not larger than a fox until, by successive steps, it developed into the true horse. How did the wild horse pass from America to Europe and Asia if there was not continuous land communication between the two continents? He seems to have existed in Europe in a wild state prior to his domestication by man.

The fossil remains of the camel are found in India, Africa, South America, and in Kansas. The existing alpacas and llamas of South America are but varieties of the camel family.

The cave bear, whose remains are found associated with the bones of the mammoth and the bones and works of man in the caves of Europe, was identical with the grizzly bear of our Rocky Mountains. The musk-ox, whose relics are found in the same deposits, now roams the wilds of Arctic America. The glutton of Northern Europe, in the Stone Age, is identical with the wolverine of the United States. According to Ruti-meyer, the ancient bison (*Bos priscus*) of Europe was identical with the existing American buffalo. "Every stage between the ancient cave bison and the European aurochs can be traced." The Norway elk, now nearly extinct, is identical with the American moose. The *Cervus Americanus* found in Kentucky was as large as the Irish elk, which it greatly resembled. The lagomys, or tailless hare, of the European caves, is now found in the colder regions of North America. The reindeer, which once occupied Europe as far down as France, was the same as the reindeer of America. Remains of the cave lion of Europe (*Felix spelœa*), a larger beast than the largest of the existing species, have been found at Natchez, Mississippi. The European cave wolf was identical with the American wolf.

Cattle were domesticated among the people of Switzerland during the earliest part of the Stone Period (Darwin's "Animals Under Domestication," vol. i., p. 103), that is to say, before the Bronze Age and the Age of Iron. Even at that remote period they had already, by long-continued selection, been developed out of wild forms akin to the American buffalo. M. Gervais ("Hist. Nat. des Mammifores," vol. xi., p. 191) concludes that the wild race from which our domestic sheep was derived is now extinct. The remains of domestic sheep are found in the debris of the Swiss lake-dwellings during the Stone Age. The domestic horse, ass, hog, and goat also date back to a like great antiquity. We have historical records 7000 years old,[†]

[†] Donnelly's Egyptian dates here and elsewhere were standard in his day, but would now be considered far too early. 4,500 to 5,000 years would be acceptable here.—E.F.B.

and during that time no similar domestication of a wild animal has been made. This fact speaks volumes as to the vast periods of time during which man must have lived in a civilized state to effect the domestication of so many and such useful animals.

And when we turn from the fauna to the flora, we find the same state of things.

An examination of the fossil beds of Switzerland of the Miocene Age reveals the remains of more than eight hundred different species of flower-bearing plants, besides mosses, ferns, etc. The total number of fossil plants catalogued from those beds, cryptogamous as well as phænogamous, is upward of three thousand. *The majority of these species have migrated to America.* There were others that passed into Asia, Africa, and even to Australia. The American types are, however, in the largest proportion. The analogues of the flora of the Miocene Age of Europe now grow in the forests of Virginia, North and South Carolina, and Florida; they include such familiar examples as magnolias, tulip-trees, evergreen oaks, maples, plane-trees, robinas, sequoias, etc. It would seem to be impossible that these trees could have migrated from Switzerland to America unless there was unbroken land communication between the two continents.

It is a still more remarkable fact that a comparison of the flora of the Old World and New goes to show that not only was there communication by land, over which the plants of one continent could extend to another, but that man must have existed, and have helped this transmigration, in the case of certain plants that were incapable of making the journey unaided.

Otto Kuntze, a distinguished German botanist, who has spent many years in the tropics, announces his conclusion that "In America and in Asia the principal domesticated tropical plants *are represented by the same species.*" He instances the *Manihot utilissima*, whose roots yield a fine flour; the tarro (*Colocasia esculenta*), the Spanish or red pepper, the tomato,

the bamboo, the guava, the mango-fruit, and especially the
banana. He denies that the American origin of tobacco,
maize, and the cocoa-nut is proved. He refers to the *Paritium
tiliaceum*, a malvaceous plant, hardly noticed by Europeans,
but very highly prized by the natives of the tropics, and cultivated everywhere in the East and West Indies; it supplies to
the natives of these regions so far apart their ropes and cord-
age. It is always seedless in a cultivated state. It existed in
America before the arrival of Columbus.

But Professor Kuntze pays especial attention to the banana,
or plantain. The banana is seedless. It is found throughout
tropical Asia and Africa. Professor Kuntze asks, "In what
way was this plant, which cannot stand a voyage through the
temperate zone, carried to America?" And yet it was generally cultivated in America before 1492. Says Professor Kuntze,
"It must be remembered that the plantain is a tree-like, herba-
ceous plant, possessing no easily transportable bulbs, like the
potato or the dahlia, nor propagable by cuttings, like the willow or the poplar. It has only a perennial root, which, once
planted, needs hardly any care, and yet produces the most
abundant crop of any known tropical plant." He then proceeds to discuss how it could have passed from Asia to America. He admits that the roots must have been transported
from one country to the other *by civilized man.* He argues
that it could not have crossed the Pacific from Asia to America, because the Pacific is nearly thrice or four times as wide as
the Atlantic. The only way he can account for the plantain
reaching America is to suppose that it was carried there when
the North Pole had a tropical climate! Is there any proof
that civilized man existed at the North Pole when it possessed
the climate of Africa?

Is it not more reasonable to suppose that the plantain, or
banana, was cultivated by the people of Atlantis, and carried
by their civilized agricultural colonies to the east and the west?
Do we not find a confirmation of this view in the fact alluded

to by Professor Kuntze in these words: "A cultivated plant which does not possess seeds must have been under culture *for a very long period*—we have not in Europe a single exclusively seedless, berry-bearing, cultivated plant—and hence it is perhaps fair to infer that these plants *were cultivated as early as the beginning of the middle of the Diluvial Period.*"

Is it possible that a plant of this kind could have been cultivated for this immense period of time in *both* Asia and America? Where are the two nations, agricultural and highly civilized, on those continents by whom it was so cultivated? What has become of them? Where are the traces of their civilization? All the civilizations of Europe, Asia, and Africa radiated from the Mediterranean; the Hindoo-Aryans advanced from the north-west; they were kindred to the Persians, who were next-door neighbors to the Arabians (cousins of the Phœnicians), and who lived along-side of the Egyptians, who had in turn derived their civilization from the Phœnicians.

It would be a marvel of marvels if *one* nation, on one continent, had cultivated the banana for such a vast period of time until it became seedless; the nation retaining a peaceful, continuous, agricultural civilization during all that time. But to suppose that two nations could have cultivated the same plant, under the same circumstances, on two different continents, for the same unparalleled lapse of time, is supposing an impossibility.

We find just such a civilization as was necessary, according to Plato, and under just such a climate, in Atlantis and nowhere else. We have found it reaching, by its contiguous islands, within one hundred and fifty miles of the coast of Europe on the one side, and almost touching the West India Islands on the other, while, by its connecting ridges, it bound together Brazil and Africa.

But it may be said these animals and plants may have passed from Asia to America across the Pacific by the continent of Lemuria; or there may have been continuous land communication at one time at Behring's Strait. True; but an examination of the flora of the Pacific States shows that very many of the trees and plants common to Europe and the Atlantic States are not to be seen west of the Rocky Mountains. The magnificent magnolias, the tulip-trees, the plane-trees, etc., which were found existing in the Miocene Age in Switzerland, and are found at the present day in the United States, are altogether lacking on the Pacific coast. The sources of supply of that region seem to have been far inferior to the sources of supply of the Atlantic States. Professor Asa Gray tells us that, out of sixty-six genera and one hundred and fifty-five species found in the forests east of the Rocky Mountains, only thirty-one genera and seventy-eight species are found west of the mountains. The Pacific coast possesses no papaw, no linden or basswood, no locust-trees, no cherry-tree large enough for a timber tree, no gum-trees, no sorrel-tree, nor kalmia; no persimmon-trees, not a holly, only one ash that may be called a timber tree, no catalpa or sassafras, not a single elm or hackberry, not a mulberry, not a hickory, or a beech, or a true chestnut. These facts would seem to indicate that the forest flora of North America entered it *from the east,* and that the Pacific States possess only those fragments of it that were able to struggle over or around the great dividing mountain-chain.

We thus see that the flora and fauna of America and Europe testify not only to the existence of Atlantis, but to the fact that in an earlier age it must have extended from the shores of one continent to those of the other; and by this bridge of land the plants and animals of one region passed to the other.

The cultivation of the cotton-plant and the manufacture of its product was known to both the Old and New World. Herodotus describes it (450 b.c.) as the tree of India that bears a fleece more beautiful than that of the sheep. Columbus found the natives of the West Indies using cotton cloth. It was also found in Mexico and Peru. It is a significant fact that the cotton-plant has been found growing wild in many parts of America, but never in the Old World. This would seem to indicate that the plant was a native of America; and this is confirmed by the superiority of American cotton, and the further fact that the plants taken from America to India constantly degenerate, while those taken from India to America as constantly improve.

There is a question whether the potato, maize, and tobacco were not cultivated in China ages before Columbus discovered America. A recent trav-

eller says, " The interior of China, along the course of the Yang-tse-Kiang, is a land full of wonders. In one place piscicultural nurseries line the banks for nearly fifty miles. All sorts of inventions, the cotton-gin included, claimed by Europeans and Americans, are to be found there forty centuries old. Plants, yielding drugs of great value, without number, the familiar tobacco and potato, maize, white and yellow corn, and other plants *believed to be indigenous to America, have been cultivated there from time immemorial.*"

Bonafous ("Histoire Naturelle du Mais," Paris, 1826) attributes a European or Asiatic origin to maize. The word *maize*, (Indian corn) is derived from *mahiz* or *mahis*, the name of the plant in the language of the Island of Hayti. And yet, strange to say, in the Lettish and Livonian languages, in the north of Europe, *mayse* signifies bread; in Irish, *maise* is food, and in the Old High German, *maz* is meat. May not likewise the Spanish *maiz* have antedated the time of Columbus, and borne testimony to early intercommunication between the people of the Old and New Worlds?

It is to Atlantis we must look for the origin of nearly all our valuable plants. Darwin says ("Animals and Plants under Domestication," vol. i., p. 374), "It has often been remarked that we do not owe a single useful plant to Australia, or the Cape of Good Hope—countries abounding to an unparalleled degree with endemic species—or to New Zealand, or to America south of the Plata; and, according to some authors, not to America north of Mexico." In other words, the domesticated plants are only found within the limits of what I shall show hereafter was the Empire of Atlantis and its colonies; for only here was to be found an ancient, long-continuing civilization, capable of developing from a wild state those plants which were valuable to man, including all the cereals on which to-day civilized man depends for subsistence. M. Alphonse de Candolle tells us that we owe 33 useful plants to Mexico, Peru, and Chili. According to the same high authority, of 157 valuable cultivated plants 85 can be traced back to their wild state; as to 40, there is doubt as to their origin; while 32 are utterly unknown in their aboriginal condition. ("Geograph. Botan. Raisonnée," 1855, pp. 810–991.) Certain roses—the imperial lily, the tuberose and the lilac—are said to have been cultivated from such a vast antiquity that they are not known in their wild state. (Darwin, "Animals and Plants," vol. i., p. 370.) And these facts are the more remarkable because, as De Candolle has shown, all the plants historically known to have been *first* cultivated in Europe still exist there in the wild state. (*Ibid.*) The inference is strong that the great cereals — wheat, oats, barley, rye, and maize—must have been first domesticated in a vast antiquity, or in some continent which has since disappeared, carrying the original wild plants with it.

Darwin quotes approvingly the opinion of Mr. Bentham ("Hist. Notes Cult. Plants"), "as the result of all the most reliable evidence that none of the Ceralia—wheat, rye, barley, and oats—exist or have existed truly wild in their present state." In the Stone Age of Europe five varieties of wheat and three of barley were cultivated. (Darwin, "Animals and Plants," vol. i., p. 382.) He says that it may be inferred, from the presence in

CEREALS OF THE AGE OF STONE IN EUROPE.

the lake habitations of Switzerland of a variety of wheat known as the Egyptian wheat, and from the nature of the weeds that grew among their crops, "that the lake inhabitants either still kept up commercial intercourse with some southern people, or had originally proceeded as colonists from the south." I should argue that they were colonists from the land where wheat and

barley were first domesticated, to wit, Atlantis. And when the
Bronze Age came, we find oats and rye making their appearance with the weapons of bronze, together with a peculiar kind
of pea. Darwin concludes (*Ibid.*, vol. i., p. 385) that wheat, barley, rye, and oats were either descended from ten or fifteen distinct species, "most of which are now unknown or extinct," or
from four or eight species closely resembling our present forms,
or so "widely different as to escape identification;" in which latter case, he says, "man must have cultivated the cereals at an
enormously remote period," and at that time practised "some
degree of selection."

Rawlinson ("Ancient Monarchies," vol. i., p. 578) expresses
the opinion that the ancient Assyrians possessed the pineapple.
"The representation on the monuments is so exact that I can
scarcely doubt the pineapple being intended." (See Layard's
"Nineveh and Babylon," p. 338.) The pineapple (*Bromelia an-
anassa*) is supposed to be of American origin, and unknown to
Europe before the time of Columbus; and yet, apart from the
revelations of the Assyrian monuments, there has been some
dispute upon this point. ("Amer. Cyclop.," vol. xiii., p. 528.)

It is not even certain that the use of tobacco was not known

ANCIENT IRISH PIPES.

to the colonists from Atlantis settled in Ireland in an age long prior to Sir Walter Raleigh. Great numbers of pipes have been found in the raths and tumuli of Ireland, which, there is every reason to believe, were placed there by men of the Prehistoric Period. The illustration on p. 63 represents some of the so-called "Danes' pipes" now in the collection of the Royal Irish Academy. The Danes entered Ireland many centuries before the time of Columbus, and if the pipes are theirs, they must have used tobacco, or some substitute for it, at that early period. It is probable, however, that the tumuli of Ireland antedate the Danes thousands of years.

Compare these pipes from the ancient mounds of Ireland with the accompanying picture of an Indian pipe of the Stone Age of New Jersey. ("Smithsonian Rep.," 1875, p. 342.)

ANCIENT INDIAN PIPE, NEW JERSEY.

Recent Portuguese travellers have found the most remote tribes of savage negroes in Africa, holding no commercial intercourse with Europeans, using strangely shaped pipes, in which they smoked a plant of the country. Investigations in America lead to the conclusion that tobacco was first burnt as an incense to the gods, the priest alone using the pipe; and from this beginning the extraordinary practice spread to the people, and thence over all the world. It may have crossed the Atlantic in a remote age, and have subsequently disappeared with the failure of retrograding colonists to raise the tobacco-plant.

PART II.

THE DELUGE.

Chapter I.

THE DESTRUCTION OF ATLANTIS DESCRIBED IN THE DELUGE LEGENDS.

HAVING demonstrated, as we think successfully, that there is no improbability in the statement of Plato that a large island, almost a continent, existed in the past in the Atlantic Ocean, nay, more, that it is a geological certainty that it did exist; and having further shown that it is not improbable but very possible that it may have sunk beneath the sea in the manner described by Plato, we come now to the next question, Is the memory of this gigantic catastrophe preserved among the traditions of mankind? We think there can be no doubt that an affirmative answer must be given to this question.

An event, which in a few hours destroyed, amid horrible convulsions, an entire country, with all its vast population—that population the ancestors of the great races of both continents, and they themselves the custodians of the civilization of their age—could not fail to impress with terrible force the minds of men, and to project its gloomy shadow over all human history. And hence, whether we turn to the Hebrews, the Aryans, the Phœnicians, the Greeks, the Cushites, or the inhabitants of America, we find everywhere traditions of the Deluge; and we shall see that all these traditions point unmistakably to the destruction of Atlantis.

François Lenormant says (*Contemp. Rev.*, Nov., 1879):

"The result authorizes us to affirm the story of the Deluge to be a universal tradition among all branches of the human race, with the one exception, however, of the black. Now, a recollection thus precise and concordant cannot be a myth voluntarily invented. No religious or cosmogonic myth presents this character of universality. It must arise from the reminiscence of a real and terrible event, so powerfully impressing the imagination of the first ancestors of our race as never to have been forgotten by their descendants. This cataclysm must have occurred near the first cradle of mankind, and before the dispersion of the families from which the principal races were to spring; for it would be at once improbable and uncritical to admit that, at as many different points of the globe as we should have to assume in order to explain the wide spread of these traditions, local phenomena so exactly alike should have occurred, their memory having assumed an identical form, and presenting circumstances that need not necessarily have occurred to the mind in such cases.

"Let us observe, however, that probably the diluvian tradition is not primitive, but imported in America; that it undoubtedly wears the aspect of an importation among the rare populations of the yellow race where it is found; and lastly, that it is doubtful among the Polynesians of Oceania. There will still remain three great races to which it is undoubtedly peculiar, *who have not borrowed it from each other*, but among whom the tradition is primitive, and goes back to the *most ancient times*, and these three races are precisely the only ones of which the Bible speaks as being *descended from Noah*—those of which it gives the ethnic filiation in the tenth chapter of Genesis. This observation, which I hold to be undeniable, attaches a singularly historic and exact value to the tradition as recorded by the Sacred Book, even if, on the other hand, it may lead to giving it a *more limited geographical and ethnological significance.* . . .

"But, as the case now stands, we do not hesitate to declare that, far from being a myth, the Biblical Deluge *is a real and historical fact*, having, to say the least, left its impress on the ancestors of three races—Aryan, or Indo-European, Semitic, or Syro-Arabian, Chamitic, or Cushite—that is to say, on the *three great civilized races of the ancient world*, those which constitute the higher humanity—before the ancestors of those races had as yet separated, and in the part of Asia they together inhabited."

Such profound scholars and sincere Christians as M. Schœbel (Paris, 1858), and M. Omalius d'Halloy (Bruxelles, 1866), deny the universality of the Deluge, and claim that "it extended only to the principal centre of humanity, to those who remained near its primitive cradle, without reaching the scattered tribes who had already spread themselves far away in almost desert regions. It is certain that the Bible narrative commences by relating facts common to the whole human species, confining itself subsequently to the annals of the race peculiarly chosen by the designs of Providence." (Lenormant and Chevallier, "Anc. Hist. of the East," p. 44.) This theory is supported by that eminent authority on anthropology, M. de Quatrefages, as well as by Cuvier; the Rev. R. P. Bellynck, S.J., admits that it has nothing expressly opposed to orthodoxy.

Plato identifies "the great deluge of all" with the destruction of Atlantis. The priest of Sais told Solon that before "the great deluge of all" Athens possessed a noble race, who performed many noble deeds, the last and greatest of which was resisting the attempts of Atlantis to subjugate them; and after this came the destruction of Atlantis, and the same great convulsion which overwhelmed that island destroyed a number of the Greeks. So that the Egyptians, who possessed the memory of many partial deluges, regarded this as "the great deluge of all."

CHAPTER II.

THE DELUGE OF THE BIBLE.

We give first the Bible history of the Deluge, as found in Genesis (chap. vi. to chap. viii.):

"And it came to pass, when men began to multiply on the face of the earth, and daughters were born unto them, that the sons of God saw the daughters of men that they were fair; and they took them wives of all which they chose.

"And the Lord said, My Spirit shall not always strive with man, for that he also is flesh: yet his days shall be a hundred and twenty years.

"There were giants in the earth in those days; and also after that, when the sons of God came in unto the daughters of men, and they bare children to them, the same became mighty men which were of old, men of renown.

"And God saw that the wickedness of man was great in the earth, and that every imagination of the thoughts of his heart was only evil continually. And it repented the Lord that he had made man on the earth, and it grieved him at his heart. And the Lord said, I will destroy man whom I have created from the face of the earth; both man, and beast, and the creeping thing, and the fowls of the air; for it repenteth me that I have made them. But Noah found grace in the eyes of the Lord.

["These are the generations of Noah: Noah was a just man and perfect in his generations, and Noah walked with God. And Noah begat three sons, Shem, Ham, and Japheth.]

"The earth also was corrupt before God; and the earth was filled with violence. And God looked upon the earth, and, behold, it was corrupt; for all flesh had corrupted his way upon the earth. And God said unto Noah, The end of all flesh is come before me; for the earth is filled with violence through them; and, behold, I will destroy them with the earth. Make thee an ark of gopher wood; rooms shalt thou make in the ark, and shalt pitch it within and without with pitch. And this is the fashion which thou shalt make it of: The length of the ark shall be three hundred cubits, the breadth of it fifty cubits, and the height of it thirty cubits. A window shalt thou make to the ark, and in a cubit shalt thou finish it above; and the door of the ark shalt thou set in the side thereof; with lower, second, and third stories shalt thou make it. And, behold, I, even I, do bring a flood of waters upon the earth, to destroy all flesh, wherein is the breath of life, from under heaven; and everything that is in the earth shall die. But with thee will I establish my covenant; and thou shalt come into the ark, thou, and thy sons, and thy wife, and thy sons' wives with thee. And of every living thing of all flesh, two of every sort shalt thou bring into the ark, to keep them alive with thee; they shall be male and female. Of fowls after their kind, and of cattle after their kind, of every creeping thing of the earth after his kind; two of every sort shall come unto thee, to keep them alive. And take thou unto thee of all food that is eaten, and thou shalt gather it to thee; and it shall be for food for thee, and for them.

"Thus did Noah; according to all that God commanded him, so did he.

"And the Lord said unto Noah, Come thou and all thy house into the ark; for thee have I seen righteous before me in this generation. Of every clean beast thou shalt take to thee by sevens, the male and his female: and of beasts that are not clean by two, the male and his female. Of fowls also of the air by sevens, the male and the female; to keep seed alive upon the face of all the earth. For yet seven days, and I will cause it to rain upon the earth forty days and forty nights; and every living substance that I have made will I destroy from off the face of the earth.

"And Noah did according unto all that the Lord commanded him. And Noah was six hundred years old when the flood of waters was upon the earth.

"And Noah went in, and his sons, and his wife, and his sons' wives with him, into the ark, because of the waters of the flood. Of clean beasts, and of beasts that are not clean, and of fowls, and of everything that creepeth upon the earth, there went in two and two unto Noah into the ark, the male and the female, as God had commanded Noah.

"And it came to pass after seven days, that the waters of the flood were upon the earth. In the six hundredth year of Noah's life, in the second month, the seventeenth day of the month, the same day were all the fountains of the great deep broken up, and the windows of heaven were opened. And the rain was upon the earth forty days and forty nights. In the self-same day entered Noah, and Shem, and Ham, and Japheth, the sons of Noah, and Noah's wife, and the three wives of his sons with them, into the ark; they, and every beast after his kind, and all the cattle after their kind, and every creeping thing that creepeth upon the earth after his kind, and every fowl after his kind, every bird of every sort. And they went in unto Noah into the ark, two and two of all flesh, wherein is the breath of life. And they that went in, went in male and female of all flesh, as God had commanded him: and the Lord shut him in.

"And the flood was forty days upon the earth; and the waters increased, and bare up the ark, and it was lifted up above the earth. And the waters prevailed, and were increased greatly upon the earth; and the ark went upon the face of the waters. And the waters prevailed exceedingly upon the earth; and all the high hills, that were under the whole heaven, were covered. Fifteen cubits upward did the waters prevail; and the mountains were covered. And all flesh died that moved upon the earth, both of fowl, and of cattle, and of beast, and of every creeping thing that creepeth upon the earth, and every man: all in whose nostrils was the breath of life, of all that was in the dry land, died. And every living substance was destroyed which was upon the face of the ground, both man, and cattle, and the creeping things, and the fowl of the heaven; and they were destroyed from the earth: and Noah only remained alive, and they that were with him in the ark. And the waters prevailed upon the earth a hundred and fifty days.

"And God remembered Noah, and every living thing, and all the cattle that was with him in the ark: and God made a wind to pass over the earth, and the waters assuaged. The fountains also of the deep and the windows of heaven were stopped, and the rain from heaven was restrained. And the waters returned from off the earth continually : and after the end of the hundred and fifty days the waters were abated. And the ark rested in the seventh month, on the seventeenth day of the month, upon the mountains of Ararat. And the waters decreased continually until the tenth month : in the tenth month, on the first day of the month, were the tops of the mountains seen.

"And it came to pass at the end of forty days, that Noah opened the window of the ark which he had made : and he sent forth a raven, which went forth to and fro, until the waters were dried up from off the earth. Also he sent forth a dove from him, to see if the waters were abated from off the face of the ground. But the dove found no rest for the sole of her foot, and she returned unto him into the ark ; for the waters were on the face of the whole earth. Then he put forth his hand, and took her, and pulled her in unto him into the ark. And he stayed yet other seven days ; and again he sent forth the dove out of the ark. And the dove came in to him in the evening, and, lo, in her mouth was an olive leaf plucked off : so Noah knew that the waters were abated from off the earth. And he stayed yet other seven days, and sent forth the dove, which returned not again unto him any more.

"And it came to pass in the six hundredth and first year, in the first month, the first day of the month, the waters were dried up from off the earth : and Noah removed the covering of the ark, and looked, and, behold, the face of the ground was dry. And in the second month, on the seven and twentieth day of the month, was the earth dried.

"And God spake unto Noah, saying, Go forth of the ark, thou, and thy wife, and thy sons, and thy sons wives with thee. Bring forth with thee every living thing that is with thee, of all flesh, both of fowl and of cattle, and of every creeping thing that creepeth upon the earth ; that they may breed abundantly in the earth, and be fruitful, and multiply upon the earth.

"And Noah went forth, and his sons, and his wife, and his sons' wives with him : every beast, every creeping thing, and every fowl, and whatsoever creepeth upon the earth, after their kinds, went forth out of the ark.

"And Noah builded an altar unto the Lord ; and took of every clean beast, and of every clean fowl, and offered burnt offerings on the altar. And the Lord smelled a sweet savour ;

and the Lord said in his heart, I will not again curse the ground any more for man's sake; for the imagination of man's heart is evil from his youth: neither will I again smite any more every thing living, as I have done. While the earth remaineth, seedtime and harvest, and cold and heat, and summer and winter, and day and night shall not cease."

Let us briefly consider this record.

It shows, taken in connection with the opening chapters of Genesis:

1. That the land destroyed by water was the country in which the civilization of the human race originated. Adam was at first naked (Gen., chap. iii., 7); then he clothed himself in leaves; then in the skins of animals (chap. iii., 21): he was the first that tilled the earth, having emerged from a more primitive condition in which he lived upon the fruits of the forest (chap. ii., 16); his son Abel was the first of those that kept flocks of sheep (chap. iv., 2); his son Cain was the builder of the first city (chap. iv., 17); his descendant, Tubal-cain, was the first metallurgist (chap. iv., 22); Jabal was the first that erected tents and kept cattle (chap. iv., 20); Jubal was the first that made musical instruments. We have here the successive steps by which a savage race advances to civilization. We will see hereafter that the Atlanteans passed through precisely similar stages of development.

2. The Bible agrees with Plato in the statement that these Antediluvians had reached great populousness and wickedness, and that it was on account of their wickedness God resolved to destroy them.

3. In both cases the inhabitants of the doomed land were destroyed in a great catastrophe by the agency of water; they were drowned.

4. The Bible tells us that in an earlier age, before their destruction, mankind had dwelt in a happy, peaceful, sinless condition in a Garden of Eden. Plato tells us the same thing of the earlier ages of the Atlanteans.

5. In both the Bible history and Plato's story the destruction of the people was largely caused by the intermarriage of the superior or divine race, " the sons of God," with an infeferior stock, " the children of men," whereby they were degraded and rendered wicked.

We will see hereafter that the Hebrews and their Flood legend are closely connected with the Phœnicians, whose connection with Atlantis is established in many ways.

It is now conceded by scholars that the genealogical table given in the Bible (Gen., chap. x.) is not intended to include the true negro races, or the Chinese, the Japanese, the Finns or Lapps, the Australians, or the American red men. It refers altogether to the Mediterranean races, the Aryans, the Cushites, the Phœnicians, the Hebrews, and the Egyptians. " The sons of Ham " were not true negroes, but the dark-brown races. (See Winchell's " Preadamites," chap. vii.)

If these races (the Chinese, Australians, Americans, etc.) are not descended from Noah they could not have been included in the Deluge. If neither China, Japan, America, Northern Europe, nor Australia were depopulated by the Deluge, the Deluge could not have been universal. But as it is alleged that it did destroy a country, and drowned all the people thereof except Noah and his family, the country so destroyed could not have been Europe, Asia, Africa, America, or Australia, for there has been no universal destruction of the people of those regions; or, if there had been, how can we account for the existence to-day of people on all of those continents whose descent Genesis does not trace back to Noah, and, in fact, about whom the writer of Genesis seems to have known nothing?

We are thus driven to one of two alternative conclusions: either the Deluge record of the Bible is altogether fabulous, or it relates to some land other than Europe, Asia, Africa, or Australia, some land that *was* destroyed by water. It is not fabulous; and the land it refers to is not Europe, Asia, Africa, or Australia—but Atlantis.   No other land is known to history or tradition that was overthrown in a great catastrophe by the agency of water; that was civilized, populous, powerful, and given over to wickedness.

That high and orthodox authority, François Lenormant, says ("Ancient Hist. of the East," vol. i., p. 64), "The descendants of Shem, Ham, and Japhet, so admirably catalogued by Moses, include one only of the races of humanity, the white race, whose three chief divisions he gives us as now recognized by anthropologists.   The other three races — yellow, black, and red—have no place in the Bible list of nations sprung from Noah."   As, therefore, the Deluge of the Bible destroyed only the land and people of Noah, it could not have been universal. The religious world does not pretend to fix the location of the Garden of Eden.   The Rev. George Leo Haydock says, "The precise situation cannot be ascertained; how great might be its extent we do not know;" and we will see hereafter that the unwritten traditions of the Church pointed to a region in the west, beyond the ocean which bounds Europe in that direction, as the locality in which "mankind dwelt before the Deluge."

It will be more and more evident, as we proceed in the consideration of the Flood legends of other nations, that the Antediluvian World was none other than Atlantis.

Chapter III.

THE DELUGE OF THE CHALDEANS.

We have two versions of the Chaldean story—unequally developed, indeed, but exhibiting a remarkable agreement. The one most anciently known, and also the shorter, is that which Berosus took from the sacred books of Babylon, and introduced into the history that he wrote for the use of the Greeks. After speaking of the last nine antediluvian kings, the Chaldean priest continues thus:

"Obartès Elbaratutu being dead, his son Xisuthros (Khasisatra) reigned eighteen sares (64,800 years). It was under him that the Great Deluge took place, the history of which is told in the sacred documents as follows: Cronos (Ea) appeared to him in his sleep, and announced that on the fifteenth of the month of Daisios (the Assyrian month Sivan—a little before the summer solstice) all men should perish by a flood. He therefore commanded him to take the beginning, the middle, and the end of whatever was consigned to writing, and to bury it in the City of the Sun, at Sippara; then to build a vessel, and to enter it with his family and dearest friends; to place in this vessel provisions to eat and drink, and to cause animals, birds, and quadrupeds to enter it; lastly, to prepare everything for navigation. And when Xisuthros inquired in what direction he should steer his bark, he was answered, 'toward the gods,' and enjoined to pray that good might come of it for men.

"Xisuthros obeyed, and constructed a vessel five stadia long and five broad; he collected all that had been prescribed to him, and embarked his wife, his children, and his intimate friends.

"The Deluge having come, and soon going down, Xisuthros

loosed some of the birds. These, finding no food nor place to alight on, returned to the ship. A few days later Xisuthros again let them free, but they returned again to the vessel, their feet full of mud. Finally, loosed the third time, the birds came no more back. Then Xisuthros understood that the earth was bare. He made an opening in the roof of the ship, and saw that it had grounded on the top of a mountain. He then descended with his wife, his daughter, and his pilot, who worshipped the earth, raised an altar, and there sacrificed to the gods; at the same moment he vanished with those who accompanied him.

"Meanwhile those who had remained in the vessel, not seeing Xisuthros return, descended too, and began to seek him, calling him by his name. They saw Xisuthros no more; but a voice from heaven was heard commanding them piety toward the gods; that he, indeed, was receiving the reward of his piety in being carried away to dwell thenceforth in the midst of the gods, and that his wife, his daughter, and the pilot of the ship shared the same honor. The voice further said that they were to return to Babylon, and, conformably to the decrees of fate, disinter the writings buried at Sippara in order to transmit them to men. It added that the country in which they found themselves was Armenia. These, then, having heard the voice, sacrificed to the gods and returned on foot to Babylon. Of the vessel of Xisuthros, which had finally landed in Armenia, a portion is still to be found in the Gordyan Mountains in Armenia, and pilgrims bring thence asphalte that they have scraped from its fragments. It is used to keep off the influence of witchcraft. As to the companions of Xisuthros, they came to Babylon, disinterred the writings left at Sippara, founded numerous cities, built temples, and restored Babylon."

"By the side of this version," says Lenormant, "which, interesting though it be, is, after all, second-hand, we are now able to place an original Chaldeo-Babylonian edition, which the lamented George Smith was the first to decipher on the cuneiform tablets exhumed at Nineveh, and now in the British Museum. Here the narrative of the Deluge appears as an episode in the eleventh tablet, or eleventh chant of the great epic of the town of Uruk. The hero of this poem, a kind of Hercules, whose name has not as yet been made out with certainty, being attacked by disease (a kind of leprosy), goes, with a view to its cure, to consult the patriarch saved from the Deluge, Khasisatra, in the distant land to which the gods have transported him, there to enjoy eternal felicity. He asks Khasisatra to reveal the secret of the events which led to his obtaining the privilege of immortality, and thus the patriarch is induced to relate the cataclysm.

"By a comparison of the three copies of the poem that the library of the palace of Nineveh contained, it has been possible to restore the narrative with hardly any breaks. These three copies were, by order of the King of Assyria, Asshurbanabal, made in the eighth century B.C., from a very ancient specimen in the sacerdotal library of the town of Uruk, founded by the monarchs of the first Chaldean empire. It is difficult precisely to fix the date of the original, copied by Assyrian scribes, but it certainly goes back to the ancient empire, seventeen centuries at least before our era, and even probably beyond; it was therefore much anterior to Moses, and nearly contemporaneous with Abraham. The variations presented by the three existing copies prove that the original was in the primitive mode of writing called the *hieratic*, a character which must have already become difficult to decipher in the eighth century B.C., as the copyists have differed as to the interpretation to be given to certain signs, and in other cases have simply reproduced exactly the forms of such as they did not understand. Finally, it results from a comparison of these variations, that the original, transcribed by order of Asshurbanabal, must itself have been a copy of some still more ancient manuscript, in which the original text had already received interlinear comments. Some of the copyists have introduced these into their text, others have omitted them. With these preliminary observations, I proceed to give integrally the narrative ascribed in the poem to Khasisatra:

" ' I will reveal to thee, O Izdhubar, the history of my preservation—and tell to thee the decision of the gods.

" ' The town of Shurippak, a town which thou knowest, is situated on the Euphrates—it was ancient, and in it [men did not honor] the gods. [I alone, I was] their servant, to the great gods—[The gods took counsel on the appeal of] Anu—[a deluge was proposed by] Bel—[and approved by Nabon, Nergal and] Adar.

" ' And the god [Ea], the immutable lord, repeated this command in a dream.—I listened to the decree of fate that he announced, and he said to me:—"Man of Shurippak, son of Ubaratutu—thou, build a vessel and finish it [quickly].—[By a deluge] I will destroy substance and life.—Cause thou to go up into the vessel the substance of all that has life.—The vessel thou shall build—600 cubits shall be the measure of its length —and 60 cubits the amount of its breadth and of its height.— [Launch it] thus on the ocean, and cover it with a roof."—I understood, and I said to Ea, my lord :—"[The vessel] that thou commandest me to build thus—[when] I shall do it,—young and old [shall laugh at me.]"—[Ea opened his mouth and] spoke. —He said to me, his servant :—"[If they laugh at thee] thou shalt say to them :—[shall be punished] he who has insulted me, [for the protection of the gods] is over me.— . . . like to caverns . . . ———— . . . I will exercise my judgment on that which is on high and that which is below . . . ———— . . . Close the vessel . . . ———— . . . At a given moment that I shall cause thee to know,—enter into it, and draw the door of the ship toward thee.—Within it, thy grains, thy furniture, thy provisions,— thy riches, thy men-servants, and thy maid-servants, and thy young people—the cattle of the field, and the wild beasts of the plain that I will assemble—and that I will send thee, shall be kept behind thy door."—Khasisatra opened his mouth and spoke ;—he said to Ea, his lord :—"No one has made [such a] ship.—On the prow I will fix . . . —I shall see . . . and the vessel . . . —the vessel thou commandest me to build [thus]— which in . . ."

" ' On the fifth day [the two sides of the bark] were raised. —In its covering fourteen in all were its rafters—fourteen in all did it count above.—I placed its roof, and I covered it.—I embarked in it on the sixth day; I divided its floors on the seventh ;—I divided the interior compartments on the eighth.

I stopped up the chinks through which the water entered in; —I visited the chinks, and added what was wanting.—I poured on the exterior three times 3600 measures of asphalte,—and three times 3600 measures of asphalte within.—Three times 3600 men, porters, brought on their heads the chests of provisions.—I kept 3600 chests for the nourishment of my family,—and the mariners divided among themselves twice 3600 chests.—For [provisioning] I had oxen slain;—I instituted [rations] for each day.—In [anticipation of the need of] drinks, of barrels, and of wine—[I collected in quantity] like to the waters of a river, [of provisions] in quantity like to the dust of the earth.—[To arrange them in] the chests I set my hand to. — ... of the sun ... the vessel was completed.— ... strong and—I had carried above and below the furniture of the ship. —[This lading filled the two-thirds.]

"'All that I possessed I gathered together; all I possessed of silver I gathered together; all that I possessed of gold I gathered—all that I possessed of the substance of life of every kind I gathered together.—I made all ascend into the vessel; my servants, male and female,—the cattle of the fields, the wild beasts of the plains, and the sons of the people, I made them all ascend.

"'Shamash (the sun) made the moment determined, and—— he announced it in these terms :—" In the evening I will cause it to rain abundantly from heaven; enter into the vessel and close the door."——The fixed moment had arrived, which he announced in these terms :—" In the evening I will cause it to rain abundantly from heaven."——When the evening of that day arrived, I was afraid,——I entered into the vessel and shut my door.——In shutting the vessel, to Buzur-shadi-rabi, the pilot,——I confided this dwelling, with all that it contained.

"'Mu-sheri-ina-namari—rose from the foundations of heaven in a black cloud;—Ramman thundered in the midst of the cloud,—and Nabon and Sharru marched before;—they marched, devastating the mountain and the plain ;—Nergal the powerful dragged chastisements after him;—Adar advanced, overthrowing before him;—the archangels of the abyss brought destruction,—in their terrors they agitated the earth.—The inundation of Ramman swelled up to the sky,—and [the earth] became without lustre, was changed into a desert.

"'They broke ... of the surface of the earth like ...;—

[they destroyed] the living beings of the surface of the earth.
—The terrible [Deluge] on men swelled up to [heaven].—
The brother no longer saw his brother; men no longer knew
each other. In heaven—the gods became afraid of the water-
spout, and—sought a refuge; they mounted up to the heaven
of Anu.—The gods were stretched out motionless, pressing
one against another like dogs.—Ishtar wailed like a child,—
the great goddess pronounced her discourse:—"Here is humanity returned into mud, and—this is the misfortune that I
have announced in the presence of the gods.—So I announced
the misfortune in the presence of the gods,—for the evil I announced the terrible [chastisement] of men who are mine.—I
am the mother who gave birth to men, and—like to the race
of fishes, there they are filling the sea;—and the gods, by reason of that—which the archangels of the abyss are doing, weep
with me."—The gods on their seats were seated in tears,—and
they held their lips closed, [revolving] future things.

"'Six days and as many nights passed; the wind, the water-
spout, and the diluvian rain were in all their strength. At the
approach of the seventh day the diluvian rain grew weaker, the
terrible water-spout—which had assailed after the fashion of
an earthquake—grew calm, the sea inclined to dry up, and the
wind and the water-spout came to an end. I looked at the
sea, attentively observing — and the whole of humanity had
returned to mud; like unto sea-weeds the corpses floated. I
opened the window, and the light smote on my face. I was
seized with sadness; I sat down and I wept;—and my tears
came over my face.

"'I looked at the regions bounding the sea: toward the
twelve points of the horizon; not any continent.—The vessel
was borne above the land of Nizir,—the mountain of Nizir
arrested the vessel, and did not permit it to pass over.—A day
and a second day the mountain of Nizir arrested the vessel,
and did not permit it to pass over;—the third and fourth day
the mountain of Nizir arrested the vessel, and did not permit
it to pass over;—the fifth and sixth day the mountain of Nizir
arrested the vessel, and did not permit it to pass over. At the
approach of the seventh day, I sent out and loosed a dove.
The dove went, turned, and—found no place to light on, and
it came back. I sent out and loosed a swallow; the swallow
went, turned, and—found no place to light on, and it came

back. I sent out and loosed a raven; the raven went and saw the corpses on the waters; it ate, rested, turned, and came not back.

"'I then sent out (what was in the vessel) toward the four winds, and I offered a sacrifice. I raised the pile of my burnt-offering on the peak of the mountain; seven by seven I disposed the measured vases,—and beneath I spread rushes, cedar, and juniper-wood. The gods were seized with the desire of it—the gods were seized with a benevolent desire of it;—and the gods assembled like flies above the master of the sacrifice. From afar, in approaching, the great goddess raised the great zones that Anu has made for their glory (the gods). These gods, luminous crystal before me, I will never leave them; in that day I prayed that I might never leave them. "Let the gods come to my sacrificial pile!—but never may Bel come to my sacrificial pile! for he did not master himself, and he has made the water-spout for the Deluge, and he has numbered my men for the pit."

"'From far, in drawing near, Bel—saw the vessel, and Bel stopped;—he was filled with anger against the gods and the celestial archangels:—

"'"No one shall come out alive! No man shall be preserved from the abyss!"—Adar opened his mouth and said; he said to the warrior Bel:—"What other than Ea should have formed this resolution?—for Ea possesses knowledge, and [he foresees] all."—Ea opened his mouth and spake; he said to the warrior Bel:—"O thou, herald of the gods, warrior,—as thou didst not master thyself, thou hast made the water-spout of the Deluge.—Let the sinner carry the weight of his sins, the blasphemer the weight of his blasphemy.—Please thyself with this good pleasure, and it shall never be infringed; faith in it never [shall be violated].—Instead of thy making a new deluge, let lions appear and reduce the number of men;—instead of thy making a new deluge, let hyenas appear and reduce the number of men;—instead of thy making a new deluge, let there be famine, and let the earth be [devastated];—instead of thy making a new deluge, let Dibbara appear, and let men be [mown down]. I have not revealed the decision of the great gods;—it is Khasisatra who interpreted a dream and comprehended what the gods had decided."

"'Then, when his resolve was arrested, Bel entered into the

vessel.—He took my hand and made me rise.—He made my wife rise, and made her place herself at my side.—He turned around us and stopped short; he approached our group.—"Until now Khasisatra has made part of perishable humanity;—but lo, now Khasisatra and his wife are going to be carried away to live like the gods,—and Khasisatra will reside afar at the mouth of the rivers."—They carried me away, and established me in a remote place at the mouth of the streams.'

"This narrative," says Lenormant, "follows with great exactness the same course as that, or, rather, as those of Genesis; and the analogies are, on both sides, striking."

When we consider these two forms of the same legend, we see many points wherein the story points directly to Atlantis.

1. In the first place, Berosus tells us that the god who gave warning of the coming of the Deluge was Chronos. Chronos, it is well known, was the same as Saturn. Saturn was an ancient king of Italy, who, far anterior to the founding of Rome, introduced civilization from some other country to the Italians. He established industry and social order, filled the land with plenty, and created the golden age of Italy. He was suddenly removed to the abodes of the gods. His name is connected, in the mythological legends, with "a great Saturnian continent" in the Atlantic Ocean, and a great kingdom which, in the remote ages, embraced Northern Africa and the European coast of the Mediterranean as far as the peninsula of Italy, and "certain islands in the sea;" agreeing, in this respect, with the story of Plato as to the dominions of Atlantis. The Romans called the Atlantic Ocean "Chronium Mare," the Sea of Chronos, thus identifying Chronos with that ocean. The pillars of Hercules were also called by the ancients "the pillars of Chronos."

Here, then, we have convincing testimony that the country referred to in the Chaldean legends was the land of Chronos, or Saturn—the ocean world, the dominion of Atlantis.

2. Hea or Ea, the god of the Nineveh tablets, was a fish-god;

he was represented in the Chaldean monuments as half man and half fish; he was described as the god, not of the rivers and seas, but of "the abyss"—to wit, the ocean. He it was who was said to have brought civilization and letters to the ancestors of the Assyrians. He clearly represented an ancient, maritime, civilized nation ; he came from the ocean, and was associated with some land and people that had been destroyed by rain and inundations. The fact that the scene of the Deluge is located on the Euphrates proves nothing, for we will see hereafter that almost every nation had its especial mountain on which, according to its traditions, the ark rested ; just as every Greek tribe had its own particular mountain of Olympos. The god Bel of the legend was the Baal of the Phœnicians, who, as we shall show, were of Atlantean origin. Bel, or Baal, was worshipped on the western and northern coasts of Europe, and gave his name to the Baltic, the Great and Little Belt, Baleshaugen, Balestranden, etc.; and to many localities in the British Islands, as, for instance, Belan and the Baal hills in Yorkshire.

3. In those respects wherein the Chaldean legend, evidently the older form of the tradition, differs from the Biblical record, we see that in each instance we approach nearer to Atlantis. The account given in Genesis is the form of the tradition that would be natural to an inland people. Although there is an allusion to "the breaking up of the fountains of the great deep" (about which I shall speak more fully hereafter), the principal destruction seems to have been accomplished by rain; hence the greater period allowed for the Deluge, to give time enough for the rain to fall, and subsequently drain off from the land. A people dwelling in the midst of a continent could not conceive the possibility of a whole world sinking beneath the sea; they therefore supposed the destruction to have been caused by a continuous down-pour of rain for forty days and forty nights.

In the Chaldean legend, on the contrary, the rain lasted but seven days; and we see that the writer had a glimpse of the fact that the destruction occurred in the midst of or near the sea. The ark of Genesis (*têbâh*) was simply a chest, a coffer, a big box, such as might be imagined by an inland people. The ark of the Chaldeans was a veritable ship; it had a prow, a helm, and a pilot, and men to manage it; and it navigated "the sea."

4. The Chaldean legend represents not a mere rain-storm, but a tremendous cataclysm. There was rain, it is true, but there was also thunder, lightning, earthquakes, wind, a water-spout, and a devastation of mountain and land by the war of the elements. All the dreadful forces of nature were fighting together over the doomed land: "the archangel of the abyss brought destruction," "the water rose to the sky," "the brother no longer saw his brother; men no longer knew each other;" the men "filled the sea like fishes;" *the sea was filled with mud*, and "the corpses floated like sea-weed." When the storm abated the land had totally disappeared—there was no longer "*any continent.*" Does not all this accord with "that dreadful day and night" described by Plato?

5. In the original it appears that Izdhubar, when he started to find the deified Khasisatra, travelled first, for nine days' journey, to the sea; then secured the services of a boatman, and, entering a ship, sailed for fifteen days before finding the Chaldean Noah. This would show that Khasisatra dwelt in a far country, one only attainable by crossing the water; and this, too, seems like a reminiscence of the real site of Atlantis. The sea which a sailing-vessel required fifteen days to cross must have been a very large body of water; in fact, an ocean.

Chapter IV.

THE DELUGE LEGENDS OF OTHER NATIONS.

A collection of the Deluge legends of other nations will throw light upon the Biblical and Chaldean records of that great event.

The author of the treatise "On the Syrian Goddess" acquaints us with the diluvian tradition of the Arameans, directly derived from that of Chaldea, as it was narrated in the celebrated Sanctuary of Hierapolis, or Bambyce.

"The generality of people," he says, "tells us that the founder of the temple was Deucalion Sisythes—that Deucalion in whose time the great inundation occurred. I have also heard the account given by the Greeks themselves of Deucalion; the myth runs thus: The actual race of men is not the first, for there was a previous one, all the members of which perished. We belong to a second race, descended from Deucalion, and multiplied in the course of time. As to the former men, they are said to have been full of insolence and pride, committing many crimes, disregarding their oath, neglecting the rights of hospitality, unsparing to suppliants; accordingly, they were punished by an immense disaster. All on a sudden enormous volumes of water issued from the earth, and rains of extraordinary abundance began to fall; the rivers left their beds, and *the sea overflowed its shores;* the whole earth was covered with water, and all men perished. Deucalion alone, because of his virtue and piety, was preserved alive to give birth to a new race. This is how he was saved: He placed himself, his children, and his wives in a great coffer that he had, in which pigs, horses, lions, serpents, and all other terrestrial animals came to seek refuge with him. He received them all; and while they were in the coffer Zeus inspired them with reciprocal amity, which prevented their devouring one another. In this man-ner, shut up within one single coffer, they floated as long as the waters remained in force. Such is the account given by the Greeks of Deucalion.

"But to this, which they equally tell, the people of Hierapo-lis add a marvellous narrative: That in their country a great chasm opened, into which all the waters of the Deluge poured. Then Deucalion raised an altar, and dedicated a temple to Hera (Atargatis) close to this very chasm. I have seen it; it is very narrow, and situated under the temple. Whether it was once large, and has now shrunk, I do not know; but I have seen it, and it is quite small. In memory of the event the following is the rite accomplished: Twice a year sea-water is brought to the temple. This is not only done by the priests, but nu-merous pilgrims come from the whole of Syria and Arabia, and even from beyond the Euphrates, bringing water. It is poured out in the temple and goes into the cleft, which, nar-row as it is, swallows up a considerable quantity. This is said to be in virtue of a religious law instituted by Deucalion to preserve the memory of the catastrophe, and of the benefits that he received from the gods. Such is the ancient tradition of the temple."

"It appears to me difficult," says Lenormant, "not to recog-nize an echo of fables popular in all Semitic countries about this chasm of Hierapolis, and the part it played in the Del-uge, in the enigmatic expressions of the Koran respecting the oven (*tannur*) which began to bubble and disgorge water all around at the commencement of the Deluge. We know that this *tannur* has been the occasion of most grotesque imagin-ings of Mussulman commentators, who had lost the tradition of the story to which Mohammed made allusion. And, more-over, the Koran formally states that the waters of the Deluge were absorbed in the bosom of the earth."

Here the Xisuthros of Berosus becomes Deucalion-*Sisythes.* The animals are not collected together by Deucalion, as in the case of Noah and Khasisatra, but they crowded into the vessel of their own accord, driven by the terror with which the storm had inspired them; as in great calamities the creatures of the forest have been known to seek refuge in the houses of men.

India affords us an account of the Deluge which, by its poverty, strikingly contrasts with that of the Bible and the Chaldeans. Its most simple and ancient form is found in the *Çatapatha Bráhmana* of the Rig-Veda. It has been translated for the first time by Max Müller.

"One morning water for washing was brought to Manu, and when he had washed himself a fish remained in his hands, and it addressed these words to him: 'Protect me, and I will save thee.' 'From what wilt thou save me?' 'A deluge will sweep all creatures away; it is from that I will save thee.' 'How shall I protect thee?' The fish replied, 'While we are small we run great dangers, for fish swallow fish. Keep me at first in a vase; when I become too large for it, dig a basin to put me into. When I shall have grown still more, throw me into the ocean; then I shall be preserved from destruction.' Soon it grew a large fish. It said to Manu, 'The very year I shall have reached my full growth the Deluge will happen. Then build a vessel and worship me. When the waters rise, enter the vessel, and I will save thee.'

"After keeping him thus, Manu carried the fish to the sea. In the year indicated Manu built a vessel and worshipped the fish. And when the Deluge came he entered the vessel. Then the fish came swimming up to him, and Manu fastened the cable of the ship to the horn of the fish, by which means the latter made it pass over the Mountain of the North. The fish said, 'I have saved thee; fasten the vessel to a tree, that the water may not sweep it away while thou art on the mountain; and in proportion as the waters decrease thou shalt descend.' Manu descended with the waters, and this is what is called the *descent of Manu* on the Mountain of the North. The Deluge had carried away all creatures, and Manu remained alone."

There is another form of the Hindoo legend in the *Puránas*. Lenormant says:

"We must also remark that in the *Puránas* it is no longer Manu Vaivasata that the divine fish saves from the Deluge, but a different personage, the King of the Dástas—*i. e.*, fishers

—Satyravata, 'the man who loves justice and truth,' strikingly corresponding to the Chaldean Khasisatra. Nor is the Puranic version of the Legend of the Deluge to be despised, though it be of recent date, and full of fantastic and often puerile details. In certain aspects it is less Aryanized than that of *Brâhmana* or than the *Mahâbhârata;* and, above all, it gives some circumstances omitted in these earlier versions, which must yet have belonged to the original foundation, since they appear in the Babylonian legend; a circumstance preserved, no doubt, by the oral tradition—popular, and not Brahmanic—with which the *Purânas* are so deeply imbued. This has already been observed by Pictet, who lays due stress on the following passage of the *Bhâgavata-Purâna:* 'In seven days,' said Vishnu to Satyravata, *'the three worlds shall be submerged.'* There is nothing like this in the *Brâhmana* nor the *Mahâbhârata,* but in Genesis the Lord says to Noah, 'Yet seven days and I will cause it to rain upon the earth;' and a little farther we read, 'After seven days the waters of the flood were upon the earth.' ... Nor must we pay less attention to the directions given by the fish-god to Satyravata for the placing of the sacred Scriptures in a safe place, in order to preserve them from Hayagriva, a marine horse dwelling in the abyss. ... We recognize in it, under an Indian garb, the very tradition of the interment of the sacred writings at Sippara by Khasisatra, such as we have seen it in the fragment of Berosus."

The references to "the three worlds" and the "fish-god" in these legends point to Atlantis. The "three worlds" probably refers to the great empire of Atlantis, described by Plato, to wit, the western continent, America, the eastern continent, Europe and Africa, considered as one, and the island of Atlantis. As we have seen, Poseidon, the founder of the civilization of Atlantis, is identical with Neptune, who is always represented riding a dolphin, bearing a trident, or three-pronged symbol, in his hand, emblematical probably of the triple kingdom. He is thus a sea-god, or fish-god, and he comes to save the representative of his country.

And we have also a new and singular form of the legend in the following. Lenormant says:

"Among the Iranians, in the sacred books containing the fundamental Zoroastrian doctrines, and dating very far back, we meet with a tradition which must assuredly be looked upon as a variety of that of the Deluge, though possessing a special character, and diverging in some essential particulars from those we have been examining. It relates how Yima, who, in the original and primitive conception, was the father of the human race, was warned by Ahuramazda, the good deity, of the earth being about to be devastated by a flood. The god ordered Yima to construct a refuge, a square garden, *vara*, protected by an enclosure, and to cause the germs of men, beasts, and plants to enter it, in order to escape annihilation. Accordingly, when the inundation occurred, the garden of Yima, with all that it contained, was alone spared, and the message of safety was brought thither by the bird Karshipta, the envoy of Ahuramazda." (" Vendûdid," vol. ii., p. 46.)

This clearly signifies that, prior to the destruction of Atlantis, a colony had been sent out to some neighboring country. These emigrants built a walled town, and brought to it the grains and domestic animals of the mother country ; and when the island of Atlantis sunk in the ocean, a messenger brought the terrible tidings to them in a ship.

"The Greeks had two principal legends as to the cataclysm by which primitive humanity was destroyed. The first was connected with the name of Ogyges, the most ancient of the kings of Bœotia or Attica—a quite mythical personage, lost in the night of ages, his very name seemingly derived from one signifying deluge in Aryan idioms, in Sanscrit *Angha*. It is said that in his time the whole land was covered by a flood, whose waters reached the sky, and from which he, together with some companions, escaped in a vessel.

"The second tradition is the Thessalian legend of Deucalion. Zeus having worked to destroy the men of the age of bronze, with whose crimes he was wroth, Deucalion, by the advice of Prometheus, his father, constructed a coffer, in which he took refuge with his wife, Pyrrha. The Deluge came ; the chest, or coffer, floated at the mercy of the waves for nine days and nine nights, and was finally stranded on Mount Parnassus. Deucalion and Pyrrha leave it, offer sacrifice, and, according

to the command of Zeus, repeople the world by throwing behind them 'the bones of the earth'—namely, stones, which
change into men. This Deluge of Deucalion is, in Grecian
tradition, what most resembles a universal deluge. Many authors affirm that it extended to the whole earth, and that the
whole human race perished. At Athens, in memory of the
event, and to appease the manes of its victims, a ceremony
called *Hydrophoria* was observed, having so close a resemblance to that in use at Hierapolis, in Syria, that we can hardly fail to look upon it as a Syro-Phœnician importation, and
the result of an assimilation established in remote antiquity
between the Deluge of Deucalion and that of Khasisatra, as
described by the author of the treatise 'On the Syrian Goddess.' Close to the temple of the Olympian Zeus a fissure in
the soil was shown, in length but one cubit, through which
it was said the waters of the Deluge had been swallowed up.
Thus, every year, on the third day of the festival of the An-
thestéria, a day of mourning consecrated to the dead—that is,
on the thirteenth of the month of Anthestérion, toward the beginning of March—it was customary, as at Bambyce, to pour
water into the fissure, together with flour mixed with honey,
poured also into the trench dug to the west of the tomb, in
the funeral sacrifices of the Athenians."

In this legend, also, there are passages which point to Atlantis. We will see hereafter that the Greek god Zeus was one
of the kings of Atlantis. "The men of the age of bronze"
indicates the civilization of the doomed people; they were
the great metallurgists of their day, who, as we will see, were
probably the source of the great number of implements and
weapons of bronze found all over Europe. Here, also, while
no length of time is assigned to the duration of the storm, we
find that the ark floated but nine days and nights. Noah was
one year and ten days in the ark, Khasisatra was not half that
time, while Deucalion was afloat only nine days.

At Megara, in Greece, it was the eponym of the city, Megaros, son of Zeus and one of the nymphs, Sithnides, who, warned by the cry of cranes of the imminence of the danger of the
coming flood, took refuge on Mount Geranien. Again, there

was the Thessalian Cerambos, who was said to have escaped
the flood by rising into the air on wings given him by the
nymphs; and it was Perirrhoos, son of Eolus, that Zeus Naios
had preserved at Dodona. For the inhabitants of the Isle of
Cos the hero of the Deluge was *Merops*, son of Hyas, who
there assembled under his rule the remnant of humanity preserved with him. The traditions of Rhodes only supposed
the Telchines, those of Crete Sasion, to have escaped the cataclysm. In Samothracia the same character was attributed to
Saon, said to be the son of Zeus or of Hermes.

It will be observed that in all these legends the name of
Zeus, King of Atlantis, reappears. It would appear probable
that many parties had escaped from the catastrophe, and had
landed at the different points named in the traditions; or else
that colonies had already been established by the Atlanteans at
those places. It would appear impossible that a maritime people could be totally destroyed; doubtless many were on shipboard in the harbors, and others going and coming on distant
voyages.

"The invasion of the East," says Baldwin ('Prehistoric Nations,' p. 396), "to which the story of Atlantis refers, seems to
have given rise to the Panathenæa, the oldest, greatest, and
most splendid festivals in honor of Athena celebrated in Attica. These festivals are said to have been established by Erichthonus in the most ancient times remembered by the historical
traditions of Athens. Boeckh says of them, in his 'Commentary on Plato:'

"'In the greater Panathenæa there was carried in procession a *peplum* of Minerva, representing the war with the giants
and the victory of the gods of Olympus. In the lesser Panathenæa they carried another *peplum* (covered with symbolic
devices), which showed how the Athenians, supported by Minerva, had the advantage in the war with the Atlantes.' A
scholia quoted from Proclus by Humboldt and Boeckh says:
'The historians who speak of the islands of the exterior sea

tell us that in their time there were seven islands consecrated to Proserpine, and three others of immense extent, of which the first was consecrated to Pluto, the second to Ammon, and the third to Neptune. The inhabitants of the latter had preserved a recollection (transmitted to them by their ancestors) of the island of Atlantis, which was extremely large, and for a long time held sway over all the islands of the Atlantic Ocean. Atlantis was also consecrated to Neptune.'" (See Humboldt's "Histoire de la Géographie du Nouveau Continent," vol. i.)

No one can read these legends and doubt that the Flood was an historical reality. It is impossible that in two different places in the Old World, remote from each other, religious ceremonies should have been established and perpetuated from age to age in memory of an event which never occurred. We have seen that at Athens and at Hierapolis, in Syria, pilgrims came from a distance to appease the god of the earthquake, by pouring offerings into fissures of the earth said to have been made at the time Atlantis was destroyed.

More than this, we know from Plato's history that the Athenians long preserved in their books the memory of a victory won over the Atlanteans in the early ages, and celebrated it by national festivals, with processions and religious ceremonies.

It is too much to ask us to believe that Biblical history, Chaldean, Iranian, and Greek legends signify nothing, and that even religious pilgrimages and national festivities were based upon a myth.

I would call attention to the further fact that in the Deluge legend of the Isle of Cos the hero of the affair was Merops. Now we have seen that, according to Theopompus, one of the names of the people of Atlantis was "Meropes."

But we have not reached the end of our Flood legends. The Persian Magi possessed a tradition in which the waters issued from the oven of an old woman. Mohammed borrowed this story, and in the Koran he refers to the Deluge as coming from an oven. "All men were drowned save Noah and his family; and then God said, 'O earth, swallow up thy waters;

and thou, O heaven, withhold thy rain;' and immediately the waters abated."

In the bardic poems of Wales we have a tradition of the Deluge which, although recent, under the concise forms of the triads, is still deserving of attention. As usual, the legend is localized in the country, and the Deluge counts among three terrible catastrophes of the island of Prydian, or Britain, the other two consisting of devastation by fire and by drought.

"The first of these events," it is said, "was the eruption of Llyn-llion, or 'the lake of waves,' and the inundation (*bawdd*) of the whole country, by which all mankind was drowned with the exception of Dwyfan and Dwyfach, who saved themselves in a vessel without rigging, and it was by them that the island of Prydian was repeopled."

Pictet here observes:

"Although the triads in their actual form hardly date far- ther than the thirteenth or fourteenth century, some of them are undoubtedly connected with very ancient traditions, and nothing here points to a borrowing from Genesis.

"But it is not so, perhaps, with another triad, speaking of the vessel *Nefyddnaf-Neifion*, which at the time of the over- flow of Llyon-llion, bore a pair of all living creatures, and rather too much resembles the ark of Noah. The very name of the patriarch may have suggested this triple epithet, obscure as to its meaning, but evidently formed on the principle of Cymric alliteration. In the same triad we have the enigmatic story of the horned oxen (*ychain banog*) of Hu the mighty, who drew out of Llyon-llion the *avanc* (beaver or crocodile?), in order that the lake should not overflow. The meaning of these enigmas could only be hoped from deciphering the chaos of barbaric monuments of the Welsh middle age; but meanwhile we cannot doubt that the Cymri possessed an indigenous tra- dition of the Deluge."

We also find a vestige of the same tradition in the Scandi- navian Ealda. Here the story is combined with a cosmogonic myth. The three sons of Borr—Othin, Wili, and We—grand- sons of Buri, the first man, slay Ymir, the father of the Hrim-

thursar, or ice giants, and his body serves them for the construction of the world.   Blood flows from his wounds in such
abundance that all the race of giants is drowned in it except
Bergelmir, who saves himself, with his wife, in a boat, and
reproduces the race.

\ In the *Edda* of *Sæmund*, "The Vala's Prophecy" (stz. 48–56,
p. 9), we seem to catch traditional glimpses of a terrible catastrophe, which reminds us of the Chaldean legend :

"Then trembles Yggdrasil's ash yet standing, groans that ancient tree, and the Jötun Loki is loosed.   The shadows groan
on the ways of Hel (the goddess of death), until the fire of
Surt has consumed *the tree.   Hyrm steers from the east, the
waters rise,* the mundane snake is coiled in jötun-rage.   The
worm beats the water and the eagle screams ; the pale of beak
tears carcasses ; (the ship) Naglfar is loosed.   Surt from the
south comes with flickering flame ; shines from his sword the
Valgod's sun.   The stony hills are dashed together, the giant-
esses totter ; men tread the path of Hel, and heaven is cloven.
The sun darkens, *earth in ocean sinks,* fall from heaven the
bright stars, fire's breath assails the all-nourishing, towering fire
plays against heaven itself."

Egypt does not contain a single allusion to the Flood.   Lenormant says :

"While the tradition of the Deluge holds so considerable a
place in the legendary memories of all branches of the Aryan
race, the monuments and original texts of Egypt, with their
many cosmogonic speculations, have not afforded one, even distant, allusion to this cataclysm.   When the Greeks told the
Egyptian priests of the Deluge of Deucalion, their reply was
that they had been preserved from it as well as from the conflagration produced by Phaëthon ; they even added that the
Hellenes were childish in attaching so much importance to
that event, as there had been several other local catastrophes
resembling it.   According to a passage in Manetho, much sus-
pected, however, of being an interpolation, Thoth, or Hermes
Trismegistus, had himself, before the cataclysm, inscribed on
stelæ, in hieroglyphical and sacred language, the principles of
all knowledge.   After it the second Thoth translated into the

vulgar tongue the contents of these stelæ. This would be the only Egyptian mention of the Deluge, the same Manetho not speaking of it in what remains to us of his 'Dynasties,' his only complete authentic work. The silence of all other myths of the Pharaonic religion on this head render it very likely that the above is merely a foreign tradition, recently introduced, and no doubt of Asiatic and Chaldean origin."

To my mind the explanation of this singular omission is very plain. The Egyptians had preserved in their annals the precise history of the destruction of Atlantis, out of which the Flood legends grew; and, as they told the Greeks, there had been no universal flood, but only local catastrophes. Possessing the real history of the local catastrophe which destroyed Atlantis, they did not indulge in any myths about a universal deluge covering the mountain-tops of all the world. They had no Ararat in their neighborhood.

The traditions of the early Christian ages touching the Deluge pointed to the quarter of the world in which Atlantis was situated.

There was a quaint old monk named Cosmos, who, about one thousand years ago, published a book, "Topographia Christiana," accompanied by a map, in which he gives his view of the world as it was then understood. It was a body surrounded by water, and resting on nothing. "The earth," says Cosmos, "presses downward, but the igneous parts tend upward," and between the conflicting forces the earth hangs suspended, like Mohammed's coffin in the old story. The accompanying illus-

THE WORLD, ACCORDING TO COSMOS.

tration (page 95) represents the earth surrounded by the ocean, and beyond this ocean was "the land where men dwelt before the Deluge."

He then gives us a more accurate map, in detail, of the known world of his day.

I copy this map, not to show how much more we know than poor Cosmos, but because he taught that all around this habitable world there was yet another world, adhering closely on all sides to the circumscribing walls of heaven. "Upon the eastern side of this transmarine land he judges man was created; and that there the paradise of gladness was located,

MAP OF EUROPE, AFTER COSMOS.

such as here on the eastern edge is described, where it received our first parents, driven out of Paradise to that extreme point of land on the sea-shore. Hence, upon the coming of the Deluge, Noah and his sons were borne by the ark to the earth we now inhabit. The four rivers he supposes to be gushing up the spouts of Paradise." They are depicted on the above map: O is the Mediterranean Sea; P, the Arabian Gulf; L, the Caspian Sea; Q, the Tigris; M, the river Pison; "*and J, the land where men dwelt before the Flood.*"

It will be observed that, while he locates Paradise in the east, he places the scene of the Deluge in the west; and he supposes that Noah came from the scene of the Deluge to Europe.

This shows that the traditions in the time of Cosmos looked to the west as the place of the Deluge, and that after the Deluge Noah came to the shores of the Mediterranean. The fact, too, that there was land in the west beyond the ocean is recognized by Cosmos, and is probably a dim echo from Atlantean times.

The following rude cut, from Cosmos, represents the high mountain in the north behind which the sun hid himself at night, thus producing the alternations of day and night. His solar majesty is just getting behind the mountain, while Luna looks calmly on at the operation. The mountain is as crooked as Culhuacan, the crooked mountain of Atzlan described by the Aztecs.

THE MOUNTAIN THE SUN GOES BEHIND AT NIGHT.

Chapter V.

THE DELUGE LEGENDS OF AMERICA.

"It is a very remarkable fact," says Alfred Maury, "that we find in America traditions of the Deluge coming infinitely nearer to that of the Bible and the Chaldean religion than among any people of the Old World. It is difficult to suppose that the emigration that certainly took place from Asia into North America by the Kourile and Aleutian Islands, and still does so in our day, should have brought in these memories, since no trace is found of them among those Mongol or Siberian populations which were fused with the natives of the New World. . . . The attempts that have been made to trace the origin of Mexican civilization to Asia have not as yet led to any sufficiently conclusive facts. Besides, had Buddhism, which we doubt, made its way into America, it could not have introduced a myth not found in its own scriptures. The cause of these similarities between the diluvian traditions of the nations of the New World and that of the Bible remains therefore unexplained."

The cause of these similarities can be easily explained: the legends of the Flood did not pass into America by way of the Aleutian Islands, or through the Buddhists of Asia, but were derived from an actual knowledge of Atlantis possessed by the people of America.

Atlantis and the western continent had from an immemorial age held intercourse with each other; the great nations of America were simply colonies from Atlantis, sharing in its civilization, language, religion, and blood. From Mexico to the peninsula of Yucatan, from the shores of Brazil to the heights of Bolivia and Peru, from the Gulf of Mexico to the head-waters of the Mississippi River, the colonies of Atlantis extended; and therefore it is not strange to find, as Alfred Maury says, American traditions of the Deluge coming nearer to that of the Bible and the Chaldean record than those of any people of the Old World.

"The most important among the American traditions are the Mexican, for they appear to have been definitively fixed by symbolic and mnemonic paintings before any contact with Europeans. According to these documents, the Noah of the Mexican cataclysm was Coxcox, called by certain peoples Teocipactli or Tezpi. He had saved himself, together with his wife Xochiquetzal, in a bark, or, according to other traditions, on a raft made of cypress-wood (*Cupressus disticha*). Paintings retracing the deluge of Coxcox have been discovered among the Aztecs, Miztecs, Zapotecs, Tlascaltecs, and Mechoacaneses. The tradition of the latter is still more strikingly in conformity with the story as we have it in Genesis, and in Chaldean sources. It tells how Tezpi embarked in a spacious vessel with his wife, his children, and several animals, and grain, whose preservation was essential to the subsistence of the human race. When the great god Tezcatlipoca decreed that the waters should retire, Tezpi sent a vulture from the bark. The bird, feeding on the carcasses with which the earth was laden, did not return. Tezpi sent out other birds, of which the humming-bird only came back with a leafy branch in its beak. Then Tezpi, seeing that the country began to vegetate, left his bark on the mountain of Colhuacan.

"The document, however, that gives the most valuable information," says Lenormant, "as to the cosmogony of the Mexicans is one known as 'Codex Vaticanus,' from the library where it is preserved. It consists of four symbolic pictures, representing the four ages of the world preceding the actual one. They were copied at Chobula from a manuscript anterior to the conquest, and accompanied by the explanatory commentary of Pedro de los Rios, a Dominican monk, who, in 1566, less than fifty years after the arrival of Cortez, devoted himself to the research of indigenous traditions as being necessary to his missionary work."

There were, according to this document, four ages of the world. The first was an age of giants (the great mammalia?)

who were destroyed by famine; the second age ended in a conflagration; the third age was an age of monkeys.

"Then comes the fourth age, *Atonatiuh*, 'Sun of Water,' whose number is $10 \times 400 + 8$, or 4008. It ends by a great inundation, a veritable deluge. All mankind are changed into fish, with the exception of one man and his wife, who save themselves in a bark made of the trunk of a cypress-tree. The picture represents Matlalcueye, goddess of waters, and consort of Tlaloc, god of rain, as darting down toward earth. Coxcox and Xochiquetzal, the two human beings preserved, are seen seated on a tree-trunk and floating in the midst of the waters. This flood is represented as the last cataclysm that devastates the earth."

The learned Abbé Brasseur de Bourbourg translates from the Aztec language of the "Codex Chimalpopoca" the following Flood legend:

"This is the sun called *Nahui-atl*, '4 water.' Now the water was tranquil for forty years, plus twelve, and men lived for the third and fourth times. When the sun *Nahui-atl* came there had passed away four hundred years, plus two ages, plus seventy-six years. Then all mankind was lost and drowned, and found themselves changed into fish. The sky came nearer the water. In a single day all was lost, and the day *Nahui-xochitl*, '4 flower,' destroyed all our flesh.

"And that year was that of *cé-calli*, '1 house,' and the day *Nahui-atl* all was lost. Even the mountains *sunk into the water*, and the water remained tranquil for fifty-two springs.

"Now at the end of the year the god Titlacahuan had warned Nata and his spouse Nena, saying, 'Make no more wine of Agave, but begin to hollow out a great cypress, and you will enter into it when in the month Tozontli the water approaches the sky.'

"Then they entered in, and when the god had closed the door, he said, 'Thou shalt eat but one ear of maize, and thy wife one also.'

"But as soon as they had finished they went out, and the water remained calm, for the wood no longer moved, and, on opening it, they began to see fish.

" Then they lit a fire, by rubbing together pieces of wood, and they roasted fish.

" The gods Citlallinicué and Citlalatonac, instantly looking down said: 'Divine Lord, what is that fire that is making there? Why do they thus smoke the sky?' At once Titlacahuan - Tezcatlipoca descended. He began to chide, saying, ' Who has made this fire here?' And, seizing hold of the fish, he shaped their loins and heads, and they were transformed into dogs (*chichime*)."

Here we note a remarkable approximation to Plato's account of the destruction of Atlantis. " In one day and one fatal night," says Plato, " there came mighty earthquakes and inundations that ingulfed that warlike people." " In a single day all was lost," says the Aztec legend. And, instead of a rainfall of forty days and forty nights, as represented in the Bible, here we see " in a single day . . . *even the mountains sunk into the water;*" not only the land on which the people dwelt who were turned into fish, but the very mountains of that land sunk into the water. Does not this describe the fate of Atlantis? In the Chaldean legend " the great goddess Ishtar wailed like a child," saying, " I am the mother who gave birth to men, and, *like to the race of fishes,* they are filling the sea."

In the account in Genesis, Noah " builded an altar unto the Lord, and took of every clean beast, and of every clean fowl, and offered burnt offerings on the altar. And the Lord smelled a sweet savor; and the Lord said in his heart, 'I will not again curse the ground any more for man's sake.'" In the Chaldean legend we are told that Khasisatra also offered a sacrifice, a burnt offering, " and the gods assembled like flies above the master of the sacrifice." But Bel came in a high state of indignation, just as the Aztec god did, and was about to finish the work of the Deluge, when the great god Ea took pity in his heart and interfered to save the remnant of mankind.

These resemblances cannot be accidental; neither can they be the interpolations of Christian missionaries, for it will be observed the Aztec legends differ from the Bible in points where they resemble on the one hand Plato's record, and on the other the Chaldean legend.

The name of the hero of the Aztec story, *Nata*, pronounced with the broad sound of the *a*, is not far from the name of Noah or Noe. The Deluge of Genesis is a Phœnician, Semitic, or Hebraic legend, and yet, strange to say, the name of Noah, which occurs in it, bears no appropriate meaning in those tongues, but is derived from Aryan sources; its fundamental root is *Na*, to which in all the Aryan language is attached the meaning of water—ναειν, to flow; νᾶμα, water; Nympha, Neptunus, water deities. (Lenormant and Chevallier, "Anc. Hist. of the East," vol. i., p. 15.) We find the root *Na* repeated in the name of this Central American Noah, *Na-ta*, and probably in the word "*Na*-hui-atl"—the age of water.

But still more striking analogies exist between the Chaldean legend and the story of the Deluge as told in the "Popul Vuh" (the Sacred Book) of the Central Americans:

"Then the waters were agitated by the will of the Heart of Heaven (Hurakan), and a great inundation came upon the heads of these creatures.... They were ingulfed, and a resinous thickness descended from heaven; ... the face of the earth was obscured, and a heavy darkening rain commenced—rain by day and rain by night.... There was heard a great noise above their heads, as if produced by fire. Then were men seen running, pushing each other, filled with despair; they wished to climb upon their houses, and the houses, tumbling down, fell to the ground; they wished to climb upon the trees, and the trees shook them off; they wished to enter into the grottoes (caves), and the grottoes closed themselves before them.... Water and fire contributed to the universal ruin at the time of the last great cataclysm which preceded the fourth creation."

Observe the similarities here to the Chaldean legend. There is the same graphic description of a terrible event. The "black cloud" is referred to in both instances; also the dreadful noises, the rising water, the earthquake rocking the trees, overthrowing the houses, and crushing even the mountain caverns; "the men running and pushing each other, filled with despair," says the "Popul Vuh;" "the brother no longer saw his brother," says the Assyrian legend.

And here I may note that this word *hurakan*—the spirit of the abyss, the god of storm, the hurricane—is very suggestive, and testifies to an early intercourse between the opposite shores of the Atlantic. We find in Spanish the word *huracan;* in Portuguese, *furacan;* in French, *ouragan;* in German, Danish, and Swedish, *orcan*—all of them signifying a storm; while in Latin *furo*, or *furio*, means to rage. And are not the old Swedish *hurra*, to be driven along; our own word *hurried;* the Icelandic word *hurra*, to be rattled over frozen ground, all derived from the same root from which the god of the abyss, Hurakan, obtained his name? The last thing a people forgets is the name of their god; we retain to this day, in the names of the days of the week, the designations of four Scandinavian gods and one Roman deity.

It seems to me certain the above are simply two versions of the same event; that while ships from Atlantis carried terrified passengers to tell the story of the dreadful catastrophe to the people of the Mediterranean shores, other ships, flying from the tempest, bore similar awful tidings to the civilized races around the Gulf of Mexico.

The native Mexican historian, Ixtlilxochitl, gave this as the Toltec legend of the Flood:

"It is found in the histories of the Toltecs that this age and *first world*, as they call it, lasted 1716 years; that men were destroyed by tremendous rains and lightning from the sky, and even all the land, without the exception of anything, and the highest mountains, were covered up and submerged in water *fifteen cubits* (caxtolmolatli); and here they added other fables of how men came to multiply from the few who escaped from this destruction in a "toptlipetlocali;" that this word nearly signifies a close chest; and how, after men had multiplied, they erected a very high "zacuali," which is to-day a tower of great height, in order to take refuge in it should the second world (age) be destroyed. Presently their languages were confused, and, not being able to understand each other, they went to different parts of the earth.

"The Toltecs, consisting of seven friends, with their wives, who understood the same language, came to these parts, having first passed great land and seas, having lived in caves, and having endured great hardships in order to reach this land; ... they wandered 104 years through different parts of the world before they reached Hue Hue Tlapalan, which was in Ce Tecpatl, 520 years after the Flood." ("Ixtlilxochitl Relaciones," in Kingsborough's "Mex. Ant.," vol. ix., pp. 321, 322.)

It will of course be said that this account, in those particulars where it agrees with the Bible, was derived from the teachings of the Spanish priests; but it must be remembered that Ixtlilxochitl was an Indian, a native of Tezcuco, a son of the queen, and that his "Relaciones" were drawn from the archives of his family and the ancient writings of his nation: he had no motive to falsify documents that were probably in the hands of hundreds at that time.

Here we see that the depth of the water over the earth, "fifteen cubits," given in the Toltec legend, is precisely the same as that named in the Bible: "fifteen cubits upward did the waters prevail." (Gen., chap. vii., 20.)

In the two curious picture-histories of the Aztecs preserved in the Boturini collection, and published by Gamelli Careri and

THE STARTING-POINT OF THE AZTECS, ACCORDING TO THE GAMELLI CARERI PICTURED MS.

THE STARTING-POINT OF THE AZTECS, ACCORDING TO THE BOTURINI PICTURED WRITING.

others, there is a record of their migrations from their original location through various parts of the North American continent until their arrival in Mexico. In both cases their starting-point is an *island*, from which they pass in a boat; and the island contains in one case a mountain, and in the other a high temple in the midst thereof. These things seem to be reminiscences of their origin in Atlantis.

In each case we see the crooked mountain of the Aztec legends, the Calhuacan, looking not unlike the bent mountain of the monk, Cosmos.

In the legends of the Chibchas of Bogota we seem to have distinct reminiscences of Atlantis. Bochica was their leading divinity. During two thousand years he employed himself in elevating his subjects. He lived in the sun, while his wife Chia occupied the moon. This would appear to be an allusion to the worship of the sun and moon. Beneath Bochica in their mythology was Chibchacum. In an angry mood he brought a deluge on the people of the table-land. Bochica punished him for this act, and obliged him ever after, like Atlas, to bear the burden of the earth on his back. Occasionally he shifts the earth from one shoulder to another, and this causes earthquakes!

Here we have allusions to an ancient people who, during thousands of years, were elevated in the scale of civilization, and were destroyed by a deluge; and with this is associated an Atlantean god bearing the world on his back. We find even the rainbow appearing in connection with this legend. When Bochica appeared in answer to prayer to quell the deluge he is seated on a rainbow. He opened a breach in the earth at Tequendama, through which the waters of the flood escaped, precisely as we have seen them disappearing through the crevice in the earth near Bambyce, in Greece.

The Toltecs traced their migrations back to a starting-point called "Aztlan," or "Atlan." This could be no other than Atlantis. (Bancroft's "Native Races," vol. v., p. 221.) "The

original home of the Nahuatlacas was Aztlan, the location of
which has been the subject of much discussion. The causes
that led to their exodus from that country can only be con-
jectured; but they may be supposed to have been driven out
by their enemies, for Aztlan is described as a land too fair
and beautiful to be left willingly in the mere hope of finding
a better." (Bancroft's "Native Races," vol. v., p. 306.) The
Aztecs also claimed to have come originally from Aztlan.
(*Ibid.*, p. 321.) Their very name, Aztecs, was derived from
Aztlan. (*Ibid.*, vol. ii., p. 125). They were Atlanteans.

The "Popul Vuh" tells us that after the migration from
Aztlan three sons of the King of the Quiches, upon the death
of their father, "determined to go as their fathers had ordered
to the East, on the shores of the sea whence their fathers had
come, to receive the royalty, 'bidding adieu to their brothers
and friends, and promising to return.' Doubtless they passed
over the sea when they went to the East to receive the royalty.
Now this is the name of the lord, of the monarch of the people of the East where they went. And when they arrived
before the lord Nacxit, the name of the great lord, the only
judge, whose power was without limit, behold he granted them
the sign of royalty and all that represents it ... and the insignia of royalty ... all the things, in fact, which they brought
on their return, and which they went to receive from the other
side of the sea—the art of painting from Tulan, *a system of
writing,* they said, *for the things recorded in their histories.*"
(Bancroft's "Native Races," vol. v., p. 553; "Popul Vuh," p.
294.)

This legend not only points to the East as the place of
origin of these races, but also proves that this land of the
East, this Aztlan, this Atlantis, exercised dominion over the
colonies in Central America, and furnished them with the es-
sentials of civilization. How completely does this agree with
the statement of Plato that the kings of Atlantis held dominion over parts of "the great opposite continent!"

Professor Valentini ("Maya Archæol.," p. 23) describes an Aztec picture in the work of Gemelli ("Il giro del mondo," vol. vi.) of the migration of the Aztecs from Aztlan:

"Out of a sheet of water there projects the peak of a mountain; on it stands a tree, and on the tree a bird spreads its wings. At the foot of the mountain-peak there comes out of the water the heads of a man and a woman. The one wears on his head the symbol of his name, *Coxcox*, a pheasant. The other head bears that of a hand with a bouquet (*xochitl*, a flower, and *quetzal*, shining in green gold). In the foreground is a boat, out of which a naked man stretches out his hand imploringly to heaven. Now turn to the sculpture in the Flood tablet (on the great Calendar stone). There you will find represented the Flood, and with great emphasis, by the accumulation of all those symbols with which the ancient Mexicans conveyed the idea of water: a tub of standing water, drops springing out—not two, as heretofore in the symbol for *Atl*, water—but four drops; the picture for moisture, a snail; above, a crocodile, the king of the rivers. In the midst of these symbols you notice the profile of a man with a fillet, and a smaller one of a woman. There can be no doubt these are the Mexican Noah, *Coxcox*, and his wife, *Xochiquetzal;* and at the same time it is evident (the Calendar stone, we know, was made in A.D., 1478) that the story of them, and the pictures representing the story, have not been invented by the Catholic clergy, but really existed among these nations long before the Conquest."

CALENDAR STONE.

The above figure represents the Flood tablet on the great Calendar stone.

When we turn to the uncivilized Indians of America, while we still find legends referring to the Deluge, they are, with one exception, in such garbled and uncouth forms that we can only see glimpses of the truth shining through a mass of fable.

The following tradition was current among the Indians of the Great Lakes:

" In former times the father of the Indian tribes dwelt *toward the rising sun.* Having been warned in a dream that a deluge was coming upon the earth, he built a raft, on which he saved himself, with his family and all the animals. He floated thus for several months. The animals, who at that time spoke, loudly complained and murmured against him. At last a new earth appeared, on which he landed with all the animals, who from that time lost the power of speech, as a punishment for their murmurs against their deliverer."

According to Father Charlevoix, the tribes of Canada and the valley of the Mississippi relate in their rude legends that all mankind was destroyed by a flood, and that the Good Spirit, to repeople the earth, had changed animals into men. It is to J. S. Kohl we owe our acquaintance with the version of the Chippeways — full of grotesque and perplexing touches — in which the man saved from the Deluge is called Menaboshu. To know if the earth be drying, he sends a bird, the diver, out of his bark; then becomes the restorer of the human race and the founder of existing society.

A clergyman who visited the Indians north-west of the Ohio in 1764 met, at a treaty, a party of Indians from the west of the Mississippi.

" They informed him that one of their most ancient traditions was that, a great while ago, they had a common father, who lived toward the rising of the sun, and governed the whole world; that all the white people's heads were under his feet; that he had twelve sons, by whom he administered the government; that the twelve sons behaved very bad, and tyrannized over the people, abusing their power; that the Great Spirit, being thus angry with them, suffered the white people to introduce spirituous liquors among them, made them drunk, stole the special gift of the Great Spirit from them, and by this means usurped power over them; and ever since the Indians' heads were under the white people's feet." (Boudinot's " Star in the West," p. 111.)

Here we note that they looked " toward the rising sun"—toward Atlantis—for the original home of their race; that this

region governed "the whole world;" that it contained white
people, who were at first a subject race, but who subsequently
rebelled, and acquired dominion over the darker races. We
will see reason hereafter to conclude that Atlantis had a com-
posite population, and that the rebellion of the Titans in Greek
mythology was the rising up of a subject population.

In 1836 C. S. Rafinesque published in Philadelphia, Pa., a
work called "The American Nations," in which he gives the
historical songs or chants of the Lenni-Lenapi, or Delaware Indians, the tribe that originally dwelt along the Delaware River.
After describing a time "when there was nothing but sea-water
on top of the land," and the creation of sun, moon, stars, earth,
and man, the legend depicts the Golden Age and the Fall in
these words: "All were willingly pleased, all were easy-think-
ing, and all were well-happified. But after a while a snake-
priest, *Powako*, brings on earth secretly the snake-worship (*Ini-
tako*) of the god of the snakes, *Wakon*. And there came wickedness, crime, and unhappiness. And bad weather was coming, distemper was coming, with death was coming. All this
happened *very long ago, at the first land, Netamaki*, beyond
the great *ocean Kitahikau*." Then follows the Song of the
Flood:

"There was, long ago, a powerful snake, *Maskanako*, when
the men had become bad beings, *Makowini*. This strong snake
had become the foe of the Jins, and they became troubled, hating each other. Both were fighting, both were spoiling, both
were never peaceful. And they were fighting, least man *Mat-
tapewi* with dead-keeper *Nihaulowit*. And the strong snake
readily resolved to destroy or fight the beings or the men. The
dark snake he brought, the monster (*Amanyam*) he brought,
snake-rushing water he brought (it). *Much water is rushing,
much go to hills, much penetrate, much destroying.* Meanwhile
at *Tula* (this is the same Tula referred to in the Central American legends), at THAT ISLAND, Nana-Bush (the great hare Nana)
becomes the ancestor of beings and men. Being born creeping, he is ready to move and dwell at *Tula*. The beings and
men all go forth from the flood creeping in shallow water or

swimming afloat, asking which is the way to the turtle-back, *Tula-pin.* But there are many monsters in the way, and some men were devoured by them. But the daughter of a spirit helped them in a boat, saying, ' Come, come;' they were coming and were helped. The name of the boat or raft is *Mo-kol.* . . . Water running off, it is drying; in the plains and the mountains, at the path of the cave, elsewhere went the powerful action or motion." Then follows Song 3, describing the condition of mankind after the Flood. Like the Aryans, they moved into a cold country : "It freezes was there; it snows was there; it is cold was there." They move to a milder region to hunt cattle; they divided their forces into tillers and hunters. "The good and the holy were the hunters;" they spread themselves north, south, east, and west. "Meantime all the snakes were afraid in their huts, and the Snake-priest *Na-kopowa* said to all, ' Let us go.' *Eastwardly* they go forth at Snakeland (*Akhokink*), and they went away earnestly grieving." Afterward the fathers of the Delawares, who "were always boating and navigating," find that the Snake-people have taken possession of a fine country; and they collect together the people from north, south, east, and west, and attempt "to pass over the waters of the frozen sea to possess that land." They seem to travel in the dark of an Arctic winter until they come to a gap of open sea. They can go no farther; but some tarry at Firland, while the rest return to where they started from, "the old turtle land."

Here we find that the land that was destroyed was the "first land;" that it was an island "beyond the great ocean." In an early age the people were happy and peaceful; they became wicked; "snake worship" was introduced, and was associated, as in Genesis, with the "fall of man;" Nana-Bush became the ancestor of the new race; his name reminds us of the Toltec *Nata* and the Hebrew *Noah.* After the flood came a dispersion of the people, and a separation into hunters and tillers of the soil.

Among the Mandan Indians we not only find flood legends, but, more remarkable still, we find an *image of the ark preserved* from generation to generation, and a religious ceremony performed which refers plainly to the destruction of Atlantis, and to the arrival of one of those who escaped from the Flood, bringing the dreadful tidings of the disaster. It must be remembered, as we will show hereafter, that many of these Mandan Indians were white men, with hazel, gray, and blue eyes, and all shades of color of the hair from black to pure white; that they dwelt in houses in fortified towns, and manufactured earthen-ware pots in which they could boil water—an art unknown to the ordinary Indians, who boiled water by putting heated stones into it.

I quote the very interesting account of George Catlin, who visited the Mandans nearly fifty years ago, lately republished in London in the "North American Indians," a very curious and valuable work. He says (vol. i., p. 88):

"In the centre of the village is an open space, or public square, 150 feet in diameter and circular in form, which is used for all public games and festivals, shows and exhibitions. The lodges around this open space front in, with their doors toward the centre; and in the middle of this stands an object of great religious veneration, on account of the importance it has in connection with the annual religious ceremonies. This object is in the form of a large hogshead, some eight or ten feet high, made of planks and hoops, containing within it some of their choicest mysteries or medicines. They call it the 'Big Canoe.'"

This is a representation of the ark; the ancient Jews venerated a similar image, and some of the ancient Greek States followed in processions a model of the ark of Deucalion. But it is indeed surprising to find this practice perpetuated, even to our own times, by a race of Indians in the heart of America. On page 158 of the first volume of the same work Catlin describes the great annual mysteries and religious ceremonials of which this image of the ark was the centre. He says:

"On the day set apart for the commencement of the ceremonies a solitary figure is seen approaching the village.

"During the deafening din and confusion within the pickets

of the village the figure discovered on the prairie continued to approach with a dignified step, and in a right line toward the village; all eyes were upon him, and he at length made his appearance within the pickets, and proceeded toward the centre of the village, where all the chiefs and braves stood ready to receive him, which they did in a cordial manner by shaking hands, recognizing him as an old acquaintance, and pronouncing his name, Nu-mohk-muck-a-nah (*the first or only man*). The body of this strange personage, which was chiefly naked, was painted with white clay, so as to resemble at a distance *a white man*. He enters the medicine lodge, and goes through certain mysterious ceremonies.

"During the whole of this day Nu-mohk-muck-a-nah (the first or only man) travelled through the village, stopping in front of each man's lodge, and crying until the owner of the lodge came out and asked who he was, and what was the matter? To which he replied by narrating *the sad catastrophe which had happened on the earth's surface by the overflowing of the waters*, saying that 'he was the *only person saved from the universal calamity;* that he landed his big canoe on a high mountain in the west, where he now resides; that he has come to open the medicine lodge, which must needs receive a present of an edged tool from the owner of every wigwam, that it may be sacrificed to the water; for,' he says, 'if this is not done there will be another flood, and no one will be saved, as it was with such tools that the big canoe was made.'

"Having visited every lodge in the village during the day, and having received such a present from each as a hatchet, a knife, etc. (which is undoubtedly always prepared ready for the occasion), he places them in the medicine lodge; and, on the last day of the ceremony, they are thrown into a deep place in the river—'sacrificed to the Spirit of the Waters.'"

Among the sacred articles kept in the great medicine lodge are four sacks of water, called *Eeh-teeh-ka*, sewed together, each of them in the form of a *tortoise* lying on its back, with a bunch of eagle feathers attached to its tail. "These four tortoises," they told me, "contained the waters from the four quarters of the world—that those waters had been contained therein *ever since the settling down of the waters.*" "I did not," says Catlin, who knew nothing of an Atlantis theory, " think it best to advance anything against such a ridiculous belief." Catlin tried to purchase one of these water-sacks, but could not obtain it for any price; he was told they were "*a society property.*"

He then describes a dance by *twelve* men around the ark: "They arrange themselves according to *the four cardinal points;* two are painted perfectly *black,* two are vermilion color, some were painted partially white. They dance a dance called '*Bel*-lohck-na-pie,'" with horns on their heads, like those used in Europe as symbolical of *Bel,* or Baal.

Could anything be more evident than the connection of these ceremonies with the destruction of Atlantis? Here we have the image of the ark; here we have a white man coming with the news that "the waters had overflowed the land," and that all the people were destroyed except himself; here we have the sacrifice to appease the spirit that caused the Flood, just as we find the Flood terminating, in the Hebrew, Chaldean, and Central American legends, with a sacrifice. Here, too, we have the image of the tortoise, which we find in other flood legends of the Indians, and which is a very natural symbol for an island. As one of our own poets has expressed it,

> "Very fair and full of promise
> Lay the island of St. Thomas;
> Like a great green turtle slumbered
> On the sea which it encumbered."

Here we have, too, the four quarters of Atlantis, divided by its four rivers, as we shall see a little farther on, represented in a dance, where the dancers arrange themselves according to the four cardinal points of the compass; the dancers are painted to represent the black and red races, while "the first and only man" represents the white race; and the name of the dance is a reminiscence of Baal, the ancient god of the races derived from Atlantis.

But this is not all. The Mandans were evidently of the race

of Atlantis. They have another singular legend, which we find in the account of Lewis and Clarke:

"Their belief in a future state is connected with this theory of their origin: The whole nation resided in one large village, underground, near a subterranean lake. A grape-vine extended its roots down to their habitation, and gave them a view of the light. Some of the most adventurous climbed up the vine, and were delighted with the sight of the earth, which they found covered with buffalo, and rich with every kind of fruit. Returning with the grapes they had gathered, their countrymen were so pleased with the taste of them that the whole nation resolved to leave their dull residence for the charms of the upper region. Men, women, and children ascended by means of the vine, but, when about half the nation had reached the surface of the earth, a corpulent woman, who was clambering up the vine, broke it with her weight, and closed upon herself and the rest of the nation the light of the sun."

This curious tradition means that the present nation dwelt in a large settlement underground, that is, beyond the land, in the sea; the sea being represented by "the subterranean lake." At one time the people had free intercourse between this "large village" and the American continent, and they founded extensive colonies on this continent; whereupon some mishap cut them off from the mother country. This explanation is confirmed by the fact that in the legends of the Iowa Indians, who were a branch of the Dakotas, or Sioux Indians, and relatives of the Mandans (according to Major James W. Lynd), "all the tribes of Indians were formerly one, and all dwelt together *on an island,* or at least across a large water *toward the east or sunrise.* They crossed this water in skin canoes, or by swimming; but they know not how long they were in crossing, or whether the water was salt or fresh." While the Dakotas, according to Major Lynd, who lived among them for nine years, possessed legends of "huge skiffs, in which the Dakotas of old floated for weeks, finally gaining dry land"—a reminiscence of ships and long sea-voyages.

The Mandans celebrated their great religious festival above described in the season when the willow is first in leaf, and a dove is mixed up in the ceremonies; and they further relate a legend that "the world was once a great tortoise, borne on the waters, and covered with earth, and that when one day, in digging the soil, a tribe of white men, who had made holes in the earth to a great depth digging for badgers, at length pierced the shell of the tortoise, it sank, and the water covering it drowned all men with the exception of one, who saved himself in a boat; and when the earth re-emerged, sent out a dove, who returned with a branch of willow in its beak."

The holes dug to find badgers were a savage's recollection of mining operations; and when the great disaster came, and the island sunk in the sea amid volcanic convulsions, doubtless men said it was due to the deep mines, which had opened the way to the central fires. But the recurrence of " white men " as the miners, and of a white man as "the last and only man," and the presence of white blood in the veins of the people, all point to the same conclusion—that the Mandans were colonists from Atlantis.

And here I might add that Catlin found the following singular resemblances between the Mandan tongue and the Welsh:

English.	Mandan.	Welsh.	Pronounced.
I.	Me.	Mi.	Me.
You.	Ne.	Chwi.	Chwe.
He.	E.	A.	A.
She.	Ea.	E.	A.
It.	Ount.	Hwynt.	Hooynt.
We.	Noo.	Ni.	Ne.
They.	Eonah.	Hona, *fem.*	Hona.
No; or there is not.	Megosh.	Nagoes.	Nagosh.
No.		Na.	
Head.	Pan.	Pen.	Pan.
The Great Spirit.	Maho Peneta.	{ Mawr { Penæthir.	{ Mosoor { Panæther.

Major Lynd found the following resemblances between the Dakota tongue and the languages of the Old World:

COMPARISON OF DAKOTA, OR SIOUX, WITH OTHER LANGUAGES.

Latin.	English.	Saxon.	Sanscrit.	German.	Danish.	Sioux.	Other Languages.	Primary Signification.
Pinso..	See, seen..	Seon...		Sehen...	Sigt....	Sin...	W., Pwynian...	Appearing, visible.
	Pound...	Punian...				Pau....		Beating.
Vado..	Went...} Wend...}	Wendan..				Winita..		Passage.
Qui..	Town...	Tun...		Zaun...	Tun....	Tonwe...	Gaelic, Dun..	
	Who...	Hwa...	Kwus...	Wir...	Vanpen..	Tuwe...		{Sionx dimin. Wi-pena.
	Weapon...	Wepn...		Wapen ...	Jeg ...	Wipe...		
Ego..	I...	Ic...	Agam...	Ich...		Mish...		
Cor..	Core...					Co...	Gr., Keap...}	Centre, heart.
	Eight...	Achta...	Aute...	Acht...	Otte...	Shaktogan..	Gr., Oktw...}	
Canna..	Cane...					Can...	Arm., Canen..} Heb., Can...} W., Cawn...}	Reed, weed, wood.
Pock..	Pock...	Poc...		Pocke...	Pukkel...	Poka...	Dutch, Poca..	Swelling.
	With...	With...		Wider...		Wita...	Goth., Gewithan.	
	Doughty...	Dohtig...		Taugen...	Digtig...}	Dita...} Ditaya..} Titan..}		Hot, brave, daring.
	Tight...}	Tian...		Dicht...	Digt...}			Strain.
Tango..	Touch..} Take..}	Taecan		Ticken	Tekkan}	Tan...} Htaka..}		Touch, take.
Tactus..	Child...	Cild...		Kind ...	Kuld...}	Cin		Progeny.
	Work...	Wercan...		Wirken...		Woccan..} Hecon...}	Dutch, Werkan.} Span., Hecho..}	Labor, motion.
	Shackle...	Seoacul...				Shka...	Ar., Shakala...} Dutch, Schakel.} Tetem, Shakalan}	To bind (a link).
	Query...					Kniva....		
	Shabby...		Schabbig....	Schabig....	Schabbig....	Shabya...		

According to Major Lynd, the Dakotas, or Sioux, belonged to the same race as the Mandans; hence the interest which attaches to these verbal similarities.

"Among the Iroquois there is a tradition that the sea and waters infringed upon the land, so that all human life was destroyed. The Chickasaws assert that the world was once destroyed by water, but that one family was saved, and two animals of every kind. The Sioux say there was a time when there was no dry land, and all men had disappeared from existence." (See Lynd's " MS. History of the Dakotas," Library of Historical Society of Minnesota.)

"The Okanagaus have a god, Skyappe, and also one called Chacha, who appear to be endowed with omniscience; but their principal divinity is their great mythical ruler and heroine, Scomalt. Long ago, when the sun was no bigger than a star, this strong medicine-woman ruled over what appears to have now become a *lost island*. At last the peace of the island was destroyed by war, and the noise of battle was heard, with which Scomalt was exceeding wroth, whereupon she rose up in her might and drove her rebellious subjects to one end of the island, and broke off the piece of land on which they were huddled and pushed it out to sea, to drift whither it would. This floating island was tossed to and fro and buffeted by the winds till all but two died. A man and woman escaped in a canoe, and arrived on the main-land; and from these the Okanagaus are descended." (Bancroft's " Native Races," vol. iii., p. 149.)

Here we have the Flood legend clearly connected with a lost island.

The Nicaraguans believed "that ages ago the world was destroyed by a flood, in which the most part of mankind perished. Afterward the *teotes*, or gods, restored the earth as at the beginning." (*Ibid.*, p. 75.) The wild Apaches, " wild from their natal hour," have a legend that " the first days of the world were happy and peaceful days;" then came a great flood, from which Montezuma and the coyote alone escaped. Montezuma became then very wicked, and attempted to build a house that would reach to heaven, but the Great

Spirit destroyed it with thunderbolts. (Bancroft's "Native Races," vol. iii., p. 76.)

The Pimas, an Indian tribe allied to the Papagos, have a peculiar flood legend. The son of the Creator was called *Szeu-kha* (Ze-us?). An eagle prophesied the deluge to the prophet of the people three times in succession, but his warning was despised; "then in the twinkling of an eye there came a peal of thunder and an awful crash, and a green mound of water reared itself over the plain. It seemed to stand upright for a second, then, cut incessantly by the lightning, goaded on like a great beast, it flung itself upon the prophet's hut. When the morning broke there was nothing to be seen alive but one man—if indeed he were a man; Szeu-kha, the son of the Creator, had saved himself by floating on a ball of gum or resin." This instantaneous catastrophe reminds one forcibly of the destruction of Atlantis. Szeu-kha killed the eagle, restored its victims to life, and repeopled the earth with them, as Deucalion repeopled the earth with the stones.

Chapter VI.

SOME CONSIDERATION OF THE DELUGE LEGENDS.

The Fountains of the Great Deep.—As Atlantis perished in a volcanic convulsion, it must have possessed volcanoes. This is rendered the more probable when we remember that the ridge of land of which it was a part, stretching from north to south, from Iceland to St. Helena, contains even now great volcanoes—as in Iceland, the Azores, the Canaries, etc.—and that the very sea-bed along the line of its original axis is, to this day, as we have shown, the scene of great volcanic disturbances.

If, then, the mountains of Atlantis contained volcanoes, of which the peaks of the Azores are the surviving representatives, it is not improbable that the convulsion which drowned it in the sea was accompanied by great discharges of water. We have seen that such discharges occurred in the island of Java, when four thousand people perished. "Immense columns of hot water and boiling mud were thrown out" of the volcano of Galung Gung; the water was projected from the mountain "like a water-spout." When a volcanic island was created near Sicily in 1831, it was accompanied by "a water-spout sixty feet high."

In the island of Dominica, one of the islands constituting the Leeward group of the West Indies, and nearest to the site of Atlantis, on the 4th of January, 1880, occurred a series of convulsions which reminds us forcibly of the destruction of Plato's island; and the similarity extends to another particular: Dominica contains, like Atlantis, we are told, numerous

hot and sulphur springs. I abridge the account given by the
New York Herald of January 28th, 1880:

"A little after 11 o'clock A.M., soon after high-mass in the
Roman Catholic cathedral, and while divine service was still
going on in the Anglican and Wesleyan chapels, all the indications of an approaching thunder-storm suddenly showed
themselves; the atmosphere, which just previously had been
cool and pleasant—slight showers falling since early morning
—became at once nearly stifling hot; the rumbling of distant
thunder was heard, and the light-blue and fleecy white of the
sky turned into a heavy and lowering black.   Soon the thun-
der-peals came near and loud, the lightning flashes, of a blue
and red color, more frequent and vivid; and the rain, first with
a few heavy drops, commenced to pour as if the floodgates
of heaven were open.   In a moment it darkened, as if night
had come; a strong, nearly overpowering smell of sulphur announced itself; and people who happened to be out in the
streets felt the rain-drops falling on their heads, backs, and
shoulders like showers of hailstones.   The cause of this was
to be noted by looking at the spouts, from which the water
was rushing like so many cataracts of molten lead, while the
gutters below ran swollen streams of thick gray mud, looking
like nothing ever seen in them before.   In the mean time
the Roseau River had worked itself into a state of mad fury,
overflowing its banks, carrying down rocks and large trees,
and threatening destruction to the bridges over it and the
houses in its neighborhood.   When the storm ceased—it lasted till twelve, mid-day—the roofs and walls of the buildings
in town, the street pavement, the door-steps and back-yards
were found covered with a deposit of volcanic débris, holding
together like clay, dark-gray in color, and in some places lying
more than an inch thick, with small, shining metallic particles
on the surface, which could be easily identified as iron pyrites.
Scraping up some of the stuff, it required only a slight examination to determine its main constituents—sandstone and mag-
nesia, the pyrites being slightly mixed, and silver showing itself
in even smaller quantity.   This is, in fact, the composition of
the volcanic mud thrown up by the *soufrières* at Watton Wa-
ven and in the Boiling Lake country, and it is found in solution as well in the lake water.   The Devil's Billiard-table,

within half a mile of the Boiling Lake, is composed wholly of
this substance, which there assumes the character of stone in
formation. Inquiries instituted on Monday morning revealed
the fact that, except on the south-east, the mud shower had not
extended beyond the limits of the town. On the north-west,
in the direction of Fond Colo and Morne Daniel, nothing but
pure rain-water had fallen, and neither Loubière nor Pointe
Michel had seen any signs of volcanic disturbance. . . .

"But what happened at Pointe Mulâtre enables us to spot
the *locale* of the eruption. Pointe Mulâtre lies at the foot of
the range of mountains on the top of which the Boiling Lake
frets and seethes. The only outlet of the lake is a cascade
which falls into one of the branches of the Pointe Mulâtre
River, the color and temperature of which, at one time and
another, shows the existence or otherwise of volcanic activity
in the lake-country. We may observe, *en passant,* that the fall
of the water from the lake is similar in appearance to the falls
on the sides of Roairama, in the interior of British Guiana;
there is no continuous stream, but the water overleaps its basin like a kettle boiling over, and comes down in detached
cascades from the top. May there not be a boiling lake on
the unapproachable summit of Roairama? The phenomena
noted at Pointe Mulâtre on Sunday were similar to what we
witnessed in Roseau, but with every feature more strongly
marked. The fall of mud was heavier, covering all the fields;
the atmospheric disturbance was greater, and the change in the
appearance of the running water about the place more surprising. The Pointe Mulâtre River suddenly began to run volcanic mud and water; then the mud predominated, and almost
buried the stream under its weight, and the odor of sulphur in
the air became positively oppressive. Soon the fish in the water—brochet, camoo, meye, crocro, mullet, down to the eel, the
crawfish, the loche, the tétar, and the dormer—died, and were
thrown on the banks. The mud carried down by the river
has formed a bank at the mouth which nearly dams up the
stream, and threatens to throw it back over the low-lying lands
of the Pointe Mulâtre estate. The reports from the Laudat
section of the Boiling Lake district are curious. The Bach-
elor and Admiral rivers, and the numerous mineral springs
which arise in that part of the island, are all running a thick
white flood, like cream milk. The face of the entire country,

from the Admiral River to the Solfatera Plain, has undergone some portentous change, which the frightened peasants who bring the news to Roseau seem unable clearly and connectedly to describe, and the volcanic activity still continues."

From this account it appears that the rain of water and mud came from a boiling lake on the mountains; it must have risen to a great height, "like a water-spout," and then fallen in showers over the face of the country. We are reminded, in this Boiling Lake of Dominica, of the Welsh legend of the eruption of the Llyn-llion, "the Lake of Waves," which "inundated the whole country." On the top of a mountain in the county of Kerry, Ireland, called Mangerton, there is a deep lake known as Poulle-i-feron, which signifies Hell-hole; it frequently overflows, and rolls down the mountain in frightful torrents. On Slieve-donart, in the territory of Mourne, in the county of Down, Ireland, a lake occupies the mountain-top, and its overflowings help to form rivers.

If we suppose the destruction of Atlantis to have been, in like manner, accompanied by a tremendous outpour of water from one or more of its volcanoes, thrown to a great height, and deluging the land, we can understand the description in the Chaldean legend of "*the terrible water-spout,*" which even "the gods grew afraid of," and which "rose to the sky," and which seems to have been one of the chief causes, together with the earthquake, of the destruction of the country. And in this view we are confirmed by the Aramæan legend of the Deluge, probably derived at an earlier age from the Chaldean tradition. In it we are told, "All on a sudden *enormous volumes of water issued from the earth,* and rains of extraordinary abundance began to fall; the rivers left their beds, and the ocean overflowed its banks." The disturbance in Dominica duplicates this description exactly: "In a moment" the water and mud burst from the mountains, "the floodgates of heaven were opened," and "the river overflowed its banks."

And here, again, we are reminded of the expression in Gen

esis, "the same day were all the fountains of the great deep broken up" (chap. vii., 11). That this does not refer to the rain is clear from the manner in which it is stated: "The same day were all the fountains of the great deep broken up, *and* the windows of heaven were opened. And the rain was upon the earth," etc. And when the work of destruction is finished, we are told "the fountains also of the deep *and* the windows of heaven were stopped." This is a reminiscence by an inland people, living where such tremendous volcanic disturbances were nearly unknown, of "the terrible water-spout" which "rose to the sky," of the Chaldean legend, and of "the enormous volumes of water issuing from the earth" of the Aramæan tradition. The Hindoo legend of the Flood speaks of "the marine god Hayagriva, who dwelt in the abyss," who produced the cataclysm. This is doubtless "the archangel of the abyss" spoken of in the Chaldean tradition.

The Mountains of the North.—We have in Plato the following reference to the mountains of Atlantis:

"The whole country was described as being very lofty and precipitous on the side of the sea. . . . The whole region of the island lies toward the south, and is sheltered from the north. . . . The surrounding mountains . . . exceeded all that are to be seen now anywhere."

These mountains were the present Azores. One has but to contemplate their present elevation, and remember the depth to which they descend in the ocean, to realize their tremendous altitude and the correctness of the description given by Plato.

In the Hindoo legend we find the fish-god, who represents Poseidon, father of Atlantis, helping Manu over "the Mountain of the North." In the Chaldean legend Khasisatra's vessel is stopped by "the Mountain of Nizir" until the sea goes down.

THE GOD OF THE FLOOD.
(From "The Walls of Nineveh.")

The Mud which Stopped Navigation.—We are told by Plato, "Atlantis disappeared beneath the sea, and then that sea became inaccessible, so that navigation on it ceased, on account of the quantity of mud which the ingulfed island left in its place." This is one of the points of Plato's story which provoked the incredulity and ridicule of the ancient, and even of the modern, world. We find in the Chaldean legend something of the same kind: Khasisatra says, "I looked at the sea attentively, observing, and the whole of humanity had returned to mud." In the "Popol Vuh" we are told that a "resinous thickness descended from heaven," even as in Dominica the rain was full of "thick gray mud," accompanied by an "overpowering smell of sulphur."

The explorations of the ship *Challenger* show that the whole of the submerged ridge of which Atlantis is a part *is to this day thickly covered with volcanic débris.*

We have but to remember the cities of Pompeii and Herculaneum, which were covered with such a mass of volcanic ashes from the eruption of A.D. 79 that for seventeen centuries they remained buried at a depth of from fifteen to thirty feet; a new population lived and labored above them; an aqueduct was constructed over their heads; and it was only when a farmer, in digging for a well, penetrated the roof of a house, that they were once more brought to the light of day and the knowledge of mankind.

We have seen that, in 1783, the volcanic eruption in Iceland covered the sea with pumice for a distance of one hundred and fifty miles, "and *ships were considerably impeded in their course.*"

The eruption in the island of Sumbawa, in April, 1815, threw out such masses of ashes as to darken the air. "The floating cinders to the west of Sumatra formed, on the 12th of April, a mass *two feet thick* and several miles in extent, *through which ships with difficulty forced their way.*"

It thus appears that the very statement of Plato which has

provoked the ridicule of scholars is in itself one of the corroborating features of his story. It is probable that the ships of
the Atlanteans, when they returned after the tempest to look
for their country, found the sea impassable from the masses
of volcanic ashes and pumice. They returned terrified to the
shores of Europe; and the shock inflicted by the destruction
of Atlantis upon the civilization of the world probably led to
one of those retrograde periods in the history of our race in
which they lost all intercourse with the Western continent.

The Preservation of a Record.—There is a singular coincidence in the stories of the Deluge in another particular.

The legends of the Phœnicians, preserved by Sanchoniathon,
tell us that Taautos, or Taut, was the inventor of the alphabet
and of the art of writing.

Now, we find in the Egyptian legends a passage of Manetho,
in which Thoth (or Hermes Trismegistus), before the Deluge,
inscribed on stelæ, or tablets, in hieroglyphics, or sacred characters, the principles of all knowledge. After the Deluge the
second Thoth translated the contents of these stelæ into the
vulgar tongue.

Josephus tells us that "The patriarch Seth, in order that
wisdom and astronomical knowledge should not perish, erected, in prevision of the double destruction by fire and water
predicted by Adam, two columns, one of brick, the other of
stone, on which this knowledge was engraved, and which existed in the Siriadic country."

In the Chaldean legends the god Ea ordered Khasisatra to
inscribe the divine learning, and the principles of all sciences,
on tables of terra-cotta, and bury them, before the Deluge, "in
the City of the Sun at Sippara."

Berosus, in his version of the Chaldean flood, says:

"The deity, Chronos, appeared to him (Xisuthros) in a vision,
and warned him that, upon the 15th day of the month Dœsius,
there would be a flood by which mankind would be destroyed.
He therefore enjoined him to write a history of the beginning,

procedure, and conclusion of all things, and to bury it in the City of the Sun at Sippara, and to build a vessel," etc.

The Hindoo Bhâgavata-Purâna tells us that the fish-god, who warned Satyravata of the coming of the Flood, directed him to place the sacred Scriptures in a safe place, "in order to preserve them from Hayagriva, a marine horse dwelling in the abyss."

Are we to find the original of these legends in the following passage from Plato's history of Atlantis?

"Now, the relations of their governments to one another were regulated by the injunctions of Poseidon, as the law had handed them down. These were inscribed by the first men on a column of orichalcum, which was situated in the middle of the island, at the Temple of Poseidon, whither the people were gathered together. . . . They received and gave judgments, and at daybreak they wrote down their sentences on a golden tablet, and deposited them as memorials with their robes. There were many special laws which the several kings had inscribed about the temples." (Critias, p. 120.)

A Succession of Disasters.—The Central American books, translated by De Bourbourg, state that originally a part of the American continent extended far into the Atlantic Ocean. This tradition is strikingly confirmed by the explorations of the ship *Challenger*, which show that the "Dolphin's Ridge" was connected with the shore of South America north of the mouth of the Amazon. The Central American books tell us that this region of the continent was destroyed by a succession of frightful convulsions, probably at long intervals apart; three of these catastrophes are constantly mentioned, and sometimes there is reference to one or two more.

"The land," in these convulsions, "was shaken by frightful earthquakes, and the waves of the sea combined with volcanic fires to overwhelm and ingulf it. . . . Each convulsion swept away portions of the land until the whole disappeared, leaving the line of coast as it now is. Most of the inhabitants, over-

taken amid their regular employments, were destroyed; but
some escaped in ships, and some fled for safety to the summits
of high mountains, or to portions of the land which for a time
escaped immediate destruction." (Baldwin's "Ancient America," p. 176.)

This accords precisely with the teachings of geology. We
know that the land from which America and Europe were
formed once covered nearly or quite the whole space now occupied by the Atlantic between the continents; and it is reasonable to believe that it went down piecemeal, and that Atlantis was but the stump of the ancient continent, which at last
perished from the same causes and in the same way.

The fact that this tradition existed among the inhabitants of
America is proven by the existence of festivals, "especially one
in the month *Izcalli,* which were instituted to commemorate
this frightful destruction of land and people, and in which, say
the sacred books, 'princes and people humbled themselves before the divinity, and besought him to withhold a return of
such terrible calamities.'"

Can we doubt the reality of events which we thus find confirmed by religious ceremonies at Athens, in Syria, and on the
shores of Central America?

And we find this succession of great destructions of the Atlantic continent in the triads of Wales, where traditions are
preserved of "three terrible catastrophes." We are told by
the explorations of the ship *Challenger* that the higher lands
reach in the direction of the British Islands; and the Celts had
traditions that a part of their country once extended far out
into the Atlantic, and was subsequently destroyed.

And the same succession of destructions is referred to in the
Greek legends, where a deluge of Ogyges—"the most ancient
of the kings of Bœotia or Attica, a quite mythical person, lost
in the night of ages"—preceded that of Deucalion.

We will find hereafter the most ancient hymns of the Aryans praying God to *hold the land firm.* The people of Atlan-

tis, having seen their country thus destroyed, section by section, and judging that their own time must inevitably come,
must have lived under a great and perpetual terror, which will
go far to explain the origin of primeval religion, and the hold
which it took upon the minds of men; and this condition of
things may furnish us a solution of the legends which have
come down to us of their efforts to perpetuate their learning
on pillars, and also an explanation of that other legend of the
Tower of Babel, which, as I will show hereafter, was common
to both continents, and in which they sought to build a tower
high enough to escape the Deluge.

All the legends of the preservation of a record prove that
the united voice of antiquity taught that the antediluvians had
advanced so far in civilization as to possess an alphabet and a
system of writing; a conclusion which, as we will see hereafter,
finds confirmation in the original identity of the alphabetical
signs used in the old world and the new.

PART III.

THE CIVILIZATION OF THE OLD WORLD AND NEW COMPARED.

CHAPTER I.

CIVILIZATION AN INHERITANCE.

MATERIAL civilization might be defined to be the result of a series of inventions and discoveries, whereby man improves his condition, and controls the forces of nature for his own advantage.

The savage man is a pitiable creature; as Menaboshu says, in the Chippeway legends, he is pursued by a "perpetual hunger;" he is exposed unprotected to the blasts of winter and the heats of summer. A great terror sits upon his soul; for every manifestation of nature—the storm, the wind, the thunder, the lightning, the cold, the heat—all are threatening and dangerous demons. The seasons bring him neither seed-time nor harvest; pinched with hunger, appeasing in part the everlasting craving of his stomach with seeds, berries, and creeping things, he sees the animals of the forest dash by him, and he has no means to arrest their flight. He is powerless and miserable in the midst of plenty. Every step toward civilization is a step of conquest over nature. The invention of the bow and arrow was, in its time, a far greater stride forward for the human race than the steam-engine or the telegraph. The savage could now reach his game; his insatiable hunger could be satisfied; the very eagle, "towering in its pride of place," was not beyond the reach of this new and wonderful weapon. The discovery of fire and the art of cooking was another immense step forward. The savage, having nothing but wooden vessels in which to cook, covered the wood with clay; the clay hardened in the fire. The savage gradually learned that he could dispense with the wood, and thus pottery was invented. Then some one (if we are to believe the Chippeway legends, on the shores of Lake Superior) found fragments of the pure copper of that region, beat them into shape, and the art of metallurgy was begun; iron was first worked in the same way by shaping meteoric iron into spear-heads.

But it must not be supposed that these inventions followed one another in rapid succession. Thousands, and perhaps tens of thousands, of years intervened between each step; many savage races have not to this day achieved some of these steps. Prof. Richard Owen says, "Unprepossessed and sober experience teaches that arts, language, literature are of slow growth, the results of gradual development."

I shall undertake to show hereafter that nearly all the arts essential to civilization which we possess date back to the time of Atlantis — certainly to that ancient Egyptian civilization which was coeval with, and an outgrowth from, Atlantis.

In six thousand years the world made no advance on the civilization which it received from Atlantis.

Phœnicia, Egypt, Chaldea, India, Greece, and Rome passed the torch of civilization from one to the other; but in all that lapse of time they added nothing to the arts which existed at the earliest period of Egyptian history. In architecture, sculpture, painting, engraving, mining, metallurgy, navigation, pottery, glass-ware, the construction of canals, roads, and aqueducts, the arts of Phœnicia and Egypt extended, without material change or improvement, to a period but two or three hundred years ago. The present age has entered upon a new era; it has added a series of wonderful inventions to the Atlantean list; it has subjugated steam and electricity to the uses of man. And its work has but commenced: it will continue until it lifts man to a plane as much higher than the present as the present is above the barbaric condition; and in the future it will be said that between the birth of civilization in Atlantis and the new civilization there stretches a period of many thousands of years, during which mankind did not invent, but simply perpetuated.

Herodotus tells us ("Euterpe," cxlii.) that, according to the information he received from the Egyptian priests, their written history dated back 11,340 years before his era, or nearly 14,000 years prior to this time. They introduced him into a spacious temple, and showed him the statues of 341 high-priests who had in turn succeeded each other; and yet the age of Columbus possessed no arts, except that of printing (which was ancient in China), which was not known to the Egyptians; and the civilization of Egypt at its first appearance was of a higher order than at any subsequent period of its history, thus testifying that it drew its greatness from a fountain higher than itself. It was in its early days that Egypt worshipped† one only God; in the later ages this simple and sublime belief was buried under the corruptions of polytheism. The greatest pyramids were built by the Fourth Dynasty, and so universal was education at that time among the people that the stones with which they were built retain to this day the writing of the workmen. The first king was Menes.

"At the epoch of Menes," says Winchell, "the Egyptians were already a civilized and numerous people. Manetho tells us that Athotis, the son of this first king, Menes, built the palace at Memphis; that he was a physician, and left anatomical books. All these statements imply that even at this early period the Egyptians were in a high state of civilization." (Winchell's "Preadamites," p. 120.) "In the time of Menes the Egyptians had long been architects, sculptors, painters, mythologists, and theologians." Professor Richard Owen says: "Egypt is recorded to have been a civilized and

† Exaggerated and incorrect.—E.F.B.

governed community *before* the time of Menes. The pastoral community of a group of nomad families, as portrayed in the Pentateuch, may be admitted as an early step in civilization. But how far in advance of this stage is a nation administered by a kingly government, consisting of grades of society, with divisions of labor, of which one kind, assigned to the priesthood, was to record or chronicle the names and dynasties of the kings, the duration and chief events of their reigns!" Ernest Renan points out that "Egypt at the beginning appears mature, old, and entirely without mythical and heroic ages, as if the country had never known youth. Its civilization has no infancy, and its art no archaic period. The civilization of the Old Monarchy did not begin with infancy. It was already mature."

We shall attempt to show that it matured in Atlantis, and that the Egyptian people were unable to maintain it at the high standard at which they had received it, as depicted in the pages of Plato. What king of Assyria, or Greece, or Rome, or even of these modern nations, has ever devoted himself to the study of medicine and the writing of medical books for the benefit of mankind? Their mission has been to kill, not to heal the people; yet here, at the very dawn of Mediterranean history, we find the son of the first king of Egypt recorded "as a physician, and as having left anatomical books."

I hold it to be incontestable that, in some region of the earth, primitive mankind must have existed during vast spaces of time, and under most favorable circumstances, to create, invent, and discover those arts and things which constitute civilization. When we have it before our eyes that for six thousand years mankind in Europe, Asia, and Africa, even when led by great nations, and illuminated by marvellous minds, did not advance one inch beyond the arts of Egypt, we may conceive what lapses, what æons, of time it must have required to bring savage man to that condition of refinement and civilization possessed by Egypt when it first comes within the purview of history.

That illustrious Frenchman, H. A. Taine ("History of English Literature," p. 23), sees the unity of the Indo-European races manifest in their languages, literature, and philosophies, and argues that these pre-eminent traits are "the great marks of an original model," and that when we meet with them " fifteen, twenty, thirty centuries before our era, in an Aryan, an Egyptian, a Chinese, they represent the work of a great many ages, perhaps of several myriads of centuries. . . . Such is the first and richest source of these master faculties from which historical events take their rise; and one sees that if it be powerful it is because this is no simple spring, but a kind of lake, a deep reservoir, wherein other springs have, for a multitude of centuries, discharged their several streams." In other words, the capacity of the Egyptian, Aryan, Chaldean, Chinese, Saxon, and Celt to maintain civilization is simply the result of civilized training during "myriads of centuries" in some original home of the race.

I cannot believe that the great inventions were duplicated spontaneously, as some would have us believe, in different countries; there is no truth in the theory that men pressed by necessity will always hit upon the same invention to relieve their wants. If this were so, all savages would have invented the boomerang; all savages would possess pottery, bows and arrows, slings, tents, and canoes; in short, all races would have risen to civilization, for certainly the comforts of life are as agreeable to one people as another.

Civilization is not communicable to all; many savage tribes are incapable of it. There are two great divisions of mankind, the civilized and the savage; and, as we shall show, every civilized race in the world has had something of civilization from the earliest ages; and as "all roads lead to Rome," so all the converging lines of civilization lead to Atlantis. The abyss between the civilized man and the savage is simply incalculable; it represents not alone a difference in arts and methods of life, but in the mental constitution, the instincts, and the predispositions of the soul. The child of the civilized races in his sports manufactures water-wheels, wagons, and houses of cobs; the savage boy amuses himself with bows and arrows: the one belongs to a building and creating race; the other to a wild, hunting stock. This abyss between savagery and civilization has never been passed by any nation through its own original force, and without external influences, during the Historic Period; those who were savages at the dawn of history are savages still; barbarian slaves may have been taught something of the arts of their masters, and conquered races have shared some of the advantages possessed by their conquerors; but we will seek in vain for any example of a savage people developing civilization of and among themselves. I may be reminded of the Gauls, Goths, and Britons; but these were not savages, they possessed written languages, poetry, oratory, and history; they were controlled by religious ideas; they believed in God and the immortality of the soul, and in a state of rewards and punishments after death. Wherever the Romans came in contact with Gauls, or Britons, or German tribes, they found them armed with weapons of iron. The Scots, according to Tacitus, used chariots and iron swords in the battle of the Grampians—"enormes gladii sine mucrone." The Celts of Gaul are stated by Diodorus Siculus to have used iron-headed spears and coats-of-mail, and the Gauls who encountered the Roman arms in B.C. 222 were armed with soft iron swords, as well as at the time when Cæsar conquered their country. Among the Gauls men would lend money to be repaid in the next world, and, we need not add, that no Christian people has yet reached that sublime height of faith; they cultivated the ground, built houses and walled towns, wove cloth, and employed wheeled vehicles; they possessed nearly all the cereals and domestic animals we have, and they wrought in iron, bronze, and steel. The Gauls had even invented a machine on wheels to cut their grain, thus anticipating our reapers and mowers by two thousand years. The difference between the civilization of the Romans under Julius Cæsar and the Gauls under Vercingetorix was a difference in degree and not in kind. The Roman civilization was simply a development and perfection of the civilization possessed by all the European populations; it was drawn from the common fountain of Atlantis.

If we find on both sides of the Atlantic precisely the same arts, sciences, religious beliefs, habits, customs, and traditions, it is absurd to say that the peoples of the two continents arrived separately, by precisely the same steps, at precisely the same ends. When we consider the resemblance of the civilizations of the Mediterranean nations to one another, no man is silly enough to pretend that Rome, Greece, Egypt, Assyria, Phœnicia, each spontaneously and separately invented the arts, sciences, habits, and opinions in which they agreed; but we proceed to trace out the thread of descent or connection from one to another. Why should a rule of interpretation prevail, as between the two sides of the Atlantic, different from that which holds good as to the two sides of the Mediterranean Sea? If, in the one case, similarity of origin has unquestionably produced similarity of arts, customs, and condition, why, in the other, should not similarity of arts, customs, and condition prove similarity of origin? Is there any instance in the world of two peoples, without knowledge of or intercourse with each other, happening upon the same invention, whether that invention be an arrow-head or a steam-engine? If it required of mankind a lapse of at least six thousand years before it began anew the work of invention, and took up the thread of original thought where Atlantis dropped it, what probability is there of three or four separate nations all advancing at the same speed to precisely the same arts and opinions? The proposition is untenable.

If, then, we prove that, on both sides of the Atlantic, civilizations were found substantially identical, we have demonstrated that they must have descended one from the other, or have radiated from some common source.

Chapter II.

THE IDENTITY OF THE CIVILIZATIONS OF THE OLD WORLD AND THE NEW.

Architecture.—Plato tells us that the Atlanteans possessed architecture; that they built walls, temples, and palaces.

We need not add that this art was found in Egypt and all the civilized countries of Europe, as well as in Peru, Mexico, and Central America. Among both the Peruvians and Egyptians the walls receded inward, and the doors were narrower at the top than at the threshold.

The obelisks of Egypt, covered with hieroglyphics, are paralleled by the round columns of Central America, and both are supposed to have originated in *Phallus-worship.* "The usual symbol of the Phallus was an erect stone, often in its rough state, sometimes sculptured." (Squier, "Serpent Symbol," p. 49; Bancroft's "Native Races," vol. iii., p. 504.) The worship of Priapus was found in Asia, Egypt, along the European shore of the Mediterranean, and in the forests of Central America.

The mounds of Europe and Asia were made in the same way and for the same purposes as those of America. Herodotus describes the burial of a Scythian king; he says, "After this they set to work to raise a vast mound above the grave, all of them vying with each other, and seeking to make it as tall as possible." "It must be confessed," says Foster ("Prehistoric Races," p. 193), "that these Scythic burial rites have a strong resemblance to those of the Mound Builders." Homer describes the erection of a great symmetrical mound over Achilles, also one over Hector. Alexander the Great raised a

MOSAICS AT MITLA, MEXICO.

great mound over his friend Hephæstion, at a cost of more than a million dollars; and Semiramis raised a similar mound over her husband. The pyramids of Egypt, Assyria, and Phœnicia had their duplicates in Mexico and Central America.

The grave-cists made of stone of the American mounds are exactly like the stone chests, or *kistvaen* for the dead, found

CARVING ON THE BUDDHIST TOWER, SÁRNÁTH, INDIA.

in the British mounds. (Foster's "Prehistoric Races," p. 109.) Tumuli have been found in Yorkshire enclosing wooden coffins, precisely as in the mounds of the Mississippi Valley. (*Ibid.*, p. 185.) The articles associated with the dead are the same in both continents: arms, trinkets, food, clothes, and funeral urns. In both the Mississippi Valley and among the

Chaldeans vases were constructed around the bones, the neck of the vase being too small to permit the extraction of the skull. (Foster's "Prehistoric Races," p. 200.)

The use of *cement* was known alike to the European and American nations.

The use of the *arch* was known on both sides of the Atlantic.[†]

The manufacture of bricks was known in both the Old and New Worlds.

The style of ornamentation in architecture was much the same on both hemispheres, as shown in the preceding designs, pages 137, 139.

Metallurgy.—The Atlanteans mined ores, and worked in metals; they used copper, tin, bronze, gold, and silver, and probably iron.

The American nations possessed all these metals. The age of bronze, or of copper combined with tin, was preceded in America, *and nowhere else*, by a simpler age of copper; and, therefore, the working of metals probably originated in America, or in some region to which it was tributary. The Mexicans manufactured bronze, and the Incas mined iron near Lake Titicaca; and the civilization of this latter region, as we will show, probably dated back to Atlantean times. The Peruvians called gold the tears of the sun: it was sacred to the sun, as silver was to the moon.

Sculpture.—The Atlanteans possessed this art; so did the American and Mediterranean nations.

Dr. Arthur Schott ("Smith. Rep.," 1869, p. 391), in describing the "Cara Gigantesca," or gigantic face, a monument of Yzamal, in Yucatan, says, "Behind and on both sides, from under the mitre, a short veil falls upon the shoulders, so as to protect the back of the head and the neck. This particular appendage vividly calls to mind the same feature in the symbolic adornments of Egyptian and Hindoo priests, and even those of the Hebrew hierarchy." Dr. Schott sees in the orbicular wheel-like plates of this statue the wheel symbol of Kronos

[†] Apart from one or two probably accidental instances the arch was not found in America. The Incas did not mine iron.—E.F.B.

and Saturn; and, in turn, it may be supposed that the wheel of Kronos was simply the cross of Atlantis, surrounded by its encircling ring.

Painting.—This art was known on both sides of the Atlantic. The paintings upon the walls of some of the temples of Central America reveal a state of the art as high as that of Egypt.

Engraving.—Plato tells us that the Atlanteans engraved upon pillars. The American nations also had this art in common with Egypt, Phœnicia, and Assyria.

Agriculture.—The people of Atlantis were pre-eminently an agricultural people; so were the civilized nations of America and the Egyptians. In Egypt the king put his hand to the plough at an annual festival, thus dignifying and consecrating the occupation of husbandry. In Peru precisely the same custom prevailed. In both the plough was known; in Egypt it was drawn by oxen, and in Peru by men. It was drawn by men in the North of Europe down to a comparatively recent period.

Public Works.—The American nations built public works as great as or greater than any known in Europe. The Peruvians had public roads, one thousand five hundred to two thousand miles long, made so thoroughly as to elicit the astonishment of the Spaniards. At every few miles taverns or hotels were established for the accommodation of travellers. Humboldt pronounced these Peruvian roads "among the most useful and stupendous works ever executed by man." They built aqueducts for purposes of irrigation some of which were five hundred miles long. They constructed magnificent bridges of stone, and had even invented suspension bridges thousands of years before they were introduced into Europe. They had, both in Peru and Mexico, a system of posts, by means of which news was transmitted hundreds of miles in a day, precisely like those known among the Persians in the time of Herodotus, and subsequently among the Romans. Stones similar to mile-stones were placed along the roads in Peru. (See Prescott's "Peru.")

Navigation.—Sailing vessels were known to the Peruvians and the Central Americans. Columbus met, in 1502, at an island near Honduras, a party of the Mayas in a large vessel, equipped with sails, and loaded with a variety of textile fabrics of divers colors.

Manufactures.—The American nations manufactured woollen and cotton goods; they made pottery as beautiful as the

ANCIENT IRISH VASE OF THE BRONZE AGE.

wares of Egypt; they manufactured glass; they engraved gems and precious stones.† The Peruvians had such immense numbers of vessels and ornaments of gold that the Inca paid with them a ransom for himself to Pizarro of the value of fifteen million dollars.

Music.—It has been pointed out that there is great resemblance between the five-toned music of the Highland Scotch

† The American nations did not manufacture glass.—E.F.B.

and that of the Chinese and other Eastern nations. ("Anthropology," p. 292.)

Weapons.—The weapons of the New World were identically the same as those of the Old World; they consisted of bows and arrows, spears, darts, short swords, battle-axes, and slings; and both peoples used shields or bucklers, and casques of wood or hide covered with metal. If these weapons had been derived from separate sources of invention, one country or the other would have possessed implements not known to the other, like the blow-pipe, the boomerang, etc. Absolute identity in so many weapons strongly argues identity of origin.

ANCIENT VASE FROM THE MOUNDS OF THE
UNITED STATES.

Religion.—The religion of the Atlanteans, as Plato tells us, was pure and simple; they made no regular sacrifices but fruits and flowers; they worshipped the sun.

In Peru a single deity was worshipped, and the sun, his most glorious work, was honored as his representative. Quetzalcoatl, the founder of the Aztecs, condemned all sacrifice but that of fruits and flowers. The first religion of Egypt was pure and simple; its sacrifices were fruits and flowers; temples were erected to the sun, *Ra*, throughout Egypt. In Peru the great festival of the sun was called *Ra*-mi. The Phœnicians worshipped Baal and Moloch; the one represented the beneficent, and the other the injurious powers of the sun.

Religious Beliefs.—The Guanches of the Canary Islands, who were probably a fragment of the old Atlantean population, believed in the immortality of the soul and the resurrection of the body, and preserved their dead as mummies. The Egyptians believed in the immortality of the soul and the resurrection of the body, and preserved the bodies of the dead by embalming them. The Peruvians believed in the immortality of the soul and the resurrection of the body, and they too preserved the bodies of their dead by embalming them. "A few mummies in remarkable preservation have been found among the Chinooks and Flatheads." (Schoolcraft, vol. v., p. 693.) The embalmment of the body was also practised in Central America and among the Aztecs. The Aztecs, like the Egyptians, mummified their dead by taking out the bowels and replacing them with aromatic substances. (Dorman, "Origin Prim. Superst.," p. 173.) The bodies of the kings of the Virginia Indians were preserved by embalming. (Beverly, p. 47.)

Here are different races, separated by immense distances of land and ocean, uniting in the same beliefs, and in the same practical and logical application of those beliefs.

The use of confession and penance was known in the religious ceremonies of some of the American nations. Baptism was a religious ceremony with them, and the bodies of the dead were sprinkled with water.

Vestal virgins were found in organized communities on both sides of the Atlantic; they were in each case pledged to celibacy, and devoted to death if they violated their vows. In both hemispheres the recreant were destroyed by being buried alive. The Peruvians, Mexicans, Central Americans, Egyptians, Phœnicians, and Hebrews each had a powerful hereditary priesthood.

The Phœnicians believed in an evil spirit called Zebub; the Peruvians had a devil called Cupay. The Peruvians burnt incense in their temples. The Peruvians, when they sacrificed animals, examined their entrails, and from these prognosticated the future.

I need not add that all these nations preserved traditions of the Deluge; and all of them possessed systems of writing.

The Egyptian priest of Sais told Solon that the myth of Phaëthon, the son of Helios, having attempted to drive the chariot of the sun, and thereby burning up the earth, referred to " a declination of the bodies moving round the earth and in the heavens" (comets), which caused a " great conflagration upon the earth," from which those only escaped who lived near rivers and seas. The " Codex Chimalpopoca "—a Nahua, Central American record — tells us that the third era of the world, or " third sun," is called *Quia Tonatiuh,* or sun of rain, " because in this age there fell a rain of fire, all which existed burned, and there fell a rain of gravel;" the rocks " boiled with tumult, and there also arose the rocks of vermilion color." In other words, the traditions of these people go back to a great cataclysm of fire, when the earth possibly encountered, as in the Egyptian story, one of " the bodies moving round the earth and in the heavens;" they had also memories of "the Drift Period," and of the outburst of Plutonic rocks. If man has existed on the earth as long as science asserts, he must have passed through many of the great catastrophes which are written upon the face of the planet; and it is very natural that in myths and legends he should preserve some recollection of events so appalling and destructive.

Among the early Greeks Pan was the ancient god; his wife was Maia. The Abbé Brasseur de Bourbourg calls attention to the fact that Pan was adored in all parts of Mexico and Central America; and at *Panuco,* or *Panca,* literally *Panopolis,* the Spaniards found, upon their entrance into Mexico, superb temples and images of Pan.† (Brasseur's Introduction in Landa's " Relacion.") The names of both Pan and Maya enter extensively into the Maya vocabulary, *Maia* being the same as Maya, the principal name of the peninsula; and *pan,* added to *Maya,* makes the name of the ancient capital Mayapan. In the Nahua language *pan,* or *pani,* signifies " equality to that which is above," and Pentecatl was the progenitor of all beings. ("North Americans of Antiquity," p. 467.)

†It is unfortunate that Donnelly took Brasseur de Bourbourg so seriously.—E.F.B.

The ancient Mexicans believed that the sun-god would destroy the world in the last night of the fifty-second year, and
that he would never come back. They offered sacrifices to
him at that time to propitiate him; they extinguished all the
fires in the kingdom; they broke all their household furniture; they hung black masks before their faces; they prayed
and fasted; and on the evening of the last night they formed
a great procession to a neighboring mountain. A human being was sacrificed exactly at midnight; a block of wood was
laid at once on the body, and fire was then produced by rapidly revolving another piece of wood upon it; a spark was carried to a funeral pile, whose rising flame proclaimed to the
anxious people the promise of the god not to destroy the world
for another fifty-two years. Precisely the same custom obtained among the nations of Asia Minor and other parts of the
continent of Asia, wherever sun-worship prevailed, at the peri-
odical reproduction of the sacred fire, but not with the same
bloody rites as in Mexico. (Valentini, "Maya Archæology,"
p. 21.)

To this day the Brahman of India "churns" his sacred fire
out of a board by boring into it with a stick; the Romans renewed their sacred fire in the same way; and in Sweden even
now a "need-fire is kindled in this manner when cholera or
other pestilence is about." (Tylor's "Anthropology," p. 262.)

A belief in ghosts is found on both continents. The American Indians think that the spirits of the dead retain the form
and features which they wore while living; that there is a hell
and a heaven; that hell is below the earth, and heaven above
the clouds; that the souls of the wicked sometimes wander the
face of the earth, appearing occasionally to mortals. The story
of Tantalus is found among the Chippewayans, who believed
that bad souls stand up to their chins in water in sight of the
spirit-land, which they can never enter. The dead passed to
heaven across a stream of water by means of a narrow and slip-
pery bridge, from which many were lost. The Zuñis set apart

a day in each year which they spent among the graves of their dead, communing with their spirits, and bringing them presents —a kind of All-souls-day. (Dorman, " Prim. Superst.," p. 35.) The Stygian flood, and Scylla and Charybdis, are found among the legends of the Caribs. (*Ibid.*, p. 37.) Even the boat of Charon reappears in the traditions of the Chippewayans.

The Oriental belief in the transmigration of souls is found in every American tribe. The souls of men passed into animals or other men. (Schoolcraft, vol. i., p. 33.) The souls of the wicked passed into toads and wild beasts. (Dorman, " Prim. Superst.," p. 50.)

Among both the Germans and the American Indians lycanthropy, or the metamorphosis of men into wolves, was believed in. In British Columbia the men-wolves have often been seen seated around a fire, with their wolf-hides hung upon sticks to dry ! The Irish legend of hunters pursuing an animal which suddenly disappears, whereupon a human being appears in its place, is found among all the American tribes.

That timid and harmless animal, the hare, was, singularly enough, an object of superstitious reverence and fear in Europe, Asia, and America. The ancient Irish killed all the hares they found on May-day among their cattle, believing them to be witches. Cæsar gives an account of the horror in which this animal was held by the Britons. The Calmucks regarded the rabbit with fear and reverence. Divine honors were paid to the hare in Mexico. Wabasso was changed into a white rabbit, and canonized in that form.

The white bull, *Apis*, of the Egyptians, reappears in the sacred white buffalo of the Dakotas, which was supposed to possess supernatural power, and after death became a god. The white doe of European legend had its representative in the white deer of the Housatonic Valley, whose death brought misery to the tribe. The transmission of spirits by the laying on of hands, and the exorcism of demons, were part of the religion of the American tribes.

The witches of Scandinavia, who produced tempests by their incantations, are duplicated in America. A Cree sorcerer sold three days of fair weather for one pound of tobacco! The Indian sorcerers around Freshwater Bay kept the winds in leather bags, and disposed of them as they pleased.

Among the American Indians it is believed that those who are insane or epileptic are "possessed of devils." (Tylor, "Prim. Cult.," vol. ii., pp. 123–126.) Sickness is caused by evil spirits entering into the sick person. (Eastman's "Sioux.") The spirits of animals are much feared, and their departure out of the body of the invalid is a cause of thanksgiving. Thus an Omaha, after an eructation, says, "Thank you, animal." (Dorman, "Prim. Superst.," p. 55.) The confession of their sins was with a view to satisfy the evil spirit and induce him to leave them. (*Ibid.*, p. 57.)

In both continents burnt-offerings were sacrificed to the gods. In both continents the priests divined the future from the condition of the internal organs of the man or animal sacrificed. (*Ibid.*, pp. 214, 226.) In both continents the future was revealed by the flight of birds and by dreams. In Peru and Mexico there were *colleges of augurs*, as in Rome, who practised divination by watching the movements and songs of birds. (*Ibid.*, p. 261.)

Animals were worshipped in Central America and on the banks of the Nile. (*Ibid.*, p. 259.)

The Ojibbeways believed that the barking of a fox was ominous of ill. (*Ibid.*, p. 225). The peasantry of Western Europe have the same belief as to the howling of a dog.

The belief in satyrs, and other creatures half man and half animal, survived in America. The Kickapoos are Darwinians. "They think their ancestors had tails, and when they lost them the impudent fox sent every morning to ask how their tails were, and the bear shook his fat sides at the joke." (*Ibid.*, p. 232.) Among the natives of Brazil the father cut a stick at the wedding of his daughter; "this was done to cut off the tails of any future grandchildren." (Tylor, vol. i., p. 384.)

Jove, with the thunder-bolts in his hand, is duplicated in the Mexican god of thunder, Mixcoatl, who is represented holding a bundle of arrows. "He rode upon a tornado, and scattered the lightnings." (Dorman, "Prim. Superst.," p. 98.)

Dionysus, or Bacchus, is represented by the Mexican god Texcatzoncatl, the god of wine. (Bancroft, vol. iii., p. 418.)

Atlas reappears in Chibchacum, the deïty of the Chibchas; he bears the world on his shoulders, and when he shifts the burden from one shoulder to another severe earthquakes are produced. (Bollært, pp. 12, 13.)

Deucalion repeopling the world is repeated in Xololt, who, after the destruction of the world, descended to Mictlan, the realm of the dead, and brought thence a bone of the perished race. This, sprinkled with blood, grew into a youth, the father of the present race. The Quiche hero-gods, Hunaphu and Xblanque, died; their bodies were burnt, their bones ground to powder and thrown into the waters, whereupon they changed into handsome youths, with the same features as before. (Dorman, "Prim. Superst.," p. 193.)

Witches and warlocks, mermaids and mermen, are part of the mythology of the American tribes, as they were of the European races. (*Ibid.*, p. 79.) The mermaid of the Ottawas was "woman to the waist and fair;" thence fish-like. (*Ibid.*, p. 278.)

The snake-locks of Medusa are represented in the snake-locks of At-otarho, an ancient culture-hero of the Iroquois.

A belief in the incarnation of gods in men, and the physical translation of heroes to heaven, is part of the mythology of the Hindoos and the American races. Hiawatha, we are told, rose to heaven in the presence of the multitude, and vanished from sight in the midst of sweet music.

The vocal statues and oracles of Egypt and Greece were duplicated in America. In Peru, in the valley of Rimac, there was an idol which answered questions and became famous as an oracle.   (Dorman, " Prim. Superst.," p. 124.)

The Peruvians believed that men were sometimes metamorphosed into stones.

The Oneidas claimed descent from a stone, as the Greeks from the stones of Deucalion.   (*Ibid.*, p. 132.)

Witchcraft is an article of faith among all the American races.   Among the Illinois Indians "they made small images to represent those whose days they have a mind to shorten, and which they stab to the heart," whereupon the person represented is expected to die.   (Charlevoix, vol. ii., p. 166.)   The witches of Europe made figures of wax of their enemies, and gradually melted them at the fire, and as they diminished the victim was supposed to sicken and die.

A writer in the *Popular Science Monthly* (April, 1881, p. 828) points out the fact that there is an absolute identity between the folk-lore of the negroes on the plantations of the South and the myths and stories of certain tribes of Indians in South America, as revealed by Mr. Herbert Smith's " Brazil, the Amazons, and the Coast."   (New York: Scribner, 1879.)   Mr. Harris, the author of a work on the folk-lore of the negroes, asks this question, " When did the negro or the North American Indian come in contact with the tribes of South America?"

Customs.—Both peoples manufactured a fermented, intoxicating drink, the one deriving it from barley, the other from maize.   Both drank toasts.   Both had the institution of marriage, an important part of the ceremony consisting in the joining of hands; both recognized divorce, and the Peruvians and Mexicans established special courts to decide cases of this kind. Both the Americans and Europeans erected arches, and had triumphal processions for their victorious kings, and both strewed the ground before them with leaves and flowers. Both celebrated important events with bonfires and illuminations; both used banners; both invoked blessings.   The Phœnicians, Hebrews, and Egyptians practised circumcision. Palacio relates that at Azori, in Honduras, the natives circumcised boys before an idol called Icelca. ("Carta," p. 84.) Lord Kingsborough tells us the Central Americans used the same rite, and McKenzie (quoted by Retzius) says he saw the ceremony performed by the Chippeways. Both had bards and minstrels, who on great festivals sung the deeds of kings and heroes. Both the Egyptians and the Peruvians held agricultural fairs; both took a census of the people. Among both the land was divided *per capita* among the people; in Judea a new division was made every fifty years. The Peruvians renewed every year all the fires of the kingdom from the Temple of the Sun, the new fire being kindled from concave mirrors by the sun's rays. The Romans under Numa had precisely the same custom. The Peruvians had theatrical plays. They chewed the leaves of the cucu mixed with lime, as the Hindoo to-day chews the leaves of the betel mixed with lime. Both the American and European nations were divided into castes; both practised planet-worship; both used scales and weights and mirrors. The Peruvians, Egyptians, and Chaldeans divided the year into twelve months, and the months into lesser divisions of weeks. Both inserted additional days, so as to give the year three hundred and sixty-five days. The Mexicans added five intercalary days; and the Egyptians, in the time of Amunoph I., had already the same practice.

Humboldt, whose high authority cannot be questioned, by an elaborate discussion ("Vues des Cordilleras," p. 148 *et seq.*, ed. 1870), has shown the relative likeness of the Nahua calendar to that of Asia. He cites the fact that the Chinese, Japanese, Calmucks, Mongols, Mantchou, and other hordes of Tartars have cycles of sixty years' duration, divided into five brief periods of twelve years each. The method of citing a date by means of signs and numbers is quite similar with Asiatics and Mexicans. He further shows satisfactorily that *the majority of the names of the twenty days employed by the Aztecs are those of a zodiac used since the most remote antiquity among the peoples of Eastern Asia.*

Cabera thinks he finds analogies between the Mexican and Egyptian calendars. Adopting the view of several writers that the Mexican year began on the 26th of February, he finds the date to correspond with the beginning of the Egyptian year.

The American nations believed in four great primeval ages, as the Hindoo does to this day.

"In the Greeks of Homer," says Volney, "I find the customs, discourse, and manners of the Iroquois, Delawares, and Miamis. The tragedies of Sophocles and Euripides paint to me almost literally the sentiments of the *red men* respecting necessity, fatality, the miseries of human life, and the rigor of blind destiny." (Volney's "View of the United States.")

The Mexicans represent an eclipse of the moon as the moon being devoured by a dragon; and the Hindoos have precisely the same figure; and both nations continued to use this expression long after they had discovered the real meaning of an eclipse.

The Tartars believe that if they cut with an axe near a fire, or stick a knife into a burning stick, or touch the fire with a knife, they will "cut the top off the fire." The Sioux Indians will not stick an awl or a needle into a stick of wood on the fire, or chop on it with an axe or a knife.

Cremation was extensively practised in the New World. The dead were burnt, and their ashes collected and placed in vases and urns, as in Europe. Wooden statues of the dead were made.

There is a very curious and apparently inexplicable custom, called the "Couvade," which extends from China to the Mississippi Valley; it demands "that, when a child is born, the father must take to his bed, while the mother attends to all the duties of the household." Marco Polo found the custom among the Chinese in the thirteenth century.

The widow tells Hudibras—

> "Chineses thus are said
> To lie-in in their ladies' stead."

The practice remarked by Marco Polo continues to this day among the hill-tribes of China. "The father of a new-born child, as soon as the mother has become strong enough to leave her couch, gets into bed himself, and there receives the congratulations of his acquaintances." (Max Müller's "Chips from a German Workshop," vol. ii., p. 272.) Strabo (vol. iii., pp. 4, 17) mentions that, among the Iberians of the North of Spain, the women, after the birth of a child, tend their husbands, putting them to bed instead of going themselves. The same custom existed among the Basques only a few years ago. "In Biscay," says M. F. Michel, "the women rise immediately after childbirth and attend to the duties of the household, while the husband goes to bed, taking the baby with him, and thus receives the neighbors' compliments." The same custom was found in France, and is said to *exist to this day in some cantons of Béarn.* Diodorus Siculus tells us that among the Corsicans the wife was neglected, and the husband put to bed and treated as the patient. Apollonius Rhodius says that among the Tibereni, at the south of the Black Sea, "when a child was born the father lay groaning, with his head tied up, while the mother tended him with food and prepared his baths." The same absurd custom extends throughout the tribes of North and South America. Among the Caribs in the West Indies (and the Caribs, Brasseur de Bourbourg says, were the same as the ancient Carians of the Mediterranean Sea) the man takes to his bed as soon as a child is born, and *kills no animals.* And herein we find an explanation of a custom otherwise inexplicable. Among the American Indians it is believed that, if the father kills an animal during the infancy of the child, the spirit of the animal will revenge itself by inflicting some disease upon the helpless little one. "For six months the Carib father must not eat birds or fish, for what ever animals he eats will impress their likeness on the child, or produce disease by entering its body." (Dorman, " Prim. Superst.," p. 58.)   Among the Abipones the husband goes to bed, fasts a number of days, " and you would think," says Dobrizhoffer, " that it was he that had had the child."   The Brazilian father takes to his hammock during and after the birth of the child, and for fifteen days eats no meat and hunts no game.   Among the Esquimaux the husbands forbear hunting during the lying-in of their wives and for some time thereafter.

Here, then, we have a very extraordinary and unnatural custom, existing to this day on both sides of the Atlantic, reaching back to a vast antiquity, and finding its explanation only in the superstition of the American races.   A practice so absurd could scarcely have originated separately in the two continents; its existence is a very strong proof of unity of origin of the races on the opposite sides of the Atlantic; and the fact that the custom and the reason for it are both found in America, while the custom remains in Europe without the reason, would imply that the American population was the older of the two.

The Indian practice of depositing weapons and food with the dead was universal in ancient Europe, and in German villages nowadays a needle and thread is placed in the coffin for the dead to mend their torn clothes with; " while all over Europe the dead man had a piece of money put in his hand to pay his way with."   (" Anthropology," p. 347.)

The American Indian leaves food with the dead; the Russian peasant puts crumbs of bread behind the saints' pictures on the little iron shelf, and believes that the souls of his forefathers creep in and out and eat them.   At the cemetery of Père-la-Chaise, Paris, on All-souls-day, they " still put cakes and sweetmeats on the graves; and in Brittany the peasants that night do not forget to make up the fire and leave the fragments of the supper on the table for the souls of the dead." (*Ibid.*, p. 351.)

The Indian prays to the spirits of his forefathers; the Chinese religion is largely " ancestor-worship ;" and the rites paid to the dead ancestors, or lares, held the Roman family together." (" Anthropology," p. 351.)

We find the Indian practice of burying the dead in a sitting posture in use among the Nasamonians, a tribe of Libyans. Herodotus, speaking of the wandering tribes of Northern Africa, says, " They bury their dead *according to the fashion of the Greeks.* . . . They bury them sitting, and are right careful, when the sick man is at the point of giving up the ghost, to make him sit, and not let him die lying down."

The dead bodies of the caciques of Bogota were protected from desecration by diverting the course of a river and making the grave in its bed, and then letting the stream return to its natural course. Alaric, the leader of the Goths, was secretly buried in the same way. (Dorman, " Prim. Superst.," p. 195.)

Among the American tribes no man is permitted to marry a wife of the same clan-name or totem as himself. In India a Brahman is not allowed to marry a wife whose clan-name (her "cow-stall," as they say) is the same as his own; nor may a Chinaman take a wife of his own surname. ("Anthropology," p. 403.) " Throughout India the hill-tribes are divided into septs or clans, and a man may not marry a woman belonging to his own clan. The Calmucks of Tartary are divided into hordes, and a man may not marry a girl of his own horde. The same custom prevails among the Circassians and the Samoyeds of Siberia. The Ostyaks and Yakuts regard it as a crime to marry a woman of the same family, or even of the same name." (Sir John Lubbock, " Smith. Rep.," p. 347, 1869.)

Sutteeism—the burning of the widow upon the funeral-pile of the husband—was extensively practised in America (West's " Journal," p. 141) ; as was also the practice of sacrificing warriors, servants, and animals at the funeral of a great chief. (Dorman, pp. 210 – 211.) Beautiful girls were sacrificed to appease the anger of the gods, as among the Mediterranean races. (Bancroft, vol. iii., p. 471.) Fathers offered up their children for a like purpose, as among the Carthaginians.

The poisoned arrows of America had their representatives in Europe. Odysseus went to Ephyra for the man-slaying drug with which to smear his bronze-tipped arrows. (Tylor's "Anthropology," p. 237.)

"The bark canoe of America was not unknown in Asia and Africa" (*Ibid.*, p. 254), while the skin canoes of our Indians and the Esquimaux were found on the shores of the Thames and the Euphrates. In Peru and on the Euphrates commerce was carried on upon rafts supported by inflated skins. They are still used on the Tigris.

The Indian boils his meat by dropping red-hot stones into a water-vessel made of hide; and Linnæus found the Bothland people brewing beer in this way—"and to this day the rude Carinthian boor drinks such *stone-beer*, as it is called." (*Ibid.*, p. 266.)

In the buffalo dance of the Mandan Indians the dancers covered their heads with a mask made of the head and horns of the buffalo. To-day in the temples of India, or among the lamas of Thibet, the priests dance the demons out, or the new year in, arrayed in animal masks (*Ibid.*, p. 297); and the "mummers" at Yule-tide, in England, are a survival of the same custom. (*Ibid.*, p. 298.) The North American dog and bear dances, wherein the dancers acted the part of those animals, had their prototype in the Greek dances at the festivals of Dionysia. (*Ibid.*, p. 298.)

Tattooing was practised in both continents. Among the Indians it was fetichistic in its origin; "every Indian had the image of an animal tattooed on his breast or arm, to charm away evil spirits." (Dorman, "Prim. Superst.," p. 156.) The sailors of Europe and America preserve to this day a custom which was once universal among the ancient races. Banners, flags, and armorial bearings are supposed to be survivals of the old totemic tattooing. The Arab woman still tattoos her face, arms, and ankles. The war-paint of the American savage reappeared in the *woad* with which the ancient Briton stained his body; and Tylor suggests that the painted stripes on the circus clown are a survival of a custom once universal. (Tylor's "Anthropolgy," p. 327.)

In America, as in the Old World, the temples of worship were built over the dead. (Dorman, " Prim. Superst.," p. 178.) Says Prudentius, the Roman bard, "there were as many temples of gods as sepulchres."

The Etruscan belief that evil spirits strove for the possession of the dead was found among the Mosquito Indians. (Bancroft, " Native Races," vol. i., p. 744.)

The belief in fairies, which forms so large a part of the folklore of Western Europe, is found among the American races. The Ojibbeways see thousands of fairies dancing in a sunbeam; during a rain myriads of them hide in the flowers. When disturbed they disappear underground. They have their dances, like the Irish fairies; and, like them, they kill the domestic animals of those who offend them. The Dakotas also believe in fairies. The Otoes located the "little people" in a mound at the mouth of Whitestone River; they were eighteen inches high, with very large heads; they were armed with bows and arrows, and killed those who approached their residence. (See Dorman's "Origin of Primitive Superstitions," p. 23.) "The Shoshone legends people the mountains of Montana with little imps, called Nirumbees, two feet long, naked, and *with a tail.*" They stole the children of the Indians, and left in their stead the young of their own baneful race, who resembled the stolen children so much that the mothers were deceived and suckled them, whereupon they died. This greatly resembles the European belief in " changelings." (*Ibid.,* p. 24.)

In both continents we find tree-worship. In Mexico and Central America cypresses and palms were planted near the temples, generally in *groups of threes;* they were tended with great care, and received offerings of incense and gifts. The same custom prevailed among the Romans—the cypress was dedicated to Pluto, and the palm to Victory.

Not only infant baptism by water was found both in the old Babylonian religion and among the Mexicans, but an offering of cakes, which is recorded by the prophet Jeremiah as part of the worship of the Babylonian goddess-mother, "the Queen of Heaven," was also found in the ritual of the Aztecs. ("Builders of Babel," p. 78.)

In Babylonia, China, and Mexico the caste at the bottom of the social scale lived upon floating islands of reeds or rafts, covered with earth, on the lakes and rivers.

In Peru and Babylonia marriages were made but once a year, at a public festival.

Among the Romans, the Chinese, the Abyssinians, and the Indians of Canada the singular custom prevails of lifting the bride over the door-step of her husband's home. (Sir John Lubbock, "Smith. Rep.," 1869, p. 352.)

"The bride-cake which so invariably accompanies a wedding among ourselves, and which must always be cut by the bride, may be traced back to the old Roman form of marriage by '*conferreatio*,' or eating together. So, also, among the Iroquois the bride and bridegroom used to partake together of a cake of sagamite, which the bride always offered to her husband." (*Ibid.*)

Among many American tribes, notably in Brazil, the husband captured the wife by main force, as the men of Benjamin carried off the daughters of Shiloh at the feast, and as the Romans captured the Sabine women. "Within a few generations the same old habit was kept up in Wales, where the bridegroom and his friends, mounted and armed as for war, carried off the bride; and in Ireland they used even to hurl spears at the bride's people, though at such a distance that no one was hurt, except now and then by accident—as happened when one Lord Hoath lost an eye, which mischance put an end to this curious relic of antiquity." (Tylor's "Anthropology," p. 409.)

Marriage in Mexico was performed by the priest. He exhorted them to maintain peace and harmony, and tied the end of the man's mantle to the dress of the woman; he perfumed them, and placed on each a shawl on which was painted a skeleton, "as a symbol *that only death could now separate them* from one another." (Dorman, "Prim. Superst.," p. 379.)

The priesthood was thoroughly organized in Mexico and Peru. They were prophets as well as priests. "They brought the newly-born infant into the religious society; they directed their training and education; they determined the entrance of the young men into the service of the state; they consecrated marriage by their blessing; they comforted the sick and assisted the dying." (*Ibid.*, p. 374.) There were five thousand priests in the temples of Mexico. They confessed and absolved the sinners, arranged the festivals, and managed the choirs in the churches. They lived in conventual discipline, but were allowed to marry; they practised flagellation and fasting, and prayed at regular hours. There were great preachers and exhorters among them. There were also convents into which females were admitted. The novice had her hair cut off and took vows of celibacy; they lived holy and pious lives. (*Ibid.*, pp. 375, 376.) The king was the high-priest of the religious orders. A new king ascended the temple naked, except his girdle; he was sprinkled four times with water which had been blessed; he was then clothed in a mantle, and on his knees took an oath to maintain the ancient religion. The priests then instructed him in his royal duties. (*Ibid.*, p. 378.) Besides the regular priesthood there were monks who were confined in cloisters. (*Ibid.*, p. 390.) Cortes says the Mexican priests were very strict in the practice of honesty and chastity, and any deviation was punished with death. They wore long white robes and burned incense.

(Dorman, " Prim. Superst.," p. 379.) The first fruits of the earth were devoted to the support of the priesthood. (*Ibid.*, p. 383.) The priests of the Isthmus were sworn to perpetual chastity.

The American doctors practised phlebotomy. They bled the sick man because they believed the evil spirit which afflicted him would come away with the blood. In Europe phlebotomy continued to a late period, but the original superstition out of which it arose, in this case as in many others, was forgotten.

There is opportunity here for the philosopher to meditate upon the perversity of human nature and the persistence of hereditary error. The superstition of one age becomes the science of another; men were first bled to withdraw the evil spirit, then to cure the disease; and a practice whose origin is lost in the night of ages is continued into the midst of civilization, and only overthrown after it has sent millions of human beings to untimely graves. Dr. Sangrado could have found the explanation of his profession only among the red men of America.

Folk-lore.—Says Max Müller: " Not only do we find the same words and the same terminations in Sanscrit and Gothic; not only do we find the same name for Zeus in Sanscrit, Latin, and German; not only is the abstract name for God the same in India, Greece, and Italy; but these very stories, these ' Mährchen ' which nurses still tell, with almost the same words, in the Thuringian forest and in the Norwegian villages, and to which crowds of children listen under the Pippal-trees of India—these stories, too, belonged to the common heirloom of the Indo-European race, and their origin carries us back to the same distant past, when no Greek had set foot in Europe, no Hindoo had bathed in the sacred waters of the Ganges."

And we find that an identity of origin can be established between the folk-lore or fairy tales of America and those of the Old World, precisely such as exists between the legends of Norway and India.

Mr. Tylor tells us the story of the two brothers in Central America who, starting on their dangerous journey to the land of Xibalba, where their father had perished, plant each a cane in the middle of their grandmother's house, that she may know by its flourishing or withering whether they are alive or dead. Exactly the same conception occurs in Grimm's "Mährchen," when the two gold-children wish to see the world and to leave their father; and when their father is sad, and asks them how he shall hear news of them, they tell him, "We leave you the two golden lilies; from these you can see how we fare. If they are fresh, we are well; if they fade, we are ill; if they fall, we are dead." Grimm traces the same idea in Hindoo stories. "Now this," says Max Müller, "is strange enough, and its occurrence in India, Germany, and Central America is stranger still."

Compare the following stories, which we print in parallel columns, one from the Ojibbeway Indians, the other from Ireland:

THE OJIBBEWAY STORY.

The birds met together one day to try which could fly the highest. Some flew up very swift, but soon got tired, and were passed by others of stronger wing. But the eagle went up beyond them all, and was ready to claim the victory, when the gray linnet, a very small bird, flew from the eagle's back, where it had perched unperceived, and, being fresh and unexhausted, succeeded in going the highest. When the birds came down and met in council to award the prize, it was given to the eagle, because that bird had not only gone up nearer to the sun than any of the larger birds, but it had carried the linnet on its back.

For this reason the eagle's feathers became the most honorable marks of distinction a warrior could bear.

THE IRISH STORY.

The birds all met together one day, and settled among themselves that whichever of them could fly highest was to be the king of all. Well, just as they were on the hinges of being off, what does the little rogue of a wren do but hop up and perch himself unbeknown on the eagle's tail. So they flew and flew ever so high, till the eagle was miles above all the rest, and could not fly another stroke, he was so tired. "Then," says he, "I'm king of the birds." "You lie!" says the wren, darting up a perch and a half above the big fellow. Well, the eagle was so mad to think how he was done, that when the wren was coming down he gave him a stroke of his wing, and from that day to this the wren was never able to fly farther than a hawthorn-bush.

Compare the following stories:

In Hindoo mythology Urvasi came down from heaven and became the wife of the son of Buddha only on condition that two pet rams should never be taken from her bedside, and that she should never behold her lord undressed. The immortals, however, wishing Urvasi back in heaven, contrived to steal the rams; and, as the king pursued the robbers with his sword in the dark, the lightning revealed his person, the compact was broken, and Urvasi disappeared. This same story is found in different forms among many people of Aryan and Turanian descent, the central idea being that of a man marrying some one of an aerial or aquatic origin, and living happily with her till he breaks the condition on which her residence with him depends; stories exactly parallel to that of Raymond of Toulouse, who chances in the hunt upon the beautiful Melusina at a fountain, and lives with her happily until he discovers her fish-nature and she vanishes.

Wampee, a great hunter, once came to a strange prairie, where he heard faint sounds of music, and looking up saw a speck in the sky, which proved itself to be a basket containing twelve most beautiful maidens, who, on reaching the earth, forthwith set themselves to dance. He tried to catch the youngest, but in vain; ultimately he succeeded by assuming the disguise of a mouse. He was very attentive to his new wife, who was really a daughter of one of the stars, but she wished to return home, so she made a wicker basket secretly, and, by help of a charm she remembered, ascended to her father.

If the legend of Cadmus recovering Europa, after she has been carried away by the white bull, the spotless cloud, means that "the sun must journey westward until he sees again the beautiful tints which greeted his eyes in the morning," it is curious to find a story current in North America to the effect that a man once had a beautiful daughter, whom he forbade to leave the lodge lest she should be carried off by the king of the buffaloes; and that as she sat, notwithstanding, outside the house combing her hair, "all of a sudden the king of the buffaloes came dashing on, with his herd of followers, and, taking her between his horns, away he cantered over plains, plunged into a river which bounded his land, and carried her safely to his lodge on the other side," whence she was finally recovered by her father.

Games.—The same games and sports extended from India to the shores of Lake Superior. The game of the Hindoos, called *pachisi*, is played upon a cross-shaped board or cloth; it is a combination of checkers and draughts, with the throwing of dice, the dice determining the number of moves; when the Spaniards entered Mexico they found the Aztecs playing a game called *patolli*, identical with the Hindoo pachisi, on a similar cross-shaped board. The game of ball, which the Indians of America were in the habit of playing at the time of the discovery of the country, from California to the Atlantic, was identical with the European *chueca, crosse,* or *hockey.*

One may well pause, after reading this catalogue, and ask himself, wherein do these peoples differ? It is absurd to pretend that all these similarities could have been the result of accidental coincidences.

These two peoples, separated by the great ocean, were baptized alike in infancy with blessed water; they prayed alike to the gods; they worshipped together the sun, moon, and stars; they confessed their sins alike; they were instructed alike by an established priesthood; they were married in the same way and by the joining of hands; they armed themselves with the same weapons; when children came, the man, on both continents, went to bed and left his wife to do the honors of the household; they tattooed and painted themselves in the same fashion; they became intoxicated on kindred drinks; their dresses were alike; they cooked in the same manner; they used the same metals; they employed the same exorcisms and bleedings for disease; they believed alike in ghosts, demons, and fairies; they listened to the same stories; they played the same games; they used the same musical instruments; they danced the same dances, and when they died they were embalmed in the same way and buried sitting; while over them were erected, on both continents, the same mounds, pyramids, obelisks, and temples. And yet we are asked to believe that there was no relationship between them, and that they had never had any ante-Columbian intercourse with each other.

If our knowledge of Atlantis was more thorough, it would no doubt appear that, in every instance wherein the people of Europe accord with the people of America, they were both in accord with the people of Atlantis; and that Atlantis was the common centre from which both peoples derived their arts, sciences, customs, and opinions. It will be seen that in every case where Plato gives us any information in this respect as to Atlantis, we find this agreement to exist. It existed in architecture, sculpture, navigation, engraving, writing, an established priesthood, the mode of worship, agriculture, the construction of roads and canals; and it is reasonable to suppose that the same correspondence extended down to all the minor details treated of in this chapter.

Chapter III.

AMERICAN EVIDENCES OF INTERCOURSE WITH EUROPE OR ATLANTIS.

1. On the monuments of Central America there are representations of bearded men. How could the beardless American Indians have imagined a bearded race?

2. All the traditions of the civilized races of Central America point to an *Eastern* origin.

The leader and civilizer of the Nahua family was Quetzalcoatl. This is the legend respecting him:

"*From the distant East,* from the fabulous Hue Hue Tlapalan, this mysterious person came to Tula, and became the patron god and high-priest of the ancestors of the Toltecs. He is described as having been *a white man,* with strong formation of body, broad forehead, large eyes, and *flowing beard.* He wore a mitre on his head, and was dressed in a long white robe reaching to his feet, and covered with red crosses. In his hand he held a sickle. His habits were ascetic, he never married, was most chaste and pure in life, and is said to have endured penance in a neighboring mountain, not for its effects upon himself, but as a warning to others. He condemned sacrifices, except of fruits and flowers, and was known as the god of peace; for, when addressed on the subject of war, he is reported to have stopped his ears with his fingers." ("North Amer. of Antiq.," p. 268.)

"He was skilled in many arts: he invented" (that is, imported) "gem-cutting and metal-casting; he originated letters, and invented the Mexican calendar. He finally returned to the land in the East from which he came: leaving the American coast at Vera Cruz, he embarked in a canoe made of serpent-skins, and '*sailed away into the East.*'" (*Ibid.,* p. 271.)

Dr. Le Plongeon says of the columns at Chichen:

"The base is formed by the head of Cukulcan, the shaft of the body of the serpent, with its feathers beautifully carved to

the very chapiter. On the chapiters of the columns that support the portico, at the entrance of the castle in Chichen Itza, may be seen the carved figures of long-bearded men, with upraised hands, in the act of worshipping sacred trees. They forcibly recall to mind the same worship in Assyria."

In the accompanying cut of an ancient vase from Tula, we see a bearded figure grasping a beardless man.

In the cut given below we see a face that might be duplicated among the old men of any part of Europe.

ANCIENT MEXICAN VASE.

The Cakchiquel MS. says: "Four persons came from Tulan, from the *direction of the rising sun*—that is one Tulan. There is another Tulan in Xibalbay, and another where the sun sets, *and it is there that we came;* and in the direction of the setting sun there is another, where is the god; so that there are four Tulans; and it is where the sun sets that we came to Tulan, *from the other side of the sea,* where this Tulan is; and it is there that we were conceived and begotten by our mothers and fathers."

BEARDED HEAD,
FROM TEOTIHUACAN.

That is to say, the birthplace of the race was in the East, across the sea, at a place called Tulan; and when they emigrated they called their first stopping-place on the American continent Tulan also; and besides this there were two other Tulans.

"Of the Nahua predecessors of the Toltecs in Mexico the Olmecs and Xicalancans were the most important. They were the forerunners of the great races that followed. According to Ixtlilxochitl, these people—which are conceded to be one— occupied the world in the third age; *they came from the East in ships or barks* to the land of Potonchan, which they commenced to populate."

3. The Abbé Brasseur de Bourbourg, in one of the notes of the Introduction of the "Popol Vuh," presents a very remarkable analogy between the kingdom of Xibalba, described in that work, and Atlantis. He says:

"Both countries are magnificent, exceedingly fertile, and abound in the precious metals. The empire of Atlantis was divided into ten kingdoms, governed by five couples of twin sons of Poseidon, the eldest being supreme over the others; and the ten constituted a tribunal that managed the affairs of the empire. Their descendants governed after them. The ten kings of Xibalba, who reigned (in couples) under Hun-Came and Vukub-Came (and who together constituted a grand council of the kingdom), certainly furnish curious points of comparison. And there is wanting neither a catastrophe—for Xibalba had a terrific inundation—nor the name of Atlas, of which the etymology is found only in the Nahuatl tongue: it comes from *atl*, water; and we know that a city of Atlan (near the water) still existed on the Atlantic side of the Isthmus of Panama at the time of the Conquest."

"In Yucatan the traditions all point to an *Eastern and foreign* origin for the race. The early writers report that the natives believe their ancestors to have *crossed the sea* by a passage which was opened for them." (Landa's "Relacion," p. 28.)

"It was also believed that part of the population came into the country from the West. Lizana says that the smaller portion, 'the little descent,' came from the East, while the greater portion, 'the great descent,' came from the West. Cogolluda considers the Eastern colony to have been the larger. . . . The culture-hero Zamna, the author of all civilization in Yucatan, is described as *the teacher of letters*, and the leader of the people from their ancient home. . . . He was the leader of a colony *from the East.*" ("North Amer. of Antiq.," p. 229.)

The ancient Mexican legends say that, after the Flood, Coxcox and his wife, after wandering one hundred and four years, landed at *Antlan,* and passed thence to Capultepec, and thence to Culhuacan, and lastly to Mexico.

Coming from Atlantis, they named their first landing-place *Antlan.*

All the races that settled Mexico, we are told, traced their origin back to an *Aztlan* (Atlan-tis). Duran describes Aztlan as "a most attractive land." ("North Amer. of Antiq.," p. 257.)

Samé, the great name of Brazilian legend, came across the ocean *from the rising sun.* He had power over the elements and tempests; the trees of the forests would recede to make room for him (cutting down the trees); the animals used to crouch before him (domesticated animals); lakes and rivers became solid for him (boats and bridges); and he taught the use of agriculture and magic. Like him, Bochica, the great law-giver of the Muyscas, and son of the sun—he who invented for them the calendar and regulated their festivals—had a white beard, a detail in which all the American culture-heroes agree. The "Samé" of Brazil was probably the "Zamna" of Yucatan.

4. We find in America numerous representations of the elephant. We are forced to one of two conclusions: either the

ELEPHANT MOUND, WISCONSIN.

monuments date back to the time of the mammoth in North America, or these people held intercourse at some time in the past with races who possessed the elephant, and from whom they obtained pictures of that singular animal. Plato tells us that the Atlanteans possessed great numbers of elephants.

There are in Wisconsin a number of mounds of earth representing different animals — men, birds, and quadrupeds.

ELEPHANT PIPE, LOUISA COUNTY, IOWA.

Among the latter is a mound representing an elephant, "so perfect in its proportions, and complete in its representation of an elephant, that its builders must have been well acquaint-ed with all the physical characteristics of the animal which they delineated." We copy the representation of this mound on page 168.

On a farm in Louisa County, Iowa, a pipe was ploughed up which also represents an elephant. We are indebted to the valuable work of John T. Short ("The North Americans of Antiquity," p. 530) for a picture of this singular object. It was found in a section where the ancient mounds were very abundant and rich in relics. The pipe is of ELEPHANT-TRUNK HEAD-DRESS, PALENQUE.
sandstone, of the ordinary Mound-Builder's
type, and has every appearance of age and usage. There can be no doubt of its genuineness. The finder had no conception of its archæological value.

In the ruined city of Palenque we find, in one of the pal-

aces, a stucco bass-relief of a priest.   His elaborate head-dress
or helmet represents very faithfully the head of an elephant.†
The cut on page 169 is from a drawing made by Waldeck.

The decoration known as "elephant-trunks" is found in
many parts of the ancient ruins of Central America, projecting from above the door-ways of the buildings.

In Tylor's "Researches into the Early History of Mankind,"
p. 313, I find a remarkable representation of an elephant, taken
from an ancient Mexican manuscript.   It is as follows:

MEXICAN REPRESENTATION OF ELEPHANT.

† Such pre-Columbian "elephants" in art are now rejected. In
the 1920's there was much serious controversy about them.—
E.F.B.

Chapter IV.

CORROBORATING CIRCUMSTANCES.

1. Lenormant insists that the human race issued from Upa-Merou, and adds that some Greek traditions point to "this locality—particularly the expression μέροπες ἄνθρωποι, which can only mean 'the men sprung from Merou.'" ("Manual," p. 21.)

Theopompus tells us that the people who inhabited Atlantis were the *Meropes*, the people of *Merou*.

2. Whence comes the word *Atlantic?* The dictionaries tell us that the ocean is named after the mountains of *Atlas;* but whence did the *Atlas* mountains get their name? †

"The words Atlas and Atlantic have no satisfactory etymology in any language known to Europe. They are not Greek, and cannot be referred to any known language of the Old World. But in the Nahuatl language we find immediately the radical *a, atl,* which signifies water, war, and the top of the head. (Molina, "Vocab. en lengua Mexicana y Castellana.") From this comes a series of words, such as atlan—on the border of or amid the water—from which we have the adjective *Atlantic.* We have also *atlaça,* to combat, or be in agony; it means likewise to hurl or dart from the water, and in the preterit makes *Atlaz.* A city named *Atlan* existed when the continent was discovered by Columbus, at the entrance of the Gulf of Uraba, in Darien. With a good harbor, it is now reduced to an unimportant pueblo named *Acla.*" (Baldwin's "Ancient America," p. 179.)

Plato tells us that Atlantis and the Atlantic Ocean were named after Atlas, the eldest son of Poseidon, the founder of the kingdom.

3. Upon that part of the African continent nearest to the site

† Atlantis is derived from Atlas, which in turn is from τλῆ̑ναι (to bear).—E.F.B.

of Atlantis we find a chain of mountains, known from the most
ancient times as the Atlas Mountains.   Whence this name Atlas, if it be not from the name of the great king of Atlantis?
And if this be not its origin, how comes it that we find it in
the most north-western corner of Africa?   And how does it
happen that in the time of Herodotus there dwelt near this
mountain-chain a people called the *Atlantes*, probably a remnant of a colony from Solon's island?   How comes it that the
people of the Barbary States were known to the Greeks, Romans, and Carthaginians as the "Atlantes," this name being
especially applied to the inhabitants of Fezzan and Bilma?
Where did they get the name from?   There is no etymology
for it east of the Atlantic Ocean.   (Lenormant's "Anc. Hist.
of the East," p. 253.)

Look at it!   An "Atlas" mountain on the shore of Africa;
an "Atlan" town on the shore of America; the "Atlantes"
living along the north and west coast of Africa; an Aztec
people from Aztlan, in Central America; an ocean rolling between the two worlds called the "Atlantic;" a mythological
deity called "Atlas" holding the world on his shoulders; and
an immemorial tradition of an island of Atlantis.   Can all
these things be the result of accident?

4. Plato says that there was a "passage west from Atlantis
to the rest of the islands, as well as from these islands to the
whole opposite continent that *surrounds* that *real* sea."   He
calls it a real sea, as contradistinguished from the Mediterranean, which, as he says, is not a real sea (or ocean) but a land-
locked body of water, like a harbor.

Now, Plato might have created Atlantis out of his imagination; but how could he have invented the islands beyond
(the West India Islands), and the whole continent (America)
enclosing that real sea?   If we look at the map, we see that
the continent of America does "surround" the ocean in a great
half-circle.   Could Plato have guessed all this?   If there had
been no Atlantis, and no series of voyages from it that re-

vealed the half-circle of the continent from Newfoundland to Cape St. Roche, how could Plato have guessed it? And how could he have known that the Mediterranean was only a harbor compared with the magnitude of the great ocean surrounding Atlantis? Long sea-voyages were necessary to establish that fact, and the Greeks, who kept close to the shores in their short journeys, did not make such voyages.

5. How can we, without Atlantis, explain the presence of the Basques in Europe, who have no lingual affinities with any other race on the continent of Europe, but whose language *is similar to the languages of America?* †

Plato tells us that the dominion of Gadeirus, one of the kings of Atlantis, extended "toward the pillars of Heracles (Hercules) as far as the country which is still called the region of Gades in that part of the world." Gades is the Cadiz of to-day, and the dominion of Gadeirus embraced the land of the Iberians or Basques, their chief city taking its name from a king of Atlantis, and they themselves being Atlanteans.

Dr. Farrar, referring to the Basque language, says:

"What is certain about it is, that its structure is polysynthetic, like the languages of America. Like them, it forms its compounds by the elimination of certain radicals in the simple words; so that *ilhun*, the twilight, is contracted from *hill*, dead, and *egun*, day; and *belhaur*, the knee, from *belhar*, front, and *oin*, leg. . . . The fact is indisputable, and is eminently noteworthy, that while the affinities of the Basque roots have never been conclusively elucidated, there has never been any doubt that this isolated language, preserving its identity in a western corner of Europe, between two mighty kingdoms, resembles, in its grammatical structure, the aboriginal languages of the vast opposite continent (America), and those alone." ("Families of Speech," p. 132.)

If there was an Atlantis, forming, with its connecting ridges, a continuous bridge of land from America to Africa, we can understand how the Basques could have passed from one conti-nent to another; but if the wide Atlantic rolled at all times un-

† Basque and the American Indian languages are not related. Some linguists relate Basque to the Caucasic languages.—E.F.B.

broken between the two continents, it is difficult to conceive of such an emigration by an uncivilized people.

6. Without Atlantis, how can we explain the fact that the early Egyptians were depicted by themselves as *red* men on their own monuments? And, on the other hand, how can we account for the representations of negroes on the monuments of Central America?

Dêsirè Charnay, now engaged in exploring those monuments, has published in the *North American Review* for December, 1880, photographs of a number of idols exhumed at San Juan de Teotihuacan, from which I select the following strikingly negroid faces:

NEGRO IDOLS FOUND IN MEXICO.

Dr. Le Plongeon says:

"Besides the sculptures of long-bearded men seen by the explorer at Chichen Itza, there were tall figures of people with small heads, thick lips, and curly short hair or wool, regarded as negroes. 'We always see them as standard or parasol bearers, but never engaged in actual warfare.'" ("Maya Archæology," p. 62.)

The following cut is from the court of the Palace of Pa-lenque, figured by Stephens. The face is strongly Ethiopian.

NEGROID FIGURE, PALENQUE.

The figure below represents a gigantic granite head, found near the volcano of Tuxtla, in the Mexican State of Vera Cruz, at Caxapa. The features are unmistakably negroid.

As the negroes have never been a sea-going race, the presence of these faces among the antiquities of Central America proves one of two things, either the existence of a land connection between America and Africa *via* Atlantis, as revealed by the deep-sea soundings of the *Challenger*, or commercial relations between America and Africa through the ships of the Atlanteans or some other civilized race, whereby the negroes were brought to America as slaves at a very remote epoch.

And we find some corroboration of the latter theory in that singular book of the Quiches, the "Popol Vuh," in which, after describing the creation of the first men "*in the region of the rising sun*" (Bancroft's "Native Races," vol. v., p. 548),

NEGRO HEAD, VERA CRUZ.

and enumerating their first generations, we are told, " All seem to have spoken one language, and to have lived in great peace, *black men and white together.* Here they awaited the rising of the sun, and prayed to the Heart of Heaven." (Bancroft's " Native Races," p. 547.) How did the red men of Central America know anything about " black men and white men ?" The conclusion seems inevitable that these legends of a primitive, peaceful, and happy land, an *Aztlan* in the East, inhabited by black and white men, to which all the civilized nations of America traced their origin, could only refer to Atlantis—that bridge of land where the white, dark, and red races met. The " Popol Vuh " proceeds to tell how this first home of the race became over-populous, and how the people under Balam-Quitze migrated ; how their language became " confounded," in other words, broken up into dialects, in consequence of separation ; and how some of the people " *went to the East,* and many came hither to Guatemala." (*Ibid.,* p. 547.)

M. A. de Quatrefages (" Human Species," p. 200) says, " Black populations have been found in America in very small numbers only, as isolated tribes in the midst of very different populations. Such are the Charruas of Brazil, the Black Carribees of Saint Vincent, in the Gulf of Mexico ; the Jamassi of Florida, and the dark-complexioned Californians. . . . Such, again, is the tribe that Balboa saw some representatives of in his passage of the Isthmus of Darien in 1513 ; . . . they were true negroes."

7. How comes it that all the civilizations of the Old World radiate from the shores of the Mediterranean ? The Mediterranean is a *cul de sac,* with Atlantis opposite its mouth. Every civilization on its shores possesses traditions that point to Atlantis. We hear of no civilization coming *to* the Mediterranean from Asia, Africa, or Europe—from north, south, or west ; but north, south, east, and west we find civilization radiating from the Mediterranean to other lands. We see the Aryans descending upon Hindostan from the direction of the Medi-

terranean; and we find the Chinese borrowing inventions from Hindostan, and claiming descent from a region not far from the Mediterranean.

The Mediterranean has been the centre of the modern world, because it lay in the path of the extension of an older civilization, whose ships colonized its shores, as they did also the shores of America. Plato says, " the nations are gathered around the shores of the Mediterranean like frogs around a marsh."

Dr. McCausland says:

" The obvious conclusion from these facts is, that at some time previous to these migrations a people speaking a language of a superior and complicated structure broke up their society, and, under some strong impulse, poured out in different directions, and gradually established themselves in all the lands now inhabited by the Caucasian race. Their territories extend from the Atlantic to the Ganges, and from Iceland to Ceylon, and are bordered on the north and east by the Asiatic Mongols, and on the south by the negro tribes of Central Africa. They present all the appearances of a later race, expanding itself between and into the territories of two pre-existing neighboring races, and forcibly appropriating the room required for its increasing population." (McCausland's " Adam and the Adamites," p. 280.)

Modern civilization is Atlantean. Without the thousands of years of development which were had in Atlantis modern civilization could not have existed. The inventive faculty of the present age is taking up the great delegated work of creation where Atlantis left it thousands of years ago.

8. How are we to explain the existence of the Semitic race in Europe without Atlantis? It is an intrusive race; a race colonized on sea-coasts. Where are its Old World affinities?

9. Why is it that the origin of wheat, barley, oats, maize, and rye—the essential plants of civilization—is totally lost in the mists of a vast antiquity? We have in the Greek mythology legends of the introduction of most of these by Atlantean kings or gods into Europe; but no European nation

claims to have discovered or developed them, and it has been impossible to trace them to their wild originals. Out of the whole *flora* of the world mankind in the last seven thousand years has not developed a single food-plant to compare in importance to the human family with these. If a wise and scientific nation should propose nowadays to add to this list, it would have to form great botanical gardens, and, by systematic and long-continued experiments, develop useful plants from the humble productions of the field and forest. Was this done in the past on the island of Atlantis?

10. Why is it that we find in Ptolemy's "Geography of Asia Minor," in a list of cities in Armenia Major in A.D. 140, the names of five cities which have their counterparts in the names of localities in Central America?

Armenian Cities.	Central American Localities.
Chol.	Chol-ula
Colua.	Colua-can.
Zuivana.	Zuivan.
Cholima.	Colima.
Zalissa.	Xalisco.

(Short's "North Americans of Antiquity," p. 497.)

11. How comes it that the sandals upon the feet of the statue of Chacmol, discovered at Chichen Itza, are "exact representations of those found on the feet of the Guanches, the early inhabitants of the Canary Islands, whose mummies are occasionally discovered in the caves of Teneriffe?" Dr. Merritt deems the axe or chisel heads dug up at Chiriqui, Central America, "almost identical in form as well as material with specimens found in Suffolk County, England." (Bancroft's "Native Races," vol. iv., p. 20.) The rock-carvings of Chiriqui are pronounced by Mr. Seemann to have a striking resemblance to the ancient incised characters found on the rocks of Northumberland, England. (*Ibid.*)

"Some stones have recently been discovered in Hierro and Las Palmas (Canary Islands), bearing sculptured symbols similar to those found on the shores of Lake Superior; and this has led M. Bertholet, the historiographer of the Canary Islands, to conclude that the first inhabitants of the Canaries and those of the great West were one in race." (Benjamin, "The Atlantic Islands," p. 130.)

12. How comes it that that very high authority, Professor Retzius ("Smithsonian Report," 1859, p. 266), declares, "With regard to the primitive dolichocephalæ of America I entertain a hypothesis still more bold, namely, that they are nearly related to the Guanches in the Canary Islands, and to the Atlantic populations of Africa, the Moors, Tuaricks, Copts, etc., which Latham comprises under the name of Egyptian-Atlantidæ. We find one and the same form of skull in the Canary Islands, in front of the African coast, and in the Carib Islands, on the opposite coast, which faces Africa. The color of the skin on both sides of the Atlantic is represented in these populations as being of a reddish-brown."

13. The Barbarians who are alluded to by Homer and Thucydides were a race of ancient navigators and pirates called *Cares,* or *Carians,* who occupied the isles of Greece before the Pelasgi, and antedated the Phœnicians in the control of the sea. The Abbé Brasseur de Bourbourg claims that these Carians were identical with the *Caribs* of the West Indies, the *Caras* of Honduras, and the *Gurani* of South America. (Landas, "Relacion," pp. 52–65.)

14. When we consider it closely, one of the most extraordinary customs ever known to mankind is that to which I have already alluded in a preceding chapter, to wit, the embalming of the body of the dead man, with a purpose that the body itself may live again in a future state. To arrive at this practice several things must coexist:

a. The people must be highly religious, and possessed of an organized and influential priesthood, to perpetuate so troublesome a custom from age to age.

b. They must believe implicitly in the immortality of the

soul; and this implies a belief in rewards and punishments after death; in a heaven and a hell.

c. They must believe in the immortality of the body, and its resurrection from the grave on some day of judgment in the distant future.

d. But a belief in the immortality of the soul and the resurrection of the body is not enough, for all Christian nations hold to these beliefs; they must supplement these with a determination that the body shall not perish; that the very flesh and blood in which the man died shall rise with him on the last day, and not a merely spiritual body.

Now all these four things must coexist before a people proceed to embalm their dead for religious purposes.† The probability that all these four things should coexist by accident in several widely separated races is slight indeed. The doctrine of chances is all against it. There is here no common necessity driving men to the same expedient, with which so many resemblances have been explained; the practice is a religious ceremony, growing out of religious beliefs by no means common or universal, to wit, that the man who is dead shall live again, and live again in the very body in which he died. Not even all the Jews believed in these things.

If, then, it should appear that among the races which we claim were descended from Atlantis this practice of embalming the dead is found, and nowhere else, we have certainly furnished evidence which can only be explained by admitting the existence of Atlantis, and of some great religious race dwelling on Atlantis, who believed in the immortality of soul and body, and who embalmed their dead. We find, as I have shown:

First. That the Guanches of the Canary Islands, supposed to be a remnant of the Atlantean population, preserved their dead as mummies.

Second. That the Egyptians, the oldest colony of Atlantis, embalmed their dead in such vast multitudes that they are

† In the 1920's and 1930's the "heliolithic" theory traced mummies and solar worship around the world.—E.F.B.

now exported by the ton to England, and ground up into manures to grow English turnips.

Third. That the Assyrians, the Ethiopians, the Persians, the Greeks, and even the Romans embalmed their dead.

Fourth. On the American continents we find that the Peruvians, the Central Americans, the Mexicans, and some of the Indian tribes, followed the same practice.

Is it possible to account for this singular custom, reaching through a belt of nations, and completely around the habitable world, without Atlantis?

15. All the traditions of the Mediterranean races look to the ocean as the source of men and gods. Homer sings of

" Ocean, the origin of gods and Mother Tethys."

Orpheus says, " The fair river of Ocean was the first to marry, and he espoused his sister Tethys, who was his mother's daughter." (Plato's " Dialogues," *Cratylus*, p. 402.) The ancients always alluded to the ocean as a river encircling the earth, as in the map of Cosmos (see page 95 *ante*); probably a reminiscence of the great canal described by Plato which surrounded the plain of Atlantis. Homer (Iliad, book xviii.) describes Tethys, "the mother goddess," coming to Achilles "from the deep abysses of the main :"

" The circling Nereids with their mistress weep,
And all the sea-green sisters of the deep."

Plato surrounds the great statue of Poseidon in Atlantis with the images of one hundred Nereids.

16. In the Deluge legends of the Hindoos (as given on page 87 *ante*), we have seen Manu saving a small fish, which subsequently grew to a great size, and warned him of the coming of the Flood. In this legend all the indications point to an ocean as the scene of the catastrophe. It says: " At the close of the last *calpa* there was a general destruction, caused by the sleep of Brahma, whence his creatures, in different worlds, *were*

drowned in a vast ocean. . . . A holy king, named Satyavrata, then reigned, a servant of *the spirit which moved on the waves*" (Poseidon?), "and so devout that *water was his only sustenance*. . . . In seven days the three worlds" (remember Poseidon's trident) "shall be *plunged in an ocean* of death." . . . "'Thou shalt enter the spacious ark, and continue in it secure from the Flood *on one immense ocean*.' . . . *The sea overwhelmed its shores*, deluged the whole earth, augmented by showers from immense clouds." ("Asiatic Researches," vol. i., p. 230.)

All this reminds us of "the fountains of the great deep and the flood-gates of heaven," and seems to repeat precisely the story of Plato as to the sinking of Atlantis in the ocean.

17. While I do not attach much weight to verbal similarities in the languages of the two continents, nevertheless there are some that are very remarkable. We have seen the Pan and Maia of the Greeks reappearing in the Pan and Maya of the Mayas of Central America. The god of the Welsh triads, "Hu the mighty," is found in the Hu-nap-hu, the hero-god of the Quiches; in Hu-napu, a hero-god; and in Hu-hu-nap-hu, in Hu-ncam, in Hu-nbatz, semi-divine heroes of the Quiches. The Phœnician deity *El* "was subdivided into a number of hypostases called the *Baalim*, secondary divinities, emanating from the substance of the deity" ("Anc. Hist. East," vol. ii., p. 219); and this word *Baalim* we find appearing in the mythology of the Central Americans, applied to the semi-divine progenitors of the human race, *Balam-Quitze, Balam-Agab*, and *Iqui-Balam*.

Chapter V.

THE QUESTION OF COMPLEXION.

The tendency of scientific thought in ethnology is in the direction of giving more and more importance to the race characteristics, such as height, color of the hair, eyes and skin, and the formation of the skull and body generally, than to language. The language possessed by a people may be merely the result of conquest or migration. For instance, in the United States to-day, white, black, and red men, the descendants of French, Spanish, Italians, Mexicans, Irish, Germans, Scandinavians, Africans, all speak the English language, and by the test of language they are all Englishmen; and yet none of them are connected by birth or descent with the country where that language was developed.

There is a general misconception as to the color of the European and American races. Europe is supposed to be peopled exclusively by white men; but in reality every shade of color is represented on that continent, from the fair complexion of the fairest of the Swedes to the dark-skinned inhabitants of the Mediterranean coast, only a shade lighter than the Berbers, or Moors, on the opposite side of that sea. Tacitus spoke of the "Black Celts," and the term, so far as complexion goes, might not inappropriately be applied to some of the Italians, Spaniards, and Portuguese, while the Basques are represented as of a still darker hue. Tylor says ("Anthropology," p. 67), "On the whole, it seems that the distinction of color, from the fairest Englishman to the darkest African, has no hard and fast lines, but varies gradually from one tint to another."

And when we turn to America we find that the popular

opinion that all Indians are "red men," and of the same hue from Patagonia to Hudson's Bay, is a gross error.

Prichard says ("Researches into the Physical History of Mankind," vol. i., p. 269, 4th ed., 1841):

"It will be easy to show that the American races show nearly as great a variety in this respect as the nations of the old continent; there are among them white races with a florid complexion, and tribes black or of a very dark hue; that their stature, figure, and countenance are almost equally diversified."

John T. Short says ("North Americans of Antiquity," p. 189):

"The Menominees, sometimes called the 'White Indians,' formerly occupied the region bordering on Lake Michigan, around Green Bay. The whiteness of these Indians, which is compared to that of white mulattoes, early attracted the attention of the Jesuit missionaries, and has often been commented on by travellers. While it is true that hybridy has done much to lighten the color of many of the tribes, still the peculiarity of the complexion of this people has been marked since the first time a European encountered them. Almost every shade, from the ash-color of the Menominees through the cinnamon-red, copper, and bronze tints, may be found among the tribes formerly occupying the territory east of the Mississippi, until we reach the dark-skinned Kaws of Kansas, who are nearly as black as the negro. The variety of complexion is as great in South America as among the tribes of the northern part of the continent."

In foot-note of p. 107 of vol. iii. of "U. S. Explorations for a Railroad Route to the Pacific Ocean," we are told,

"Many of the Indians of Zuni (New Mexico) are white. They have a fair skin, blue eyes, chestnut or auburn hair, and are quite good-looking. They claim to be full-blooded Zunians, and have no tradition of intermarriage with any foreign race. The circumstance creates no surprise among this people, for from time immemorial a similar class of people has existed among the tribe."

Winchell says:

"The ancient Indians of California, in the latitude of forty-two degrees, were as black as the negroes of Guinea, while in Mexico were tribes of an olive or reddish complexion, relatively light. Among the black races of tropical regions we find, generally, some light-colored tribes interspersed. These sometimes have light hair and blue eyes. This is the case with the Tuareg of the Sahara, the Afghans of India, and the aborigines of the banks of the Oronoco and the Amazon." (Winchell's "Preadamites," p. 185.)

William Penn said of the Indians of Pennsylvania, in his letter of August, 1683:

"The natives . . . are generally tall, straight, well-built, and of singular proportion; they tread strong and clever, and mostly walk with a lofty chin. . . . Their eye is little and black, not unlike a straight-looked Jew. . . . I have seen among them as comely European-like faces of both sexes as on your side of the sea; and truly an Italian complexion hath not much more of the white, and the noses of several of them have as much of the Roman. . . . For their original, I am ready to believe them to be of the Jewish race—I mean of the stock of the ten tribes —and that for the following reasons: first, . . .; in the next place, I find them to be of the like countenance, and their children of so lively a resemblance that a man would think himself in Duke's Place or Berry Street in London when he seeth them. But this is not all: they agree in rites, they reckon by moons, they offer their first-fruits, they have a kind of feast of tabernacles, they are said to lay their altars upon twelve stones, their mourning a year, customs of women, with many other things that do not now occur."

Upon this question of complexion Catlin, in his "Indians of North America," vol. i., p. 95, etc., gives us some curious information. We have already seen that the Mandans preserved an image of the ark, and possessed legends of a clearly Atlantean character. Catlin says:

"A stranger in the Mandan village is first struck with the different shades of complexion and various colors of hair which

he sees in a crowd about him, and is at once disposed to ex-
claim, 'These are not Indians.' There are a great many of
these people whose complexions appear as light as half-breeds;
and among the women particularly there are many whose skins
are almost white, with the most pleasing symmetry and proportion of feature; with hazel, with gray, and with blue eyes;
with mildness and sweetness of expression and excessive modesty of demeanor, which render them exceedingly pleasing and
beautiful.   Why this diversity of complexion I cannot tell,
nor can they themselves account for it.   Their traditions,
so far as I can learn them, afford us no information of their
having had any knowledge of white men before the visit of
Lewis and Clarke, made to their village thirty-three years ago.
Since that time until now (1835) there have been very few
visits of white men to this place, and surely not enough to
have changed the complexions and customs of a nation.   And
I recollect perfectly well that Governor Clarke told me, before
I started for this place, that I would find the Mandans a strange
people and half white.

"Among the females may be seen every shade and color of
hair that can be seen in our own country except red or auburn,
which is not to be found. . . . There are very many of both
sexes, and of every age, from infancy to manhood and old age,
with hair of a bright silvery-gray, and in some instances almost
perfectly white.   This unaccountable phenomenon is not the
result of disease or habit, but it is unquestionably an hereditary
characteristic which runs in families, and indicates no inequali-
ty in disposition or intellect.   And by passing this hair through
my hands I have found it uniformly to be as coarse and harsh
as a horse's mane, differing materially from the hair of other
colors, which, among the Mandans, is generally as fine and soft
as silk.

"The stature of the Mandans is rather below the ordinary
size of man, with beautiful symmetry of form and proportion,
and wonderful suppleness and elasticity."

Catlin gives a group (54) showing this great diversity in
complexion: one of the figures is painted almost pure white,
and with light hair.   The faces are European.

Major James W. Lynd, who lived among the Dakota Indians
for nine years, and was killed by them in the great outbreak of

GOVERNOR AND OTHER INDIANS OF THE PUEBLO OF SAN DOMINGO, NEW MEXICO.

1862, says (MS. " Hist. of Dakotas," Library, Historical Society, Minnesota, p. 47), after calling attention to the fact that the
different tribes of the Sioux nation represent several different
degrees of darkness of color:

" The Dakota child is of lighter complexion than the young
brave; this one lighter than the middle-aged man, and the
middle-aged man lighter than the superannuated *homo,* who,
by smoke, paint, dirt, and a drying up of the vital juices, appears to be the true copper-colored Dakota. The color of the
Dakotas varies with the nation, and also with the age and condition of the individual. It may be set down, however, *as a
shade lighter than olive;* yet it becomes still lighter by change
of condition or mode of life, and nearly vanishes, even in the
child, under constant ablutions and avoiding of exposure.
Those children in the Mission at Hazlewood, who are taken
very young, and not allowed to expose themselves, lose almost
entirely the olive shade, and become quite as white as the
American child. The Mandans are as light as the peasants of
Spain, while their brothers, the Crows, are as dark as the Arabs.
Dr. Goodrich, in the ' Universal Traveller,' p. 154, says that the
modern Peruvians, in the warmer regions of Peru, are as fair as
the people of the south of Europe."

The Aymaras, the ancient inhabitants of the mountains of
Peru and Bolivia, are described as having an olive-brown complexion, with regular features, large heads, and a thoughtful and
melancholy cast of countenance. They practised in early times
the deformation of the skull.

Professor Wilson describes the hair of the ancient Peruvians,
as found upon their mummies, as " a lightish brown, and of a
fineness of texture which equals that of the Anglo-Saxon race."
" The ancient Peruvians," says Short ("North Americans of
Antiquity," p. 187), " appear, from numerous examples of hair
found in their tombs, to have been an auburn-haired race." Gar-
cilasso, who had an opportunity of seeing the body of the king,
Viracocha, describes the hair of that monarch as snow-white.
Haywood tells us of the discovery, at the beginning of this
century, of three mummies in a cave on the south side of the

Cumberland River (Tennessee), who were buried in baskets, as the Peruvians were occasionally buried, and whose skin was fair and white, and their hair auburn, and of a fine texture. ("Natural and Aboriginal History of Tennessee," p. 191.)

CHOOTAW.

Neither is the common opinion correct which asserts all the American Indians to be of the same type of features. The portraits on this page and on pages 187 and 191, taken from the "Report of the U. S. Survey for a Route for a Pacific Railroad," present features very much like those of Europeans; in fact, every face here could be precisely matched among the inhabitants of the southern part of the old continent.

On the other hand, look at the portrait of the great Italian orator and reformer, Savonarola, on page 193. It looks more

SHAWNEES.

like the hunting Indians of North-western America than any of the preceding faces. In fact, if it was dressed with a scalp-lock it would pass muster anywhere as a portrait of the "Man-afraid-of-his-horses," or "Sitting Bull."

SAVONAROLA.

Adam was, it appears, a *red* man. Winchell tells us that Adam is derived from the *red* earth. The radical letters ÂDàM are found in ADaMaH, "something out of which vegetation was made to germinate," to wit, the earth. ÂDôM and ÂDOM signifies *red, ruddy, bay-colored*, as of a horse, the color of a red heifer. "ÂDàM, a man, a human being, male or female, *red, ruddy.*" ("Preadamites," p. 161.)

"The Arabs distinguished mankind into two races, one *red, ruddy*, the other black." (*Ibid.*) They classed themselves among the red men.

Not only was Adam a red man, but there is evidence that, from the highest antiquity, red was a sacred color; the gods of the ancients were always painted *red*. The Wisdom of Solomon refers to this custom: "The carpenter carved it elegantly, and formed it by the skill of his understanding, and fashioned it to the shape of a man, or made it like some vile beast, laying it over with vermilion, and with paint, coloring it *red*, and covering every spot therein."

The idols of the Indians were also painted red, and red was the religious color. (Lynd's MS. "Hist. of Dakotas," Library, Hist. Society, Minn.)

The Cushites and Ethiopians, early branches of the Atlantean stock, took their name from their "sunburnt" complexion; they were red men.

The name of the Phœnicians signified *red*. *Himyar*, the prefix of the Himyaritic Arabians, also means red, and the Arabs were painted red on the Egyptian monuments.

The ancient Egyptians were red men. They recognized four races of men—the red, yellow, black, and white men. They themselves belonged to the "*Rot*," or red men; the yellow men they called "*Namu*"—it included the Asiatic races; the black men were called "*Nahsu*," and the white men "*Tamhu*." The following figures are copied from Nott and Gliddon's "Types of Mankind," p. 85, and were taken by them from the great works of Belzoni, Champollion, and Lepsius.

In later ages so desirous were the Egyptians of preserving the aristocratic distinction of the color of their skin, that they represented themselves on the monuments as of a crimson hue —an exaggeration of their original race complexion.

In the same way we find that the ancient Aryan writings divided mankind into four races—the white, red, yellow, and black: the four castes of India were founded upon these distinctions in color; in fact, the word for color in Sanscrit (*varna*) means caste. The red men, according to the *Mahâbhârata*, were the Kshatriyas—the warrior caste—who were afterward

engaged in a fierce contest with the whites—the Brahmans—
and were nearly exterminated, although some of them survived,
and from their stock Buddha was born. So that not only the
Mohammedan and Christian but the Buddhistic religion seem
to be derived from branches of the Hamitic or red stock. The
great Manu was also of the red race.

Red.   Yellow.   Black   White.

THE RACES OF MEN ACCORDING TO THE EGYPTIANS.

The Egyptians, while they painted themselves red-brown,
represented the nations of Palestine as yellow-brown, and the
Libyans yellow-white. The present inhabitants of Egypt
range from a yellow color in the north parts to a deep *bronze.*
Tylor is of opinion ("Anthropology," p. 95) that the ancient
Egyptians belonged to a brown race, which embraced the
Nubian tribes and, to some extent, the Berbers of Algiers and
Tunis. He groups the Assyrians, Phœnicians, Persians, Greeks,
Romans, Andalusians, Bretons, dark Welshmen, and people of
the Caucasus into one body, and designates them as "dark-
whites." The Himyarite Arabs, as I have shown, derived
their name originally from their red color, and they were con-
stantly depicted on the Egyptian monuments as red or light

brown.   Herodotus tells us that there was a nation of Libyans, called the Maxyans, who claimed descent from the people of Troy (the walls of Troy, we shall see, were built by Poseidon; that is to say, Troy was an Atlantean colony).   These Maxyans painted their whole bodies red.   The Zavecians, the ancestors of the Zuavas of Algiers (the tribe that gave their name to the French Zouaves), also painted themselves red.   Some of the Ethiopians were "copper-colored."   ("Amer. Cyclop.," art. *Egypt,* p. 464.)   Tylor says ("Anthropology," p. 160) : "The language of the ancient Egyptians, though it cannot be classed in the Semitic family with Hebrew, has important points of correspondence, whether due to the long intercourse between the two races in Egypt *or to some deeper ancestral connection;* and such analogies also appear in the Berber languages of North Africa."

These last were called by the ancients the Atlanteans.

"If a congregation of twelve representatives from Malacca, China, Japan, Mongolia, Sandwich Islands, Chili, Peru, Brazil, Chickasaws, Comanches, etc., were dressed alike, or undressed and unshaven, the most skilful anatomist could not, from their appearance, separate them."   (Fontaine's "How the World was Peopled," pp. 147, 244.)

Ferdinand Columbus, in his relation of his father's voyages, compares the inhabitants of Guanaani to the Canary Islanders (an Atlantean race), and describes the inhabitants of San Domingo as still more beautiful and fair.   In Peru the Charanzanis, studied by M. Angraud, also resemble the Canary Islanders. L'Abbé Brasseur de Bourbourg imagined himself surrounded by Arabs when all his Indians of Rabinal were around him; for they had, he said, their complexion, features, and beard. Pierre Martyr speaks of the Indians of the Parian Gulf as having fair hair.   ("The Human Species," p. 201.)   The same author believes that tribes belonging to the Semitic type are also found in America.   He refers to "certain traditions of

Guiana, and *the use in the country of a weapon entirely characteristic of the ancient Canary Islanders.*"

When science is able to disabuse itself of the Mortonian
theory that the aborigines of America are all red men, and all
belong to one race, we may hope that the confluence upon the
continent of widely different races from different countries may
come to be recognized and intelligently studied. There can be
no doubt that red, white, black, and yellow men have united to
form the original population of America. And there can be
as little doubt that the entire population of Europe and the
south shore of the Mediterranean is a mongrel race—a combination, in varying proportions, of a dark-brown or red race
with a white race; the characteristics of the different nations
depending upon the proportions in which the dark and light
races are mingled, for peculiar mental and moral characteristics
go with these complexions. The red-haired people are a distinct variety of the white stock; there were once whole tribes
and nations with this color of hair; their blood is now intermingled with all the races of men, from Palestine to Iceland.
Everything in Europe speaks of vast periods of time and long-
continued and constant interfusion of bloods, until there is not
a fair-skinned man on the Continent that has not the blood of
the dark-haired race in his veins; nor scarcely a dark-skinned
man that is not lighter in hue from intermixture with the
white stock.

Chapter VI.

GENESIS CONTAINS A HISTORY OF ATLANTIS.

The Hebrews are a branch of the great family of which that powerful commercial race, the Phœnicians, who were the merchants of the world fifteen hundred years before the time of Christ, were a part. The Hebrews carried out from the common storehouse of their race a mass of traditions, many of which have come down to us in that oldest and most venerable of human compositions, the Book of Genesis. I have shown that the story of the Deluge plainly refers to the destruction of Atlantis, and that it agrees in many important particulars with the account given by Plato. The people destroyed were, in both instances, the ancient race that had created civilization; they had formerly been in a happy and sinless condition; they had become great and wicked; they were destroyed for their sins—they were destroyed by water.

But we can go farther, and it can be asserted that there is scarcely a prominent fact in the opening chapters of the Book of Genesis that cannot be duplicated from the legends of the American nations, and scarcely a custom known to the Jews that does not find its counterpart among the people of the New World.

Even in the history of the Creation we find these similarities:

The Bible tells us (Gen. i., 2) that in the beginning the earth was without form and void, and covered with water. In the Quiche legends we are told, " at first all was sea—no man, animal, bird, or green herb—there was nothing to be seen but the sea and the heavens."

The Bible says (Gen. i., 2), "And the Spirit of God moved upon the face of the waters." The Quiche legend says, "The Creator—the Former, the Dominator—the feathered serpent —those that give life, moved upon the waters like a glowing light."

The Bible says (Gen. i., 9), "And God said, Let the waters under the heaven be gathered together unto one place, and let the dry land appear: and it was so." The Quiche legend says, "The creative spirits cried out 'Earth!' and in an instant it was formed, and rose like a vapor-cloud; immediately the plains and the mountains arose, and the cypress and pine appeared."

The Bible tells us, "And God saw that it was good." The Quiche legend says, "Then Gucumatz was filled with joy, and cried out, 'Blessed be thy coming, O Heart of Heaven, Hurakan, thunder-bolt.'"

The order in which the vegetables, animals, and man were formed is the same in both records.

In Genesis (chap. ii., 7) we are told, "And the Lord God formed man of the dust of the ground." The Quiche legend says, "The first man was made of clay; but he had no intelligence, and was consumed in the water."

In Genesis the first man is represented as naked. The Aztec legend says, "The sun was much nearer the earth then than now, and his grateful warmth rendered clothing unnecessary."

Even the temptation of Eve reappears in the American legends. Lord Kingsborough says: "The Toltecs had paintings of a garden, with a single tree standing in the midst; round the root of the tree is entwined a serpent, whose head appearing above the foliage displays the face of a woman. Torquemada admits the existence of this tradition among them, and agrees with the Indian historians, who affirm that this was the first woman in the world, who bore children, and from whom all mankind are descended." ("Mexican Antiquities," vol. viii., p. 19.) There is also a legend of Suchiquecal, who disobediently gathered roses from a tree, and thereby disgraced and injured herself and all her posterity. ("Mexican Antiquities," vol. vi., p. 401.)

The legends of the Old World which underlie Genesis, and were used by Milton in the "Paradise Lost," appear in the Mexican legends of a war of angels in heaven, and the fall of *Zoutem-que* (*Soutem, Satan*—Arabic, *Shatana?*) and the other rebellious spirits.

We have seen that the Central Americans possessed striking parallels to the account of the Deluge in Genesis.

There is also a clearly established legend which singularly resembles the Bible record of the Tower of Babel.

Father Duran, in his MS. "Historia Antiqua de la Nueva Espana," A.D. 1585, quotes from the lips of a native of Cholula, over one hundred years old, a version of the legend as to the building of the great pyramid of Cholula. It is as follows:

"In the beginning, before the light of the sun had been created, this land (Cholula) was in obscurity and darkness, and void of any created thing; all was a plain, without hill or elevation, encircled in every part by water, without tree or created thing; and immediately *after the light and the sun arose in the east* there appeared gigantic men of deformed stature and possessed the land, and desiring to see the nativity of the sun, as well as his occident, proposed to go and seek them. Dividing themselves into two parties, some journeyed to the west and others toward the east; these travelled until the sea cut off their road, whereupon they determined to return to the place from which they started, and arriving at this place (Cholula), not finding the means of reaching the sun, enamored of his light and beauty, they determined to build a tower so high that its summit should reach the sky. Having collected materials for the purpose, they found a very adhesive clay and bitumen, with which they speedily commenced to build the tower; and having reared it to the greatest possible altitude, so that they say it reached to the sky, the Lord of the Heavens, enraged, said to the inhabitants of the sky, 'Have you observed how they of the earth have built a high and haughty tower to mount hither, being enamored of the light of the sun and

RUINS OF THE PYRAMID OF CHOLULA.

his beauty? Come and confound them, because it is not right
that they of the earth, living in the flesh, should mingle with
us.' Immediately the inhabitants of the sky sallied forth like
flashes of lightning; they destroyed the edifice, and divided
and scattered its builders to all parts of the earth."

One can recognize in this legend the recollection, by a ruder
race, of a highly civilized people; for only a highly civilized
people would have attempted such a vast work. Their mental
superiority and command of the arts gave them the character
of giants who arrived from the East; who had divided into
two great emigrations, one moving eastward (toward Europe),
the other westward (toward America). They were sun-wor-

shippers; for we are told "they were enamored of the light and beauty of the sun," and they built a high place for his worship.

The pyramid of Cholula is one of the greatest constructions ever erected by human hands. It is even now, in its ruined condition, 160 feet high, 1400 feet square at the base, and covers forty-five acres; we have only to remember that the greatest pyramid of Egypt, Cheops, covers but twelve or thirteen acres, to form some conception of the magnitude of this American structure.

It must not be forgotten that this legend was taken down by a Catholic priest, shortly after the conquest of Mexico, from the lips of an old Indian who was born before Columbus sailed from Spain.

Observe the resemblances between this legend and the Bible account of the building of the Tower of Babel:

"All was a plain without hill or elevation," says the Indian legend. "They found a plain in the land of Shinar, and they dwelt there," says the Bible. They built of brick in both cases. "Let us build us a tower whose top may reach unto heaven," says the Bible. "They determined to build a tower so high that its summit should reach the sky," says the Indian legend. "And the Lord came down to see the city and the tower which the children of men had builded. And the Lord said, Behold . . . nothing will be restrained from them which they have imagined to do. Go to, let us go down and confound them," says the Bible record. "The Lord of the Heavens, enraged, said to the inhabitants of the sky, 'Have you observed,' etc. Come and confound them," says the Indian record. "And the Lord scattered them abroad from thence on all the face of the earth," says the Bible. "They scattered its builders to all parts of the earth," says the Mexican legend.

Can any one doubt that these two legends must have sprung in some way from one another, or from some common source? There are enough points of difference to show that the American is not a servile copy of the Hebrew legend. In the former the story comes from a native of Cholula: it is told under the shadow of the mighty pyramid it commemorates; it is a *local* legend which he repeats. The men who built it, according to his account, were foreigners. They built it to reach the sun—that is to say, as a sun-temple; while in the Bible record Babel was built to perpetuate the glory of its architects. In the Indian legend the gods stop the work by a great storm, in the Bible account by confounding the speech of the people.

Both legends were probably derived from Atlantis, and referred to some gigantic structure of great height built by that people; and when the story emigrated to the east and west, it was in the one case affixed to the tower of the Chaldeans, and in the other to the pyramid of Cholula, precisely as we find the ark of the Deluge resting upon separate mountain-chains all the way from Greece to Armenia. In one form of the Tower of Babel legend, that of the Toltecs, we are told that the pyramid of Cholula was erected "as a means of escape from a second flood, should another occur."

But the resemblances between Genesis and the American legends do not stop here.

We are told (Gen. ii., 21) that "the Lord God caused a deep sleep to fall upon Adam," and while he slept God made Eve out of one of his ribs. According to the Quiche tradition, there were four men from whom the races of the world descended (probably a recollection of the red, black, yellow, and white races); and these men were without wives, and the Creator made wives for them "while they slept."

Some wicked misanthrope referred to these traditions when he said, "And man's first sleep became his last repose."

In Genesis (chap. iii., 22), "And the Lord God said, Behold, the man is become as one of us, to know good and evil: and now, lest he put forth his hand, and take also of the tree of life, and eat, and live forever:" therefore God drove him out of the garden. In the Quiche legends we are told, "The gods feared that they had made men too perfect, and they breathed a cloud of mist over their vision."

When the ancestors of the Quiches migrated to America the Divinity parted the sea for their passage, as the Red Sea was parted for the Israelites.

The story of Samson is paralleled in the history of a hero named Zipanca, told of in the "Popol Vuh," who, being captured by his enemies and placed in a pit, pulled down the building in which his captors had assembled, and killed four hundred of them.

"There were giants in those days," says the Bible. A great deal of the Central American history is taken up with the doings of an ancient race of giants called Quinames.

This parallelism runs through a hundred particulars:

Both the Jews and Mexicans worshipped toward the east. Both called the south "the right hand of the world."

Both burnt incense toward the four corners of the earth.

Confession of sin and sacrifice of atonement were common to both peoples.

Both were punctilious about washings and ablutions.

Both believed in devils, and both were afflicted with leprosy.

Both considered women who died in childbirth as worthy of honor as soldiers who fell in battle.

Both punished adultery with stoning to death.

As David leaped and danced before the ark of the Lord, so did the Mexican monarchs before their idols.

Both had an ark, the abiding-place of an invisible god.

Both had a species of serpent-worship.

Compare our representation of the great serpent-mound in Adams County, Ohio, with the following description of a great serpent-mound in Scotland:

"*Serpent-worship in the West.*—Some additional light appears to have been thrown upon ancient serpent-worship in the West by the recent archæological explorations of Mr. John S. Phené, F.G.S., F.R.G.S., in Scotland. Mr. Phené has just investigated

a curious earthen mound in Glen Feechan, Argyleshire, referred
to by him, at the late meeting of the British Association in
Edinburgh, as being in the form of a serpent or saurian. The
mound, says the *Scotsman*, is a most perfect one. The head
is a large cairn, and the body of the earthen reptile 300 feet
long; and in the centre of the head there were evidences, when
Mr. Phené first visited it, of an altar having been placed there.
The position with regard to Ben Cruachan is most remarkable.

GREAT SERPENT-MOUND, OHIO.

The three peaks are seen over the length of the reptile when a
person is standing on the head, or cairn. The shape can only
be seen so as to be understood when looked down upon from
an elevation, as the outline cannot be understood unless the
whole of it can be seen. This is most perfect when the spec-
tator is on the head of the animal form, or on the lofty rock to
the west of it. This mound corresponds almost entirely with
one 700 feet long in America, an account of which was lately
published, after careful survey, by Mr. Squier. The altar toward
the head in each case agrees. In the American mound three
rivers (also objects of worship with the ancients) were evidently identified. The number three was a sacred number in all
ancient mythologies. The sinuous winding and articulations
of the vertebral spinal arrangement are anatomically perfect

in the Argyleshire mound. The gentlemen present with Mr.
Phené during his investigation state that beneath the cairn
forming the head of the animal was found a megalithic chamber, in which was a quantity of charcoal and burnt earth and
charred nutshells, a flint instrument, beautifully and minutely
serrated at the edge, and burnt bones. The back or spine
of the serpent, which, as already stated, is 300 feet long, was
found, beneath the peat moss, to be formed by a careful adjust-
ment of stones, the formation of which probably prevented the
structure from being obliterated by time and weather." (*Pall
Mall Gazette.*)

We find a striking likeness between the works of the Stone
Age in America and Europe, as shown in the figures here given.

Stone Axe, Illinois.

Stone Axe, North Germany.

Stone Arrow-head, Switzerland.   Stone Arrow-heads, America.

STONE IMPLEMENTS OF EUROPE AND AMERICA.

The same singular custom which is found among the Jews and the Hindoos, for "a man to raise up seed for his deceased brother by marrying his widow," was found among the Central American nations. (Las Casas, MS. "Hist. Apoloq.," cap. ccxiii., ccxv. Torquemada, "Monarq. Ind.," tom. ii., 377–8.)

No one but the Jewish high-priest might enter the Holy of Holies. A similar custom obtained in Peru. Both ate the flesh of the sacrifices of atonement; both poured the blood of the sacrifice on the earth; they sprinkled it, they marked persons with it, they smeared it upon walls and stones. The Mexican temple, like the Jewish, faced the east. "As among the Jews the ark was a sort of portable temple, in which the Deity was supposed to be continually present, so among the Mexicans, the Cherokees, and the Indians of Michoacan and Honduras, an ark was held in the highest veneration, and was considered an object too sacred to be touched by any but the priests." (Kingsborough, "Mex. Antiq.," vol. viii., p. 258.)

The Peruvians believed that the rainbow was a sign that the earth would not be again destroyed by a deluge. (*Ibid.*, p. 25.)

The Jewish custom of laying the sins of the people upon the head of an animal, and turning him out into the wilderness, had its counterpart among the Mexicans, who, to cure a fever, formed a dog of maize paste and left it by the roadside, saying the first passer-by would carry away the illness. (Dorman, "Prim. Super.," p. 59.) Jacob's ladder had its duplicate in the vine or tree of the Ojibbeways, which led from the earth to heaven, up and down which the spirits passed. (*Ibid.*, p. 67.)

Both Jews and Mexicans offered water to a stranger that he might wash his feet; both ate dust in token of humility; both anointed with oil; both sacrificed prisoners; both periodically separated the women, and both agreed in the strong and universal idea of uncleanness connected with that period.

Both believed in the occult power of water, and both practised baptism.

"Then the Mexican midwife gave the child to taste of the water, putting her moistened fingers in its mouth, and said, 'Take this; by this thou hast to live on the earth, to grow and to flourish; through this we get all things that support existence on the earth; receive it.' Then with moistened fingers she touched the breast of the child, and said, 'Behold the pure water that washes and cleanses thy heart, that removes all filthiness; receive it: may the goddess see good to purify and cleanse thine heart.' Then the midwife poured water upon the head of the child, saying, 'O my grandson—my son—take this water of the Lord of the world, which is thy life, invigorating and refreshing, washing and cleansing. I pray that this celestial water, blue and light blue, may enter into thy body, and there live; I pray that it may destroy in thee and put away from thee all the things evil and adverse that were *given thee before the beginning of the world.* . . . Wheresoever thou art in this child, O thou hurtful thing, begone! leave it, put thyself apart; for now does it live anew, and *anew is it born;* now again is it purified and cleansed; now again is it shaped and engendered by our mother, the goddess of water." (Bancroft's "Native Races," vol. iii., p. 372.)

Here we find many resemblances to the Christian ordinance of baptism: the pouring of the water on the head, the putting of the fingers in the mouth, the touching of the breast, the new birth, and the washing away of the original sin. The Christian rite, we know, was not a Christian invention, but was borrowed from ancient times, from the great storehouse of Asiatic traditions and beliefs.

The Mexicans hung up the heads of their sacrificed enemies; this was also a Jewish custom:

"And the Lord said unto Moses, Take all the heads of the people, and hang them up before the Lord against the sun, that the fierce anger of the Lord may be turned away from Israel. And Moses said unto the judges of Israel, Slay ye every one his men that were joined unto Baal-peor." (Numb., xxv., 4, 5.)

The Scythians, Herodotus tells us, scalped their enemies,

and carried the scalp at the pommel of their saddles; the Jews probably scalped their enemies:

"But God shall wound the head of his enemies, and the hairy scalp of such a one as goeth on still in his trespasses." (Psa., lxviii., 21.)

The ancient Scandinavians practised scalping. When Harold Harefoot seized his rival, Alfred, with six hundred followers, he " had them maimed, blinded, hamstrung, *scalped*, or embowelled." (Taine's " Hist. Eng. Lit.," p. 35.)

Herodotus describes the Scythian mode of taking the scalp: " He makes a cut round the head near the ears, and shakes the skull out." This is precisely the Indian custom. " The more scalps a man has," says Herodotus, " the more highly he is esteemed among them."

The Indian scalp-lock is found on the Egyptian monuments as one of the characteristics of the Japhetic Libyans, who shaved all the head except one lock in the middle.

The Mantchoos of Tartary wear a scalp-lock, as do the modern Chinese.

Byron describes the heads of the dead Tartars under the walls of Corinth, devoured by the wild dogs:

> "Crimson and green were the shawls of their wear,
> And each scalp had a single long tuft of hair,
> All the rest was shaven and bare."

These resemblances are so striking and so numerous that repeated attempts have been made to prove that the inhabitants of America are the descendants of the Jews; some have claimed that they represented " the lost tribes " of that people. But the Jews were never a maritime or emigrating people; they formed no colonies; and it is impossible to believe (as has been asserted) that they left their flocks and herds, marched across the whole face of Asia, took ships and sailed across the greatest of the oceans to a continent of the existence of which they had no knowledge.

If we seek the origin of these extraordinary coincidences in opinions and habits, we must go far back of the time of the lost tribes. We must seek it in the relationship of the Jews to the family of Noah, and in the identity of the Noachic race destroyed in the Deluge with the people of the drowned Atlantis.

Nor need it surprise us to find traditions perpetuated for thousands upon thousands of years, especially among a people having a religious priesthood.

The essence of religion is conservatism; little is invented; nothing perishes; change comes from without; and even when one religion is supplanted by another its gods live on as the demons of the new faith, or they pass into the folk-lore and fairy stories of the people. We see Votan, a hero in America, become the god Odin or Woden in Scandinavia; and when his worship as a god dies out Odin survives (as Dr. Dasent has proved) in the Wild Huntsman of the Hartz, and in the Robin Hood (Oodin) of popular legend. The Hellequin of France becomes the Harlequin of our pantomimes. William Tell never existed; he is a myth; a survival of the sun-god Apollo, Indra, who was worshipped on the altars of Atlantis.

> "Nothing here but it doth change
> Into something rich and strange."

The rite of circumcision dates back to the first days of Phœnicia, Egypt, and the Cushites. It, too, was probably an Atlantean custom, invented in the Stone Age. Tens of thousands of years have passed since the Stone Age; the ages of copper, bronze, and iron have intervened; and yet to this day the Hebrew rabbi performs the ceremony of circumcision with a *stone* knife.

Frothingham says, speaking of St. Peter's Cathedral, in Rome:

"Into what depths of antiquity the ceremonies carried me back! To the mysteries of Eleusis; to the sacrificial rites of Phœnicia. The boys swung the censors as censors had been swung in the adoration of Bacchus. The girdle and cassock of the priests came from Persia; the veil and tonsure were from Egypt; the alb and chasuble were prescribed by Numa Pompilius; the stole was borrowed from the official who used to throw it on the back of the victim that was to be sacrificed; the white surplice was the same as described by Juvenal and Ovid."

Although it is evident that many thousands of years must have passed since the men who wrote in Sanscrit, in North-western India, could have dwelt in Europe, yet to this day they preserve among their ancient books maps and descriptions of the western coast of Europe, and even of England and Ireland; and we find among them a fuller knowledge of the vexed question of the sources of the Nile than was possessed by any nation in the world twenty-five years ago.

This perpetuation of forms and beliefs is illustrated in the fact that the formulas used in the Middle Ages in Europe to exorcise evil spirits were Assyrian words, imported probably thousands of years before from the magicians of Chaldea. When the European conjurer cried out to the demon, "*Hilka, hilka, besha, besha,*" he had no idea that he was repeating the very words of a people who had perished ages before, and that they signified *Go away, go away, evil one, evil one.* (Lenormant, "Anc. Hist. East," vol. i., p. 448.)

Our circle of 360 degrees; the division of a chord of the circle equal to the radius into 60 equal parts, called degrees; the division of these into 60 minutes, of the minute into 60 seconds, and the second into 60 thirds; the division of the day into 24 hours, each hour into 60 minutes, each minute into 60 seconds; the division of the week into seven days, and the very order of the days—all have come down to us from the Chaldeo-Assyrians; and these things will probably be perpetuated among our posterity "to the last syllable of recorded time."

We need not be surprised, therefore, to find the same legends and beliefs cropping out among the nations of Central America and the people of Israel. Nay, it should teach us to regard the Book of Genesis with increased veneration, as a relic dating from the most ancient days of man's history on earth; its roots cross the great ocean; every line is valuable; a word, a letter, an accent may throw light upon the gravest problems of the birth of civilization.

The vital conviction which, during thousands of years, at all times pressed home upon the Israelites, was that they were a "chosen people," selected out of all the multitudes of the earth, to perpetuate the great truth that there was but one God—an illimitable, omnipotent, paternal spirit, who rewarded the good and punished the wicked—in contradistinction from the multifarious, subordinate, animal and bestial demi-gods of the other nations of the earth. This sublime monotheism could only have been the outgrowth of a high civilization, for man's first religion is necessarily a worship of "stocks and stones," and history teaches us that the gods decrease in number as man increases in intelligence. It was probably in Atlantis that monotheism was first preached. The proverbs of "Ptah-hotep," the oldest book of the Egyptians, show that this most ancient colony from Atlantis received the pure faith from the mother-land at the very dawn of history: this book preached the doctrine of *one* God, "the rewarder of the good and the punisher of the wicked." (Reginald S. Poole, *Contemporary Rev.*, Aug., 1881, p. 38.) "In the early days the Egyptians worshipped one only God, the maker of all things, without beginning and without end. To the last the priests preserved this doctrine and taught it privately to a select few." ("Amer. Encycl.," vol. vi., p. 463.) The Jews took up this great truth where the Egyptians dropped it, and over the heads and over the ruins of Egypt, Chaldea, Phœnicia, Greece, Rome, and India this handful of poor shepherds—ignorant, debased, and despised—have carried down to our own times a conception which could only have originated in the highest possible state of human society.

And even skepticism must pause before the miracle of the

continued existence of this strange people, wading through the ages, bearing on their shoulders the burden of their great trust, and pressing forward under the force of a perpetual and irresistible impulse. The speech that may be heard to-day in the synagogues of Chicago and Melbourne resounded two thousand years ago in the streets of Rome; and, at a still earlier period, it could be heard in the palaces of Babylon and the shops of Thebes—in Tyre, in Sidon, in Gades, in Palmyra, in Nineveh. How many nations have perished, how many languages have ceased to exist, how many splendid civilizations have crumbled into ruin, how many temples and towers and towns have gone down to dust since the sublime frenzy of monotheism first seized this extraordinary people! All their kindred nomadic tribes are gone; their land of promise is in the hands of strangers; but Judaism, with its offspring, Christianity, is taking possession of the habitable world; and the continuous life of one people—one poor, obscure, and wretched people—spans the tremendous gulf between "Ptah-hotep" and this nineteenth century.

If the Spirit of which the universe is but an expression—of whose frame the stars are the infinite molecules—can be supposed ever to interfere with the laws of matter and reach down into the doings of men, would it not be to save from the wreck and waste of time the most sublime fruit of the civilization of the drowned Atlantis—a belief in the one, only, just God, the father of all life, the imposer of all moral obligations?

ONE of the most marvellous inventions for the advancement of mankind is the phonetic alphabet, or a system of signs representing the sounds of human speech. Without it our present civilization could scarcely have been possible.

No solution of the origin of our European alphabet has yet been obtained: we can trace it back from nation to nation, and form to form, until we reach the Egyptians, and the archaic forms of the Phœnicians, Hebrews, and Cushites, but beyond this the light fails us.

The Egyptians spoke of their hieroglyphic system of writing not as their own invention, but as "the language of the gods." (Lenormant and Cheval, "Anc. Hist. of the East," vol. ii., p. 208.) "The gods" were, doubtless, their highly civilized ancestors—the people of Atlantis—who, as we shall hereafter see, became the gods of many of the Mediterranean races.

"According to the Phœnicians, the art of writing was invented by Taautus, or Taut, 'whom the Egyptians call Thouth,' and the Egyptians said it was invented by Thouth, or Thoth, otherwise called 'the first Hermes,' in which we clearly see that both the Phœnicians and Egyptians referred the invention to a period older than their own separate political existence, and to an older nation, from which both peoples received it." (Baldwin's "Prehistoric Nations," p. 91.)

The "first Hermes," here referred to (afterward called Mercury by the Romans), was a son of Zeus and *Maia*, a daughter of Atlas. This is the same *Maia* whom the Abbé Brasseur de Bourbourg identifies with the Maya of Central America.

Sir William Drummond, in his " Origines," said:

" There seems to be no way of accounting either for the early use of letters among so many different nations, or for the resemblance which existed between some of the graphic systems employed by those nations, than by supposing hieroglyphical writing, if I may be allowed the term, to have been in use among the Tsabaists in the first ages after the Flood, when Tsabaism (planet-worship) was the religion of almost every country that was yet inhabited."

Sir Henry Rawlinson says:

" So great is the analogy between the first principles of the science of writing, as it appears to have been pursued in Chaldea, and as we can actually trace its progress in Egypt, that we can hardly hesitate to assign the original invention *to a period before the Hamitic race had broken up and divided.*"

It is not to be believed that such an extraordinary system of sound-signs could have been the invention of any one man or even of any one age. Like all our other acquisitions, it must have been the slow growth and accretion of ages; it must have risen step by step from picture-writing through an intermediate condition like that of the Chinese, where each word or thing was represented by a separate sign. The fact that so old and enlightened a people as the Chinese have never reached a phonetic alphabet, gives us some indication of the greatness of the people among whom it was invented, and the lapse of time before they attained to it.

Humboldt says:

" According to the views which, since Champollion's great discovery, have been gradually adopted regarding the earlier condition of the development of alphabetical writing, the Phœnician as well as the Semitic characters are to be regarded as a phonetic alphabet that has originated from pictorial writing; as one in which the ideal signification of the symbols is wholly disregarded, and the characters are regarded as mere signs for sounds." (" Cosmos," vol. ii., p. 129.)

Baldwin says ("Prehistoric Nations," p. 93):

"The nation that became mistress of the seas, established communication with every shore, and monopolized the commerce of the known world, must have substituted a phonetic alphabet for the hieroglyphics as it gradually grew to this eminence; while isolated Egypt, less affected by the practical wants and tendencies of commercial enterprise, retained the hieroglyphic system, and carried it to a marvellous height of perfection."

It must be remembered that some of the letters of our alphabet are inventions of the later nations. In the oldest alphabets there was no *c*, the *g* taking its place. The Romans converted the *g* into *c;* and then, finding the necessity for a *g* sign, made one by adding a tail-piece to the *c* (*C*, *G*). The Greeks added to the ancient alphabet the *upsilon*, shaped like our V or Y, the two forms being used at first indifferently: they added the X sign; they converted the t̲ of the Phœnicians into *th*, or *theta;* *z* and *s* into signs for double consonants; they turned the Phœnician *y* (*yod*) into *i* (*iota*). The Greeks converted the Phœnician alphabet, which was partly consonantal, into one purely phonetic — "a perfect instrument for the expression of spoken language." The *w* was also added to the Phœnician alphabet. The Romans added the *y*. At first *i* and *j* were both indicated by the same sound; a sign for *j* was afterward added. We have also, in common with other European languages, added a double U, that is, VV, or W, to represent the *w* sound.

The letters, then, which we owe to the Phœnicians, are A, B, C, D, E, H, I, K, L, M, N, O, P, Q, R, S, T, Z. If we are to trace out resemblances with the alphabet of any other country, it must be with these signs.

Is there any other country to which we can turn which possessed a phonetic alphabet in any respect kindred to this Phœnician alphabet? It cannot be the Chinese alphabet, which has more signs than words; it cannot be the cuneiform alphabet of Assyria, with its seven hundred arrow-shaped characters, none of which bear the slightest affinity to the Phœnician letters.

It is a surprising fact that *we find in Central America a phonetic alphabet.* This is in the alphabet of the Mayas, the ancient people of the peninsula of Yucatan, who claim that their civilization came to them *across the sea in ships from the east,* that is, from the direction of Atlantis. The Mayas succeeded to the Colhuas, whose era terminated one thousand years before the time of Christ; from them they received their alphabet. It has come to us through Bishop Landa, one of the early missionary bishops, who confesses to having burnt a great number of Maya books because they contained nothing but the works of the devil. He fortunately, however, preserved for posterity the alphabet of this people. We present it herewith.

Diego de Landa was the first bishop of Yucatan. He wrote a history of the Mayas and their country, which was preserved in manuscript at Madrid in the library of the Royal Academy of History. . . . It contains a description and explanation of the phonetic alphabet of the Mayas. Landa's manuscript seems to have lain neglected in the library, for little or nothing was heard of it until it was discovered by the French priest Brasseur de Bourbourg, who, by means of it, has deci-

LANDA'S ALPHABET.
(From "North Amer. of Antiquity," p. 424.)

phered some of the old American writings. He says, 'the alphabet and signs explained by Landa have been to me a Rosetta stone.'" (Baldwin's "Ancient America," p. 191.)

When we observe, in the table of alphabets of different European nations which I give herewith, how greatly the forms of the Phœnician letters have been modified, it would surprise us to find any resemblance between the Maya alphabet of two or three centuries since and the ancient European forms. It must, however, be remembered that the Mayas are one of the most conservative peoples in the world. They still adhere with striking pertinacity to the language they spoke when Columbus landed on San Salvador; and it is believed that that language is the same as the one inscribed on the most ancient monuments of their country. Señor Pimental says of them, "The Indians have preserved this idiom with such tenacity that they will speak no other; it is necessary for the whites to address them in their own language to communicate with them." It is therefore probable, as their alphabet did not pass from nation to nation, as did the Phœnician, that it has not departed so widely from the original forms received from the Colhuas.

But when we consider the vast extent of time which has elapsed, and the fact that we are probably without the intermediate stages of the alphabet which preceded the archaic Phœnician, it will be astonishing if we find resemblances between *any* of the Maya letters and the European forms, even though we concede that they are related. If we find decided affinities between two or three letters, we may reasonably presume that similar coincidences existed as to many others which have disappeared under the attrition of centuries.

The first thought that occurs to us on examining the Landa alphabet is the complex and ornate character of the letters. Instead of the two or three strokes with which we indicate a sign for a sound, we have here rude pictures of objects. And we find that these are themselves simplifications of older forms

The Alphabet.

	Maya	Mayoc	Supposed Intermediate Forms	From the Stone of Moab 890 B.C.	Archaic Phoenician	Phoenician & Carthaginian	Old Greek	Old Hebrew	Samaritan	Ethiopian	Irish	Later Greek	Hieratic Egyptian
A												A	
B												B	
G												Γ	
D												Δ	
HE.												E	
V												F	
Z												Z	
C.H.												H	
T												Θ	
I												I	
K												K	
L												Λ	
M												M	
N												N	
XX.												Ξ	
O												O	
P												Π	
Q													
R												P	
S												Σ	

of a still more complex character. Take, for instance, the letter *pp* in Landa's alphabet, ⌊⫿⌋ : here are evidently the traces
of a face. † The same appear, but not so plainly, in the sign
for *x*, which is ◧. Now, if we turn to the ancient hieroglyphics upon the monuments of Central America, we will find
the human face appearing in a great many of them, as in
the following, which we copy from the Tablet of the Cross at
Palenque. We take the hieroglyphs from the left-hand side
of the inscription. Here it will be seen that, out of
seven hieroglyphical figures, six contain human faces.
And we find that in the whole inscription of the Tablet of the Cross there are 33 figures out of 108 that
are made up in part of the human countenance.

We can see, therefore, in the Landa alphabet a
tendency to simplification. And this is what we
would naturally expect. When the emblems—which
were probably first intended for religious inscriptions, where they could be slowly and carefully elab-
orated—were placed in the hands of a busy, active,
commercial people, such as were the Atlanteans, and afterward
the Phœnicians, men with whom time was valuable, the natural
tendency would be to simplify and condense them ; and when
the original meaning of the picture was lost, they would naturally slur it, as we find in the letters *pp* and *x* of the Maya
alphabet, where the figure of the human face remains only in
rude lines.

The same tendency is plainly shown in the two forms of
the letter *h*, as given in Landa's alphabet; the original form
is more elaborate than the variation of it. The original form
is ⫿. The variation is given as ⫿. Now let us suppose
this simplification to be carried a step farther : we have seen
the upper and lower parts of the first form shrink into a smaller
and less elaborate shape ; let us imagine that the same tendency does away with them altogether ; we would then have the

† The following analysis of the Landa alphabet and Eurasian
alphabets is fanciful and worthless.—E.F.B.

letter H of the Maya alphabet represented by this figure, ⊟ ; now, as it takes less time to make a single stroke than a double one, this would become in time ⊟. We turn now to the archaic Greek and the old Hebrew, and we find the letter *h* indicated by this sign, ⊟, precisely the Maya letter *h* simplified. We turn to the archaic Hebrew, and we find it ⊟. Now it is known that the Phœnicians wrote from right to left, and just as we in writing from left to right slope our letters to the right, so did the Phœnicians slope their letters to the left. Hence the Maya sign becomes in the archaic Phœnician this, ⋈ · In some of the Phœnician alphabets we even find the letter *h* made with the double strokes above and below, as in the Maya *h*. The Egyptian hieroglyph for *h* is ⊏⊐ while *ch* is ⊓ · In time the Greeks carried the work of simplification still farther, and eliminated the top lines, as we have supposed the Atlanteans to have eliminated the double strokes, and they left the letter as it has come down to us, H.

Now it may be said that all this is coincidence. If it is, it is certainly remarkable. But let us go a step farther :

We have seen in Landa's alphabet that there are two forms of the letter *m*. The first is 🐚. But we find also an *m* combined with the letter *o*, *a*, or *e*, says Landa, in this form, o—⌐—o. The *m* here is certainly indicated by the central part of this combination, the figure ⌐⌐; where does that come from? It is clearly taken from the heart of the original figure wherein it appears. What does this prove? That the Atlanteans, or Mayas, when they sought to simplify their letters and combine them with others, took from the centre of the ornate hieroglyphical figure some characteristic mark with which they represented the whole figure. Now let us apply this rule :

We have seen in the table of alphabets that in every language, from our own day to the time of the Phœnicians, *o* has been represented by a circle or a circle within a circle. Now where did the Phœnicians get it? Clearly from the Mayas. There are two figures for *o* in the Maya alphabet; they are and ; now, if we apply the rule which we have seen to exist in the case of the Maya *m* to these figures, the essential characteristic found in each is the circle, in the first case pendant from the hieroglyph; in the other, in the centre of the lower part of it. And that this circle was withdrawn from the hieroglyph, and used alone, as in the case of the *m*, is proved by the very sign used at the foot of Landa's alphabet, which is, o—⊓—o. Landa calls this *ma*, *me*, or *mo;* it is probably the latter, and in it we have the circle detached from the hieroglyph.

We find the precise Maya *o* a circle in a circle, or a dot within a circle, repeated in the Phœnician forms for *o*, thus, ⊙ and ◎, and by exactly the same forms in the Egyptian hieroglyphics; in the Runic we have the circle in the circle; in one form of the Greek *o* the dot was placed along-side of the circle instead of below it, as in the Maya.

Are these another set of coincidences?

Take another letter:

The letter *n* of the Maya alphabet is represented by this sign, itself probably a simplification of some more ornate form, Ƨ. This is something like our letter S, but quite unlike our N. But let us examine into the pedigree of our *n*. We find in the archaic Ethiopian, a language as old as the Egyptian, and which represents the Cushite branch of the Atlantean stock, the sign for *n* (*na*) is ⚡; in archaic Phœnician it comes still closer to the S shape, thus, Ƨ, or in this form, Ƨ; we have but to curve these angles to approximate it very closely to the Maya *n;* in Troy this form was found, Ƨ. The Samaritan makes it ㄅ; the old Hebrew Ƨ; the Moab stone inscription gives it Ƴ; the later Phœnicians simplified the archaic form still further, until it became ⁊; then it passed into Ƴ: the archaic Greek form is ⤳; the later Greeks made Ν, from which it passed into the present form, N. All these forms seem to be representations of a serpent; we turn to the valley of the Nile, and we find that the Egyptian hieroglyphic for *n* was the serpent, ∽ᶜ; the Pelasgian *n* was ʔ; the Arcadian, ϟ; the Etruscan, ʔ .

Can anything be more significant than to find the serpent the sign for *n* in Central America, and in all these Old World languages?

Now turn to the letter *k*. The Maya sign for *k* is 🔣. This does not look much like our letter K; but let us examine it. Following the precedent established for us by the Mayas in the case of the letter *m*, let us see what is the distinguishing feature here; it is clearly the figure of a serpent standing erect, with its tail doubled around its middle, forming a circle. It has already been remarked by Savolini that this erect serpent is very much like the Egyptian *Uræus*, an erect serpent with an enlarged body—a sacred emblem found in the hair of their deities. We turn again to the valley of the Nile, and we find that the Egyptian hieroglyphic for *k* was a serpent with a convolution or protuberance in the middle, precisely as in the Maya, thus, 𓆓 ; this was transformed into the Egyptian letter ∫ ; the serpent and the protuberance reappear in one of the Phœnician forms of *k*, to wit, ϟ ; while in the Punic we have these forms, ℘ and ♣ . Now suppose a busy people trying to give this sign: instead of drawing the serpent in all its details they would abbreviate it into something like this, ℘ ; now we turn to the ancient Ethiopian sign for *k* (*ka*), and we have ⸙, or the Himyaritic Arabian ◁; while in the Phœnician it becomes ⸢; in the archaic Greek, ⸤; and in the later Greek, when they changed the writing from left to right, K . So that the two lines projecting from the upright stroke of our English K are a reminiscence of the convolution of the serpent in the Maya original and the Egyptian copy.

Turn now to the Maya sign for *t*: it is 🔣. What is the distinctive mark about this figure? It is the cross composed of two curved lines, thus, ⏦. It is probable that in this

Maya sign the cross is united at the bottom, like a figure 8. Here again we turn to the valley of the Nile, and we find that the Egyptian hieroglyph for *t* is ♂ and ♂; and in the Syriac *t* it is ♂. We even find the curved lines of the Maya *t*, which give it something of the appearance of the numeral 8, repeated accurately in the Mediterranean alphabets; thus the Punic *t* repeats the Maya form almost exactly as X and X. Now suppose a busy people compelled to make this mark every day for a thousand years, and generally in a hurry, and the cross would soon be made without curving the lines; it would become ✕. But before it reached even that simplified form it had crossed the Atlantic, and appeared in the archaic Ethiopian sign for *tsa*, thus, ⋋. In the archaic Phœnician the sign for *t* is ⊕ and ✕; the oldest Greek form is ⊗, or X, and the later Greeks gave it to the Romans T, and modified this into ⊖; the old Hebrew gave it as ✕ and +; the Moab stone as ✕; this became in time ✝ and T.

Take the letter *a*. In the Maya there are three forms given for this letter. The first is ⬭; the third is ⬭. The first looks very much like the foot of a lion or tiger; the third is plainly a foot or boot. If one were required to give hurriedly a rude outline of either of these, would he not represent it thus, ɗ; and can we not conceive that this could have been in time modified into the Phœnician *a*, which was ⅄? The hieratic Egyptian *a* was ℥; the ancient Hebrew, which was ⋋, or ✦; the ancient Greek was the foot reversed, ∆; the later Greek became our A.

Turn next to the Maya sign for *q* (*ku*): it is ⬭. Now what is the peculiarity of this hieroglyph? The circle below is not significant, for there are many circular figures in the Maya alphabet. Clearly, if one was called upon to simplify this, he would retain the two small circles joined side by side at the top, and would indicate the lower circle with a line or dash. And when we turn to the Egyptian *q* we find it in this shape,

⨂ ; we turn to the Ethiopian *q* (*khua*), and we find it ⤶ᵒ, or as *qua*, ⨂₀ ; while the Phœnician comes still nearer the supposed Maya form in ϙ; the Moab stone was φ; the Himyaritic Arabian form became Ϙ ; the Greek form was Ϙ, which graduated into the Roman Q. But a still more striking proof of the descent of the Phœnician alphabet from the Maya is found in the other form of the *q*, the Maya *cu*, which is ⓧ. Now, if we apply the Maya rule to this, and discard the outside circle, we have this left, ⤵. In time the curved line would be made straight, and the figure would assume this form, X| ; the next step would be to make the cross *on* the straight line, thus, ⵟ. One of the ancient Phœnician forms is ⴼ. Can all this be accident?

The letter *c* or *g* (for the two probably gave the same sound as in the Phœnician) is given in the Maya alphabet as follows, ⓌⓌ. This would in time be simplified into a figure representing the two sides of a triangle with the apex upward, thus, Λ. This is precisely the form found by Dr. Schliemann in the ruins of Troy, Λ. What is the Phœnician form for *g*, as found on the Moab stone? It is ⟋. The Carthaginian Phœnicians gave it more of a rounded form, thus, ⋂. The hieratic Egyptian figure for *g* was ⟋ℳ ; in the earlier Greek form the left limb of the figure was shortened, thus, ⟈; the later Greeks reversed it, and wrote it Γ; the Romans changed this into ⟨, and it finally became C.

In the Maya we have one sign for *p*, and another for *pp*. The first contains a curious figure, precisely like our *r* laid on its back, ⌂. There is, apparently, no *r* in the Maya alphabet; and the Roman *r* grew out of the later Phœnician *r* formed thus, ⟁ ; it would appear that the earliest Phœnician alphabet did not contain the letter *r*. But if we now turn to the Phœnician alphabet, we will find one of the curious forms of the *p* given thus, ⌣, a very fair representation of an *r* lying upon its face. Is it not another remarkable coincidence that the *p*, in both Maya and Phœnician, should contain this singular sign?

The form of *pp* in the Maya alphabet is this, ⎨⎬. If we are asked, on the principle already indicated, to reduce this to its elements, we would use a figure like this, ⊦⊦; in time the tendency would be to shorten one of these perpendicular lines, thus, ⊦⊦ ; and this we find is very much like the Phœnician *p*, ⌐. The Greek *ph* is Φ.

The letter *l* in the Maya is in two forms; one of these is ⌖, the other is ⌁. Now, if we again apply the rule which we observed to hold good with the letter *m*—that is, draw from the inside of the hieroglyph some symbol that will briefly indicate the whole letter — we will have one of two forms, either a right-angled figure formed thus, ⌐, or an acute angle formed by joining the two lines which are unconnected, thus, ∠; and either of these forms brings us quite close to the letter *l* of the Old World. We find *l* on the Moab stone thus formed, 6. The archaic Phœnician form of *l* was ∠, or ∟; the archaic Hebrew was ∠ and ∟; the hieratic Egyptian was ⌐; the Greek form was ∧—the Roman L.

The Maya letter *b* is shaped thus, ⌸. Now, if we turn to the Phœnician, we find that *b* is represented by the same crescent-like figure which we find in the middle of this hieroglyph, but reversed in the direction of the writing, thus,); while in the archaic Hebrew we have the same crescent figure as in the Maya, turned in the same direction, but accompanied by a line drawn downward, and to the left, thus, ⊆; a similar form is also found in the Phœnician ᑫ; and this in the earliest Greek changed into ᕑ, and in the later Greek into B. One of the Etruscan signs for *b* was ᕪ, while the Pelasgian *b* was represented thus, 🝊🝊; the Chaldaic *b* was ⊐; the Syriac sign for *b* was ⟋⟍; the Illyrian *b* was ◺.

The Maya *e* is ⊚; this became in time ⟑⟍; then ⎯⎯ (we see this form on the Maya monuments); the dots in time were indicated by strokes, and we reach the hieratic Egyptian form, 𝍇: we even find in some of the ancient Phœnician inscriptions the original Maya circles preserved in making the letter *e*, thus, ⊒; then we find the old Greek form, 🝳; the old Hebrew, ∃; and the later Phœnician, 🝳: when the direction of the writing was changed this became **E**. Dr. Schliemann found a form like this on inscriptions deep in the ruins of Troy, 𝍇. This is exactly the form found on the American monuments.

The Maya *i* is ⊛; this became in time 𝍝; this developed into a still simpler form, 𝈜; and this passed into the Phœnician form, ⊓. The Samaritan *i* was formed thus, ⫟⫟; the Egyptian letter *i* is ⟨⟩: gradually in all these the left-hand line was dropped, and we come to the figure used on the stone of Moab, 𝈜 and ⎯⎰; this in time became the old Hebrew 𝈜 or 𝈜; and this developed into the Greek ‡.

We have seen the complicated symbol for *m* reduced by the Mayas themselves into this figure, ⎍: if we attempt to write this rapidly, we find it very difficult to always keep the base lines horizontal; naturally we form something like this, ⌇: the distinctive figure within the sign for *m* in the Maya is ⊓ or ⊏. We see this repeated in the Egyptian hieroglyphics for *m*, ⊏, and 𝍓, and ⊐; in the Chaldaic *m*, ▢; and in the Ethiopic ⊓⊓. We find one form of the Phœnician where the *m* is made thus, ⌐⊓; and in the Punic it appears thus, 𝍓; and this is not unlike the *m* on the stone of Moab, ⩊, or the ancient Phœnician forms, ⩊, ⩊, and the old Greek ⋀, or the ancient Hebrew ⩊, ⩊.

The χ, *x*, of the Maya alphabet is a hand pointing downward, ; this, reduced to its elements, would be expressed something like this, ⫽⫽\ or ⫼⫽\; and this is very much like the *x* of the archaic Phœnician, ; or the Moab stone, ; or the later Phœnician, ; or the Hebrew, , ; or the old Greek, : the later Greek form was Ξ.

The Maya alphabet contains no sign for the letter *s ;* there is, however, a symbol called *ca* immediately above the letter *k ;* it is probable that the sign *ca* stands for the soft sound of *c*, as in our words *citron, circle, civil, circus*, etc. As it is written in the Maya alphabet *ca*, and not *k*, it evidently represents a different sound. The sign *ca* is this, . A somewhat similar sign is found in the body of the symbol for *k*, thus, ⌁; this would appear to be a simplification of *ca*, but turned downward. If now we turn to the Egyptian letters we find the sign *k* represented by this figure , simplified again into ; while the sign for *k* in the Phœnician inscription on the stone of Moab is . If now we turn to the *s* sound, indicated by the Maya sign *ca*, , we find the resemblance still more striking to kindred European letters. The Phœnician *s* is ⊔⌐ ⋃ ⊔⊔; in the Greek this becomes M ⋀; the Hebrew is ⋁⋁ ⋓; the Samaritan, . The Egyptian hieroglyph for *s* is ; the Egyptian letter *s* is ; the Ethiopic, ; the Chaldaic, ; and the Illyrian *s c* is .

We have thus traced back the forms of eighteen of the ancient letters to the Maya alphabet. In some cases the pedigree is so plain as to be indisputable.

For instance, take the *h :*

Maya, ; old Greek, ⊟; old Hebrew, ; Phœnician, .
Or take the letter *o :*
Maya, o ; old Greek, o ; old Hebrew, o ; Phœnician, o.
Or take the letter *t :*
Maya, ⊗ ; old Greek, ⊗; old Phœnician, (+) and ✕.

Or take the letter *q :*

Maya, 🐘 ; old Phœnician, ϙ and ϙ ; Greek, ϙ.

Or take the letter *k :*

Maya, (🐘) ; Egyptian, 🐘 ; Ethiopian, Φ ; Phœnician, 𐤊.

Or take the letter *n :*

Maya, S ; Egyptian, 🐍 ; Pelasgian, ς ; Arcadian, S ;
Phœnician, 𐤍.

Surely all this cannot be accident!

But we find another singular proof of the truth of this theory:

It will be seen that the Maya alphabet lacks the letter *d* and
the letter *r.* The Mexican alphabet possessed a *d.* The sounds
d and *t* were probably indicated in the Maya tongue by the
same sign, called *t* in the Landa alphabet. The Finns and
Lapps do not distinguish between these two sounds. In the
oldest known form of the Phœnician alphabet, that found on
the Moab stone, we find in the same way but one sign to express the *d* and *t. D* does not occur on the Etruscan monuments, *t* being used in its place. It would, therefore, appear
that after the Maya alphabet passed to the Phœnicians they
added two new signs for the letters *d* and *r ;* and it is a singular fact that their poverty of invention seems to have been such
that they used to express both *d* and *r,* the same sign, with
very little modification, which they had already obtained from
the Maya alphabet as the symbol for *b.* To illustrate this we
place the signs side by side:

	b			d		r	
Phœnician	ᖁ	ᖁ	ᖁ	◁	ᖁ	◁	ᖁ
Old Greek	ᖁ				△	◁	ᖁ
Old Hebrew	◁	ᖁ	Ч	△	Ƴ	◁	ᖁ

It thus appears that the very signs *d* and *r,* in the Phœnician, early Greek, and ancient Hebrew, which are lacking in the

Maya, were supplied by imitating the Maya sign for *b;* and it is a curious fact that while the Phœnician legends claim that Taaut invented the art of writing, yet they tell us that Taaut made records, and "delivered them to his successors and to foreigners, of whom one was Isiris (Osiris, the Egyptian god), *the inventor of the three letters.*" Did these three letters include the *d* and *r*, which they did not receive from the Atlantean alphabet, as represented to us by the Maya alphabet?

In the alphabetical table which we herewith append we have represented the sign V, or vau, or *f*, by the Maya sign for U. "In the present so-called Hebrew, as in the Syriac, Sabæic, Palmyrenic, and some other kindred writings, the *vau* takes the place of F, and indicates the sounds of *v* and *u*. F occurs in the same place also on the Idalian tablet of Cyprus, in Lycian, also in Tuarik (Berber), and some other writings." ("American Cyclopædia," art. *F.*)

Since writing the above, I find in the "Proceedings of the American Philosophical Society" for December, 1880, p. 154, an interesting article pointing out other resemblances between the Maya alphabet and the Egyptian. I quote:

"It is astonishing to notice that while Landa's first B is, ac- cording to Valentini, represented by a footprint, and that path and footprint are pronounced *Be* in the Maya dictionary, the Egyptian sign for B was the human leg.

"Still more surprising is it that the H of Landa's alphabet is a tie of cord, while the Egyptian H is a twisted cord. . . . But the most striking coincidence of all occurs in the coiled or curled line representing Landa's U; *for it is absolutely identical with the Egyptian* curled U. The Mayan word for to wind or bend is Uuc; but why should Egyptians, confined as they were to the valley of the Nile, and abhorring as they did the sea and sailors, write their U precisely like Landa's alphabet U in Central America? There is one other remarkable coincidence between Landa's and the Egyptian alphabets; and, by-the-way, the English and other Teutonic dialects have a curious share in it. Landa's D (T) is a disk with lines inside the four quarters, the allowed Mexican symbol for a day or sun.

So far as sound is concerned, the English *day* represents it; so far as the form is concerned, the Egyptian 'cake,' ideograph for (1) country and (2) the sun's orbit is essentially the same."

It would appear as if both the Phœnicians and Egyptians drew their alphabet from a common source, of which the Maya is a survival, but did not borrow from one another. They followed out different characteristics in the same original hieroglyph, as, for instance, in the letter *b*. And yet I have shown that the closest resemblances exist between the Maya alphabet and the Egyptian signs—in the *c*, *h*, *t*, *i*, *k*, *l*, *m*, *n*, *o*, *q*, and *s*— eleven letters in all; in some cases, as in the *n* and *k*, the signs are identical; the *k*, in both alphabets, is not only a serpent, but a serpent with a protuberance or convolution in the middle! If we add to the above the *b* and *u*, referred to in the "Proceedings of the American Philosophical Society," we have thirteen letters out of sixteen in the Maya and Egyptian related to each other. Can any theory of accidental coincidences account for all this? And it must be remembered that these resemblances are found between *the only two phonetic systems of alphabet in the world*.

Let us suppose that two men agree that each shall construct apart from the other a phonetic alphabet of sixteen letters; that they shall employ only simple forms—combinations of straight or curved lines—and that their signs shall not in anywise resemble the letters now in use. They go to work apart; they have a multitudinous array of forms to draw from—the thousand possible combinations of lines, angles, circles, and curves; when they have finished, they bring their alphabets together for comparison. Under such circumstances it is possible that out of the sixteen signs one sign might appear in both alphabets; there is one chance in one hundred that such might be the case; but there is not one chance in five hundred that this sign should in both cases represent the same sound. It is barely possible that two men working thus apart should hit upon two or three identical forms, but altogether impossible that these forms should have the same significance; and by no stretch of the imagination can it be supposed that in these alphabets so created, without correspondence, thirteen out of sixteen signs should be the same in form and the same in meaning.

It is probable that a full study of the Central American monuments may throw stronger light upon the connection between the Maya and the European alphabets, and that further discoveries of inscriptions in Europe may approximate the alphabets of the New and Old World still more closely by supplying intermediate forms.

We find in the American hieroglyphs peculiar signs which take the place of pictures, and which probably, like the hieratic symbols mingled with the hieroglyphics of Egypt, represent alphabetical sounds. For instance, we find this sign on the walls of the palace of Palenque, ☐ ; this is not unlike the form of the Phœnician *t* used in writing, ☐ and ☐; we find also upon these monuments the letter *o* represented by a small circle, and entering into many of the hieroglyphs; we also find the *tau* sign (thus ☐) often repeated; also the sign which we have supposed to represent *b*, ☐ ; also this sign, ☐, which we think is the simplification of the letter *k*; also this sign, which we suppose to represent *e*, ☐; also this figure, ☐ ; and this, ∞. There is an evident tendency to reduce the complex figures to simple signs whenever the writers proceed to form words.

Although it has so far been found difficult, if not impossible, to translate the compound words formed from the Maya alphabet, yet we can go far enough to see that they used the system of simpler sounds for the whole hieroglyph to which we have referred.

Bishop Landa gives us, in addition to the alphabet, the signs which represent the days and months, and which are evidently compounds of the Maya letters. For instance, we have this figure as the representative of the month *Mol*, ☐. Here we

see very plainly the letter � for *m*, the sign ⊙ for *o;* and we will possibly find the sign for *l* in the right angle to the right of the *m* sign, and which is derived from the figure in the second sign for *l* in the Maya alphabet.

One of the most ancient races of Central America is the Chiapenec, a branch of the Mayas. They claim to be the first settlers of the country. They came, their legends tell us, from the East, from beyond the sea.

And even after the lapse of so many thousand years most remarkable resemblances have been found to exist between the Chiapenec language and the Hebrew, the living representative of the Phœnician tongue.

The Mexican scholar, Señor Melgar ("North Americans of Antiquity," p. 475) gives the, following list of words taken from the Chiapenec and the Hebrew:

English.	Chiapenec.	Hebrew.
Son	Been	Ben.
Daughter	Batz	Bath.
Father	Abagh	Abba.
Star in Zodiac	Chimax	Chimah.
King	Molo	Maloc.
Name applied to Adam	Abagh	Abah.
Afflicted	Chanam	Chanan.
God	Elab	Elab.
September	Tsiquin	Tischiri.
More	Chic	Chi.
Rich	Chabin	Chabic.
Son of Seth	Enot	Enos.
To give	Votan	Votan.

Thus, while we find such extraordinary resemblances between the Maya alphabet and the Phœnician alphabet, we find equally surprising coincidences between the Chiapenec tongue, a branch of the Mayas, and the Hebrew, a branch of the Phœnician.

Attempts have been repeatedly made by European scholars to trace the letters of the Phœnician alphabet back to the elaborate hieroglyphics from which all authorities agree they must have been developed, but all such attempts have been failures. But here, in the Maya alphabet, we are not only able to extract from the heart of the hieroglyphic the typical sign for the sound, but we are able to go a step farther, and, by means of the inscriptions upon the monuments of Copan and Palenque, deduce the alphabetical hieroglyph itself from an older and more ornate figure; we thus not only discover the relationship of the European alphabet to the American, but we trace its descent in the very mode in which reason tells us it must have been developed. All this proves that the similarities in question did not come from Phœnicians having accidentally visited the shores of America, but that we have before us the origin, the source, the very matrix in which the Phœnician alphabet was formed. In the light of such a discovery the inscriptions upon the monuments of Central America assume incalculable importance; they take us back to a civilization far anterior to the oldest known in Europe; they represent the language of antediluvian times.

It may be said that it is improbable that the use of an alphabet could have ascended to antediluvian times, or to that prehistoric age when intercourse existed between ancient Europe and America; but it must be remembered that if the Flood legends of Europe and Asia are worth anything they prove that the art of writing existed at the date of the Deluge, and that records of antediluvian learning were preserved by those who escaped the Flood; while Plato tells us that the people of Atlantis engraved their laws upon columns of bronze and plates of gold.

There was a general belief among the ancient nations that the art of writing was known to the antediluvians. The Druids believed in books more ancient than the Flood. They styled them "the books of Pheryllt," and "the writings of Pridian or Hu." "Ceridwen consults them before she prepares the mysterious caldron which shadows out the awful catastrophe of the Deluge." (Faber's "Pagan Idolatry," vol. ii., pp. 150, 151.)

In the first *Avatar* of Vishnu we are told that "the divine ordinances were stolen by the demon Haya-Griva. Vishnu became a fish; and after the Deluge, when the waters had subsided, he recovered the holy books *from the bottom of the ocean.*" Berosus, speaking of the time before the Deluge, says: "Oannes wrote concerning the generations of mankind and their civil polity." The Hebrew commentators on Genesis say, "Our rabbins assert that Adam, our father of blessed memory, composed a book of precepts, which were delivered to him by God in Paradise." (Smith's "Sacred Annals," p. 49.) That is to say, the Hebrews preserved a tradition that the Ad-ami, the people of Ad, or Adlantis, possessed, while yet dwelling in Paradise, the art of writing. It has been suggested that without the use of letters it would have been impossible to preserve the many details as to dates, ages, and measurements, as of the ark, handed down to us in Genesis. Josephus, quoting Jewish traditions, says, "The births and deaths of illustrious men, between Adam and Noah, were noted down at the time with great accuracy." (Ant., lib. 1, cap. iii., sec. 3.) Suidas, a Greek lexicographer of the eleventh century, expresses tradition when he says, "Adam was the author of arts and letters." The Egyptians said that their god Anubis was an antediluvian, and "wrote annals *before* the Flood." The Chinese have traditions that the earliest race of their nation, prior to history, "taught all the arts of life and wrote books." "The Goths always had the use of letters;" and Le Grand affirms that before or soon after the Flood "there were found the acts of great men engraved in letters on large stones." (Fosbroke's "Encyclopædia of Antiquity," vol. i., p. 355.) Pliny says, "Letters were always in use." Strabo says, "The inhabitants of Spain possessed records *written before the Deluge.*" (Jackson's "Chronicles of Antiquity," vol. iii., p. 85.) Mitford ("History of Greece," vol. i., p. 121) says, "Nothing appears to us so probable as that it (the alphabet) was derived from the antediluvian world."

Chapter VIII.

THE BRONZE AGE IN EUROPE.

There exist in Europe the evidences of three different ages of human development : †

1. The Stone Age, which dates back to a vast antiquity. It is subdivided into two periods : an age of rough stone implements; and a later age, when these implements were ground smooth and made in improved forms.

2. The Bronze Age, when the great mass of implements were manufactured of a compound metal, consisting of about nine parts of copper and one part of tin.

3. An age when iron superseded bronze for weapons and cutting tools, although bronze still remained in use for ornaments. This age continued down to what we call the Historical Period, and embraces our present civilization; its more ancient remains are mixed with coins of the Gauls, Greeks, and Romans.

The Bronze Period has been one of the perplexing problems of European scientists. Articles of bronze are found over nearly all that continent, but in especial abundance in Ireland and Scandinavia. They indicate very considerable refinement and civilization upon the part of the people who made them; and a wide diversity of opinion has prevailed as to who that people were and where they dwelt.

In the first place, it was observed that the age of bronze (a compound of copper and tin) must, in the natural order of things, have been preceded by an age when copper and tin were used separately, before the ancient metallurgists had dis-

† Donnelly's assumption, general in his day, was not justified. —E.F.B.

covered the art of combining them, and yet in Europe the remains of no such age have been found. Sir John Lubbock says ("Prehistoric Times," p. 59), "The absence of implements made either of copper or tin seems to me to indicate that *the art of making bronze was introduced into, not invented in, Europe.*" The absence of articles of copper is especially marked; nearly all the European specimens of copper implements have been found in Ireland; and yet out of twelve hundred and eighty-three articles of the Bronze Age, in the great museum at Dublin, only thirty celts and one sword-blade are said to be made of pure copper; and even as to some of these there seems to be a question.

Where on the face of the earth are we to find a Copper Age? Is it in the barbaric depths of that Asia out of whose uncivilized tribes all civilization is said to have issued? By no means. Again we are compelled to turn to the West. In America, from Bolivia to Lake Superior, we find everywhere the traces of a long-enduring Copper Age; bronze existed, it is true, in Mexico, but it held the same relation to the copper as the copper held to the bronze in Europe—it was the exception as against the rule. And among the Chippeways of the shores of Lake Superior, *and among them alone,* we find any traditions of the origin of the manufacture of copper implements; and on the shores of that lake we find pure copper, out of which the first metal tools were probably hammered before man had learned to reduce the ore or run the metal into moulds. And on the shores of this same American lake we find the ancient mines from which some people, thousands of years ago, derived their supplies of copper.

Sir W. R. Wilde says, " It is remarkable that so few antique copper implements have been found (in Europe), although a knowledge of that metal must have been the preliminary stage in the manufacture of bronze." He thinks that this may be accounted for by supposing that "but a short time elapsed between the knowledge of smelting, and casting copper ore

Irish Mould for casting Bronze Celts.

Bronze Reaping-hook, Switzerland.

Finger-ring.

Ear-ring.

Bronze Chisel.

Bronze Hammer.

Ancient Adze, Ireland.

IMPLEMENTS AND ORNAMENTS OF THE BRONZE AGE.

and the introduction of tin, and the subsequent manufacture and use of bronze."

But here we have in America the evidence that thousands of years must have elapsed during which copper was used alone, before it was discovered that by adding one-tenth part of tin it gave a harder edge, and produced a superior metal.

The Bronze Age cannot be attributed to the Roman civilization. Sir John Lubbock shows ("Prehistoric Times," p. 21) that bronze weapons have never been found associated with Roman coins or pottery, or other remains of the Roman Period; that bronze articles have been found in the greatest abundance in countries like Ireland and Denmark, which were never invaded by Roman armies; and that the character of the ornamentation of the works of bronze is not Roman in character, and that the Roman bronze contained a large proportion of lead, which is never the case in that of the Bronze Age.

It has been customary to assume that the Bronze Age was due to the Phœnicians, but of late the highest authorities have taken issue with this opinion. Sir John Lubbock (*Ibid.*, p. 73) gives the following reasons why the Phœnicians could not have been the authors of the Bronze Age: First, the ornamentation is different. In the Bronze Age "this always consists of geometrical figures, and we rarely, if ever, find upon them representations of animals and plants, while on the ornamented shields, etc., described by Homer, as well as in the decoration of Solomon's Temple, animals and plants were abundantly represented." The cuts on p. 242 will show the character of the ornamentation of the Bronze Age. In the next place, the form of burial is different in the Bronze Age from that of the Phœnicians. "In the third place, the Phœnicians, so far as we know them, were well acquainted with the use of iron; in Homer we find the warriors already armed with iron weapons, and the tools used in preparing the materials for Solomon's Temple were of this metal."

This view is also held by M. de Fallenberg, in the "Bulletin

Gold Ornament of the Bronze Age, Ireland.

Bronze Bracelet.

Bronze Bracelet, Switzerland.   Amulet.

ORNAMENTS OF THE BRONZE AGE.

de la Société des Sciences" of Berne.   (See "Smithsonian Rep.," 1865–66, p. 383.)   He says,

"It seems surprising that the nearest neighbors of the Phœnicians—the Greeks, the Egyptians, the Etruscans, and the Romans—should have manufactured *plumbiferous* bronzes, while the Phœnicians carried to the people of the North only pure bronzes without the alloy of lead. If the civilized people of the Mediterranean added lead to their bronzes, it can scarcely be doubted that the calculating Phœnicians would have done as much, and, at least, with distant and half-civilized tribes, have replaced the more costly tin by the cheaper metal. . . . On the whole, then, I consider that the first knowledge of bronze may have been conveyed to the populations of the period under review not only by the Phœnicians, but by other civilized people dwelling more to the south-east."

Professor E. Desor, in his work on the " Lacustrian Constructions of the Lake of Neuchatel," says,

"The Phœnicians certainly knew the use of iron, and it can scarcely be conceived why they should have excluded it from their commerce on the Scandinavian coasts. . . . The Etruscans, moreover, were acquainted with the use of iron as well as the Phœnicians, and it has already been seen that the composition of their bronzes is different, since it contains lead, which is entirely a stranger to our bronze epoch. . . . We must look, then, *beyond* both the Etruscans and Phœnicians in attempting to identify the commerce of the Bronze Age of our palafittes. It will be the province of the historian to inquire whether, exclusive of Phœnicians and Carthaginians, there may not have been some maritime and commercial people who carried on a traffic through the ports of Liguria with the populations of the age of bronze of the lakes of Italy *before the discovery of iron.* We may remark, in passing, that there is nothing to prove that the Phœnicians were the first navigators. History, on the contrary, positively mentions prisoners, under the name of Tokhari, who were vanquished in a naval battle fought by Rhamses III. in the thirteenth century before our era, and whose physiognomy, according to Morton, would indicate the Celtic type. Now there is room to suppose that if these Tokhari were energetic enough to measure their strength on the sea with one of the powerful kings of Egypt, they must, with stronger reason, have been in a condition to carry on a commerce along the coasts of the Mediterranean, and perhaps of the Atlantic. If such a commerce really existed before the time of the Phœnicians, it would not be limited to the southern slope of the Alps ; it would have extended also to the people of the age of bronze in Switzerland. The introduction of bronze would thus ascend to a very high antiquity, doubtless beyond the limits of the most ancient European races."

For the merchants of the Bronze Age we must look beyond even the Tokhari, who were contemporaries of the Phœnicians. The Tokhari, we have seen, are represented as taken prisoners in a sea-fight with Rhamses III., of the twentieth dynasty,

CELTIC WARRIOR, FROM EGYPTIAN MONUMENTS.

about the thirteenth century B.C. They are probably the *Tochari* of Strabo. The accompanying figure represents one of these people as they appear upon the Egyptian monuments. (See Nott and Gliddon's "Types of Mankind," p. 108.) Here we have, not an inhabitant of Atlantis, but probably a representative of one of the mixed races that sprung from its colonies.

Dr. Morton thinks these people, as painted on the Egyptian monuments, to have "strong Celtic features. Those familiar with the Scotch Highlanders may recognize a speaking likeness."

It is at least interesting to have a portrait of one of the daring race who more than three thousand years ago left the west of Europe in their ships to attack the mighty power of Egypt.

They were troublesome to the nations of the East for many centuries; for in 700 B.C. we find them depicted on the Assyrian monuments. This figure represents one of the Tokhari of the time of Sennacherib. It will be observed that the head-dress (apparently of feathers) is the same in both portraits, although separated by a period of six hundred years.

It is more reasonable to suppose that the authors of the

Bronze Age of Europe were the people described by Plato, who were workers in metal, who were highly civilized, who preceded in time all the nations which we call ancient. It was this people who passed through an age of copper before they reached the age of bronze, and whose colonies in America represented this older form of metallurgy as it existed for many generations.

Professor Desor says:

CELTIC WARRIOR, FROM ASSYRIAN MONUMENTS.

" We are asked if the preparation of bronze was not an indigenous invention which had originated on the slopes of the Alps?... In this idea we acquiesced for a moment. But we are met by the objection that, if this were so, the natives, like the ancient tribes of America, would have commenced by manufacturing utensils of *copper;* yet thus far no utensils of this metal have been found except a few in the strand of Lake Garda. The great majority of metallic objects is of bronze, which necessitated the employment of tin, and this could not be obtained except by commerce, inasmuch as it is a stranger to the Alps. It would appear, therefore, more natural to admit that the art of combining tin with copper—in other words, *that the manufacture of bronze—was of foreign importation.*" He then shows that, although copper ores are found in the Alps, the probability is that even " the copper also was of foreign importation. Now, in view of the prodigious quantity of bronze manufactured at that epoch, this single branch of commerce must itself have *necessitated the most incessant commercial communications.*"

And as this commerce could not, as we have seen, have been carried on by the Romans, Greeks, Etruscans, or Phœnicians, because their civilizations flourished during the Iron Age, to which this age of bronze was anterior, where then are we to look for a great maritime and commercial people, who carried vast quantities of copper, tin, and bronze (unalloyed by the lead of the south of Europe) to Denmark, Norway, Sweden, Ireland, England, France, Spain, Switzerland, and Italy? Where can we find them save in that people of Atlantis, whose ships, docks, canals, and commerce provoked the astonishment of the ancient Egyptians, as recorded by Plato. The Toltec root for water is *Atl;* the Peruvian word for copper is *Anti* (from which, probably, the Andes derived their name, as there was a province of Anti on their slopes) : may it not be that the name of Atlantis is derived from these originals, and signified the copper island, or the copper mountains in the sea? And from these came the thousands of tons of copper and tin that must, during the Bronze Age, have been introduced into Europe? There are no ancient works to indicate that the tin mines of Cornwall were worked for any length of time in the early days (see " Prehistoric Times," p. 74). Morlot has pointed out that the bronze implements of Hallstadt, in Austria, were of foreign origin, because they contain no lead or silver.

Or, if we are to seek for the source of the vast amount of copper brought into Europe somewhere else than in Atlantis, may it not be that these supplies were drawn in large part from the shores of Lake Superior in America? The mining operations of some ancient people were there carried on upon a gigantic scale, not only along the shores of the lake but even far out upon its islands. At Isle Royale vast works were found, reaching to a depth of sixty feet; great intelligence was shown in following up the richest veins even when interrupted; the excavations were drained by underground drains. On three sections of land on this island the amount of mining exceeded that mined in twenty years in one of our largest mines, with a numerous force constantly employed. In one place the excavations extended in a nearly continuous line for two miles. No remains of the dead and no mounds are found near these mines; it would seem, therefore, that the miners came from a distance, and carried their dead back with them. Henry Gillman ("Smithsonian Rep.," 1873, p. 387) supposes that the curious so-called "Garden Beds" of Michigan were the fields from which they drew their supplies of food. He adds,

"The discoveries in Isle Royale throw a new light on the character of the 'Mound Builders,' giving us a totally distinct conception of them, and dignifying them with something of the prowess and spirit of adventure which we associate with the higher races. The copper, the result of their mining, to be available, must, in all probability, have been conveyed in vessels, great or small, across a treacherous and stormy sea, whose dangers are formidable to us now, being dreaded even by our largest craft, and often proving their destruction. Leaving their homes, those men dared to face the unknown, to brave the hardships and perils of the deep and of the wilderness, actuated by an ambition which we to-day would not be ashamed to acknowledge."

Such vast works in so remote a land must have been inspired by the commercial necessities of some great civilization; and why not by that ancient and mighty people who covered Europe, Asia, and Africa with their manufactures of bronze—and who possessed, as Plato tells us, enormous fleets trading to all parts of the inhabited world—whose cities roared with the continual tumult of traffic, whose dominion extended to Italy and Egypt, and who held parts of "the great opposite continent" of America under their control? A continuous water-way led from the island of Atlantis to the Gulf of Mexico, and thence up the Mississippi River and its tributaries almost to these very mines of Lake Superior.

Arthur Mitchell says ("The Past in the Present," p. 132),

"The discovery of bronze, and the knowledge of how to make it, may, as a mere intellectual effort, be regarded as rather above than below the effort which is involved in the discovery and use of iron. As regards bronze, there is first the discovery of copper, and the way of getting it from its ore; then the discovery of tin, and the way to get it from its ore; and then the further discovery that, by an admixture of tin with copper in proper proportions, an alloy with the qualities of a hard metal can be produced. It is surely no mistake to say that there goes quite as much thinking to this as to the getting of iron from its ore, and the conversion of that iron into steel. There is a considerable leap from stone to bronze, but the leap from bronze to iron is comparatively small. . . . It seems highly improbable, if not altogether absurd, that the human mind, at some particular stage of its development, should here, there, and everywhere—independently, and as the result of reaching that stage—discover that an alloy of copper and tin yields a hard metal useful in the manufacture of tools and weapons. There is nothing analogous to such an occurrence in the known history of human progress. It is infinitely more probable that bronze was discovered in one or more centres by one or more men, and that its first use was solely in such centre or centres. That the invention should then be perfected, and its various applications found out, and that it should thereafter spread more or less broadly over the face of the earth, is a thing easily understood."

We will find the knowledge of bronze wherever the colonies of Atlantis extended, and nowhere else; and Plato tells us that the people of Atlantis possessed and used that metal.

The indications are that the Bronze Age represents the coming in of a new people—a civilized people. With that era, it is believed, appears in Europe for the first time the domesticated animals—the horse, the ox, the sheep, the goat, and the hog. (Morlot, "Smithsonian Rep.," 1860, p. 311.) It was a small race, with very small hands; this is shown in the size of the sword-hilts: they are not large enough to be used by the present races of Europe. They were a race with long skulls, as contradistinguished from the round heads of the Stone Period. The drawings on the following page represent the types of the two races.

This people must have sent out colonies to the shores of France, Spain, Italy, Ireland, Denmark, and Norway, who bore

A SKULL OF THE AGE OF STONE, DENMARK (¼ NATURAL SIZE).

A SKULL OF THE EARLIEST TIMES OF THE AGE OF IRON, DENMARK (¼ NATURAL SIZE). †

with them the arts and implements of civilized life. They raised crops of grain, as is proved by the bronze sickles found in different parts of Europe.

It is not even certain that their explorations did not reach to Iceland. Says Humboldt,

"When the Northmen first landed in Iceland (A.D. 875), although the country was uninhabited, they found there Irish books, mass-bells, and other objects which had been left behind by earlier visitors, called Papar; these papæ (fathers) were the clerici of Dicuil. If, then, as we may suppose from the testimony here referred to, these objects belonged to Irish monks (papar), who had come from the Faroe Islands, why should they have been termed in the native sagas 'West men' (Vestmen), '*who had come over the sea from the westward*' (kommer til vestan um haf)?" (Humboldt's "Cosmos," vol. ii., p. 238.)

If they came "from the West" they could not have come from Ireland; and the Scandinavians may easily have mistaken Atlantean books and bells for Irish books and mass-bells. They do not say that there were any evidences that these relics belonged to a people who had *recently* visited the island; and, as they found the island uninhabited, it would be impossible for them to tell how many years or centuries had elapsed since the books and bells were left there.

† The comparative size of the skulls is misleading.—E.F.B.

The fact that the implements of the Bronze Age came from some common centre, and did not originate independently in different countries, is proved by the striking similarity which exists between the bronze implements of regions as widely separated as Switzerland, Ireland, Denmark, and Africa. It is not to be supposed that any overland communication existed in that early age between these countries; and the coincidence of design which we find to exist can only be accounted for by the fact that the articles of bronze were obtained from some sea-going people, who carried on a commerce at the same time with all these regions.

Compare, for instance, these two decorated bronze celts, the first from Ireland, the second from Denmark; and then com-

IRISH CELT.   DANISH CELT.

Ireland.

Switzerland.

Denmark.

Sweden.

Leaf-shaped Stone Sword, from ancient Earthwork on Big Harpeth River, Tennessee. (¼ natural size.)

LEAF-SHAPED BRONZE SWORDS.

pare both these with a stone celt found in a mound in Tennessee, given below. Here we have the same form precisely.

Compare the bronze swords in the four preceding illustrations—from Ireland, Sweden, Switzerland, and Denmark—and
then observe the same very peculiar shape—
the leaf-shape, as it is called — in the stone
sword from Big Harpeth River, Tennessee.

We shall find, as we proceed, that the Phœnicians were unquestionably identified with
Atlantis, and that it was probably from Atlantis they derived their god Baal, or Bel, or
El, whose name crops out in the Bel of the
Babylonians, the Elohim, and the Beelzebub
of the Jews, and the Allah of the Arabians.
And we find that this great deity, whose worship extended so widely among the Mediterranean races, was known and adored also upon
the northern and western coasts of Europe.

STONE CELT, MOUND
IN TENNESSEE.

Professor Nilsson finds traces of Baal worship in Scandinavia;
he tells us that the festival of Baal, or Balder, was celebrated
on midsummer's night in Scania, and far up into Norway, almost to the Loffoden Islands, until within the last fifty years.
The feast of Baal, or Beltinne, was celebrated in Ireland to a
late period. I argue from these facts, not that the worship of
Baal came to Ireland and Norway from Assyria or Arabia, but
that the same great parent-race which carried the knowledge
of Baal to the Mediterranean brought it also to the western
coasts of Europe, and with the adoration of Baal they imported also the implements of bronze now found in such abundance
in those regions.

The same similarity of form exists in the bronze knives from
Denmark and Switzerland, as represented in the illustrations
on p. 254.

In the central figure we have a representation of an Egyp-
tian-looking man holding a cup before him. We shall see, as

we proceed, that the magnetic needle, or "mariner's compass," dates back to the days of Hercules, and that it consisted of a bar of magnetized iron floating upon a piece of wood *in a*

BRONZE KNIVES FROM DENMARK.

BRONZE KNIVES FROM SWITZERLAND.

cup. It is possible that in this ancient relic of the Bronze Age we have a representation of the magnetic cup. The magnetic needle must certainly have been an object of great interest to a people who, through its agency, were able to carry on commerce on all the shores of Europe, from the Mediterranean to the Baltic. The second knife represented above has upon its handle a wheel, or cross surrounded by a ring, which, we shall see hereafter, was pre-eminently the symbol of Atlantis.

If we are satisfied that these implements of bronze were the work of the artisans of Atlantis—of the antediluvians—they must acquire additional and extraordinary interest in our eyes, and we turn to them to learn something of the habits and customs of "that great, original, broad-eyed, sunken race."

We find among the relics of the Bronze Age an urn, which probably gives us some idea of the houses of the Atlanteans: it is evidently made to represent a house, and shows us even the rude fashion in which they fast-

HUT URN, ALBANO.

ened their doors. The Mandan Indians built round houses very much of this appearance.

The museum at Munich contains a very interesting piece of pottery, which is supposed to represent one of the lake

BRONZE LAKE VILLAGE.

villages or hamlets of the era when the people of Switzerland dwelt in houses erected on piles driven into the bottom of the lakes of that country. The accompanying illustration represents it. The double spiral ornament upon it shows that it belongs to the Bronze Age.

Among the curious relics of the Bronze Age are a number of razor-like knives; from which we may conclude that the habit of shaving the whole or some part of the face or head

dates back to a great antiquity. The illustrations below represent them.

These knives were found in Denmark. The figures upon
them represent ships, and it is not impossible that their curious appendages may have been a primitive kind of sails.

An examination of the second of these bronze knives reveals
a singular feature: Upon the handle of the razor there are *ten*

BRONZE RAZOR-KNIVES.

series of lines; the stars in the sky are *ten* in number; and
there were probably *ten* rings at the left-hand side of the figure, two being obliterated. There were, we are told, ten sub-
kingdoms in Atlantis; and precisely as the thirteen stripes on
the American flag symbolize the thirteen original States of the
Union, so the recurrence of the figure ten in the emblems upon

this bronze implement may have reference to the ten sub-divisions of Atlantis. The large object in the middle of this ship may be in-tended to represent a palm-tree — the symbol, as we shall see, in America, of Aztlan, or Atlantis. We have but to compare the pictures of the ships upon these ancient razor-knives with the ac-

ANCIENT GALLEY, FROM A
ROMAN COIN.

companying representations of a Roman galley and a ship of William the Conqueror's time, to see that there can be no question that they represented the galleys of that remote age. They are doubtless faithful portraits of the great vessels which Plato described as filling the harbors of Atlantis.

SHIP OF WILLIAM THE CONQUEROR.

We give on page 258 a representation of a bronze dagger found in Ireland, a strongly-made weapon. The cut below it represents the only implement of the Bronze Age yet found con-taining an inscription. It has been impossible to decipher it, or even to tell to what group of languages its alphabet belongs.

IRISH BRONZE DAGGER.

It is proper to note, in connection with a discussion of the Bronze Age, that our word bronze is derived from the Basque, or Iberian *broncea*, from which the Spanish derive *bronce*, and the Italians *bronzo*. The copper mines of the Basques were extensively worked at a very early age of the world, either by the people of Atlantis or by the Basques themselves, a colony from Atlantis. The probabilities are that the name for bronze, as well as the metal itself, dates back to Plato's island.

I give some illustrations on pages 239 and 242 of ornaments and implements of the Bronze Age, which may serve to throw light upon the habits of the ancient people. It will be seen that they had reached a considerable degree of civilization; that they raised crops of grain, and cut them with sickles; that their women ornamented themselves with bracelets, armlets, earrings, finger-rings, hair-pins, and amulets; that their mechanics used hammers, adzes, and chisels; and that they possessed very fair specimens of pottery. Sir John Lubbock argues ("Prehistoric Times," pp. 14, 16, etc.):

"A new civilization is indicated not only by the mere presence of bronze

INSCRIBED CELT.

but by the beauty and variety of the articles made from it. We find not only, as before, during the Stone Age, axes, arrows, and knives, but, in addition, swords, lances, sickles, fish-hooks, ear-rings, bracelets, pins, rings, and a variety of other articles."

If the bronze implements of Europe had been derived from the Phœnicians, Greeks, Etruscans, or Romans, the nearer we approached the site of those nations the greater should be the number of bronze weapons we would find; but the reverse is the case. Sir John Lubbock ("Prehistoric Times," p. 20) shows that more than three hundred and fifty bronze swords have been found in Denmark, and that the Dublin Museum contains twelve hundred and eighty-three bronze weapons found in Ireland; "while," he says, "I have only been able to hear of six bronze swords in all Italy." This state of things is inexplicable unless we suppose that Ireland and Denmark received their bronze implements directly from some maritime nation whose

BRONZE HAIR-PINS.

site was practically as near their shores as it was to the shores of the Mediterranean. We have but to look at our map on page 43, *ante,* to see that Atlantis was considerably nearer to Ireland than it was to Italy.

The striking resemblance between the bronze implements found in the different portions of Europe is another proof that they were derived from one and the same source—from some great mercantile people who carried on their commerce at the same time with Denmark, Norway, Ireland, Spain, Greece, Italy, Egypt, Switzerland, and Hungary. Mr. Wright ("Essays on Archæology," p. 120) says, "Whenever we find the bronze swords or celts, whether in Ireland, in the far west, in Scotland, in distant Scandinavia, in Germany, or still farther east, in the Sclavonic countries, they are the same—*not similar in character, but identical.*" Says Sir John Lubbock ("Prehistoric Times," p. 59), "Not only are the several varieties of celts

VASES FROM MOUNDS IN THE MISSISSIPPI VALLEY.

found throughout Europe alike, but some of the swords, knives, daggers, etc., are so similar that they seem as if they must have been cast by the same maker."

What race was there, other than the people of Atlantis, that existed before the Iron Age—before the Greek, Roman, Etrus-

can, and Phœnician—that was civilized, that worked in metals,
that carried on a commerce with all parts of Europe? Does
history or tradition make mention of any such?

We find a great resemblance between the pottery of the
Bronze Age in Europe and the pottery of the ancient inhabitants of America. The two figures on page 260 represent vases
from one of the mounds of the Mississippi Valley. Compare
them with the following from the lake dwellings of Switzerland :

VASES FROM SWITZERLAND.

It will be seen that these vases could scarcely stand upright
unsupported; and we find that
the ancient inhabitants of Switzerland had circles or rings of
baked earth in which they placed
them when in use, as in the annexed figure. The Mound Builders used the same contrivance.

The illustrations of discoidal
stones on page 263 are from the
"North Americans of Antiquity,"
p. 77. The objects represented
were taken from an ancient
mound in Illinois. It would be
indeed surprising if two distinct

ANCIENT SWISS VASE AND SUP-
PORTER.

peoples, living in two different continents, thousands of miles apart, should, without any intercourse with each other, not only form their vases in the same inconvenient form, but should hit upon the same expedient as a remedy.

We observe, in the American spear-head and the Swiss hatchets, on the opposite page, the same overlapping of the metal around the staff, or handle—a very peculiar mode of uniting them together, which has now passed out of use.

A favorite design of the men of the Bronze Age in Europe is the spiral or double-spiral form. It appears on the face of the urn in the shape of a lake dwelling, which is given on p. 255; it also appears in the rock sculptures of Argyleshire, Scotland, here shown.

Central America.   Switzerland.
BRONZE CHISELS.

SPIRALS, FROM SCOTLAND.

We find the same figure in an ancient fragment of pottery from the Little Colorado, as given in the

SPIRAL, FROM NEW MEXICO.

"United States Pacific Railroad Survey Report," vol. iii., p. 49, art. *Pottery.* It was part of a large vessel. The annexed illustration represents this.

The same design is also found in ancient rock etchings of the Zuñis of New Mexico, of which the cut on p. 265 is an illustration.

DISCOIDAL STONES, ILLINOIS.

COPPER SPEAR-HEAD,
LAKE SUPERIOR.

BRONZE HATCHETS, SWITZERLAND.

We also find this figure repeated upon a vase from a Mississippi Valley mound, which we give elsewhere. (See p. 260.)

SPIRAL, FROM NEW MEXICO.

It is found upon many of the monuments of Central America. In the Treasure House of Atreus, at Mycenæ, Greece, a fragment of a pillar was found which is literally covered with this double-spiral design. (See "Rosengarten's Architectural Styles," p. 59.)

This Treasure House of Atreus is one of the oldest buildings in Greece.

We find the double-spiral figure upon a shell ornament found on the breast of a skeleton, in a carefully constructed stone coffin, in a mound near Nashville, Tennessee.

Lenormant remarks ("Anc. Civil.," vol. ii., p. 158) that the bronze implements found in Egypt, near Memphis, had been buried for six thousand years; and that at that time, as the Egyptians had a horror of the sea, some commercial nation must have brought

SHELL ORNAMENT, MOUND NEAR NASHVILLE, TENNESSEE.

the tin, of which the bronze was in part composed, from India, the Caucasus, or Spain, the nearest points to Egypt in which tin is found.

Heer has shown that the civilized plants of the lake dwellings are not of Asiatic, but of African, and, to a great extent, of Egyptian origin. Their stone axes are made largely of jade or nephrite, "a mineral which, strange to say, geologists *have*

not found in place on the continent of Europe." (Foster's "Prehistoric Races," p. 44.)

Compare this picture of a copper axe from a mound near Laporte, Indiana, with this representation of a copper axe of the Bronze Age, found near Waterford, Ire-

COPPER AXE, FROM A MOUND NEAR LAPORTE, INDIANA.

COPPER AXE, WATER-FORD, IRELAND.

land. Professor Foster pronounces them almost identical.

Compare this specimen of pottery from the lake dwellings of Switzerland with the following specimen from San José,

FRAGMENT OF POTTERY, LAKE NEUF-CHATEL, SWITZERLAND.

FRAGMENT OF POTTERY, SAN JOSÉ, MEXICO.

Mexico. Professor Foster calls attention to the striking resemblance in the designs of these two widely separated works of art, one belonging to the Bronze Age of Europe, the other to the Copper Age of America.

These, then, in conclusion, are our reasons for believing that the Bronze Age of Europe has relation to Atlantis:

1. The admitted fact that it is anterior in time to the Iron Age relegates it to a great antiquity.

2. The fact that it is anterior in time to the Iron Age is

conclusive that it is not due to any of the known European or Asiatic nations, all of which belong to the Iron Age. †

3. The fact that there was in Europe, Asia, or Africa no copper or tin age prior to the Bronze Age, is conclusive testimony that the manufacture of bronze was an importation into those continents from some foreign country.

4. The fact that in America alone of all the world is found the Copper Age, which must necessarily have preceded the Bronze Age, teaches us to look to the westward of Europe and beyond the sea for that foreign country.

5. We find many similarities in forms of implements between the Bronze Age of Europe and the Copper Age of America.

6. If Plato told the truth, the Atlanteans were a great commercial nation, trading to America and Europe, and, at the same time, they possessed bronze, and were great workers in the other metals.

7. We shall see hereafter that the mythological traditions of Greece referred to a Bronze Age which preceded an Iron Age, and placed this in the land of the gods, which was an island in the Atlantic Ocean, beyond the Pillars of Hercules; and this land was, as we shall see, clearly Atlantis.

8. As we find but a small development of the Bronze Age in America, it is reasonable to suppose that there must have been some intermediate station between America and Europe, where, during a long period of time, the Bronze Age was developed out of the Copper Age, and immense quantities of bronze implements were manufactured and carried to Europe.

† Donnelly ignored the question of relative age. He should have known that the Indian material was thousands of years younger than the European.—E.F.B.

Chapter IX.

ARTIFICIAL DEFORMATION OF THE SKULL.

An examination of the American monuments shows (see figure on page 269) that the people represented were in the habit of flattening the skull by artificial means. The Greek and Roman writers had mentioned this practice, but it was long totally forgotten by the civilized world, until it was discovered, as an unheard-of wonder, to be the usage among the Carib Islanders, and several Indian tribes in North America. It was afterward found that the ancient Peruvians and Mexicans practised this art: several flattened Peruvian skulls are depicted in Morton's "Crania Americana." It is still in use among the Flat-head Indians of the north-western part of the United States.

In 1849 a remarkable memoir appeared from the pen of M. Rathke, showing that similar skulls had been found near Kertsch, in the Crimea, and calling attention to the book of Hippocrates, "De Aeris, Aquis et Locu," lib. iv., and a passage of Strabo, which speaks of the practice among the Scythians. In 1854 Dr. Fitzinger published a learned memoir on the skulls of the Avars, a branch of the Uralian race of Turks. He shows that the practice of flattening the head had existed from an early date throughout the East, and described an ancient skull, greatly distorted by artificial means, which had lately been found in Lower Austria. Skulls similarly flattened have been found in Switzerland and Savoy. The Huns under Attila had the same practice of flattening the heads. Professor Anders Retzius proved (see "Smithsonian Report," 1859) that the custom *still exists in the south of France, and in parts of Turkey.*

"Not long since a French physician surprised the world by the fact that nurses in Normandy were still giving the children's heads a sugar-loaf shape by bandages and a tight cap,

STUCCO BASS-RELIEF IN THE PALACE OF PALENQUE.

while in Brittany they preferred to press it round. No doubt they are doing so to this day." (Tylor's "Anthropology," p. 241.)

Professor Wilson remarks:

"Trifling as it may appear, it is not without interest to have the fact brought under our notice, by the disclosures of ancient

barrows and cysts, that the same practice of nursing the child
and carrying it about, bound to a flat cradle-board, prevailed in
Britain and the north of Europe long before the first notices of
written history reveal the presence of man beyond the Baltic or
the English Channel, and that in all probability the same custom prevailed continuously from the shores of the German Ocean
to Behring's Strait." ("Smithsonian Report," 1862, p. 286.)

Dr. L. A. Gosse testifies to the prevalence of the same custom
among the Caledonians and Scandinavians in the earliest times;
and Dr. Thurman has treated of the same peculiarity among
the Anglo-Saxons. ("Crania Britannica," chap. iv., p. 38.)

ANCIENT SWISS SKULL.

Here, then, is an extraordinary and unnatural practice which has existed from
the highest antiquity, over
vast regions of country, on
both sides of the Atlantic,
and which is perpetuated
unto this day in races as
widely separated as the
Turks, the French, and the
Flat-head Indians. Is it
possible to explain this except by supposing that it
originated from some com-
mon centre?

The annexed cut repre-
sents an ancient Swiss skull,
from a cemetery near Lau-
sanne, from a drawing of Frederick Troyon. Compare this with
the illustration given on page 271, which represents a Peruvian
flat-head, copied from Morton's "Ethnography and Archæology
of the American Aborigines," 1846. This skull is shockingly
distorted. The dotted lines indicate the course of the bandages by which the skull was deformed.

PERUVIAN SKULL.

CHINOOK (FLAT-HEAD), AFTER CATLIN.

The following heads are from Del Rio's "Account of Palenque," copied into Nott and Gliddon's "Types of Mankind," p. 440. They show that the receding forehead was a natural characteristic of the ancient people of Central America. The same form of head has been found even in fossil skulls. We may therefore conclude that the skull-flattening, which we find to have been practised in both the Old and New Worlds, was

an attempt of other races to imitate the form of skull of a people whose likenesses are found on the monuments of Egypt
and of America. It has been shown that this peculiar form
of the head was present even in the fœtus of the Peruvian
mummies.

Hippocrates tells us that the practice among the Scythians
was for the purpose of giving a certain aristocratic distinction.

HEADS FROM PALENQUE.

Amedée Thierry, in his "History of Attila," says the Huns
used it for the same reason; and the same purpose influences
the Indians of Oregon.

Dr. Lund, a Swedish naturalist, found in the bone caves
of Minas-Geraes, Brazil, ancient human bones associated with
the remains of extinct quadrupeds. "These skulls," says Lund,
"show not only the peculiarity of the American race but in an
excessive degree, *even to the entire disappearance of the forehead.*" Sir Robert Schomburgh found on some of the affluents
of the Orinoco a tribe known as Frog Indians, whose heads
were flattened by Nature, as shown in newly-born children.

In the accompanying plate we show the difference in the conformation of the forehead in various races. The upper dotted line, A, represents the shape of the European forehead; the next line, B, that of the Australian; the next, C, that of the Mound Builder of the United States; the next, D, that of the

OUTLINES OF SKULLS OF DIFFERENT RACES.

Guanche of the Canary Islands; and the next, E, that of a skull from the Inca cemetery of Peru. We have but to compare these lines with the skulls of the Egyptians, Kurds, and the heroic type of heads in the statues of the gods of Greece, to see that there was formerly an ancient race marked by a receding forehead; and that the practice of flattening the skull was probably an attempt to approximate the shape of the head to this standard of an early civilized and dominant people.

Not only do we find the same receding forehead in the skulls of the ancient races of Europe and America, and the same attempt to imitate this natural and peculiar conformation by artificial flattening of the head, but it has been found (see Henry Gillman's "Ancient Man in Michigan," "Smithsonian Report," 1875, p. 242) that the Mound Builders and Peruvians of America, and the Neolithic people of France and *the Canary Islands*, had alike an extraordinary custom of boring a circular hole in the top of the skulls of their dead, so that the soul might readily pass in and out. More than this, it has been found that in all these ancient populations the skeletons exhibit a remarkable degree of *platicnemism*, or flattening of the *tibiæ* or leg bones. (*Ibid.*, 1873, p. 367.) In this respect the Mound Builders of Michigan were identical with the man of Cro Magnon and the ancient inhabitants of Wales.

The annexed ancient Egyptian heads, copied from the monuments, indicate either that the people of the Nile deformed their heads by pressure upon the front of the skull, or that

EGYPTIAN HEADS.

there was some race characteristic which gave this appearance to their heads. These heads are all the heads of priests, and therefore represented the aristocratic class.

The first illustration below is taken from a stucco relief

CENTRAL AMERICAN HEAD.   EGYPTIAN HEAD.

found in a temple at Palenque, Central America. The second is from an Egyptian monument of the time of Rameses IV.

The outline drawing on the following page shows the form

of the skull of the royal Inca line : the receding forehead here seems to be natural, and not the result of artificial compression.

Both illustrations at the bottom of the preceding page show the same receding form of the forehead, due to either artificial deformation of the skull or to a common race characteristic.

We must add the fact that the extraordinary practice of deforming the skull was found all over Europe and America to the catalogue of other proofs that the people of both continents were originally united in blood and race. With the couvade, the practice of circumcision, unity of religious beliefs and customs, folk-lore, and alphabetical signs, language and flood legends, we array together a mass of unanswerable proofs of prehistoric identity of race.

PERUVIAN INCA SKULL, FROM THE ANCIENT CEMETERY OF PACHACAMAC.

PART IV.

THE MYTHOLOGIES OF THE OLD WORLD
A RECOLLECTION OF ATLANTIS.

Chapter I.
TRADITIONS OF ATLANTIS.

We find allusions to the Atlanteans in the most ancient traditions of many different races.

The great *antediluvian* king of the Mussulman was Shedd-Ad-Ben-Ad, or Shed-Ad, the son of Ad, or Atlantis.

Among the Arabians the first inhabitants of that country are known as the *Adites*, from their progenitor, who is called *Ad*, the grandson of Ham. These *Adites* were probably the people of Atlantis or Ad-lantis. "They are personified by a monarch *to whom everything is ascribed,* and to whom is assigned several centuries of life." ("Ancient History of the East," Lenormant and Chevallier, vol. ii., p. 295.) Ad came from the northeast. "He married a thousand wives, had four thousand sons, and lived twelve hundred years. His descendants multiplied considerably. After his death his sons Shadid and Shedad reigned in succession over the Adites. In the time of the latter the people of Ad were a thousand tribes, each composed of several thousands of men. Great conquests are attributed to Shedad; he subdued, it is said, all Arabia and Irak. The migration of the Canaanites, their establishment in Syria, and the Shepherd invasion of Egypt are, by many Arab writers, attributed to an expedition of Shedad." (*Ibid.,* p. 296.)

Shedad built a palace ornamented with superb columns, and surrounded by a magnificent garden. It was called Irem. " It was a paradise that Shedad had built in imitation of the celestial Paradise, of whose delights he had heard." ("Ancient History of the East," p. 296.) In other words, an ancient, sun-worshipping, powerful, and conquering race overran Arabia at the very dawn of history; they were the sons of Adlantis: their king tried to create a palace and garden of Eden like that of Atlantis.

The Adites are remembered by the Arabians as a great and civilized race. " They are depicted as men of gigantic stature; their strength was equal to their size, and they easily moved enormous blocks of stone." (*Ibid.*) They were architects and builders. " They raised many monuments of their power; and hence, among the Arabs, arose the custom of calling great ruins " buildings of the Adites." To this day the Arabs say " as old as Ad." In the Koran allusion is made to the edifices they built on " high places for vain uses;" expressions proving that their " idolatry was considered to have been tainted with Sabæism or star-worship." (*Ibid.*) " In these legends," says Lenormant, " we find traces of a wealthy nation, constructors of great buildings, with an advanced civilization, analogous to that of Chaldea, professing a religion similar to the Babylonian; a nation, in short, with whom material progress was allied to great moral depravity and obscene rites. These facts must be true and strictly historical, for they are everywhere met with among the Cushites, as among the Canaanites, their brothers by origin."

Nor is there wanting a great catastrophe which destroys the whole Adite nation, except a very few who escape because they had renounced idolatry. A black cloud assails their country, from which proceeds a terrible hurricane (the water-spout?) which sweeps away everything.

The first Adites were followed by a second Adite race; probably the colonists who had escaped the Deluge. The centre of its power was the country of Sheba proper. This empire endured for a thousand years. The Adites are represented upon the Egyptian monuments as very much like the Egyptians themselves; in other words, they were a red or sunburnt race : their great temples were pyramidal, surmounted by buildings. ("Ancient History of the East," p. 321.) "The Sabæans," says Agatharchides ("De Mari Erythræo," p. 102), "have in their houses an incredible number of vases, and utensils of all sorts, of gold and silver, beds and tripods of silver, and all the furniture of astonishing richness. Their buildings have porticos with columns sheathed with gold, or surmounted by capitals of silver. On the friezes, ornaments, and the framework of the doors they place plates of gold incrusted with precious stones."

All this reminds one of the descriptions given by the Spaniards of the temples of the sun in Peru.

The Adites worshipped the gods of the Phœnicians under names but slightly changed; " their religion was especially solar. . . . It was originally a religion without images, without idolatry, and without a priesthood." (*Ibid.*, p. 325.) They " worshipped the sun from the tops of pyramids." (*Ibid.*) They believed in the immortality of the soul.

In all these things we see resemblances to the Atlanteans.

The great Ethiopian or Cushite Empire, which in the earliest ages prevailed, as Mr. Rawlinson says, "from the Caucasus to the Indian Ocean, from the shores of the Mediterranean to the mouth of the Ganges," was the empire of Dionysos, the empire of "Ad," the empire of Atlantis. El Eldrisi called the language spoken to this day by the Arabs of Mahrah, in Eastern Arabia, "the language of the people of Ad," and Dr. J. H. Carter, in the *Bombay Journal* of July, 1847, says, "It is the softest and sweetest language I have ever heard." It would be interesting to compare this primitive tongue with the languages of Central America.

The god Thoth of the Egyptians, who was the god of a foreign country, and who invented letters, was called *At*-hothes.

We turn now to another ancient race, the Indo-European family—the Aryan race.

In Sanscrit *Adim* means *first.* Among the Hindoos the first man was *Ad*-ima, his wife was Heva. They *dwelt upon an island,* said to be Ceylon ; they left the island and reached the main-land, when, by a great convulsion of nature, their communication with the parent land was forever cut off. (See " Bible in India.")

Here we seem to have a recollection of the destruction of Atlantis.

Mr. Bryant says, "Ad and Ada signify *the first.*" The Persians called the first man " Ad-amah." " Adon " was one of the names of the Supreme God of the Phœnicians ; from it was derived the name of the Greek god "Ad-onis." The Arv-*ad* of Genesis was the Ar-*Ad* of the Cushites ; it is now known as Ru-*Ad.* It is a series of connected cities *twelve miles in length,* along the coast, full of the most massive and gigantic ruins.

Sir William Jones gives the tradition of the Persians as to the earliest ages. He says : " Moshan assures us that in the opinion of the best informed Persians the first monarch of Iran, *and of the whole earth,* was Mashab-*Ad;* that he received from the Creator, and promulgated among men a sacred book, *in a heavenly language,* to which the Mussulman author gives the Arabic title of ' Desatir,' or ' Regulations.' Mashab-*Ad* was, in the opinion of the ancient Persians, the person left at the end of the last great cycle, and consequently *the father of the present world.* He and his wife having survived the former cycle, were blessed with a numerous progeny ; he planted *gardens,* invented ornaments, forged weapons, taught men to take the fleece from sheep and make clothing ; he built cities, constructed palaces, fortified towns, and introduced arts and commerce."

We have already seen that the primal gods of this people are identical with the gods of the Greek mythology, and were originally kings of Atlantis. But it seems that these ancient divinities are grouped together as "*the Aditya;*" and in this name "Ad-itya" we find a strong likeness to the Semitic "Adites," and another reminiscence of Atlantis, or Adlantis. In corroboration of this view we find,

1. The gods who are grouped together as the Aditya are the most ancient in the Hindoo mythology.

2. They are all gods of light, or solar gods. (Whitney's "Oriental and Linguistic Studies," p. 39.)

3. There are *twelve* of them. (*Ibid.*)

4. These twelve gods presided over twelve months in the year.

5. They are a dim recollection of a very remote past. Says Whitney, "It seems as if here was an attempt on the part of the Indian religion to take a new development in a moral direction, which a change in the character and circumstances of the people has caused to fail in the midst, and fall back again into forgetfulness, while yet half finished and indistinct." (*Ibid.*)

6. These gods are called "the sons of Aditi," just as in the Bible we have allusions to "the sons of Adah," who were the first metallurgists and musicians. "Aditi" is not a goddess. She is addressed as a queen's daughter, "she of fair children."

7. The Aditya "are elevated above all imperfections; they do not sleep or wink." The Greeks represented their gods as equally wakeful and omniscient. "Their character is all truth; they hate and punish guilt." We have seen the same traits ascribed by the Greeks to the Atlantean kings.

8. The sun is sometimes addressed as an Aditya.

9. Among the Aditya is Varuna, the equivalent of Uranos, whose identification with Atlantis I have shown. In the vedas Varuna is "the god of the *ocean.*"

10. The Aditya represent an earlier and purer form of religion: "While in hymns to the other deities long life, wealth, power, are the objects commonly prayed for, of the Aditya is

craved purity, forgiveness of sin, freedom from guilt, and repentance." ("Oriental and Linguistic Studies," p. 43.)

11. The Aditya, like the Adites, are identified with the doctrine of the immortality of the soul. Yama is the god of the abode beyond the grave. In the Persian story he appears as Yima, and "*is made ruler of the golden age and founder of the Paradise.*" (*Ibid.*, p. 45.) (See "Zamna," p. 167 *ante*.)

In view of all these facts, one cannot doubt that the legends of the "sons of Ad," "the Adites," and "the Aditya," all refer to Atlantis.

Mr. George Smith, in the Chaldean account of the Creation (p. 78), deciphered from the Babylonian tablets, shows that there was an original race of men at the beginning of Chaldean history, a dark race, the *Zalmat-qaqadi*, who were called *Ad-mi*, or *Ad-ami;* they were the race "who had fallen," and were contradistinguished from "the *Sarku*, or light race." The "fall" probably refers to their destruction by a deluge, in consequence of their moral degradation and the indignation of the gods. The name *Adam* is used in these legends, but as the name of a race, not of a man.

Genesis (chap. v., 2) distinctly says that God created man male and female, and "called *their* name Adam." That is to say, the people were the Ad-ami, the people of "Ad," or Atlantis. "The author of the Book of Genesis," says M. Schœbel, "in speaking of the men who were swallowed up by the Deluge, always describes them as 'Haadam,' 'Adamite humanity.'" The race of Cain lived and multiplied far away from the land of Seth; in other words, far from the land destroyed by the Deluge. Josephus, who gives us the primitive traditions of the Jews, tells us (chap. ii., p. 42) that "Cain travelled over many countries" before he came to the land of Nod. The Bible does not tell us that the race of Cain perished in the Deluge. "Cain went out from the presence of Jehovah;" he did not call on his name; the people that were destroyed were the "sons of Jehovah." All this indicates that large colonies had been sent out by the mother-land before it sunk in the sea.

Across the ocean we find the people of Guatemala claiming their descent from a goddess called *At-tit*, or grandmother, who lived for four hundred years, and first taught the worship of the true God, which they afterward forgot. (Bancroft's " Native Races," vol. iii., p. 75.) While the famous Mexican calendar stone shows that the sun was commonly called *tonatiuh*, but when it was referred to as the god of the Deluge it was then called *Atl-tona-ti-uh*, or *At-onatiuh*. (Valentini's " Mexican Calendar Stone," art. *Maya Archæology*, p. 15.)

We thus find the sons of *Ad* at the base of all the most ancient races of men, to wit, the Hebrews, the Arabians, the Chaldeans, the Hindoos, the Persians, the Egyptians, the Ethiopians, the Mexicans, and the Central Americans; testimony that all these races traced their beginning back to a dimly-remembered Ad-lantis.

Chapter II.

THE KINGS OF ATLANTIS BECOME THE GODS OF THE GREEKS.

Lord Bacon said:

"The mythology of the Greeks, which their oldest writers do not pretend to have invented, was no more than a light air, which had passed from a more ancient people into the flutes of the Greeks, which they modulated to such descants as best suited their fancies."

This profoundly wise and great man, who has illuminated every subject which he has touched, guessed very close to the truth in this utterance.

The Hon. W. E. Gladstone has had quite a debate of late with Mr. Cox as to whether the Greek mythology was underlaid by a nature worship, or a planetary or solar worship.

Peru, worshipping the sun and moon and planets, probably represents very closely the simple and primitive religion of Atlantis, with its sacrifices of fruits and flowers. This passed directly to their colony in Egypt. We find the Egyptians in their early ages sun and planet worshippers. Ptah was the object of their highest adoration. He is the father of the god of the sun, the ruler of the region of light. Ra was the sun-god. He was the supreme divinity at On, or Heliopolis, near Memphis. His symbol was the solar disk, supported by two rings. He created all that exists below the heavens.

The Babylonian trinity was composed of Hea, Anu, and Bel. Bel represented the sun, and was the favorite god. Sin was the goddess of the moon.

The Phœnicians were also sun-worshippers. The sun was

represented by Baal-Samin, the great god, the god of light and the heavens, the creator and rejuvenator.

"The attributes of both Baal and Moloch (the good and bad powers of the sun) were united in the Phœnician god Melkart, "king of the city," whom the inhabitants of Tyre considered their special patron. The Greeks called him "Melicertes," and identified him with Hercules. By his great strength and power he turned evil into good, brought life out of destruction, pulled back the sun to the earth at the time of the solstices, lessened excessive heat and cold, and rectified the evil signs of the zodiac. In Phœnician legends *he conquers the savage races of distant coasts*, founds the ancient settlements on the Mediterranean, and plants the rocks in the Straits of Gibraltar. ("American Cyclopædia," art. *Mythology*.)

The Egyptians worshipped the sun under the name of Ra; the Hindoos worshipped the sun under the name of Rama; while the great festival of the sun, of the Peruvians, was called Ray-mi.

Sun-worship, as the ancient religion of Atlantis, underlies all the superstitions of the colonies of that country. The Samoyed woman says to the sun, "When thou, god, risest, I too rise from my bed." Every morning even now the Brahmans stand on one foot, with their hands held out before them and their faces turned to the east, adoring the sun. "In Germany or France one may still see the peasant take off his hat to the rising sun." ("Anthropology," p. 361.) The Romans, even, in later times, worshipped the sun at Emesa, under the name of Elagabalus, "typified in the form of a black conical stone, which it was believed had fallen from heaven." The conical stone was the emblem of Bel. Did it have relation to the mounds and pyramids?

Sun-worship was the primitive religion of the red men of America. It was found among all the tribes. (Dorman, "Origin of Primitive Superstitions, p. 338.) The Chichimecs called the sun their father. The Comanches have a similar belief.

But, compared with such ancient nations as the Egyptians

and Babylonians, the Greeks were children. A priest of Sais said to Solon,

"You Greeks are novices in knowledge of antiquity. You are ignorant of what passed either here or among yourselves in days of old. The history of eight thousand years is deposited in our sacred books; but I can ascend to a much higher antiquity, and tell you what our fathers have done for nine thousand years; I mean their institutions, their laws, and their most brilliant achievements."

The Greeks, too young to have shared in the religion of Atlantis, but preserving some memory of that great country and its history, proceeded to convert its kings into gods, and to depict Atlantis itself as the heaven of the human race. Thus we find a great solar or nature worship in the elder nations, while Greece has nothing but an incongruous jumble of gods and goddesses, who are born and eat and drink and make love and ravish and steal and die; and who are worshipped as immortal in presence of the very monuments that testify to their death.

"These deities, to whom the affairs of the world were intrusted, were, it is believed, immortal, though not eternal in their existence. In Crete there was even a story of the death of Zeus, his tomb being pointed out." (Murray's "Mythology," p. 2.)

The history of Atlantis is the key of the Greek mythology. There can be no question that these gods of Greece were human beings. The tendency to attach divine attributes to great earthly rulers is one deeply implanted in human nature. The savages who killed Captain Cook firmly believed that he was immortal, that he was yet alive, and would return to punish them. The highly civilized Romans made gods out of their dead emperors. Dr. Livingstone mentions that on one occasion, after talking to a Bushman for some time about the Deity, he found that the savage thought he was speaking of Sekomi, the principal chief of the district.

We find the barbarians of the coast of the Mediterranean re-

garding the civilized people of Atlantis with awe and wonder:
"Their physical strength was extraordinary, the earth shaking
sometimes under their tread. Whatever they did was done
speedily. They moved through space almost without the loss
of a moment of time." This probably alluded to the rapid
motion of their sailing-vessels. "They were wise, and communicated their wisdom to men." That is to say, they civilized the people they came in contact with. "They had a strict
sense of justice, and punished crime rigorously, and rewarded
noble actions, though it is true they were less conspicuous for
the latter." (Murray's "Mythology," p. 4.) We should understand this to mean that where they colonized they established
a government of law, as contradistinguished from the anarchy
of barbarism.

"There were tales of personal visits and adventures of the
gods among men, taking part in battles and appearing in
dreams. They were conceived to possess the form of human
beings, and to be, like men, subject to love and pain, but always characterized by the highest qualities and grandest forms
that could be imagined." (*Ibid.*)

Another proof that the gods of the Greeks were but the deified kings of Atlantis is found in the fact that "the gods were
not looked upon as having created the world." They succeeded to the management of a world already in existence.

The gods dwelt on Olympus. They lived together like human beings; they possessed palaces, storehouses, stables, horses,
etc.; "they dwelt in a social state which was but a magnified
reflection of the social system on earth. Quarrels, love passages, mutual assistance, and such instances as characterize human life, were ascribed to them." (*Ibid.*, p. 10.)

Where was Olympus? It was in Atlantis. "The ocean encircled the earth with a great stream, and was a region of wonders of all kinds." (*Ibid.*, p. 23.) It was a great island, the
then civilized world. The "encircling ocean" was spoken of
in all the ancient legends. "Okeanos lived there with his wife

Tethys: these were the *Islands of the Blessed*, the garden of the gods, the sources of the nectar and ambrosia on which the gods lived." (Murray's " Mythology," p. 23.) Nectar was probably a fermented intoxicating liquor, and ambrosia bread made from wheat. Soma was a kind of whiskey, and the Hindoos deified it. "The gods lived on nectar and ambrosia" simply meant that the inhabitants of these blessed islands were civilized, and possessed a liquor of some kind and a species of food superior to anything in use among the barbarous tribes with whom they came in contact.

This blessed land answers to the description of Atlantis. It was an island full of wonders. It lay spread out in the ocean "like a disk, with the mountains rising from it." (*Ibid.*) On the highest point of this mountain dwelt Zeus (the king), "while the mansions of the other deities were arranged upon plateaus, or in ravines lower down the mountain. These deities, including Zeus, were twelve in number: Zeus (or Jupiter), Hera (or Juno), Poseidon (or Neptune), Demeter (or Ceres), Apollo, Artemis (or Diana), Hephæstos (or Vulcan), Pallas Athena (or Minerva), Ares (or Mars), Aphrodite (or Venus), Hermes (or Mercury), and Hestia (or Vesta)." These were doubtless the twelve gods from whom the Egyptians derived their kings. Where two names are given to a deity in the above list, the first name is that bestowed by the Greeks, the last that given by the Romans.

It is not impossible that our division of the year into twelve parts is a reminiscence of the twelve gods of Atlantis. Diodorus Siculus tells us that among the Babylonians there were twelve gods of the heavens, each personified by one of the signs of the zodiac, and worshipped in a *certain month of the year.* The Hindoos had twelve primal gods, "the Aditya." Moses erected twelve pillars at Sinai. The Mandan Indians celebrated the Flood with twelve typical characters, who danced around the ark. The Scandinavians believed in the twelve gods, the Aesir, who dwelt on Asgard, the Norse Olympus.

Diligent investigation may yet reveal that the number of a modern jury, twelve, is a survival of the ancient council of Asgard.

"According to the traditions of the Phœnicians, the Gardens of the Hesperides were in *the remote west.*" (Murray's "Manual of Mythology," p. 258.) Atlas lived in these gardens. (*Ibid.,* p. 259.) Atlas, we have seen, was king of Atlantis. "The Elysian Fields (the happy islands) were commonly placed in *the remote west.* They were ruled over by Chronos." (*Ibid.,* p. 60.) Tartarus, the region of Hades, the gloomy home of the dead, was also located "under the mountains of an island in the *midst of the ocean* in the remote west." (*Ibid.,* p. 58.) Atlas was described in Greek mythology as " an enormous giant, who stood upon the *western confines of the earth,* and supported the heavens on his shoulders, in a region of the west where the sun continued to shine after he had set upon Greece." (*Ibid.,* p. 156.)

Greek tradition located the island in which Olympus was situated "in the far west," "in the ocean beyond Africa," "on the western boundary of the known world," "where the sun shone when it had ceased to shine on Greece," and where the mighty Atlas "held up the heavens." And Plato tells us that the land where Poseidon and Atlas ruled was Atlantis.

"The Garden of the Hesperides" (another name for the dwelling-place of the gods) "was situated *at the extreme limit of Africa.* Atlas was said to have surrounded it on every side with high mountains." (Smith's " Sacred Annals, Patriarchal Age," p. 131.) Here were found the golden apples.

This is very much like the description which Plato gives of the great plain of Atlantis, covered with fruit of every kind, and surrounded by precipitous mountains descending to the sea.

The Greek mythology, in speaking of the Garden of the Hesperides, tells us that "the outer edge of the garden was slightly raised, so that the water might not run in and overflow the land." Another reminiscence of the surrounding mountains of Atlantis as described by Plato, and as revealed by the deep-sea soundings of modern times.

Chronos, or Saturn, Dionysos, Hyperion, Atlas, Hercules, were all connected with "a great Saturnian continent;" they were kings that ruled over countries on the western shores of the Mediterranean, Africa and Spain.   One account says : "Hyperion, Atlas, and Saturn, or Chronos, were sons of Uranos, who reigned over a great kingdom composed of countries around the western part of the Mediterranean, *with certain islands in the Atlantic.*   Hyperion succeeded his father, and was then killed by the Titans.   The kingdom was then divided between Atlas and Saturn—Atlas taking Northern Africa, with the Atlantic islands, and Saturn the countries on the opposite shore of the Mediterranean to Italy and Sicily."   (Baldwin's "Prehistoric Nations," p. 357.)

Plato says, speaking of the traditions of the Greeks ("Dialogues, Laws," c. iv., p. 713), "There is a tradition of the happy life of mankind in the days when all things were spontaneous and abundant. . . . In like manner God in his love of mankind placed over us the demons, who are a superior race, and they, with great care and pleasure to themselves and no less to us, taking care of us and giving us place and reverence and order and justice never failing, made the tribes of men happy and peaceful . . . for Cronos knew that no human nature, invested with supreme power, is able to order human affairs and not overflow with insolence and wrong."

In other words, this tradition refers to an ancient time when the forefathers of the Greeks were governed by Chronos, of the Cronian Sea (the Atlantic), king of Atlantis, through civilized Atlantean governors, who by their wisdom preserved peace and created a golden age for all the populations under their control —they were the demons, that is, "the knowing ones," the civilized.

Plato puts into the mouth of Socrates these words ("Dialogues, Cratylus," p. 397) : "My notion would be that the sun, moon, and stars, earth, and heaven, which are still the gods of many barbarians, were the only gods known to the aboriginal Hellenes. . . . What shall follow the gods ?   Must not demons

and heroes and men come next ? . . . Consider the real meaning
of the word demons.   You know Hesiod uses the word.   He
speaks of ' a golden race of men ' who came first.   He says of
them,

> " ' But now that fate has *closed over this race*,
>   They are holy demons upon earth,
>   Beneficent averters of ills, guardians of mortal men.'

He means by the golden men not men literally made of gold,
but good and noble men ; he says we are of the ' age of iron.'
He called them demons because they were δαήμονες (knowing
or wise)."

This is made the more evident when we read that this region
of the gods, of Chronos and Uranos and Zeus, passed through,
first, a Golden Age, then a Silver Age — these constituting a
great period of peace and happiness; then it reached a Bronze
Age; then an Iron Age, and finally *perished by a great flood*,
sent upon these people by Zeus as a punishment for their sins.
We read :

"Men were rich then (in the Silver Age), as in the Golden
Age of Chronos, and lived in plenty ; but still they wanted the
innocence and contentment which were the true sources of human happiness in the former age ; and accordingly, while living in luxury and delicacy, they became overbearing in their
manners to the highest degree, were never satisfied, and forgot
the gods, to whom, in their confidence of prosperity and com-
fort, they denied the reverence they owed. . . . Then followed
the Bronze Age, a period of constant quarrelling and deeds of
violence.   Instead of cultivated lands, and a life of peaceful
occupations and orderly habits, there came a day when everywhere might was right, and men, big and powerful as they
were, became physically worn out. . . . Finally came the Iron
Age, in which enfeebled mankind had to toil for bread with
their hands, and, bent on gain, did their best to overreach
each other.   Dike, or Astræa, the goddess of justice and good
faith, modesty and truth, turned her back on such scenes, and
retired to Olympus, while Zeus determined to destroy the human race *by a great flood*.   The whole of Greece lay under water, and none but Deucalion and his wife Pyrrha were saved."
(Murray's " Mythology," p. 44.)

It is remarkable that we find here the same succession of the Iron Age after the Bronze Age that has been revealed to scientific men by the patient examination of the relics of antiquity in Europe. And this identification of the land that was destroyed by a flood — the land of Chronos and Poseidon and Zeus — with the Bronze Age, confirms the view expressed in Chapter VIII. (page 237, *ante*), that the bronze implements and weapons of Europe were mainly imported from Atlantis.

And here we find that the Flood that destroyed this land of the gods was the Flood of Deucalion, and the Flood of Deucalion was the Flood of the Bible, and this, as we have shown, was "the last great Deluge of all," according to the Egyptians, which destroyed Atlantis.

The foregoing description of the Golden Age of Chronos, when "men were rich and lived in plenty," reminds us of Plato's description of the happy age of Atlantis, when "men despised everything but virtue, not caring for their present state of life, and thinking lightly of the possession of gold and other property;" a time when, as the chants of the Delaware Indians stated it (page 109, *ante*), "all were willingly pleased, all were well-happified." While the description given by Murray in the above extract of the degeneracy of mankind in the land of the gods, "a period of constant quarrelling and deeds of violence, when might was right," agrees with Plato's account of the Atlanteans, when they became "aggressive," "unable to bear their fortune," "unseemly," "base," "filled with unrighteous avarice and power," and "in a most wretched state." And here again I might quote from the chant of the Delaware Indians—"they became troubled, hating each other; both were fighting, both were spoiling, both were never peaceful." And in all three instances the gods punished the depravity of mankind by a great deluge. Can all these precise coincidences be the result of accident?

May we not even suppose that the very word "Olympus" is a transformation from "Atlantis," in accordance with the laws that regulate the changes of letters of the same class into each other? Olympus was written by the Greeks "Olumpos." The letter *a* in Atlantis was sounded by the ancient world broad and full, like the *a* in our words *all* or *altar;* in these words it approximates very closely to the sound of *o.* It is not far to go to convert Otlontis into Oluntos, and this into Olumpos. We may, therefore, suppose that when the Greeks said that their gods dwelt in "Olympus," it was the same as if they said that they dwelt in "Atlantis."

Nearly all the gods of Greece are connected with Atlantis. We have seen the twelve principal gods all dwelling on the mountain of Olympus, in the midst of an island in the ocean in the far west, which was subsequently destroyed by a deluge on account of the wickedness of its people. And when we turn to Plato's description of Atlantis (p. 13, *ante*) we find that Poseidon and Atlas dwelt upon a mountain in the midst of the island; and on this mountain were their magnificent temples and palaces, where they lived, separated by great walls from their subjects.

It may be urged that Mount Olympus could not have referred to any mountain in Atlantis, because the Greeks gave that name to a group of mountains partly in Macedonia and partly in Thessaly. But in Mysia, Lycia, Cyprus, and elsewhere there were mountains called Olympus; and on the plain of Olympia, in Elis, there was an eminence bearing the same designation. There is a natural tendency among uncivilized peoples to give a "local habitation" to every general tradition.

"Many of the oldest myths," says Baldwin ("Prehistoric Nations," p. 376), "relate to Spain, North-western Africa, and other regions on the Atlantic, such as those concerning Hercules, the Cronidæ, the Hyperboreans, the Hesperides, and the Islands of the Blessed. Homer described the Atlantic region of Europe in his account of the wanderings of Ulysses. . . . In the ages previous to the decline of Phœnician influence in Greece and around the Ægean Sea, the people of those regions must have had a much better knowledge of Western

Europe than prevailed there during the Ionian or Hellenic period."

The mythology of Greece is really a history of the kings of Atlantis. The Greek heaven was Atlantis. Hence the refer-ences to statues, swords, etc., that fell from heaven, and were preserved in the temples of the different states along the shores of the Mediterranean from a vast antiquity, and which were regarded as the most precious possessions of the people. They were relics of the lost race received in the early ages. Thus we read of the brazen or bronze anvil that was preserved in one city, which fell from heaven, and was nine days and nine nights in falling; in other words, it took nine days and nights of a sailing-voyage to bring it from Atlantis.

The modern theory that the gods of Greece never had any personal existence, but represented atmospheric and meteoro-logical myths, the movements of clouds, planets, and the sun, is absurd. Rude nations repeat, they do not invent; to sup-pose a barbarous people creating their deities out of clouds and sunsets is to reverse nature. Men first worship stones, then other men, then spirits. Resemblances of names prove noth-ing; it is as if one would show that the name of the great Napoleon meant "the lion of the desert" (Napo-leon), and should thence argue that Napoleon never existed, that he was a myth, that he represented power in solitude, or some such stuff. When we read that Jove whipped his wife, and threw her son out of the window, the inference is that Jove was a man, and actually did something like the thing described; certainly gods, sublimated spirits, aerial sprites, do not act after this fashion; and it would puzzle the myth-makers to prove that the sun, moon, or stars whipped their wives or flung recalcitrant young men out of windows. The history of Atlantis could be in part reconstructed out of the mythology of Greece; it is a history of kings, queens, and princes; of love-making, adulteries, rebellions, wars, murders, sea-voyages, and colonizations; of palaces, tem-ples, workshops, and forges; of sword-making, engraving and metallurgy; of wine, barley, wheat, cattle, sheep, horses, and agriculture generally. Who can doubt that it represents the history of a real people?

Uranos was the first god; that is to say, the first king of the great race. As he was at the commencement of all things, his symbol was the sky. He probably represented the race previous even to the settlement of Atlantis. He was a son of Gæa (the earth). He seems to have been the parent of three races—the Titans, the Hekatoncheires, and the Kyklopes or Cyclops.

I incline to the belief that these were civilized races, and that the peculiarities ascribed to the last two refer to the vessels in which they visited the shores of the barbarians.

The empire of the Titans was clearly the empire of Atlantis. "The most judicious among our mythologists" (says Dr. Rees, "New British Cyclopædia," art. *Titans*)—"such as Gerard Vossius, Marsham, Bochart, and Father Thomassin—are of opinion that the partition of the world among the sons of Noah—Shem, Ham, and Japheth—was the original of the tradition of *the same partition among Jupiter, Neptune, and Pluto,*" upon the breaking up of the great empire of the Titans. "The learned Pezron contends that the division which was made of this vast empire came, in after-times, to be taken for the partition of the whole world; that Asia remaining in the hands of Jupiter (Zeus), the most potent of the three brothers, made him looked upon as the god of Olympus; that the sea and islands which fell to Neptune occasioned their giving him the title of 'god of the sea;' and that Spain, the extremity of the then known world, thought to be a very low country in respect of Asia, and famous for its excellent mines of gold and silver, falling to Pluto, occasioned him to be taken for the 'god of the infernal regions.'" We should suppose that Pluto possibly ruled over the transatlantic possessions of Atlantis in America, over those "portions of the opposite continent" which Plato tells us were dominated by Atlas and his posterity, and which, being far beyond or below sunset, were the "under-world" of

THE EMPIRE OF ATLANTIS.

the ancients; while Atlantis, the Canaries, etc., constituted the island division with Western Africa and Spain. Murray tells us ("Mythology," p. 58) that Pluto's share of the kingdom was supposed to lie "in the remote west." The under-world of the dead was simply the world below the western horizon; "the home of the dead has to do with that *far west* region where the sun dies at night." ("Anthropology," p. 350.) "On the coast of Brittany, where Cape Raz stands out *westward into the ocean*, there is 'the Bay of Souls,' the launching-place where the departed spirits *sail off across the sea.*" (*Ibid.*) In like manner, Odysseus found the land of the dead in the ocean beyond the Pillars of Hercules. There, indeed, was the land of the mighty dead, the grave of the drowned Atlanteans.

"However this be," continues F. Pezron, "the empire of the Titans, according to the ancients, was very extensive; they possessed Phrygia, Thrace, a part of Greece, the island of Crete, and several other provinces to the inmost recesses of Spain. To these Sanchoniathon seems to join Syria; and Diodorus adds a part of Africa, and the kingdoms of Mauritania." The kingdoms of Mauritania embraced all that north-western region of Africa nearest to Atlantis in which are the Atlas Mountains, and in which, in the days of Herodotus, dwelt the Atlantes.

Neptune, or Poseidon, says, in answer to a message from Jupiter,

> No vassal god, nor of his train am I.
> Three brothers, deities, from Saturn came,
> And ancient Rhea, earth's immortal dame;
> Assigned by lot our triple rule we know;
> Infernal Pluto sways the shades below:
> O'er the wide clouds, and o'er the starry plain
> Ethereal Jove extends his high domain;
> My court beneath the hoary waves I keep,
> And hush the roaring of the sacred deep.
>
> *Iliad,* book xviii.

Homer alludes to Poseidon as

> "The god whose liquid arms are hurled
> Around the globe, whose earthquakes rock the world."

Mythology tells us that when the Titans were defeated by Saturn they retreated into the interior of Spain; Jupiter followed them up, and beat them for the last time near Tartessus, and thus terminated a ten-years' war. Here we have a real battle on an actual battle-field.

If we needed any further proof that the empire of the Titans was the empire of Atlantis, we would find it in the names of the Titans: among these were *Oceanus*, Saturn or Chronos, and *Atlas;* they were all the sons of Uranos. Oceanus was at the base of the Greek mythology. Plato says ("Dialogues," Timæus, vol. ii., p. 533): "Oceanus and Tethys were the children of Earth and Heaven, and from these sprung Phorcys, and Chronos, and Rhea, and many more with them; and from Chronos and Rhea sprung Zeus and Hera, and *all those whom we know as their brethren, and others who were their children.*" In other words, all their gods came out of the ocean; they were rulers over some ocean realm; Chronos was the son of Oceanus, and Chronos was an Atlantean god, and from him the Atlantic Ocean was called by the ancients "the Chronian Sea." The elder Minos was called "the Son of the Ocean:" he first gave civilization to the Cretans; he engraved his laws on brass, precisely as Plato tells us the laws of Atlantis were engraved on pillars of brass.

The wanderings of Ulysses, as detailed in the "Odyssey" of Homer, are strangely connected with the Atlantic Ocean. The islands of the Phæacians were apparently in mid-ocean:

> We dwell apart, afar
> Within the unmeasured deep, amid its waves
> The most remote of men; no other race
> Hath commerce with us.—*Odyssey*, book vi.

The description of the Phæacian walls, harbors, cities, palaces, ships, etc., seems like a recollection of Atlantis. The island of Calypso appears also to have been in the Atlantic Ocean, twenty days' sail from the Phæacian isles; and when Ulysses goes to the land of Pluto, "the under-world," the home of the dead, he

"Reached the far confines of Oceanus,"

beyond the Pillars of Hercules. It would be curious to inquire how far the poems of Homer are Atlantean in their relations and inspiration. Ulysses's wanderings were a prolonged struggle with Poseidon, the founder and god of Atlantis.

"The Hekatoncheires, or Cetimæni, beings each with a hundred hands, were three in number — Kottos, Gyges or Gyes, and Briareus—and represented the frightful crashing of waves, and its resemblance to the convulsions of earthquakes." (Murray's "Mythology," p. 26.) Are not these hundred arms the oars of the galleys, and the frightful crashing of the waves their movements in the water?

"The Kyklopes also were three in number—Brontes, with his thunder; Steröpes, with his lightning; and Arges, with his stream of light. They were represented as having only one eye, which was placed at the juncture between the nose and brow. It was, however, a large, flashing eye, as became beings who were personifications of the storm-cloud, with its flashes of destructive lightning and peals of thunder."

We shall show hereafter that the invention of gunpowder dates back to the days of the Phœnicians, and may have been derived by them from Atlantis. It is not impossible that in this picture of the Kyklopes we see a tradition of sea-going ships, with a light burning at the prow, and armed with some explosive preparation, which, with a roar like thunder, and a flash like lightning, destroyed those against whom it was employed? It at least requires less strain upon our credulity to suppose these monsters were a barbarian's memory of great ships than to believe that human beings ever existed with a hundred arms, and with one eye in the middle of the forehead, and giving out thunder and lightning.

The natives of the West India Islands regarded the ships of Columbus as living creatures, and that their sails were wings.

Berosus tells us, speaking of the ancient days of Chaldea, "In the first year there appeared, from that part of the Erythræan Sea which borders upon Babylonia, an animal endowed with reason, by name Oannes, whose whole body (according to the account of Apollodorus) was that of a fish; that under the fish's head he had another head, with feet also below, similar to those of a man, subjoined to the fish's tail. His voice too and language was articulate and human, and a representation of him is preserved even unto this day. This being was accustomed to pass the day among men, but took no food at that season, and he gave them an insight into letters and arts of all kinds. He taught them to construct cities, to found temples, to compile laws, and explained to them the principles of geometrical knowledge. He made them distinguish the seeds of the earth, and showed them how to collect the fruits; in short, he instructed them in everything which could tend to soften manners and humanize their laws. *From that time nothing material has been added by way of improvement to his instructions.* And when the sun set, this being, Oannes, retired again into the sea, and passed the night in the deep, for he was amphibious. After this there appeared other animals like Oannes."

This is clearly the tradition preserved by a barbarous people of the great ships of a civilized nation, who colonized their coast and introduced the arts and sciences among them. And here we see the same tendency to represent the ship as a living thing, which converted the war-vessels of the Atlanteans (the Kyklopes) into men with one blazing eye in the middle of the forehead.

Uranos was deposed from the throne, and succeeded by his son Chronos. He was called "the ripener, the harvest-god," and was probably identified with the beginning of the Agricultural Period. He married his sister Rhea, who bore him Pluto, *Poseidon,* Zeus, Hestia, Demeter, and Hera. He anticipated that his sons would dethrone him, as he had dethroned his father, Uranos, and he swallowed his first five children, and would have swallowed the sixth child, Zeus, but that his wife Rhea deceived him with a stone image of the child; and Zeus was conveyed to the island of Crete, and there concealed in a cave

and raised to manhood. Subsequently Chronos " yielded back
to the light the children he had swallowed." This myth probably means that Chronos had his children raised in some secret
place, where they could not be used by his enemies as the
instruments of a rebellion against his throne; and the stone
image of Zeus, palmed off upon him by Rhea, was probably
some other child substituted for his own. His precautions
seem to have been wise; for as soon as the children returned
to the light they commenced a rebellion, and drove the old
gentleman from his throne. A rebellion of the Titans followed. The struggle was a tremendous one, and seems to
have been decided at last by the use of gunpowder, as I shall
show farther on.

We have seen Chronos identified with the Atlantic, called
by the Romans the "Chronian Sea." He was known to the
Romans under the name of Saturn, and ruled over "a great Saturnian continent" in the Western Ocean. Saturn, or Chronos,
came to Italy: he presented himself to the king, Janus, "and
proceeded to instruct the subjects of the latter in agriculture,
gardening, and many other arts then quite unknown to them;
as, for example, how to tend and cultivate the vine. By such
means he at length raised the people from a rude and comparatively barbarous condition to one of order and peaceful occupations, in consequence of which he was everywhere held in high
esteem, and, in course of time, was selected by Janus to share
with him the government of the country, which thereupon assumed the name of *Saturnia*—'a land of seed and fruit.' The
period of Saturn's government was sung in later days by poets
as a happy time, when sorrows were unknown, when innocence,
freedom, and gladness reigned throughout the land in such a
degree as to deserve the title of the Golden Age." (Murray's
"Mythology," p. 32.)

All this accords with Plato's story. He tells us that the rule
of the Atlanteans extended to Italy; that they were a civilized,
agricultural, and commercial people. The civilization of Rome

was therefore an outgrowth directly from the civilization of Atlantis.

The Roman *Saturnalia* was a remembrance of the Atlantean colonization. It was a period of joy and festivity; master and slave met as equals; the distinctions of poverty and wealth were forgotten; no punishments for crime were inflicted; servants and slaves went about dressed in the clothes of their masters; and children received presents from their parents or relatives. It was a time of jollity and mirth, a recollection of the Golden Age. We find a reminiscence of it in the Roman " Carnival."

The third and last on the throne of the highest god 'was Zeus. We shall see him, a little farther on, by the aid of some mysterious engine overthrowing the rebels, the Titans, who rose against his power, amid the flash of lightning and the roar of thunder. He was called "the thunderer," and "the mighty thunderer." He was represented with thunder-bolts in his hand and an eagle at his feet.

During the time of Zeus Atlantis seems to have reached its greatest height of power. He was recognized as the father of the whole world; he everywhere rewarded uprightness, truth, faithfulness, and kindness; he was merciful to the poor, and punished the cruel. To illustrate his rule on earth the following story is told:

" Philemon and Baukis, an aged couple of the poorer class, were living peacefully and full of piety toward the gods in their cottage in Phrygia, when Zeus, who often visited the earth, disguised, to inquire into the behavior of men, paid a visit, in passing through Phrygia on such a journey, to these poor old people, and was received by them very kindly as a weary traveller, which he pretended to be. Bidding him welcome to the house, they set about preparing for their guest, who was accompanied by Hermes, as excellent a meal as they could afford, and for this purpose were about to kill the only goose they had left, when Zeus interfered; for he was touched by their kindliness and genuine piety, and that all the more because he had observed among the other inhabitants of the district nothing but cruelty of disposition and a habit of reproaching and despising the gods. To punish this conduct he determined to visit the country with a flood, but to save from it Philemon and Baukis, the good aged couple, and to reward them in a striking manner. To this end he revealed himself to them before opening the gates of the great flood, transformed their poor cottage on the hill into a splendid temple, installed the aged pair as his priest and priestess, and granted their prayer that they might both die together. When, after many years, death overtook them, they were changed into two trees, that grew side by side in the neighborhood—an oak and a linden." (Murray's "Mythology," p. 38.)

Here we have another reference to the Flood, and another identification with Atlantis.

Zeus was a kind of Henry VIII., and took to himself a number of wives. By Demeter (Ceres) he had Persephone (Proserpine); by Leto, Apollo and Artemis (Diana); by Dione, Aphrodite (Venus); by Semele, Dionysos (Bacchus); by Maia, Hermes (Mercury); by Alkmene, Hercules, etc., etc.

We have thus the whole family of gods and goddesses traced back to Atlantis.

Hera, or Juno, was the first and principal wife of Zeus. There were numerous conjugal rows between the royal pair, in which, say the poets, Juno was generally to blame. She was naturally jealous of the other wives of Zeus. Zeus on one occasion beat her, and threw her son Hephæstos out of Olympus; on another occasion he hung her out of Olympus with her arms tied and two great weights attached to her feet—a very brutal and ungentlemanly trick—but the Greeks transposed this into a beautiful symbol: the two weights, they say, represent the earth and sea, "an illustration of how all the phenomena of the visible sky were supposed to hang dependent on the highest god of heaven!" (*Ibid.*, p. 47.) Juno probably regarded the transaction in an altogether different light; and she therefore united with Poseidon, the king's brother, and his daughter

Athena, in a rebellion to put the old fellow in a strait-jacket, "and would have succeeded had not Thetis brought to his aid the sea-giant Ægæon," probably a war-ship. She seems in the main, however, to have been a good wife, and was the type of all the womanly virtues.

Poseidon, the first king of Atlantis, according to Plato, was, according to Greek mythology, a brother of Zeus, and a son of Chronos. In the division of the kingdom he fell heir to the ocean and its islands, and to the navigable rivers; in other words, he was king of a maritime and commercial people. His symbol was the horse. "He was the first to train and employ horses;" that is to say, his people first domesticated the horse. This agrees with what Plato tells us of the importance attached to the horse in Atlantis, and of the baths and race-courses provided for him. He was worshipped in the island of Tenos "in the character of a physician," showing that he represented an advanced civilization. He was also master of an agricultural people; "the ram with the golden fleece for which the Argonauts sailed was the offspring of Poseidon." He carried in his hand a three-pronged symbol, the trident, doubtless an emblem of the three continents that were embraced in the empire of Atlantis. He founded many colonies along the shores of the Mediterranean; "he helped to build the walls of Troy;" the tradition thus tracing the Trojan civilization to an Atlantean source. He settled Attica and founded Athens, named after his niece Athena, daughter of Zeus, who had no mother, but had sprung from the head of Zeus, which probably signified that her mother's name was not known—she was a foundling. Athena caused the first olive-tree to grow on the Acropolis of Athens, parent of all the olive-trees of Greece. Poseidon seems to have had settlements at Corinth, Ægina, Naxos, and Delphi. Temples were erected to his honor in nearly *all the seaport towns of Greece.* He sent a sea-monster, to wit, a ship, to ravage part of the Trojan territory.

In the "Iliad" Poseidon appears "as ruler of the sea, inhab-

iting a brilliant palace in its depths, traversing its surface in a
chariot, or stirring the powerful billows *until the earth shakes*
as they crash upon the shores. . . . He is also associated with
well - watered plains and valleys." (Murray's "Mythology,"
p. 51.) The palace in the depths of the sea was the palace
upon Olympus in Atlantis; the traversing of the sea referred
to the movements of a mercantile race; the shaking of the

POSEIDON, OR NEPTUNE.

earth was an association with earthquakes; the " well-watered
plains and valleys" remind us of the great plain of Atlantis
described by Plato.

All the traditions of the coming of civilization into Europe
point to Atlantis.

For instance, Keleos, who lived at Eleusis, near Athens, hos-
pitably received Demeter, the Greek Ceres, the daughter of Poseidon, when she landed; and in return she taught him the use
of the plough, and presented his son with the seed of barley,
and sent him out to teach mankind how to sow and utilize that
grain. Dionysos, grandson of Poseidon, travelled " through all

the known world, even into the remotest parts of India, instructing the people, as he proceeded, how to tend the vine, and how to practise many other arts of peace, besides teaching them the value of just and honorable dealings." (Murray's "Mythology," p. 119.) The Greeks celebrated great festivals in his honor down to the coming of Christianity.

"The Nymphs of Grecian mythology were a kind of middle beings between the gods and men, communicating with both, loved and respected by both; . . . living like the gods on ambrosia. In extraordinary cases they were summoned, it was believed, to the councils of the Olympian gods; but they usually remained in their particular spheres, in secluded grottoes and peaceful valleys, occupied in spinning, weaving, bathing, singing sweet songs, dancing, sporting, or accompanying deities who passed through their territories—hunting with Artemis (Diana), rushing about with Dionysos (Bacchus), making merry with Apollo or Hermes (Mercury), but always in a hostile attitude toward the wanton and excited Satyrs."

The Nymphs were plainly the female inhabitants of Atlantis dwelling on the plains, while the aristocracy lived on the higher lands. And this is confirmed by the fact that part of them were called *Atlantids*, offspring of Atlantis. The Hesperides were also "daughters of Atlas;" their mother was Hesperis, a personification of "the region of the West." Their home was "an island in the ocean," off the north or west coast of Africa.

And here we find a tradition which not only points to Atlantis, but also shows some kinship to the legend in Genesis of the tree and the serpent.

Titæa, "a goddess of the earth," gave Zeus a tree bearing golden apples on it. This tree was put in the care of the Hesperides, but they *could not resist the temptation to pluck and eat its fruit;* thereupon a *serpent* named Ladon was put to watch the tree. Hercules slew the serpent, and gave the apples to the Hesperides.

Heracles (Hercules), we have seen, was a son of Zeus, king of Atlantis. One of his twelve labors (the tenth) was the carrying off the cattle of Geryon. The meaning of Geryon is "the red glow of the *sunset*." He dwelt on the island of "Erythea, in the *remote west*, beyond the Pillars of Hercules." Hercules took a ship, and after encountering a storm, reached the island and placed himself on Mount Abas. Hercules killed Geryon, stole the cattle, put them on the ship, and landed them safely, driving them "through Iberia, Gaul, and over the Alps down into Italy." (Murray's "Mythology," p. 257.) This was simply the memory of a cattle raid made by an uncivilized race upon the civilized, cattle-raising people of Atlantis.

It is not necessary to pursue the study of the gods of Greece any farther. They were simply barbarian recollections of the rulers of a great civilized people who in early days visited their shores, and brought with them the arts of peace.

Here then, in conclusion, are the proofs of our proposition that the gods of Greece had been the kings of Atlantis:

1. They were not the makers, but the rulers of the world.

2. They were human in their attributes; they loved, sinned, and fought battles, the very sites of which are given; they founded cities, and civilized the people of the shores of the Mediterranean.

3. They dwelt upon an island in the Atlantic, "in the remote west, . . . where the sun shines after it has ceased to shine on Greece."

4. Their land was destroyed in a deluge.

5. They were ruled over by Poseidon and Atlas.

6. Their empire extended to Egypt and Italy and the shores of Africa, precisely as stated by Plato.

7. They existed during the Bronze Age and at the beginning of the Iron Age.

The entire Greek mythology is the recollection, by a degenerate race, of a vast, mighty, and highly civilized empire, which in a remote past covered large parts of Europe, Asia, Africa, and America.

Chapter III.

THE GODS OF THE PHŒNICIANS ALSO KINGS OF ATLANTIS.

Not alone were the gods of the Greeks the deified kings of Atlantis, but we find that the mythology of the Phœnicians was drawn from the same source.

For instance, we find in the Phœnician cosmogony that the Titans (Rephaim) derive their origin from the Phœnician gods Agrus and Agrotus. This connects the Phœnicians with that island in the remote west, in the midst of ocean, where, according to the Greeks, the Titans dwelt.

According to Sanchoniathon, *Ouranos* was the son of Autochthon, and, according to Plato, Autochthon was one of the ten kings of Atlantis. He married his sister *Ge.* He is the *Uranos* of the Greeks, who was the son of *Gœa* (the earth), whom he married. The Phœnicians tell us, " Ouranos had by Ge four sons: Ilus (El), who is called Chronos, and Betylus (Beth-El), and Dagon, which signifies bread-corn, and Atlas (Tammuz?)." Here, again, we have the names of two other kings of Atlantis. These four sons probably represented four races, the offspring of the earth. The Greek Uranos was the father of Chronos, and the ancestor of Atlas. The Phœnician god Ouranos had a great many other wives: his wife *Ge* was jealous; they quarrelled, and he attempted to kill the children he had by her. This is the legend which the Greeks told of Zeus and Juno. In the Phœnician mythology Chronos raised a rebellion against Ouranos, and, after a great battle, dethroned him. In the Greek legends it is Zeus who attacks and overthrows his father, Chronos. Ouranos had a daughter called Astarte (Ashtoreth), another called Rhea. "And Dagon, after he had found out bread-corn and the plough, was called Zeus-Aro-trius."

We find also, in the Phœnician legends, mention made of Poseidon, founder and king of Atlantis.

Chronos gave Attica to his daughter Athena, as in the Greek legends. In a time of plague he sacrificed his son to Ouranos, and "circumcised himself, and compelled his allies to do the same thing." It would thus appear that this singular rite, practised as we have seen by the Atlantidæ of the Old and New Worlds, the Egyptians, the Phœnicians, the Hebrews, the Ethiopians, the Mexicans, and the red men of America, dates back, as we might have expected, to Atlantis.

"Chronos visits the different regions of the habitable world."

He gave Egypt as a kingdom to the god Taaut, who had invented the alphabet. The Egyptians called him Thoth, and he was represented among them as "the god of letters, the clerk of the under-world," bearing a tablet, pen, and palm-branch.

This not only connects the Phœnicians with Atlantis, but shows the relations of Egyptian civilization to both Atlantis and the Phœnicians.

There can be no doubt that the royal personages who formed the gods of Greece were also the gods of the Phœnicians. We have seen the Autochthon of Plato reappearing in the Autochthon of the Phœnicians; the Atlas of Plato in the Atlas of the Phœnicians; the Poseidon of Plato in the Poseidon of the Phœnicians; while the kings Mestor and Mneseus of Plato are probably the gods Misor and Amynus of the Phœnicians.

Sanchoniathon tells us, after narrating all the discoveries by which the people advanced to civilization, that the Cabiri set down their records of the past by the command of the god Taaut, "and they delivered them to their successors and to foreigners, of whom one was Isiris (Osiris), the inventor of the three letters, the brother of Chua, who is called the first Phœnician." (Lenormant and Chevallier, "Ancient History of the East," vol. ii., p. 228.)

This would show that the first Phœnician came long after this line of the kings or gods, and that he was a foreigner, as compared with them; and, therefore, that it could not have been the Phœnicians proper who made the several inventions narrated by Sanchoniathon, but some other race, from whom the Phœnicians might have been descended.

And in the delivery of their records to the foreigner Osiris, the god of Egypt, we have another evidence that Egypt derived her civilization from Atlantis.

Max Müller says:

"The Semitic languages also are all varieties of one form of speech. Though we do not know that primitive language from which the Semitic dialects diverged, yet we know that at one time such language must have existed. . . . We cannot derive Hebrew from Sanscrit, or Sanscrit from Hebrew; but we can well understand how both may have proceeded from one common source. They are both channels supplied from one river, and they carry, though not always on the surface, floating materials of language which challenge comparison, and have already yielded satisfactory results to careful analyzers." ("Outlines of Philosophy of History," vol. i., p. 475.)

There was an ancient tradition among the Persians that the Phœnicians migrated from the shores of the Erythræan Sea, and this has been supposed to mean the Persian Gulf; but there was a very old city of Erythia, in utter ruin in the time of Strabo, which was built in some ancient age, long before the founding of Gades, near the site of that town, on the Atlantic coast of Spain. May not this town of Erythia have given its name to the adjacent sea? And this may have been the starting-point of the Phœnicians in their European migrations. It would even appear that there was an island of Erythea. In the Greek mythology the tenth labor of Hercules consisted in driving away the cattle of Geryon, who lived in the island of Erythea, "an island somewhere in the remote west, *beyond the*

Pillars of Hercules." (Murray's " Mythology," p. 257.) Hercules stole the cattle from this remote oceanic island, and, returning, drove them "through Iberia, Gaul, over the Alps, and
through Italy." (*Ibid.*) It is probable that a people emigrat·
ing from the Erythræan Sea, that is, from the Atlantic, first
gave their name to a town on the coast of Spain, and at a later
date to the Persian Gulf—as we have seen the name of York
carried from England to the banks of the Hudson, and then to
the Arctic Circle.

The builders of the Central American cities are reported to
have been a bearded race. The Phœnicians, in common with
the Indians, practised human sacrifices to a great extent; they
worshipped fire and water, adopted the names of the animals
whose skins they wore—that is to say, they had the totemic
system—telegraphed by means of fires, poisoned their arrows,
offered peace before beginning battle, and used drums. (Bancroft's " Native Races," vol. v., p. 77.)

The extent of country covered by the commerce of the Phœnicians represents to some degree the area of the old Atlantean
Empire. Their colonies and trading-posts extended east and
west from the shores of the Black Sea, through the Mediterranean to the west coast of Africa and of Spain, and around to
Ireland and England ; while from north to south they ranged
from the Baltic to the Persian Gulf. They touched every point
where civilization in later ages made its appearance. Strabo
estimated that they had three hundred cities along the west
coast of Africa. When Columbus sailed to discover a new
world, or re-discover an old one, he took his departure from a
Phœnician seaport, founded by that great race two thousand
five hundred years previously. This Atlantean sailor, with his
Phœnician features, sailing from an Atlantean port, simply
re-opened the path of commerce and colonization which had
been closed when Plato's island sunk in the sea. And it is
a curious fact that Columbus had the antediluvian world in
his mind's eye even then, for when he reached the mouth of

the Orinoco he thought it was the river Gihon, that flowed out of Paradise, and he wrote home to Spain, " There are here great indications suggesting the proximity of the earthly Paradise, for not only does it correspond in mathematical position with the opinions of the holy and learned theologians, but all other signs concur to make it probable."

Sanchoniathon claims that the learning of Egypt, Greece, and Judæa was derived from the Phœnicians. It would appear probable that, while other races represent the conquests or colonizations of Atlantis, the Phœnicians succeeded to their arts, sciences, and especially their commercial supremacy; and hence the close resemblances which we have found to exist between the Hebrews, a branch of the Phœnician stock, and the people of America.

> Upon the Syrian sea the people live
> Who style themselves Phœnicians. . . .
> These were *the first great founders of the world*—
> Founders of cities and of mighty states—
> Who showed a path through seas before unknown.
> In the first ages, when the sons of men
> Knew not which way to turn them, they assigned
> To each his first departraent; they bestowed
> Of land a portion and of sea a lot,
> And sent each wandering tribe far off to share
> A different soil and climate. Hence arose
> The great diversity, so plainly seen,
> 'Mid nations widely severed.
>
> *Dyonysius of Susiana,* A.D. 300.

CHAPTER IV.

THE GOD ODIN, WODEN, OR WOTAN.

In the Scandinavian mythology the chief god was Odin, the Woden, Wotan, or Wuotan of the Germans. He is represented with many of the attributes of the Greek god Zeus, and is supposed by some to be identical with him. He dwelt with the *twelve* Æsir, or gods, upon Asgard, the Norse Olympus, which arose out of Midgard, a land half-way between the regions of frost and fire (to wit, in a temperate climate). The Scandinavian Olympus was probably Atlantis. Odin is represented as a grave-looking elderly man with a long beard, carrying in his hand a spear, and accompanied by two dogs and two ravens. He was the father of poetry, and the inventor of Runic writing.

The Chiapenese of Central America (the people whose language we have seen furnishing such remarkable resemblances to Hebrew) claim to have been the first people of the New World. Clavigero tells us ("Hist. Antiq. del Messico," Eng. trans., 1807, vol. i.) that according to the traditions of the Chiapenese there was a Votan who was the grandson of the man who built the ark to save himself and family from the Deluge; he was one of those who undertook to build the tower that should reach to heaven. The Lord ordered him to people America. "He came *from the East.*" He brought seven families with him. He had been preceded in America by two others, Igh and Imox. He built a great city in America called "Nachan," City of the Serpents (the serpent that tempted Eve was Nahash), from his own race, which was named Chan, a serpent. This Nachan is supposed to have been Palenque. The date of his journey is placed in the legends in the year 3000 of the world, and in the tenth century B.C. He also founded three tributary monarchies, whose capitals were Tulan, Mayapan, and Chiquimala. He wrote a book containing a history of his deeds, and proofs that he belonged to the tribe of Chanes (serpents). He states that " he is the third of the Votans; that he conducted seven families from Valum-Votan to this continent, and assigned lands to them; that he determined to travel until he came to the root of heaven and found his relations, the Culebres, and made himself known to them; that he accordingly made four voyages to Chivim; that he arrived in Spain; that he went to Rome; that he saw the house of God building; that he went by the road which his brethren, the Culebres, had bored; that he marked it, and that he passed by the houses of the thirteen Culebres. He relates that, in returning from one of his voyages, he found seven other families of the Tzequil nation who had joined the first inhabitants, and recognized in them the same origin as his own, that is, of the Culebres; he speaks of the place where they built the first town, which from its founders received the name of Tzequil; he affirms that, having taught them the refinement of manners in the use of the table, table-cloths, dishes, basins, cups, and napkins, they taught him the knowledge of God and his worship; his first ideas of a king, and obedience to him; that he was chosen captain of all these united families."

It is probable that Spain and Rome are interpolations. Cabrera claims that the Votanites were Carthaginians. He thinks the Chivim of Votan were the Hivim, or Givim, who were descended of Heth, son of Canaan, Phœnicians; they were the builders of Accaron, Azotus, Ascalon, and Gaza. The Scriptures refer to them as Hivites (Givim) in Deuteronomy (chap. ii., verse 32), and Joshua (chap. xiii., verse 4). He claims that Cadmus and his wife Hermione were of this stock; and according to Ovid they were metamorphosed into snakes (Culebres). The name Hivites in Phœnician signifies a snake.

Votan may not, possibly, have passed into Europe; he may have travelled altogether in Africa. His singular allusion to "a way which the Culebres had bored" seems at first inexplicable; but Dr. Livingstone's last letters, published 8th November, 1869, in the "Proceedings of the Royal Geographical Society," mention that "tribes live in underground houses in Rua. Some excavations are said to be thirty miles long, and have running rills in them; a whole district can stand a siege in them. The 'writings' therein, I have been told by some of the people, are drawings of animals, and not letters; otherwise I should have gone to see them. People very dark, well made, and outer angle of eyes slanting inward."

And Captain Grant, who accompanied Captain Speke in his famous exploration of the sources of the Nile, tells of a tunnel or subway under the river Kaōma, on the highway between Loowemba and Marunga, near Lake Tanganyika. His guide Manua describes it to him:

"I asked Manua if he had ever seen any country resembling it. His reply was, 'This country reminds me of what I saw in the country to the south of the Lake Tanganyika, when travelling with an Arab's caravan from Unjanyembeh. There is a river there called the Kaōma, running into the lake, the sides of which are similar in precipitousness to the rocks before us.' I then asked, 'Do the people cross this river in boats?' 'No; they have no boats; and even if they had, the people could not land, as the sides are too steep: they pass underneath the river by a natural tunnel, or subway.' He and all his party went through it on their way from Loowemba to Ooroongoo, and returned by it. He described its length as having taken them from sunrise till noon to pass through it, and so high that, if mounted upon camels, they could not touch the top. Tall reeds, the thickness of a walking-stick, grew inside; the road was strewed with white pebbles, and so wide — four hundred yards — that they could see their way tolerably well while passing through it. The rocks looked as if they had been planed by artificial means. Water never came through from the river overhead; it was procured by digging wells. Manua added that the people of Wambweh take shelter in this tunnel, and live there with their families and cattle, when molested by the Watuta, a warlike race, descended from the Zooloo Kafirs."

But it is interesting to find in this book of Votan, however little reliance we may place in its dates or details, evidence that there was actual intercourse between the Old World and the New in remote ages.

Humboldt remarks:

"We have fixed the special attention of our readers upon this Votan, or Wodan, an American who appears of the same family with the Wods or Odins of the Goths and of the people of Celtic origin.   Since, according to the learned researches of Sir William Jones, Odin and Buddha are probably the same person, it is curious to see the names of *Bondvar*, *Wodansdag*, and *Votan* designating in India, Scandinavia, and in Mexico the day of a brief period."   ("Vues des Cordilleras," p. 148, ed. 1810.)

There are many things to connect the mythology of the Gothic nations with Atlantis; they had, as we have seen, flood legends; their gods Krodo and Satar were the Chronos and Saturn of Atlantis; their Baal was the Bel of the Phœnicians, who were closely connected with Poseidon and Atlas; and, as we shall see hereafter, their language has a distinct relationship with the tongues of the Arabians, Cushites, Chaldeans, and Phœnicians.

CHAPTER V.

THE PYRAMID, THE CROSS, AND THE GARDEN OF EDEN.

No fact is better established than the reverence shown to the sign of the Cross in all the ages prior to Christianity. We cannot do better than quote from an able article in the *Edinburgh Review* of July, 1870, upon this question:

"From the dawn of organized Paganism in the Eastern world to the final establishment of Christianity in the Western, the Cross was undoubtedly one of the commonest and most sacred of symbolical monuments; and, to a remarkable extent, it is so still in almost every land where that of Calvary is unrecognized or unknown. Apart from any distinctions of social or intellectual superiority, of caste, color, nationality, or location in either hemisphere, it appears to have been the aboriginal possession of every people in antiquity—the elastic girdle, so to say, which embraced the most widely separated heathen communities—the most significant token of a universal brotherhood, to which all the families of mankind were severally and irresistibly drawn, and by which *their common descent was emphatically expressed,* or by means of which each and all preserved, amid every vicissitude of fortune, a knowledge of *the primeval happiness and dignity of their species.* Where authentic history is silent on the subject, the material relics of past and long since forgotten races are not wanting to confirm and strengthen this supposition. Diversified forms of the symbol are delineated more or less artistically, according to the progress achieved in civilization at the period, on the ruined walls of temples and palaces, on natural rocks and sepulchral galleries, on the hoariest monoliths and the rudest statuary; on coins, medals, and vases of every description; and, in not a few instances, are preserved in the architectural proportions of sub-

terranean as well as superterranean structures, of tumuli as well
as fanes. The extraordinary sanctity attaching to the symbol,
in every age and under every variety of circumstance, justified
any expenditure incurred in its fabrication or embellishment;
hence the most persistent labor, the most consummate ingenuity, were lavished upon it. Populations of essentially different
culture, tastes, and pursuits—the highly-civilized and the demi-
civilized, the settled and nomadic—vied with each other in their
efforts to extend the knowledge of its exceptional import and
virtue among their latest posterities. The marvellous rock-
hewn caves of Elephanta and Ellora, and the stately temples of
Mathura and Terputty, in the East, may be cited as characteristic examples of one laborious method of exhibiting it; and the
megalithic structures of Callernish and Newgrange, in the West,
of another; while a third may be instanced in the great temple
at Mitzla, 'the City of the Moon,' in Ojaaca, Central America.
also excavated in the living rock, and manifesting the same stupendous labor and ingenuity as are observable in the cognate
caverns of Salsette—of endeavors, we repeat, made by peoples
as intellectually as geographically distinct, and followers withal
of independent and unassociated deities, to magnify and perpetuate some grand primeval symbol. . . .

"Of the several varieties of the Cross still in vogue, as national or ecclesiastical emblems, in this and other European states,
and distinguished by the familiar appellations of St. George,
St. Andrew, the Maltese, the Greek, the Latin, etc., etc., there
is not one among them the existence of which may not be
traced to the remotest antiquity. They were the common
property of the Eastern nations. No revolution or other casu-
alty has wrought any perceptible difference in their several
forms or delineations; they have passed from one hemisphere
to the other intact; have survived dynasties, empires, and races;
have been borne on the crest of each successive wave of Aryan
population in its course toward the West; and, having been re-
consecrated in later times by their lineal descendants, are still
recognized as military and national badges of distinction. . . .

"Among the earliest known types is the *crux ansata*, vulgarly
called 'the key of the Nile,' because of its being found sculptured or otherwise represented so frequently upon Egyptian and
Coptic monuments. It has, however, a very much older and
more sacred signification than this. It was the symbol of

symbols, the mystical Tau, 'the hidden wisdom,' not only of the ancient Egyptians but also of the Chaldeans, Phœnicians, Mexicans, Peruvians, and of every other ancient people commemorated in history, in either hemisphere, and is formed very similarly to our letter T, with a roundlet, or oval, placed immediately above it. Thus it was figured on the gigantic emerald or glass statue of Serapis, which was transported (293 B.C.) by order of Ptolemy Soter from Sinope, on the southern shores of the Black Sea, re-erected within that famous labyrinth which encompassed the banks of Lake Mœris, and destroyed by the victorious army of Theodosius (A.D. 389), despite the earnest entreaties of the Egyptian priesthood to spare it, because it was the emblem of their god

EGYPTIAN TAU.

and of 'the life to come.' Sometimes, as may be seen on the breast of an Egyptian mummy in the museum of the London University, the simple T only is planted on the frustum of a cone; and sometimes it is represented as springing from a heart; in the first instance signifying goodness; in the second, hope or expectation of reward. As in the oldest temples and catacombs of Egypt, so this type likewise abounds in the ruined cities of Mexico and Central America, graven as well upon the most ancient cyclopean and polygonal walls as upon the more modern and perfect examples of masonry; and is displayed in an equally conspicuous manner upon the breasts of innumerable bronze statuettes which have been recently disinterred from the cemetery of Juigalpa (of unknown antiquity) in Nicaragua."

CROSS FROM MONUMENTS OF PALENQUE.

When the Spanish missionaries first set foot upon the soil of America, in the fifteenth century, they were amazed to find the Cross was as devoutly worshipped by the red Indians as by themselves, and were in doubt whether to ascribe the fact to the pious labors of St. Thomas or to the cunning device of the Evil One. The hallowed symbol challenged their atten-

ANCIENT IRISH CROSS.

tion on every hand and in almost every variety of form. It appeared on the bass-reliefs of ruined and deserted as well as on those of inhabited palaces, and was the most conspicuous ornament in the great temple of Gozumel, off the coast of Yucatan. According to the particular locality, and the purpose which it served, it was formed of various materials — of marble and gypsum in the open spaces of cities and by the way-side; of wood in the teocallis or chapels on pyramidal summits and in subterranean sanctuaries; and of emerald or jasper in the palaces of kings and nobles.

When we ask the question how it comes that the sign of the Cross has thus been reverenced from the highest antiquity by the races of the Old and New Worlds, we learn that it is a reminiscence of the Garden of Eden, in other words, of Atlantis.

Professor Hardwicke says:

CENTRAL AMERICAN CROSS.

"All these and similar traditions are but mocking satires of the old Hebrew story—jarred and broken notes of the same strain; but with all their exaggerations they intimate how in the background of man's vision lay a paradise of holy joy—a paradise secured from every kind of profanation, and made inaccessible to the guilty; a paradise full of objects that were calculated to delight the senses and to elevate the mind; a paradise that granted to its tenant rich and rare immunities, and that fed with its perennial streams the tree of life and immortality."

COPPER COIN—
TEOTIHUACAN.

To quote again from the writer in the *Edinburgh Review*, already cited:

"Its undoubted antiquity, no less than its extraordinary diffusion, evidences that it must have been, as it may be said to
be still in unchristianized lands, emblematical of some fundamental doctrine or mystery. The reader will not have failed
to observe that it is most usually associated with *water;* it was
'the key of the Nile,' that mystical instrument by means of
which, in the popular judgment of his Egyptian devotees, Osiris produced the annual revivifying inundations of the sacred
stream ; it is discernible in that mysterious pitcher or vase portrayed on the brazen table of Bembus, before-mentioned, with
its four lips discharging as many streams of water in opposite
directions ; it was the emblem of the water-deities of the Babylonians in the East and of the Gothic nations in the West, as

ANCIENT IRISH CROSS—PRE-CHRISTIAN—KILNABOY.

well as that of the rain-deities respectively of the mixed population in America. We have seen with what peculiar rites the
symbol was honored by those widely-separated races in the
western hemisphere ; and the monumental slabs of Nineveh,
now in the museums of London and Paris, show us how it was
similarly honored by the successors of the Chaldees in the
eastern. . . .

"In Egypt, Assyria, and Britain it was emblematical of creative power and eternity ; in India, China, and Scandinavia, of
heaven and immortality ; in the two Americas, of rejuvenes-
cence and freedom from physical suffering ; while in both hemispheres it was the common symbol of the resurrection, or 'the
sign of the life to come ;' and, finally, in all heathen communi-

ties, without exception, it was the emphatic type, the sole en-during evidence, of the Divine Unity. This circumstance alone determines its extreme antiquity—an antiquity, in all likeli-hood, long antecedent to the foundation of either of the three great systems of religion in the East. And, lastly, we have seen how, as a rule, it is found in conjunction with a stream or streams of water, with exuberant vegetation, and with a hill or a mountainous region—in a word, *with a land of beauty, fertili-ty, and joy.* Thus it was expressed upon those circular and sacred cakes of the Egyptians, composed of the richest materi-als—of flour, of honey, of milk—and with which the serpent

and bull, as well as other reptiles and beasts con-secrated to the service of Isis and their higher divinities, were daily fed; and upon certain festi-vals were eaten with extraordinary ceremony by the people and their priests. 'The cross-cake,' says Sir Gardner Wilkinson, 'was their hiero-glyph for civilized land;' obviously *a land su-perior to their own, as it was, indeed, to all other mundane territories;* for it was that *distant, traditional country of sempiternal contentment and repose,* of exquisite delight and serenity, where Nature, unassisted by man, produces all that is necessary for his sustentation."

And this land was the Garden of Eden of our race. This was the Olympus of the Greeks, where

> "This same mild season gives the blooms to blow,
>   The buds to harden and the fruits to grow."

In the midst of it was a sacred and glorious eminence—the *umbilicus orbis terrarum*—"toward which the heathen in all parts of the world, and in all ages, turned a wistful gaze in ev-ery act of devotion, and to which they hoped to be admitted, or, rather, to be restored, at the close of this transitory scene."

In this "glorious eminence" do we not see Plato's moun-tain in the middle of Atlantis, as he describes it:

"Near the plain and in the centre of the island there was a mountain, not very high on any side. In this mountain there dwelt one of the earth-born primeval men of that country, whose name was Evenor, and he had a wife named Leucippe, and they had an only daughter, who was named Cleito. Poseidon married her. He enclosed the hill in which she dwelt all around, making alternate zones of sea and land, larger and smaller, encircling one another; there were two of land and three of water . . . so that no man could get to the island. . . . He brought streams of water under the earth to this mountain-island, and made all manner of food to grow upon it. This island became the seat of Atlas, the over-king of the whole island; upon it they built the great temple of their nation; they continued to ornament it in successive generations, every king surpassing the one who came before him to the utmost of his power, until they made the building a marvel to behold for size and beauty. . . . And they had such an amount of wealth as was never before possessed by kings and potentates—as is not likely ever to be again."

The gardens of Alcinous and Laertes, of which we read in Homeric song, and those of Babylon, were probably transcripts of Atlantis. "The sacred eminence in the midst of a superabundant, happy region figures more or less distinctly in almost every mythology, ancient or modern. It was the Mesomphalos of the earlier Greeks, and the Omphalium of the Cretans, dominating the Elysian fields, upon whose tops, bathed in pure, brilliant, incomparable light, the gods passed their days in ceaseless joys."

"The Buddhists and Brahmans, who together constitute nearly half the population of the world, tell us that the decussated figure (the cross), whether in a simple or a complex form, symbolizes the traditional happy abode of their primeval ancestors — that 'Paradise of Eden toward the East,' as we find it expressed in the Hebrew. And, let us ask, what better picture, or more significant characters, in the complicated alphabet of symbolism, could have been selected for the purpose than a circle and a cross: the one to denote a region of absolute purity and perpetual felicity; the other, those four perennial streams that divided and watered the several quarters of it?" (*Edinburgh Review*, January, 1870.)

And when we turn to the mythology of the Greeks, we find

that the origin of the world was ascribed to *Okeanos*, the ocean. The world was at first an island surrounded by the ocean, as by a great stream :

"It was a region of wonders of all kinds ; Okeanos lived there with his wife Tethys : these were the Islands of the Blessed, the gardens of the gods, the sources of nectar and ambrosia, on which the gods lived.   Within this *circle of water* the earth lay spread out like a disk, *with mountains rising from it*, and the vault of heaven appearing to rest upon its outer edge all around."   (Murray's "Manual of Mythology," pp. 23, 24, *et seq.*)

On the mountains dwelt the gods ; they had palaces on these mountains, with store-rooms, stabling, etc.

"The Gardens of the Hesperides, with their golden apples, were believed to exist *in some island of the ocean*, or, as it was sometimes thought, *in the islands* off the north or *west coast of Africa.*   They were far famed in antiquity ; for it was there that springs of nectar flowed by the couch of Zeus, and there that the earth displayed the rarest blessings of the gods ; it was another Eden."   (*Ibid.*, p. 156.)

Homer described it in these words :

> "Stern winter smiles on that auspicious clime,
> The fields are florid with unfading prime,
> From the bleak pole no winds inclement blow,
> Mould the round hail, or flake the fleecy snow ;
> But from the breezy deep the bless'd inhale
> The fragrant murmurs of the western gale."

"It was the sacred Asgard of the Scandinavians, springing from the centre of a fruitful land, which was watered by *four primeval rivers* of milk, severally flowing in the direction of the cardinal points, 'the abode of happiness, and the height of bliss.'   It is the Tien-Chan, 'the celestial mountain-land, . . . the enchanted gardens' of the Chinese and Tartars, watered by the *four perennial fountains* of Tychin, or Immortality ; it is the hill-encompassed Ilá of the Singhalese and Thibetians, 'the everlasting dwelling-place of the wise and just.'   It is the Sineru of the Buddhist, on the summit of which is Tawrutisa, the habitation of Sekrá, the supreme god, from which proceed the *four sacred streams*, running in as many contrary directions.

It is the Slávratta, 'the celestial earth,' of the Hindoo, the summit of his golden mountain *Meru*, the city of Brahma, in the centre of Jambadwípa, and from the four sides of which gush forth the *four primeval rivers*, reflecting in their passage the colorific glories of their source, and severally flowing northward, southward, eastward, and westward."

It is the Garden of Eden of the Hebrews :

" And the Lord God planted a garden eastward in Eden ; and there he put the man whom he had formed. And out of the ground made the Lord God to grow every tree that is pleasant to the sight, and good for food ; the tree of life also in the midst of the garden, and the tree of knowledge of good and evil. And a river went out of Eden to water the garden ; and from thence it was parted, and became into *four* heads. The name of the first is Pison ; that is it which compasseth the whole land of Havilah, where there is gold ; and the gold of that land is good : there is bdellium and the onyx stone. And the name of the second river is Gihon : the same is it that compasseth the whole land of Ethiopia. And the name of the third river is Hiddekel : that is it which goeth toward the east of Assyria. And the fourth river is Euphrates. And the Lord God took the man and put him into the Garden of Eden to dress it and to keep it." (Gen. ii., 8–15.)

As the four rivers named in Genesis are not branches of any one stream, and head in very different regions, it is evident that there was an attempt, on the part of the writer of the Book, to adapt an ancient tradition concerning another country to the known features of the region in which he dwelt.

Josephus tells us (chap. i., p. 41), " Now the garden (of Eden) was watered by one river, *which ran round about the whole earth*, and was parted into four parts." Here in the four parts we see the origin of the Cross, while in the river running around the whole earth we have the wonderful canal of Atlantis, described by Plato, which was " carried around the whole of the plain," and received the streams which came down from the mountains. The streams named by Josephus would seem to represent the migrations of people from Atlantis to its colo nies. "Phison," he tells us, "denotes a multitude; it ran into India; the Euphrates and Tigris go down into the Red Sea; while the Geon runs through Egypt."

We are further told (chap. ii., p. 42) that when Cain, after the murder of Abel, left the land of Adam, "he travelled over many countries" before he reached the land of Nod; *and the land of Nod was to the eastward of Adam's home.* In other words, the original seat of mankind was in the West, that is to say, in the direction of Atlantis. Wilson tells us that the Aryans of India believed that they originally came "from the West." Thus the nations on the west of the Atlantic look to the *east* for their place of origin; while on the east of the Atlantic they look to the *west:* thus all the lines of tradition converge upon Atlantis.

But here is the same testimony that in the Garden of Eden there were four rivers radiating from one parent stream. And these four rivers, as we have seen, we find in the Scandinavian traditions, and in the legends of the Chinese, the Tartars, the Singhalese, the Thibetians, the Buddhists, the Hebrews, and the Brahmans.

And not only do we find this tradition of the Garden of Eden in the Old World, but it meets us also among the civilized races of America. The elder Montezuma said to Cortez, "Our fathers dwelt in that happy and prosperous place which they called Aztlan, which means *whiteness.* . . . In this place *there is a great mountain in the middle of the water* which is called Culhuacan, because it has the point somewhat turned over toward the bottom; and for this cause it is called Culhuacan, which means 'crooked mountain.'" He then proceeds to describe the charms of this favored land, abounding in birds, game, fish, trees, "fountains enclosed with elders and junipers, and alder-trees both large and beautiful." The people planted "maize, red peppers, tomatoes, beans, and all kinds of plants, *in furrows.*"

Here we have the same mountain in the midst of the water

which Plato describes — the same mountain to which all the legends of the most ancient races of Europe refer.

The inhabitants of Aztlan were *boatmen.* (Bancroft's " Native Races," vol. v., p. 325.) E. G. Squier, in his "Notes on Central America," p. 349, says, " It is a significant fact that in the map of their migrations, presented by Gemelli, the place of the origin of the Aztecs is designated by the sign of water, *Atl* standing for *Atzlan*, a *pyramidal temple* with grades, and near these a *palm-tree.*" This circumstance did not escape the attention of Humboldt, who says, " I am astonished at finding a palm-tree near this teocalli. This tree certainly does not indicate a northern origin. . . . The possibility that an unskilful artist should unintentionally represent a tree of which he had no knowledge is so great, that any argument dependent on it hangs upon a slender thread." ("North Americans of Antiquity," p. 266.)

The Miztecs, a tribe dwelling on the outskirts of Mexico, had a tradition that the gods, " in the day of obscurity and darkness," built " a sumptuous palace, a masterpiece of skill, in which they made their abode upon a mountain. The rock was called 'The Place of Heaven;' there the gods first abode on earth, living many years in great rest and content, as in a happy and delicious land, though the world still lay in obscurity and darkness. The children of these gods made to themselves a garden, in which they put many trees, and fruit-trees, and flowers, and roses, and odorous herbs. Subsequently there came a great deluge, in which many of the sons and daughters of the gods perished." (Bancroft's "Native Races," vol. iii., p. 71.) Here we have a distinct reference to Olympus, the Garden of Plato, and the destruction of Atlantis.

And in Plato's account of Atlantis we have another description of the Garden of Eden and the Golden Age of the world:

" Also, whatever fragrant things there are in the earth, whether roots, or herbage, or woods, or distilling drops of flowers and fruits, grew and thrived in that land; and again the cultivated fruits of the earth, both the edible fruits and other species of food which we call by the name of legumes, and the fruits having a hard rind, affording drinks and meats and ointments . . . all these that sacred island, lying beneath the sun, brought forth in abundance. . . . For many generations, as long as the divine nature lasted in them, they were obedient to the laws, and well-affectioned toward the gods, who were their kinsmen; for they possessed true and in every way great spirits, practising gentleness and wisdom in the various chances of life, and in their intercourse with one another. They despised everything but virtue, not caring for their present state of life, and thinking lightly of the possession of gold and other property, which seemed only a burden to them; neither were they intoxicated by luxury; nor did wealth deprive them of their self-control; but they were sober, and saw clearly that all these goods were increased by virtuous friendship with one another, and that by excessive zeal for them, and honor of them, the good of them is lost, and friendship perishes with them."

All this cannot be a mere coincidence; it points to a common tradition of a veritable land, where four rivers flowed down in opposite directions from a central mountain-peak. And these four rivers, flowing to the north, south, east, and west, constitute the origin of that sign of the Cross which we have seen meeting us at every point among the races who were either descended from the people of Atlantis, or who, by commerce and colonization, received their opinions and civilization from them.

Let us look at the question of the identity of the Garden of Eden with Atlantis from another point of view:

If the alphabet of the Phœnicians is kindred with the Maya alphabet, as I think is clear, then the Phœnicians were of the same race, or of some race with which the Mayas were connected; in other words, they were from Atlantis.

Now we know that the Phœnicians and Hebrews were of the same stock, used the same alphabet, and spoke almost precisely the same language.

The Phœnicians preserved traditions, which have come down

to us in the writings of Sanchoniathon, of all the great essential inventions or discoveries which underlie civilization. The
first two human beings, they tell us, were Protogonos and Aion
(Adam and 'Havath), who produce Genos and Genea (Qên and
Qênath), from whom again are descended three brothers, named
Phos, Phur, and Phlox (Light, Fire, and Flame), because they
"have discovered how to produce fire by the friction of two
pieces of wood, and have taught the use of this element." In
another fragment, at the origin of the human race we see in
succession the fraternal couples of Autochthon and Technites
(Adam and Quen — Cain?), inventors of the manufacture of
bricks; Agros and Agrotes (Sade and Cêd), fathers of the agriculturists and hunters; then Amynos and Magos, "who taught
to dwell in villages and rear flocks."

The connection between these Atlantean traditions and the
Bible record is shown in many things. For instance, "the
Greek text, in expressing the invention of Amynos, uses the
words κώμας καὶ ποίμνας, which are precisely the same as the
terms *ôhel umiqneh*, which the Bible uses in speaking of the
dwellings of the descendants of Jabal (Gen., chap. iv., v. 20).
In like manner Lamech, both in the signification of his name
and also in the savage character attributed to him by the legend attached to his memory, is a true synonyme of Agrotes."

"And the title of 'Αλῆται, given to Agros and Agrotes in
the Greek of the Phœnician history, fits in wonderfully with
the physiognomy of the race of the Cainites in the Bible narrative, whether we take ἁλῆται simply as a Hellenized transcription of the Semitic *Elîm*, 'the strong, the mighty,' or whether
we take it in its Greek acceptation, 'the wanderers;' for such is
the destiny of Cain and his race according to the very terms of
the condemnation which was inflicted upon him after his crime
(Gen. iv., 14), and this is what is signified by the name of his
grandson 'Yirad. Only, in Sanchoniathon the genealogy does
not end with Amynos and Magos, as that of the Cainites in the
Bible does with the three sons of Lamech. These two personages are succeeded by Misôr and Sydyk, 'the released and the

just,' as Sanchoniathon translates them, but rather the 'upright and the just' (Mishôr and Çüdüq), 'who invent the use of salt.' To Misôr is born Taautos (Taût), to whom we owe letters; and to Sydyk the Cabiri or Corybantes, the institutors of navigation." (Lenormant, "Genealogies between Adam and the Deluge." *Contemporary Review*, April, 1880.)

We have, also, the fact that the Phœnician name for their goddess Astynome (Ashtar No'emâ), whom the Greeks called Nemaun, was the same as the name of the sister of the three sons of Lamech, as given in Genesis—Na'emah, or Na'amah.

If, then, the original seat of the Hebrews and Phœnicians was the Garden of Eden, to the west of Europe, and if the Phœnicians are shown to be connected, through their alphabets, with the Central Americans, who looked to an island in the sea, to the eastward, as their starting-point, the conclusion becomes irresistible that Atlantis and the Garden of Eden were one and the same.

The Pyramid.—Not only are the Cross and the Garden of Eden identified with Atlantis, but in Atlantis, the habitation of the gods, we find the original model of all those pyramids which extend from India to Peru.

This singular architectural construction dates back far beyond the birth of history. In the *Purânas* of the Hindoos we read of pyramids long anterior in time to any which have survived to our day. Cheops was preceded by a countless host of similar erections which have long since mouldered into ruins.

If the reader will turn to page 104 of this work he will see, in the midst of the picture of Aztlan, the starting-point of the Aztecs, according to the Botturini pictured writing, a pyramid with worshippers kneeling before it.

Fifty years ago Mr. Faber, in his "Origin of Pagan Idolatry," placed artificial tumuli, pyramids, and pagodas in the same category, conceiving that all were transcripts of the holy mountain which was generally supposed to have stood in the centre of Eden; or, rather, as intimated in more than one place by the Psalmist, the garden itself was situated on an eminence. (Psalms, chap. iii., v. 4, and chap. lxviii., vs. 15, 16, 18.)

The pyramid is one of the marvellous features of that problem which confronts us everywhere, and which is insoluble without Atlantis.

The Arabian traditions linked the pyramid with the Flood. In a manuscript preserved in the Bodleian Library, and translated by Dr. Sprenger, Abou Balkhi says:

" The wise men, *previous to the Flood*, foreseeing an impending judgment from heaven, either by *submersion* or fire, which would destroy every created thing, built upon the tops of the mountains in Upper Egypt many pyramids of stone, in order to have some refuge against the approaching calamity. Two of these buildings exceeded the rest in height, being four hundred cubits high and as many broad and as many long. They were built with large blocks of marble, and they were so well put together that the joints were scarcely perceptible. Upon the exterior of the building every charm and wonder of physic was inscribed."

This tradition locates these monster structures upon the mountains of Upper Egypt, but there are no buildings of such dimensions to be found anywhere in Egypt. Is it not probable that we have here another reference to the great record preserved in the land of the Deluge? Were not the pyramids of Egypt and America imitations of similar structures in Atlantis? Might not the building of such a gigantic edifice have given rise to the legends existing on both continents in regard to a Tower of Babel?

How did the human mind hit upon this singular edifice— the pyramid? By what process of development did it reach it? Why should these extraordinary structures crop out on the banks of the Nile, and amid the forests and plains of America? And why, in both countries, should they stand with their sides square to the four cardinal points of the compass? Are they in this, too, a reminiscence of the Cross, and of the four rivers of Atlantis that ran to the north, south, east, and west?

"There is yet a third combination that demands a specific notice. The decussated symbol is not unfrequently planted upon what Christian archæologists designate 'a calvary,' that is, upon a *mount* or a *cone.* Thus it is represented in both hemispheres. The megalithic structure of Callernish, in the island of Lewis before mentioned, is the most perfect example of the practice extant in Europe. The mount is preserved to this day. This, to be brief, was the recognized conventional mode of expressing a particular primitive truth or mystery from the days of the Chaldeans to those of the Gnostics, or from one extremity of the civilized world to the other. It is seen in the treatment of the ash Yggdrasill of the Scandinavians, as well as in that of the Bo-tree of the Buddhists. The proto-type was not the Egyptian, but the Babylonian *crux ansata*, the lower member of which constitutes a conical support for the oval or sphere above it. With the Gnostics, who occupied the debatable ground between primitive Christianity and philosophic paganism, and who inscribed it upon their tombs, the cone symbolized death as well as life. In every heathen mythology it was the universal emblem of the goddess or mother of heaven, by whatsoever name she was addressed—whether as Mylitta, Astarte, Aphrodite, Isis, Mata, or Venus; and the several eminences consecrated to her worship were, like those upon which Jupiter was originally adored, of a conical or pyramidal shape. This, too, is the ordinary form of the altars dedicated to the Assyrian god of fertility. In exceptional instances the cone is introduced upon one or the other of the sides, or is distinguishable in the always accompanying mystical tree." (*Edinburgh Review*, July, 1870.)

If the reader will again turn to page 104 of this work he will see that the tree appears on the top of the pyramid or mountain in both the Aztec representations of Aztlan, the original island-home of the Central American races.

The writer just quoted believes that Mr. Faber is correct in his opinion that the pyramid is a transcript of the sacred mountain which stood in the midst of Eden, the Olympus of Atlantis. He adds:

"Thomas Maurice, who is no mean authority, held the same view. He conceived the use to which pyramids in particular were anciently applied to have been threefold — namely, as tombs, temples, and observatories; and this view he labors to establish in the third volume of his 'Indian Antiquities.' Now, whatever may be their actual date, or with whatsoever people they may have originated, whether in Africa or Asia, in the lower valley of the Nile or in the plains of Chaldea, the pyramids of Egypt were unquestionably destined to very opposite purposes. According to Herodotus, they were introduced by the Hyksos; and Proclus, the Platonic philosopher, connects them with the science of astronomy—a science which, he adds, the Egyptians derived from the Chaldeans. Hence we may reasonably infer that they served as well for temples for planetary worship as for observatories. Subsequently to the descent of the shepherds, their hallowed precincts were invaded by royalty, from motives of pride and superstition; and the principal chamber in each was used as tombs."

The pyramidal imitations, dear to the hearts of colonists of the sacred mountain upon which their gods dwelt, was devoted, as perhaps the mountain itself was, to sun and fire worship. The same writer says:

"That Sabian worship once extensively prevailed in the New World is a well-authenticated fact; it is yet practised to some extent by the wandering tribes on the Northern continent, and was the national religion of the Peruvians at the time of the Conquest. That it was also the religion of their more highly civilized predecessors on the soil, south of the equator more especially, is evidenced by the remains of fire-altars, both round and square, scattered about the shores of lakes Umayu and Titicaca, and which are the counterparts of the Gueber dokhmehs overhanging the Caspian Sea. Accordingly, we find, among these and other vestiges of antiquity that indissolubly connected those long-since extinct populations in the New with the races of the Old World, the well-defined symbol of the Maltese Cross. On the Mexican feroher before alluded to, and which is most elaborately carved in bass-relief on a massive piece of polygonous granite, constituting a portion of a cyclopean wall, the cross is enclosed within the ring, and accompanying it are four tassel-like ornaments, graved equally well. Those accompaniments, however, are disposed without any particular regard to order, but the four arms of the cross, never theless, severally and accurately point to the *cardinal quarters.* The same regularity is observable on a much smaller but not less curious monument, which was discovered some time since in an ancient Peruvian huaca or catacomb—namely, a syrinx, or pandean pipe, cut out of a solid mass of *lapis ollaris,* the sides of which are profusely ornamented, not only with Maltese crosses, but also with other symbols very similar in style to those inscribed on the obelisks of Egypt and on the monoliths of this country. The like figure occurs on the equally ancient Otrusco black pottery. But by far the most remarkable example of this form of the Cross in the New World is that which appears on a second type of the Mexican feroher, engraved on a tablet of gypsum, and which is described at length by its discoverer, Captain du Paix, and depicted by his friend, M. Baradère. Here the accompaniments—a shield, a hamlet, and a couple of bead-annulets or rosaries—are, with a single exception, identical in even the minutest particular with an Assyrian monument emblematical of the Deity. . . .

"No country in the world can compare with India for the exposition of the pyramidal cross. There the stupendous labors of Egypt are rivalled, and sometimes surpassed. Indeed, but for the fact of such monuments of patient industry and unexampled skill being still in existence, the accounts of some others which have long since disappeared, having succumbed to the ravages of time and the fury of the bigoted Mussulman, would sound in our ears as incredible as the story of Porsenna's tomb, which 'o'ertopped old Pelion,' and made 'Ossa like a wart.' Yet something not very dissimilar in character to it was formerly the boast of the ancient city of Benares, on the banks of the Ganges. We allude to the great temple of Bindh Madhu, which was demolished in the seventeenth century by the Emperor Aurungzebe. Tavernier, the French baron, who travelled thither about the year 1680, has preserved a brief description of it. The body of the temple was constructed in the figure of a colossal cross (*i. e.,* a St. Andrew's Cross), with a lofty dome at the centre, above which rose a massive structure of a pyramidal form. At the four extremities of the cross there were four other pyramids of proportionate dimensions, and which were ascended from the outside by steps, with balconies at **stated distances** for places of rest, reminding us of the temple of Belus, as described in the pages of Herodotus. The remains of a similar building are found at Mhuttra, on the banks of the Jumna. This and many others, including the subterranean temple at Elephanta and the caverns of Ellora and Salsette, are described at length in the well-known work by Maurice; who adds that, besides these, there was yet another device in which the Hindoo displayed the all-pervading sign; this was by pyramidal towers placed crosswise. At the famous temple of Chillambrum, on the Coromandel coast, there were seven lofty walls, one within the other, round the central quadrangle, and as many pyramidal gate-ways in the midst of each side which forms the limbs of a vast cross."

In Mexico pyramids were found everywhere. Cortez, in a letter to Charles V., states that he counted four hundred of them at Cholula. Their temples were on those "high places." The most ancient pyramids in Mexico are at Teotihuacan, eight leagues from the city of Mexico; the two largest were dedicated to the sun and moon respectively, each built of cut stone, with a level area at the summit, and four stages leading up to it. The larger one is 680 feet square at the base, about 200 feet high, and covers an area of eleven acres. The Pyramid of Cholula, measured by Humboldt, is 160 feet high, 1400 feet square at the base, and covers forty-five acres! The great pyramid of Egypt, Cheops, is 746 feet square, 450 feet high, and covers between twelve and thirteen acres. So that it appears that the base of the Teotihuacan structure is nearly as large as that of Cheops, while that of Cholula covers nearly four times as much space. The Cheops pyramid, however, exceeds very much in height both the American structures.

Señor Garcia y Cubas thinks the pyramids of Teotihuacan (Mexico) were built for the same purpose as those of Egypt. He considers the analogy established in eleven particulars, as follows: 1, the site chosen is the same; 2, the structures are orientated with slight variation; 3, the line through the centres of the structures is in the astronomical meridian; 4, the construction in grades and steps is the same; 5, in both cases the larger pyramids are dedicated to the sun; 6, the Nile has "a valley of the dead," as in Teotihuacan there is "a street of the dead;" 7, some monuments in each class have the nature of fortifications; 8, the smaller mounds are of the same nature and for the same purpose; 9, both pyramids have a small mound joined to one of their faces; 10, the openings discovered in the Pyramid of the Moon are also found in some Egyptian pyramids; 11, the interior arrangements of the pyramids are analogous. ("Ensayo de un Estudio.")

It is objected that the American edifices are different in form from the Egyptian, in that they are truncated, or flattened at the top; but this is not an universal rule.

"In many of the ruined cities of Yucatan one or more pyramids have been found upon the summit of which no traces of any building could be discovered, although upon surrounding pyramids such structures could be found. There is also some reason to believe that perfect pyramids have been found in America. Waldeck found near Palenque two pyramids in a state of perfect preservation, square at the base, pointed at the top, and thirty-one feet high, their sides forming equilateral triangles." (Bancroft's "Native Races," vol. v., p. 58.)

Bradford thinks that "some of the Egyptian pyramids, and those which with some reason it has been supposed are the most ancient, are precisely similar to the Mexican *teocalli.*" ("North Americans of Antiquity" p. 423.)

And there is in Egypt another form of pyramid called the *mastaba*, which, like the Mexican, was flattened on the top; while in Assyria structures flattened like the Mexican are found. "In fact," says one writer, "this form of temple (the flat-topped) has been found from Mesopotamia to the Pacific Ocean." The Phœnicians also built pyramids. In the thirteenth century the Dominican Brocard visited the ruins of the Phœnician city of Mrith or Marathos, and speaks in the strongest terms of admiration of those pyramids of surprising grandeur, constructed of blocks of stone from twenty-six to twenty-

eight feet long, whose thickness exceeded the stature of a tall
man. ("Prehistoric Nations," p. 144.)

"If," says Ferguson, "we still hesitate to pronounce that
there was any connection between the builders of the pyramids of Suku and Oajaca, or the temples of Xochialco and
Boro Buddor, we must at least allow that the likeness is startling, and difficult to account for on the theory of mere accidental coincidence."

The Egyptian pyramids all stand with their sides to the car-

PYRAMIDS OF EGYPT.

dinal points, while many of the Mexican pyramids do likewise.
The Egyptian pyramids were penetrated by small passage-ways;
so were the Mexican. The Pyramid of Teotihuacan, according
to Almarez, has, at a point sixty-nine feet from the base, a gallery large enough to admit a man crawling on hands and knees.

which extends inward, on an incline, a distance of twenty-five feet, and terminates in two square wells or chambers, each five feet square, and one of them fifteen feet deep.   Mr. Löwenstern

PYRAMIDS OF TEOTIHUACAN.

states, according to Mr. Bancroft ("Native Races," vol. iv., p. 533), that "the gallery is one hundred and fifty-seven feet long, increasing in height to over six feet and a half as it penetrates the pyramid; that the well is over six feet square, extending (apparently) down to the base and up to the summit; and that other cross-galleries are blocked up by débris." In the Pyramid of Cheops there is a similar opening or passage-way forty-nine feet above the base; it is three feet eleven inches high, and three feet five and a half inches wide; it leads down a slope to a sepulchral chamber or well, and connects with other passage-ways leading up into the body of the pyramid.

THE GREAT MOUND, NEAR MIAMISBURG, OHIO.

In both the Egyptian and the American pyramids the outside of the structures was covered with a thick coating of smooth, shining cement.

Humboldt considered the Pyramid of Cholula of the same type as the Temple of Jupiter Belus, the pyramids of Meidoun Dachhour, and the group of Sakkarah, in Egypt.

GREAT PYRAMID OF XCOOH, MEXICO.

In both America and Egypt the pyramids were used as places of sepulture; and it is a remarkable fact that the system of earthworks and mounds, kindred to the pyramids, is found even in England. Silsbury Hill, at Avebury, is an artificial mound *one hundred and seventy feet high.* It is connected with ramparts, avenues (fourteen hundred and eighty yards long), circular ditches, and stone circles, almost identical with those found in the valley of the Mississippi. In Ireland the dead were buried in vaults of stone, and the earth raised over them in pyramids flattened on the top. They were called "moats" by the people. We have found the stone vaults at the base of similar truncated pyramids in Ohio. There can be no doubt that the pyramid was a developed and perfected mound, and that the parent form of these curious structures is to be found in Silsbury Hill, and in the mounds of earth of Central America and the Mississippi Valley.

We find the emblem of the Cross in pre-Christian times venerated as a holy symbol on both sides of the Atlantic; and we find it explained as a type of the four rivers of the happy island where the civilization of the race originated.

We find everywhere among the European and American nations the memory of an Eden of the race, where the first men dwelt in primeval peace and happiness, and which was afterward destroyed by water.

We find the pyramid on both sides of the Atlantic, with its four sides pointing, like the arms of the Cross, to the four cardinal points—a reminiscence of Olympus; and in the Aztec representation of Olympos (Aztlan) we find the pyramid as the central and typical figure.

Is it possible to suppose all these extraordinary coincidences to be the result of accident? We might just as well say that the similarities between the American and English forms of government were not the result of relationship or descent, but that men placed in similar circumstances had spontaneously and necessarily reached the same results.

Chapter VI.

GOLD AND SILVER THE SACRED METALS OF ATLANTIS.

Money is the instrumentality by which man is lifted above the limitations of barter. Baron Storch terms it "the marvellous instrument to which we are indebted for our wealth and civilization."

It is interesting to inquire into the various articles which have been used in different countries and ages as money. The following is a table of some of them:

Articles of Utility.

India .... Cakes of tea.
China .... Pieces of silk.
Abyssinia .... Salt.
Iceland and Newfoundland.......... Codfish.
Illinois (in early days).............. Coon-skins.
Bornoo (Africa) .... Cotton shirts.
Ancient Russia.................... Skins of wild animals.
West India Islands (1500) .... Cocoa-nuts.
Massachusetts Indians .... Wampum and musket-balls.
Virginia (1700) .... Tobacco.
British West India Islands.......... Pins, snuff, and whiskey.
Central South America .... Soap, chocolate, and eggs.
Ancient Romans.................... Cattle.
     "   Greece.................... Nails of copper and iron.
The Lacedemonians................ Iron.
The Burman Empire .... Lead.
Russia (1828 to 1845).............. Platinum.
Rome (under Numa Pompilius) .... Wood and leather.
     "   ("   the Cæsars) .... Land.

Articles of Utility—Continued.

Carthaginians....................Leather.
Ancient Britons ....Cattle, slaves, brass, and iron.
England (under James II.)..........Tin, gun-metal, and pewter.
South Sea Islands ....Axes and hammers.

Articles of Ornament.

Ancient Jews ....Jewels.
The Indian Islands and Africa........Cowrie shells.

Conventional Signs.

Holland (1574)...................Pieces of pasteboard.
China (1200) ....Bark of the mulberry-tree.

It is evident that every primitive people uses as money those
articles upon which they set the highest value—as cattle, jewels, slaves, salt, musket-balls, pins, snuff, whiskey, cotton shirts,
leather, axes, and hammers; or those articles for which there
was a foreign demand, and which they could trade off to the
merchants for articles of necessity—as tea, silk, codfish, coon-
skins, cocoa-nuts, and tobacco. Then there is a later stage,
when the stamp of the government is impressed upon paper,
wood, pasteboard, or the bark of trees, and these articles are
given a legal-tender character.

When a civilized nation comes in contact with a barbarous
people they seek to trade with them for those things which
they need; a metal-working people, manufacturing weapons of
iron or copper, will seek for the useful metals, and hence we
find iron, copper, tin, and lead coming into use as a standard
of values—as money; for they can always be converted into
articles of use and weapons of war. But when we ask how it
chanced that gold and silver came to be used as money, and
why it is that gold is regarded as so much more valuable than
silver, no answer presents itself. It was impossible to make
either of them into pots or pans, swords or spears; they were
not necessarily more beautiful than glass or the combinations
of tin and copper. Nothing astonished the American races

more than the extraordinary value set upon gold and silver by
the Spaniards; they could not understand it. A West Indian
savage traded a handful of gold-dust with one of the sailors accompanying Columbus for some tool, and then ran for his life
to the woods lest the sailor should repent his bargain and call
him back. The Mexicans had coins of tin shaped like a letter
T. We can understand this, for tin was necessary to them in
hardening their bronze implements, and it may have been the
highest type of metallic value among them. A round copper
coin with a serpent stamped on it was found at Palenque, and
T-shaped copper coins are very abundant in the ruins of Central America. This too we can understand, for copper was necessary in every work of art or utility.

All these nations were familiar with gold and silver, but they
used them as *sacred metals* for the adornment of the temples
of the sun and moon. The color of gold was something of the
color of the sun's rays, while the color of silver resembled the
pale light of the moon, and hence they were respectively sacred to the gods of the sun and moon. And this is probably
the origin of the comparative value of these metals: they became the precious metals because they were the sacred metals,
and gold was more valuable than silver—just as the sun-god
was the great god of the nations, while the mild moon was
simply an attendant upon the sun.

The Peruvians called gold "the tears wept by the sun." It
was not used among the people for ornament or money. The
great temple of the sun at Cuzco was called the "Place of
Gold." It was, as I have shown, literally a mine of gold.
Walls, cornices, statuary, plate, ornaments, all were of gold;
the very ewers, pipes, and aqueducts — even the agricultural
implements used in the garden of the temple—were of gold
and silver. The value of the jewels which adorned the temple
was equal to one hundred and eighty millions of dollars! The
riches of the kingdom can be conceived when we remember
that from a pyramid in Chimu a Spanish explorer named

Toledo took, in 1577, $4,450,284 in gold and silver. ("New American Cyclopædia," art. *American Antiquities.*) The gold and silver of Peru largely contributed to form the metallic currency upon which Europe has carried on her commerce during the last three hundred years.

Gold and silver were not valued in Peru for any intrinsic usefulness; they were regarded as sacred because reserved for the two great gods of the nation. As we find gold and silver mined and worked on both sides of the Atlantic at the earliest periods of recorded history, we may fairly conclude that they were known to the Atlanteans; and this view is confirmed by the statements of Plato, who represents a condition of things in Atlantis exactly like that which Pizarro found in Peru. Doubtless the vast accumulations of gold and silver in both countries were due to the fact that these metals were not permitted to be used by the people. In Peru the annual taxes of the people were paid to the Inca in part in gold and silver from the mines, and they were used to ornament the temples; and thus the work of accumulating the sacred metals went on from generation to generation. The same process doubtless led to the vast accumulations in the temples of Atlantis, as described by Plato.

Now, as the Atlanteans carried on an immense commerce with all the countries of Europe and Western Asia, they doubtless inquired and traded for gold and silver for the adornment of their temples, and they thus produced a demand for and gave a value to the two metals otherwise comparatively useless to man—a value higher than any other commodity which the people could offer their civilized customers; and as the reverence for the great burning orb of the sun, master of all the manifestations of nature, was tenfold as great as the veneration for the smaller, weaker, and variable goddess of the night, so was the demand for the metal sacred to the sun ten times as great as for the metal sacred to the moon. This view is confirmed by the fact that the root of the word by which the Celts, the Greeks, and the Romans designated gold was the Sanscrit word *harat,* which means, "*the color of the sun.*" Among the Assyrians gold and silver were respectively consecrated to the sun and moon precisely as they were in Peru. A pyramid belonging to the palace of Nineveh is referred to repeatedly in the inscriptions. It was composed of seven stages, equal in height, and each one smaller in area than the one beneath it; each stage was covered with stucco of different colors, "a different color representing each of the heavenly bodies, the least important being at the base: white (Venus); black (Saturn); purple (Jupiter); blue (Mercury); vermillion (Mars); *silver* (the Moon); and *gold* (the Sun)." (Lenormant's "Ancient History of the East," vol. i., p. 463.) "In England, to this day the new moon is saluted with a bow or a courtesy, as well as the curious practice of 'turning one's silver,' which seems a relic of the offering of *the moon's proper metal.*" (Tylor's "Anthropology, p. 361.) The custom of wishing, when one first sees the new moon, is probably a survival of moon-worship; the wish taking the place of the prayer.

And thus has it come to pass that, precisely as the physicians of Europe, fifty years ago, practised bleeding, because for thousands of years their savage ancestors had used it to draw away the evil spirits out of the man, so the business of our modern civilization is dependent upon the superstition of a past civilization, and the bankers of the world are to-day perpetuating the adoration of "the tears wept by the sun" which was commenced ages since on the island of Atlantis.

And it becomes a grave question—when we remember that the rapidly increasing business of the world, consequent upon an increasing population, and a civilization advancing with giant steps, is measured by the standard of a currency limited by natural laws, decreasing annually in production, and incapable of expanding proportionately to the growth of the world— whether this Atlantean superstition may not yet inflict more incalculable injuries on mankind than those which resulted from the practice of phlebotomy.

PART V.

THE COLONIES OF ATLANTIS.

Chapter I.

THE CENTRAL AMERICAN AND MEXICAN COLONIES.

The western shores of Atlantis were not far distant from the West India Islands; a people possessed of ships could readily pass from island to island until they reached the continent. Columbus found the natives making such voyages in open canoes. If, then, we will suppose that there was no original connection between the inhabitants of the main-land and of Atlantis, the commercial activity of the Atlanteans would soon reveal to them the shores of the Gulf. Commerce implies the plantation of colonies; the trading-post is always the nucleus of a settlement; we have seen this illustrated in modern times in the case of the English East India Company and the Hudson Bay Company. We can therefore readily believe that commercial intercourse between Atlantis and Yucatan, Honduras and Mexico, created colonies along the shores of the Gulf which gradually spread into the interior, and to the high table-lands of Mexico. And, accordingly, we find, as I have already shown, that all the traditions of Central America and Mexico point to some country in the East, and beyond the sea, as the source of their first civilized people; and this region, known among them as "Aztlan," lived in the memory of the people as a beautiful and happy land, where their ancestors had dwelt in peace for many generations.

Dr. Le Plongeon, who spent four years exploring Yucatan, says:

"One-third of this tongue (the Maya) is pure Greek. Who brought the dialect of Homer to America? or who took to Greece that of the Mayas? Greek is the offspring of the Sanscrit. Is Maya? or are they coeval? . . . The Maya is not devoid of words from the Assyrian."

That the population of Central America (and in this term I include Mexico) was at one time very dense, and had attained to a high degree of civilization, higher even than that of Europe in the time of Columbus, there can be no question; and it is also probable, as I have shown, that they originally belonged to the white race. Dèsirè Charnay, who is now exploring the ruins of Central America, says (*North American Review*, January, 1881, p. 48), "The Toltecs were *fair, robust, and bearded*. I have often seen Indians of pure blood with blue eyes." Quetzalcoatl was represented as large, "with a big head and a heavy beard." The same author speaks (page 44) of "the ocean of ruins all around, not inferior in size to those of Egypt." At Teotihuacan he measured one building two thousand feet wide on each side, and fifteen pyramids, each nearly as large in the base as Cheops. "The city is indeed of vast extent . . . the whole ground, over a space of five or six miles in diameter, is covered with heaps of ruins—ruins which at first make no impression, so complete is their dilapidation." He asserts the great antiquity of these ruins, because he found the very highways of the ancient city to be composed of broken bricks and pottery, the débris left by earlier populations. "This continent," he says (page 43), "is the land of mysteries; we here enter an infinity whose limits we cannot estimate. . . . I shall soon have to quit work in this place. The long avenue on which it stands is lined with ruins of public buildings and palaces, forming continuous lines, as in the streets of modern cities. Still, all these edifices and halls were as nothing compared with the vast substructures which strengthened their foundations."

We find the strongest resemblances to the works of the an·
cient European races: the masonry is similar; the cement is
the same; the sculptures are alike; both peoples used the arch;
in both continents we find bricks, glassware, and even porcelain
(*North American Review*, December, 1880, pp. 524, 525), " with
blue figures on a white ground;" also bronze composed of the
same elements of copper and tin in like proportions; coins
made of copper, round and T-shaped, and even metallic can-
dlesticks.

Dèsirè Charnay believes that he has found in the ruins of Tula
the bones of swine, sheep, oxen, and horses, in a *fossil* state, indicating an immense antiquity.   The Toltecs possessed a pure
and simple religion, like that of Atlantis, as described by Plato,
with the same sacrifices of fruits and flowers; they were farmers; they raised and wove cotton; they cultivated fruits; they
used the sign of the Cross extensively; they cut and engraved
precious stones; among their carvings have been found representations of the elephant and the lion, both animals not known
in America.   The forms of sepulture were the same as among
the ancient races of the Old World; they burnt the bodies
of their great men, and enclosed the dust in funeral urns; some
of their dead were buried in a sitting position, others reclined
at full length, and many were embalmed like the Egyptian
mummies.

When we turn to Mexico, the same resemblances present
themselves.

The government was an elective monarchy, like that of Po-
land, the king being selected from the royal family by the
votes of the nobles of the kingdom.   There was a royal family, an aristocracy, a privileged priesthood, a judiciary, and a
common people.   Here we have all the several estates into
which society in Europe is divided.

There were thirty grand nobles in the kingdom, and the
vastness of the realm may be judged by the fact that each of
these could muster one hundred thousand vassals from their

own estates, or a total of three millions. And we have only to read of the vast hordes brought into the field against Cortez to know that this was not an exaggeration.

They even possessed that which has been considered the crowning feature of European society, the feudal system. The nobles held their lands upon the tenure of military service.

But the most striking feature was the organization of the judiciary. The judges were independent even of the king, and held their offices for life. There were supreme judges for the larger divisions of the kingdom, district judges in each of the provinces, and magistrates chosen by the people throughout the country.

There was also a general legislative assembly, congress, or parliament, held every eighty days, presided over by the king, consisting of all the judges of the realm, to which the last appeal lay.

"The rites of marriage," says Prescott, "were celebrated with as much formality as in any Christian country; and the institution was held in such reverence that a tribunal was instituted for the sole purpose of determining questions relating to it. Divorces could not be obtained until authorized by a sentence of the court, after a patient hearing of the parties."

Slavery was tolerated, but the labors of the slave were light, his rights carefully guarded, and his children were free. The slave could own property, and even other slaves.

Their religion possessed so many features similar to those of the Old World, that the Spanish priests declared the devil had given them a bogus imitation of Christianity to destroy their souls. "The devil," said they, "stole all he could."

They had confessions, absolution of sins, and baptism. When their children were named, they sprinkled their lips and bosoms with water, and "the Lord was implored to permit the holy drops to wash away the sin that was given it before the foundation of the world."

The priests were numerous and powerful. They practised

fasts, vigils, flagellations, and many of them lived in monastic seclusion.

The Aztecs, like the Egyptians, had progressed through all the three different modes of writing—the picture-writing, the symbolical, and the phonetic. They recorded all their laws, their tribute-rolls specifying the various imposts, their mythology, astronomical calendars, and rituals, their political annals and their chronology. They wrote on cotton-cloth, on skins prepared like parchment, on a composition of silk and gum, and on a species of paper, soft and beautiful, made from the aloe. Their books were about the size and shape of our own, but the leaves were long strips folded together in many folds.

They wrote poetry and cultivated oratory, and paid much attention to rhetoric. They also had a species of theatrical performances.

Their proficiency in astronomy is thus spoken of by Prescott:

"That they should be capable of accurately adjusting their festivals by the movements of the heavenly bodies, and should fix the true length of the tropical year *with a precision unknown to the great philosophers of antiquity*, could be the result only of a long series of nice and patient observations, evincing no slight progress in civilization."

"Their women," says the same author, "are described by the Spaniards as pretty, though with a serious and rather melancholy cast of countenance. Their long, black hair might generally be seen wreathed with flowers, or, among the richer people, with strings of precious stones and pearls from the Gulf of California. They appear to have been treated with much consideration by their husbands; and passed their time in indolent tranquillity, or in such feminine occupations as spinning, embroidery, and the like; while their maidens beguiled the hours by the rehearsal of traditionary tales and ballads.

"Numerous attendants of both sexes waited at the banquets. The halls were scented with perfumes, and the courts strewed with odoriferous herbs and flowers, which were distributed in profusion among the guests as they arrived. Cotton napkins and ewers of water were placed before them as they took their seats at the board. Tobacco was then offered, in pipes, mixed with aromatic substances, or in the form of cigars inserted in tubes of tortoise-shell or silver. It is a curious fact that the Aztecs also took the dried tobacco leaf in the pulverized form of snuff.

"The table was well supplied with substantial meats, especially game, among which the most conspicuous was the turkey. Also, there were found vegetables and fruits of every delicious variety native to the continent. Their palate was still further regaled by confections and pastry, for which their maize-flower and sugar furnished them ample materials. The meats were kept warm with chafing-dishes. The table was ornamented

COMMON FORM OF ARCH, CENTRAL AMERICA.

with vases of silver and sometimes gold of delicate workmanship. The favorite beverage was *chocolatl,* flavored with vanilla and different spices. The fermented juice of the maguey, with a mixture of sweets and acids, supplied various agreeable drinks of different degrees of strength."

It is not necessary to describe their great public works, their floating gardens, their aqueducts, bridges, forts, temples, pal-

SECTION OF THE TREASURE-HOUSE OF ATREUS AT MYCENÆ.

aces, and gigantic pyramids, all ornamented with wonderful statuary.

We find a strong resemblance between the form of arch
used in the architecture of Central America and that of the
oldest buildings of Greece. The Palenque arch is made by
the gradual overlapping of the strata of the building, as shown
in the accompanying cut from Baldwin's "Ancient America,"
page 100. It was the custom of these ancient architects to
fill in the arch itself with masonry, as shown in the picture

ARCH OF LAS MONJAS, PALENQUE, CENTRAL AMERICA.

on page 355 of the Arch of Las Monjas, Palenque. If now we look at the representation of the "Treasure-house of Atreus" at Mycenæ, on page 354 — one of the oldest structures in Greece—we find precisely the same form of arch, filled in in the same way.

Rosengarten ("Architectural Styles," p. 59) says:

"The base of these treasure-houses is circular, and the covering of a dome shape; it does not, however, form an arch, but courses of stone are laid horizontally over one another in such a way that each course projects beyond the one below it, till the space at the highest course becomes so narrow that a single stone covers it. Of all those that have survived to the present day the treasure-house at Atreus is the most venerable."

The same form of arch is found among the ruins of that interesting people, the Etruscans.

"Etruscan vaults are of two kinds. The more curious and probably the most ancient are *false arches*, formed of horizontal courses of stone, each a little overlapping the other, and carried on until the aperture at the top could be closed by a single superincumbent slab. Such is the construction of the Regulini-Galassi vault, at Cervetere, the ancient Cære." (Rawlinson's "Origin of Nations," p. 117.)

It is sufficient to say, in conclusion, that Mexico, under European rule, or under her own leaders, has never again risen to her former standard of refinement, wealth, prosperity, or civilization.

Chapter II.

THE EGYPTIAN COLONY.

WHAT proofs have we that the Egyptians were a colony from Atlantis?

1. They claimed descent from "the twelve great gods," which must have meant the twelve gods of Atlantis, to wit, Poseidon and Cleito and their ten sons.

2. According to the traditions of the Phœnicians, the Egyptians derived their civilization from them; and as the Egyptians far antedated the rise of the Phœnician nations proper, this must have meant that Egypt derived its civilization from the same country to which the Phœnicians owed their own origin. The Phœnician legends show that Misor, from whom the Egyptians were descended, was the child of the Phœnician gods Amynus and Magus. Misor gave birth to Taaut, the god of letters, the inventor of the alphabet, and Taaut became Thoth, the god of history of the Egyptians. Sanchoniathon tells us that "Chronos (king of Atlantis) visited the South, and gave all Egypt to the god Taaut, that it might be his kingdom." "Misor" is probably the king "Mestor" named by Plato.

3. According to the Bible, the Egyptians were descendants of Ham, who was one of the three sons of Noah who escaped from the Deluge, to wit, the destruction of Atlantis.

4. The great similarity between the Egyptian civilization and that of the American nations.

5. The fact that the Egyptians claimed to be *red* men.

6. The religion of Egypt was pre-eminently sun-worship; and *Ra* was the sun-god of Egypt, Rama, the sun of the Hin-

doos, Rana, a god of the Toltecs, Raymi, the great festival of
the sun of the Peruvians, and Rayam, a god of Yemen.

7. The presence of pyramids in Egypt and America.

8. The Egyptians were the only people of antiquity who
were well-informed as to the history of Atlantis. The Egyptians were never a maritime people, and the Atlanteans must
have brought that knowledge to them. They were not likely
to send ships to Atlantis.

9. We find another proof of the descent of the Egyptians
from Atlantis in their belief as to the "under-world." This
land of the dead was situated in the *West*—hence the tombs
were all placed, whenever possible, on the west bank of the
Nile. The constant cry of the mourners as the funeral procession moved forward was, "To the west; to the west." This
under-world was *beyond the water*, hence the funeral procession always crossed a body of water. "Where the tombs were,
as in most cases, on the west bank of the Nile, the Nile was
crossed; where they were on the eastern shore the procession
passed over a sacred lake." (R. S. Poole, *Contemporary Review*, August, 1881, p. 17.) In the procession was "*a sacred
ark* of the sun."

All this is very plain: the under-world in the West, the
land of the dead, was Atlantis, the drowned world, the world
beneath the horizon, beneath the sea, to which the peasants of
Brittany looked from Cape Raz, the most western cape projecting into the Atlantic. It was only to be reached from Egypt
by crossing the water, and it was associated with the ark, the
emblem of Atlantis in all lands.

The soul of the dead man was supposed to journey to the
under-world by "a *water progress*" (*Ibid.*, p. 18), his destina-
tion was the Elysian Fields, where mighty corn grew, and where
he was expected to cultivate the earth; "this task was of supreme importance." (*Ibid.*, p. 19.) The Elysian Fields were
the "Elysion" of the Greeks, the abode of the blessed, which
we have seen was an island *in the remote west.*" The Egyp-

tian belief referred to a real country; they described its cities, mountains, and rivers; one of the latter was called *Uranes*, a name which reminds us of the Atlantean god Uranos. In connection with all this we must not forget that Plato described Atlantis as "that *sacred* island lying beneath the sun." Everywhere in the ancient world we find the minds of men looking to the west for the land of the dead. Poole says, "How then can we account for this strong conviction? Surely it must be a survival of an ancient belief which flowed in the very veins of the race." (*Contemporary Review*, 1881, p. 19.) It was based on an universal tradition that under "an immense ocean," in "the far west," there was an "under-world," a world comprising millions of the dead, a mighty race, that had been suddenly swallowed up in the greatest catastrophe known to man since he had inhabited the globe.

10. There is no evidence that the civilization of Egypt was developed in Egypt itself; it must have been transported there from some other country. To use the words of a recent writer in *Blackwood*,

"Till lately it was believed that the use of the papyrus for writing was introduced about the time of Alexander the Great; then Lepsius found the hieroglyphic sign of the papyrus-roll on monuments of the twelfth dynasty; afterward he found the same sign on monuments of the fourth dynasty, which is getting back pretty close to Menes, the protomonarch; and, indeed, little doubt is entertained that the art of writing on papyrus was understood as early as the days of Menes himself. The fruits of investigation in this, as in many other subjects, are truly most marvellous. Instead of exhibiting the rise and progress of any branches of knowledge, they tend to prove that nothing had any rise or progress, but that everything is referable to the very earliest dates. The experience of the Egyptologist must teach him to reverse the observation of Topsy, and to ''spect that nothing growed,' but that as soon as men were planted on the banks of the Nile they were *already the cleverest men that ever lived, endowed with more knowledge and more power than their successors for centuries and centuries could at-*

tain to. Their system of writing, also, is found to have been complete from the very first. . . .

"But what are we to think when the antiquary, grubbing in the dust and silt of five thousand years ago to discover some traces of infant effort—some rude specimens of the ages of Magog and Mizraim, in which we may admire the germ that has since developed into a wonderful art—breaks his shins against an article so perfect that it equals if it does not excel the supreme stretch of modern ability? How shall we support the theory if it come to our knowledge that, before Noah was cold in his grave, his descendants were adepts in construction and in the fine arts, and that their achievements were for magnitude such as, if we possess the requisite skill, we never attempt to emulate? . . .

"As we have not yet discovered any trace of the rude, savage Egypt, but have seen her in her very earliest manifestations already skilful, erudite, and strong, it is impossible to determine the order of her inventions. Light may yet be thrown upon her rise and progress, but our deepest researches have hitherto shown her to us as only the mother of a most accomplished race. How they came by their knowledge is matter for speculation; that they possessed it is matter of fact. We never find them without the ability to organize labor, or shrinking from the very boldest efforts in digging canals and irrigating, in quarrying rock, in building, and in sculpture."

The explanation is simple: the waters of the Atlantic now flow over the country where all this magnificence and power were developed by slow stages from the rude beginnings of barbarism.

And how mighty must have been the parent nation of which this Egypt was a colony!

Egypt was the magnificent, the golden bridge, ten thousand years long, glorious with temples and pyramids, illuminated and illustrated by the most complete and continuous records of human history, along which the civilization of Atlantis, in a great procession of kings and priests, philosophers and astronomers, artists and artisans, streamed forward to Greece, to Rome, to Europe, to America. As far back in the ages as the eye can penetrate, even where the perspective dwindles almost to a point, we can still see the swarming multitudes, possessed of all the arts of the highest civilization, pressing forward from out that other and greater empire of which even this wonder-working Nile-land is but a faint and imperfect copy.

Look at the record of Egyptian greatness as preserved in her works: The pyramids, still in their ruins, are the marvel of mankind. The river Nile was diverted from its course by monstrous embankments to make a place for the city of Memphis. The artificial lake of Mœris was created as a reservoir for the waters of the Nile: it was *four hundred and fifty miles in circumference* and three hundred and fifty feet deep, with subterranean channels, flood-gates, locks, and dams, by which the wilderness was redeemed from sterility. Look at the magnificent mason-work of this ancient people! Mr. Kenrick, speaking of the casing of the Great Pyramid, says, "The joints are scarcely perceptible, and *not wider than the thickness of silver-paper*, and the cement so tenacious that fragments of the casing-stones still remain in their original position, notwithstanding the lapse of so many centuries, and the violence by which they were detached." Look at the ruins of the Labyrinth, which aroused the astonishment of Herodotus; it had three thousand chambers, half of them above ground and half below —a combination of courts, chambers, colonnades, statues, and pyramids. Look at the Temple of Karnac, covering a square each side of which is eighteen hundred feet. Says a recent writer, "Travellers one and all appear to have been unable to find words to express the feelings with which these sublime remains inspired them. They have been astounded and overcome by the magnificence and the prodigality of workmanship here to be admired. Courts, halls, gate-ways, pillars, obelisks, monolithic figures, sculptures, rows of sphinxes, are massed in such profusion that the sight is too much for modern comprehension." Denon says, "It is hardly possible to believe, after having seen it, in the reality of the existence of so many buildings collected on a single point—in their dimensions, in the resolute perseverance which their construction required, and in the incalculable expense of so much magnificence." And again, " It is necessary that the reader should fancy what is before him to be a dream, as he who views the objects themselves occasionally yields to the doubt whether he be perfectly awake." There were lakes and mountains within the periphery of the sanctuary. " *The cathedral of Notre Dame at Paris could be set inside one of the halls of Karnac, and not touch the walls! . . .* The whole valley and delta of the Nile, from the Catacombs to the sea, was covered with temples, palaces, tombs, pyramids, and pillars." Every stone was covered with inscriptions.

The state of society in the early days of Egypt approximated very closely to our modern civilization. Religion consisted in the worship of one God and the practice of virtue; forty-two commandments prescribed the duties of men to themselves, their neighbors, their country, and the Deity; a heaven awaited the good and a hell the vicious; there was a judgment-day when the hearts of men were weighed:

> " He is sifting out the hearts of men
> Before his judgment-seat."

Monogamy was the strict rule; not even the kings, in the early days, were allowed to have more than one wife. The wife's rights of separate property and her dower were protected by law; she was "the lady of the house;" she could "buy, sell, and trade on her own account;" in case of divorce her dowry was to be repaid to her, with interest at a high rate. The marriage-ceremony embraced an oath not to contract any other matrimonial alliance. The wife's status was as high in the earliest days of Egypt as it is now in the most civilized nations of Europe or America.

Slavery was permitted, but the slaves were treated with the greatest humanity. In the confessions, buried with the dead, the soul is made to declare that "I have not incriminated the slave to his master." There was also a clause in the commandments "which protected the laboring man against the exaction of more than his day's labor." They were merciful to the captives made in war; no picture represents torture inflicted upon them; while the representation of a sea-fight shows them saving their drowning enemies. Reginald Stuart Poole says (*Contemporary Review*, August, 1881, p. 43):

"When we consider the high ideal of the Egyptians, as proved by their portrayals of a just life, the principles they laid down as the basis of ethics, the elevation of women among them, their humanity in war, we must admit that their moral place ranks very high among the nations of antiquity.

"The true comparison of Egyptian life is with that of modern nations. This is far too difficult a task to be here undertaken. Enough has been said, however, to show that we need not think that in all respects they were far behind us."

Then look at the proficiency in art of this ancient people.

They were the first mathematicians of the Old World. Those Greeks whom we regard as the fathers of mathematics were simply pupils of Egypt. They were the first land-surveyors. They were the first astronomers, calculating eclipses, and watching the periods of planets and constellations. They knew the rotundity of the earth, which it was supposed Columbus had discovered! †

"The signs of the zodiac were certainly in use among the Egyptians 1722 years before Christ. One of the learned men of our day, who for fifty years labored to decipher the hieroglyphics of the ancients, found upon a mummy-case in the British Museum a delineation of the signs of the zodiac, and the position of the planets; the date to which they pointed was the autumnal equinox of the year 1722 B.C. Professor Mitchell, to whom the fact was communicated, employed his assistants to ascertain the exact position of the heavenly bodies belonging to our solar system on the equinox of that year. This was done, and a diagram furnished by parties ignorant of his object, which showed that on the 7th of October, 1722 B.C.,

† Incorrect.—E.F.B.

the moon and planets occupied the exact point in the heavens marked upon the coffin in the British Museum." (Goodrich's " Columbus," p. 22.)

They had clocks and dials for measuring time. They possessed gold and silver money. They were the first agriculturists of the Old World, raising all the cereals, cattle, horses, sheep, etc. They manufactured linen of so fine a quality that in the days of King Amasis (600 years B.C.) a single thread of a garment was composed of three hundred and sixty-five minor threads. They worked in gold, silver, copper, bronze, and iron; they tempered iron to the hardness of steel. They were the first chemists. The word " chemistry " comes from *chemi*, and *chemi* means Egypt. They manufactured glass and all kinds of pottery; they made boats out of earthenware; and, precisely as we are now making railroad car-wheels of paper, they manufactured vessels of paper. Their dentists filled teeth with gold; their farmers hatched poultry by artificial heat. They were the first musicians; they possessed guitars, single and double pipes, cymbals, drums, lyres, harps, flutes, the sambric, ashur, etc.; they had even castanets, such as are now used in Spain. In medicine and surgery they had reached such a degree of perfection that several hundred years B.C. the operation for the removal of cataract from the eye was performed among them; one of the most delicate and difficult feats of surgery, only attempted by us in the most recent times. " The papyrus of Berlin " states that it was discovered, rolled up in a case, under the feet of an Anubis in the town of Sekhém, in the days of Tet (or Thoth), after whose death it was transmitted to King Sent, and was then restored to the feet of the statue. King Sent belonged to the second dynasty, which flourished 4751 B.C., and the papyrus was old in his day.† This papyrus is a medical treatise; there are in it no incantations or charms; but it deals in reasonable remedies, draughts, unguents and injections. The later medical papyri contain a great deal of magic and incantations.

† Outdated chronology. About 2,500 years too early.—E.F.B.

"Great and splendid as are the things which we know about oldest Egypt, she is made a thousand times more sublime by our uncertainty as to the limits of her accomplishments. She presents not a great, definite idea, which, though hard to receive, is, when once acquired, comprehensible and clear. Under the soil of the modern country are hid away thousands and thousands of relics which may astonish the world for ages to come, and change continually its conception of what Egypt was. The effect of research seems to be to prove the objects of it to be much older than we thought them to be—some things thought to be wholly modern having been proved to be repetitions of things Egyptian, and other things known to have been Egyptian being by every advance in knowledge carried back more and more toward the very beginning of things. She shakes our most rooted ideas concerning the world's history; she has not ceased to be a puzzle and a lure: there is a spell over her still."

Renan says, "It has no archaic epoch." Osborn says, "It bursts upon us at once in the flower of its highest perfection." Seiss says ("A Miracle in Stone," p. 40), "It suddenly takes its place in the world in all its matchless magnificence, without father, without mother, and as clean apart from all evolution as if it had dropped from the unknown heavens." It had dropped from Atlantis.

Rawlinson says ("Origin of Nations," p. 13):

"Now, in Egypt, it is notorious that there is no indication of any early period of savagery or barbarism. All the authorities agree that, however far back we go, we find in Egypt no rude or uncivilized time out of which civilization is developed. Menes, the first king, changes the course of the Nile, makes a great reservoir, and builds the temple of Phthah at Memphis. . . . We see no barbarous customs, not even the habit, so slowly abandoned by all people, of wearing arms when not on military service."

Tylor says ("Anthropology," p. 192):

"Among the ancient cultured nations of Egypt and Assyria handicrafts had already come to a stage which could only have been reached by thousands of years of progress. In museums still may be examined the work of their joiners, stone-cutters, goldsmiths, wonderful in skill and finish, and often putting to shame the modern artificer. . . . To see gold jewellery of the highest order, the student should examine that of the ancients, such as the Egyptian, Greek, and Etruscan."

The carpenters' and masons' tools of the ancient Egyptians were almost identical with those used among us to-day.

There is a plate showing an Aztec priestess in Delafield's "Antiquities of America," p. 61, which presents a head-dress strikingly Egyptian. In the celebrated "tablet of the cross," at Palenque, we see a cross with a bird perched upon it, to which (or to the cross) two priests are offering sacrifice. In Mr. Stephens's representation from the Vocal Memnon we find almost the same thing, the difference being that, instead of an ornamented Latin cross, we have a *crux commissa*, and instead of one bird there are two, not on the cross, but immediately above it. In both cases the hieroglyphics, though the characters are of course different, are disposed upon the stone in much the same manner. (Bancroft's "Native Races," vol. v., p. 61.)

Even the obelisks of Egypt have their counterpart in America.

Quoting from Molina ("History of Chili," tom. i., p. 169), McCullough writes, "Between the hills of Mendoza and La Punta is a pillar of stone *one hundred and fifty feet high,* and twelve feet in diameter." ("Researches," pp. 171, 172.) The columns of Copan stand detached and solitary, so do the obelisks of Egypt; both are square or four-sided, and covered with sculpture. (Bancroft's "Native Races," vol. v., p. 60.)

In a letter by Jomard, quoted by Delafield, we read,

"I have recognized in your memoir on the division of time among the Mexican nations, compared with those of Asia, some very striking analogies between the Toltec characters and institutions observed on the banks of the Nile. Among these analogies there is one which is worthy of attention—it is the use of the vague year of three hundred and sixty-five days, composed of equal months, and of five complementary days, equally employed at Thebes and Mexico—a distance of three thousand leagues. . . . In reality, the intercalation of the Mexicans being thirteen days on each cycle of fifty-two years, comes to the same thing as that of the Julian calendar, which is one day in four years; and consequently supposes the duration of the year to be three hundred and sixty-five days *six hours.* Now such was the length of the year among the Egyptians— they intercalated an entire year of three hundred and seventy-five days every one thousand four hundred and sixty years. . . . The fact of the intercalation (by the Mexicans) of thirteen days every cycle—that is, the use of a year of three hundred and sixty-five days and a quarter—is a proof that it was borrowed from the Egyptians, *or that they had a common origin.*" ("Antiquities of America," pp. 52, 53.)

The Mexican century began on the 26th of February, and the 26th of February was celebrated from the time of Nabonassor, 747 B.C., because the Egyptian priests, conformably to their astronomical observations, had fixed the beginning of the month *Toth,* and the commencement of their year, at noon on that day. The five intercalated days to make up the three hundred and sixty-five days were called by the Mexicans *Nemontemi,* or useless, and on them they transacted no business; while the Egyptians, during that epoch, celebrated the festival of the birth of their gods, as attested by Plutarch and others.

It will be conceded that a considerable degree of astronomical knowledge must have been necessary to reach the conclusion that the true year consisted of three hundred and sixty-five days *and six hours* (modern science has demonstrated that it consists of three hundred and sixty-five days and five hours, less ten seconds); and a high degree of civilization was requisite to insist that the year must be brought around, by the intercalation of a certain number of days in a certain period of time, to its true relation to the seasons. Both were the outgrowth of a vast, ancient civilization of the highest order, which transmitted some part of its astronomical knowledge to its colonies through their respective priesthoods.

Can we, in the presence of such facts, doubt the statements of the Egyptian priests to Solon, as to the glory and greatness of Atlantis, its monuments, its sculpture, its laws, its religion, its civilization?

In Egypt we have the oldest of the Old World children of Atlantis; in her magnificence we have a testimony to the development attained by the parent country; by that country whose kings were the gods of succeeding nations, and whose kingdom extended to the uttermost ends of the earth.

The Egyptian historian, Manetho, referred to a period of thirteen thousand nine hundred years as "the reign of the gods," and placed this period at the very beginning of Egyptian history. These thirteen thousand nine hundred years were probably a recollection of Atlantis. Such a lapse of time, vast as it may appear, is but as a day compared with some of our recognized geological epochs.

Chapter III.

THE COLONIES OF THE MISSISSIPPI VALLEY.

If we will suppose a civilized, maritime people to have plant-ed colonies, in the remote past, along the headlands and shores of the Gulf of Mexico, spreading thence, in time, to the table-lands of Mexico and to the plains and mountains of New Mex-ico and Colorado, what would be more natural than that these adventurous navigators, passing around the shores of the Gulf, should, sooner or later, discover the mouth of the Mississippi River; and what more certain than that they would enter it, ex-plore it, and plant colonies along its shores, wherever they found a fertile soil and a salubrious climate. Their outlying provinces would penetrate even into regions where the severity of the climate would prevent great density of population or develop-ment of civilization.

The results we have presupposed are precisely those which we find to have existed at one time in the Mississippi Valley.

The Mound Builders of the United States were pre-eminent-ly a river people. Their densest settlements and greatest works were near the Mississippi and its tributaries. Says Foster ("Pre-historic Races," p. 110), "The navigable streams were the great highways of the Mound Builders."

Mr. Fontaine claims ("How the World was Peopled") that this ancient people constructed "levees" to control and utilize the bayous of the Mississippi for the purpose of agri-culture and commerce. The Yazoo River is called *Yazoo-ok-hinnah*—the River of Ancient Ruins. "There is no evidence that they had reached the Atlantic coast; no authentic remains of the Mound Builders are found in the New England States, nor even in the State of New York." (" North Americans of Antiquity," p. 28.) This would indicate that the civilization of this people advanced up the Mississippi River and spread out over its tributaries, but did not cross the Alleghany Mountains. They reached, however, far up the Missouri and Yellowstone rivers, and thence into Oregon. The head-waters of the Missouri became one of their great centres of population; but their chief sites were upon the Mississippi and Ohio rivers. In Wisconsin we find the northern central limit of their work; they seem to have occupied the southern counties of the State, and the western shores of Lake Michigan. Their circular mounds are found in Minnesota and Iowa, and some very large ones in Dakota. Illinois and Indiana were densely populated by them: it is believed that the vital centre of their colonies was near the junction of the Ohio and Mississippi rivers.

The chief characteristic of the Mound Builders was that from which they derived their name—the creation of great structures of earth or stone, not unlike the pyramids of Mexico and Egypt. Between Alton and East St. Louis is the great mound of Cahokia, which may be selected as a type of their works: it rises ninety-seven feet high, while its square sides are 700 and 500 feet respectively. There was a terrace on the south side 160 by 300 feet, reached by a graded way; the summit of the pyramid is flattened, affording a platform 200 by 450 feet. It will thus be seen that the area covered by the mound of Cahokia is about as large as that of the greatest pyramid of Egypt, Cheops, although its height is much less.

The number of monuments left by the Mound Builders is extraordinarily great. In Ohio alone there are more than ten thousand tumuli, and from one thousand to fifteen hundred enclosures. Their mounds were not cones but four-sided pyramids—their sides, like those of the Egyptian pyramids, corresponding with the cardinal points. (Foster's " Prehistoric Races," p. 112.)

The Mound Builders had attained a considerable degree of civilization; they were able to form, in the construction of their works, perfect circles and perfect squares of great accuracy, carried over the varying surface of the country. One large enclosure comprises exactly forty acres. At Hopetown, Ohio, are two walled figures—one a square, the other a circle—each containing precisely twenty acres. They must have possessed regular scales of measurement, and the means of determining angles and of computing the area to be enclosed by the square and the circle, so that the space enclosed by each might exactly correspond.

"The most skilful engineer of this day would find it difficult," says Mr. Squier, "without the aid of instruments, to lay down an accurate square of the great dimensions above represented, measuring, as they do, more than four-fifths of a mile in circumference. . . . But we not only find accurate squares and perfect circles, but also, as we have seen, octagons of great dimensions."

They also possessed an accurate system of weights; bracelets of copper on the arms of a skeleton have been found to be of uniform size, measuring each two and nine-tenth inches, and each weighing *precisely four ounces.*

They built great military works surrounded by walls and ditches, with artificial lakes in the centre to supply water. One work, Fort Ancient, on the Little Miami River, Ohio, has a circuit of between four and five miles; the embankment was twenty feet high; the fort could have held a garrison of sixty thousand men with their families and provisions.

Not only do we find pyramidal structures of earth in the Mississippi Valley very much like the pyramids of Egypt, Mexico, and Peru, but a very singular structure is repeated in Ohio and Peru: I refer to the double walls or prolonged pyramids, if I may coin an expression, shown in the cut page 375.

The Mound Builders possessed chains of fortifications reaching from the southern line of New York diagonally across the

GRADED WAY NEAR PIKETON, OHIO.

country, through Central and Northern Ohio to the Wabash. It would appear probable, therefore, that while they advanced

WALLS AT GRAN-CHIMU, PERU.

from the south it was from the north-east the savage races came who drove them south or exterminated them.

At Marietta, Ohio, we find a combination of the cross and pyramid. (See p. 334, *ante.*) At Newark, Ohio, are extensive

CROSS AND PYRAMID MOUND, OHIO.

and intricate works: they occupy an area two miles square, embraced within embankments twelve miles long. One of the mounds is a threefold symbol, like a bird's foot; the central mound is 155 feet long, and the other two each 110 feet in length. Is this curious design a reminiscence of Atlantis and the three-pronged trident of Poseidon? (See 4th fig., p. 242, *ante.*)

The Mound Builders made sun-dried brick mixed with rushes, as the Egyptians made sun-dried bricks mixed with straw; they worked in copper, silver, lead, and there are evidences, as we shall see, that they wrought even in iron.

Copper implements are very numerous in the mounds. Copper axes, spear-heads, hollow buttons, bosses for ornaments, bracelets, rings, etc., are found in very many of them strikingly similar to those of the Bronze Age in Europe. In one in Butler County, Ohio, was found a copper fillet around the head of a skeleton, with strange devices marked upon it.

Silver ornaments have also been found, but not in such great numbers. They seem to have attached a high value to silver, and it is often found in thin sheets, no thicker than paper, wrapped over copper or stone ornaments so neatly as almost to escape detection. The great esteem in which they held a metal so intrinsically valueless as silver, is another evidence that they must have drawn their superstitions from the same source as the European nations.

Copper is also often found in this manner *plated* over stone pipes, presenting an unbroken metallic lustre, the overlapping edges so well polished as to be scarcely discoverable. Beads and stars made of shells have sometimes been found doubly plated, first with copper then with silver.

The Mound Builders also understood the art of casting metals, or they held intercourse with some race who did; a copper axe "cast" has been found in the State of New York. (See Lubbock's "Prehistoric Times," p. 254, note.) Professor Foster ("Prehistoric Races," p. 259) also proves that the ancient people of the Mississippi Valley possessed this art, and he gives us representations of various articles plainly showing the marks of the mould upon them.

A rude article in the shape of an axe, composed of pure lead, weighing about half a pound, was found in sinking a well within the trench of the ancient works at Circleville. There can be no doubt it was the production of the Mound Builders, as galena has often been found on the altars in the mounds.

It has been generally thought, by Mr. Squier and others, that there were no evidences that the Mound Builders were acquainted with the use of iron, or that their plating was more than a simple *overlaying* of one metal on another, or on some foreign substance.

Some years since, however, a mound was opened at Marietta, Ohio, which seems to have refuted these opinions. Dr. S. P. Hildreth, in a letter to the American Antiquarian Society, thus speaks of it:

"Lying immediately over or on the forehead of the body were found three large circular bosses, or ornaments for a sword-belt or buckler; they are composed of copper overlaid with a thick plate of silver. The fronts are slightly convex, with a depression like a cup in the centre, and they measure two inches and a quarter across the face of each. On the back side, opposite the depressed portion, is a copper rivet or nail, around which are two separate plates by which they were fastened to the leather. Two small pieces of leather were found lying between the plates of one of the bosses; they resemble the skin of a mummy, and seem to have been preserved by the salts of copper. Near the side of the body was found a plate of silver, which appears to have been the upper part of a sword scabbard; it is six inches in length, two in breadth, and weighs one ounce. It seems to have been fastened to the scabbard by three or four rivets, the holes of which remain in the silver.

"Two or three pieces of copper tube were also found, *filled with iron rust.* These pieces, from their appearance, composed the lower end of the scabbard, near the point of the sword. No signs of the sword itself were discovered, except the rust above mentioned.

"The mound had every appearance of being as old as any in the neighborhood, and was at the first settlement of Marietta covered with large trees. It seems to have been made for this single personage, as this skeleton alone was discovered. The bones were very much decayed, and many of them crumbled to dust upon exposure to the air."

Mr. Squier says, "These articles have been critically examined, and it is beyond doubt that the copper bosses were absolutely *plated*, not simply *overlaid*, with silver. Between the copper and the silver exists a connection such as, it seems to me, could only be produced by heat; and if it is admitted that these are genuine relics of the Mound Builders, it must, at the same time, be admitted that they possessed the difficult art of plating one metal upon another. There is but one alternative, viz., that they had occasional or constant intercourse with a people advanced in the arts, from whom these articles were obtained. Again, if Dr. Hildreth is not mistaken, *oxydized iron* or steel was also discovered in connection with the above remains, from which also follows the extraordinary conclusion that *the Mound Builders were acquainted with the use of iron*, the conclusion being, of course, subject to the improbable alternative already mentioned."

In connection with this subject, we would refer to the interesting evidences that the copper mines of the shore of Lake Superior had been at some very remote period worked by the Mound Builders. There were found deep excavations, with rude ladders, huge masses of rock broken off, also numerous stone tools, and all the evidences of extensive and long-continued labor. It is even said that the great Ontonagon mass of pure copper which is now in Washington was excavated by these ancient miners, and that when first found its surface showed numerous marks of their tools.

There seems to be no doubt, then, that the Mound Builders were familiar with the use of copper, silver, and lead, and in all probability of iron. They possessed various mechanical contrivances. They were very probably acquainted with *the lathe*. Beads of shell have been found, looking very much like ivory, and showing the *circular striæ, identical with those produced by turning in a lathe*.

In a mound on the Scioto River was found around the neck

of a skeleton triple rows of beads, made of marine shells and the tusks of some animal. "Several of these," says Squier, "still retain their polish, and bear marks which seem to indicate that they were turned in some machine, instead of being carved or rubbed into shape by hand."

"Not among the least interesting and remarkable relics," continues the same author, "obtained from the mounds are the stone tubes. They are all carved from fine-grained materials, capable of receiving a polish, and being made ornamental as well as useful. The finest specimen yet discovered, and which can scarcely be surpassed in the delicacy of its workmanship, was found in a mound in the immediate vicinity of Chillicothe. It is composed of a compact variety of slate. This stone cuts with great clearness, and receives a fine though not glaring polish. The tube under notice is thirteen inches long by one and one-tenth in diameter; one end swells slightly, and the other terminates in a broad, flattened, triangular mouth-piece of fine proportions, which is carved *with mathematical precision.* It is *drilled* throughout; the bore is seven-tenths of an inch in diameter at the cylindrical end of the tube, and retains that calibre until it reaches the point where the cylinder subsides into the mouth-piece, when it contracts gradually to one-tenth of an inch. The inner surface of the tube is perfectly smooth till within a short distance of the point of contraction. *For the remaining distance the circular striœ, formed by the drill in boring, are distinctly marked.* The carving upon it is very fine."

That they possessed *saws* is proved by the fact that on some fossil teeth found in one of the mounds the *striœ* of the teeth of the saw could be distinctly perceived.

When we consider that some of their porphyry carvings will turn the edge of the best-tempered knife, we are forced to conclude that they possessed that singular process, known to the Mexicans and Peruvians, of tempering copper to the hardness of steel.

We find in the mounds adzes similar in shape to our own, with the edges bevelled from the inside.

Drills and gravers of copper have also been found, with chisel-shaped edges or sharp points.

"It is not impossible," says Squier, "but, on the contrary, very probable, from a close inspection of the mound pottery, that the ancient people possessed the simple approximation toward the potter's wheel; and the polish which some of the finer vessels possess is due to other causes than vitrification."

Their sculptures show a considerable degree of progress. They consist of figures of birds, animals, reptiles, and the faces of men, carved from various kinds of stones, upon the bowls of pipes, upon toys, upon rings, and in distinct and separate figures. We give the opinions of those who have examined them.

Mr. Squier observes: "Various though not abundant specimens of their skill have been recovered, which in elegance of model, delicacy, and finish, as also in fineness of material, come fully up to the best Peruvian specimens, to which they bear, in many respects, a close resemblance. The bowls of most of the stone pipes are carved in miniature figures of animals, birds, reptiles, etc. All of them are executed with strict fidelity to nature, and with exquisite skill. Not only are the features of the objects faithfully represented, but their peculiarities and habits are in some degree exhibited. . . . The two heads here presented, intended to represent the eagle, are far superior in point of finish, spirit, and truthfulness, to any miniature carvings, ancient or modern, which have fallen under the notice of the authors. The peculiar defiant expression of the king of birds is admirably preserved in the carving, which in this respect, more than any other, displays the skill of the artist."

Traces of cloth with "doubled and twisted fibre" have been found in the mounds; also matting; also shuttle-like tablets, used in weaving. There have also been found numerous musical pipes, with mouth-pieces and stops; lovers' pipes, curiously and delicately carved, reminding us of Bryant's lines—

FROM THE MOUNDS OF THE OHIO VALLEY.

> "Till twilight came, and lovers walked and wooed
> In a forgotten language; and old tunes,
> From instruments of unremembered forms,
> Gave the soft winds a voice."

There is evidence which goes to prove that the Mound Builders had relations with the people of a semi-tropical region in the direction of Atlantis. Among their sculptures, in Ohio, we find accurate representations of the lamantine, manatee, or sea-cow—found to-day on the shores of Florida, Brazil, and Central America—and of the toucan, a tropical and almost exclusively South American bird. Sea-shells from the Gulf, pearls from the Atlantic, and obsidian from Mexico, have also been found side by side in their mounds.

The antiquity of their works is now generally conceded. "From the ruins of Nineveh and Babylon," says Mr. Gliddon, "we have bones of at least two thousand five hundred years old; from the pyramids and the catacombs of Egypt both mummied and unmummied crania have been taken, of still higher antiquity, in perfect preservation; nevertheless, the skeletons deposited in our Indian mounds, from the Lakes to the Gulf, are crumbling into dust through age alone."

All the evidence points to the conclusion that civilized or semi-civilized man has dwelt on the western continent from a vast antiquity. Maize, tobacco, quinoa, and the mandico plants have been cultivated so long that their wild originals have quite disappeared.

"The only species of palm cultivated by the South American Indians, that known as the *Gulielma speciosa*, has lost through that culture its original nut-like seed, and is dependent on the hands of its cultivators for its life. Alluding to the above-named plants Dr. Brinton (" Myths of the New World," p. 37) remarks, 'Several are sure to perish unless fostered by human care. What numberless ages does this suggest? How many centuries elapsed ere man thought of cultivating Indian corn? How many more ere it had spread over nearly a hundred degrees of latitude and lost all resemblance to its original form?'

In the animal kingdom certain animals were domesticated by the aborigines from so remote a period that scarcely any of their species, as in the case of the lama of Peru, were to be found in a state of unrestrained freedom at the advent of the Spaniards." (Short's "North Americans of Antiquity," p. 11.)

The most ancient remains of man found in Europe are distinguished by a flattening of the tibia; and this peculiarity is found to be present in an exaggerated form in some of the American mounds. This also points to a high antiquity.

"None of the works, mounds, or enclosures are found on the lowest formed of the river terraces which mark the subsidence of the streams, and as there is no good reason why their builders should have avoided erecting them on that terrace while they raised them promiscuously on all the others, it follows, not unreasonably, that this terrace has been formed since the works were erected." (Baldwin's "Ancient America," p. 47.)

We have given some illustrations showing the similarity between the works of the Mound Builders and those of the Stone and Bronze Age in Europe. (See pp. 251, 260, 261, 262, 265, 266, *ante.*)

The Mound Builders retreated southward toward Mexico, and probably arrived there some time between A.D. 29 and A.D. 231, under the name of Nahuas. They called the region they left in the Mississippi Valley "Hue Hue Tlapalan"—*the old, old red land*—in allusion, probably, to the red-clay soil of part of the country.

In the mounds we find many works of copper but none of bronze. This may indicate one of two things: either the colonies which settled the Mississippi Valley may have left Atlantis prior to the discovery of the art of manufacturing bronze, by mixing one part of tin with nine parts of copper, or, which is more probable, the manufactures of the Mound Builders may have been made on the spot; and as they had no tin within their territory they used copper alone, except, it may be, for such tools as were needed to carve stone, and these, perhaps, were hardened with tin. It is known that the Mexicans possessed the art of manufacturing true bronze; and the intercourse which evidently existed between Mexico and the Mississippi Valley, as proved by the presence of implements of obsidian in the mounds of Ohio, renders it probable that the same commerce which brought them obsidian brought them also small quantities of tin, or tin-hardened copper implements necessary for their sculptures.

The proofs, then, of the connection of the Mound Builders with Atlantis are:

1. Their race identity with the nations of Central America who possessed Flood legends, and whose traditions all point to an eastern, over-sea origin; while the many evidences of their race identity with the ancient Peruvians indicate that they were part of one great movement of the human race, extending from the Andes to Lake Superior, and, as I believe, from Atlantis to India.

2. The similarity of their civilization, and their works of stone and bronze, with the civilization of the Bronze Age in Europe.

3. The presence of great truncated mounds, kindred to the pyramids of Central America, Mexico, Egypt, and India.

4. The representation of tropical animals, which point to an intercourse with the regions around the Gulf of Mexico, where the Atlanteans were colonized.

5. The fact that the settlements of the Mound Builders were confined to the valley of the Mississippi, and were apparently densest at those points where a population advancing up that stream would first reach high, healthy, and fertile lands.

6. The hostile nations which attacked them came from the north; and when the Mound Builders could no longer hold the country, or when Atlantis sunk in the sea, they retreated in the direction whence they came, and fell back upon their kindred races in Central America, as the Roman troops in

Gaul and Britain drew southward upon the destruction of Rome.

7. The Natchez Indians, who are supposed to have descended from the Mound Builders, kept a perpetual fire burning before an altar, watched by old men who were a sort of priesthood, as in Europe.

8. If the tablet said to have been found in a mound near Davenport, Iowa, is genuine, which appears probable, the Mound Builders must either have possessed an alphabet, or have held intercourse with some people who did. (See "North Americans of Antiquity," p. 38.) This singular relic exhibits what appears to be a sacrificial mound with a fire upon it; over it are the sun, moon, and stars, and above these a mass of hieroglyphics which bear some resemblance to the letters of European alphabets, and especially to that unknown alphabet which appears upon the inscribed bronze celt found near Rome. (See p. 258 of this work.) For instance, one of the letters on the celt is this, ⟁; on the Davenport tablet we find this sign, ⟐; on the celt we have ⟑; on the tablet, ⟄; on the celt we have ⟅; on the tablet, ⟆.

Chapter IV.

THE IBERIAN COLONIES OF ATLANTIS.

At the farthest point in the past to which human knowledge extends a race called Iberian inhabited the entire peninsula of Spain, from the Mediterranean to the Pyrenees. They
also extended over the southern part of Gaul as far as the Rhone.

"It is thought that the Iberians from Atlantis and the
north-west part of Africa," says Winchell, "settled in the south-
west of Europe at a period earlier than the settlement of the
Egyptians in the north-east of Africa. The Iberians spread
themselves over Spain, Gaul, and the British Islands as early
as 4000 or 5000 b.c. . . . The fourth dynasty (of the Egyptians), according to Brugsch, dates from about 3500 b.c. At
this time the Iberians had become sufficiently powerful to attempt the conquest of the known world." ("Preadamites,"
p. 443.)
"The Libyan-Amazons of Diodorus—that is to say, the Libyans of the Iberian race—must be identified with the Libyans
with brown and grizzly skin, of whom Brugsch has already
pointed out the representations figured on the Egyptian monuments of the fourth dynasty." (*Ibid.*)

The Iberians, known as Sicanes, colonized Sicily in the
ancient days. They were the original settlers in Italy and
Sardinia. They are probably the source of the dark-haired
stock in Norway and Sweden. Bodichon claims that the Iberians embraced the Ligurians, Cantabrians, Asturians, and Aqui-
tanians. Strabo says, speaking of the Turduli and Turdetani,
"they are the most cultivated of all the Iberians; they employ
the art of writing, and have written books containing memori-

als of ancient times, and also poems and laws set in verse, for which they claim an antiquity of six thousand years." (Strabo, lib. iii., p. 139.)

The Iberians are represented to-day by the Basques.

The Basques are "of middle size, compactly built, robust and agile, *of a darker complexion than the Spaniards,* with gray eyes and black hair. They are simple but proud, impetuous, merry, and hospitable. The women are beautiful, skilful in performing men's work, and remarkable for their vivacity and grace. The Basques are much attached to dancing, and are very fond of the music of the bagpipe." ("New American Cyclopædia," art. *Basques.*)

"According to Paul Broca their language stands quite alone, or has mere *analogies with the American type.* Of all Europeans, we must provisionally hold the Basques to be the oldest inhabitants of our quarter of the world." (Peschel, "Races of Men," p. 501.)

The Basque language—the Euscara—"has some common traits with the Magyar, Osmanli, and other dialects of the Altai family, as, for instance, with the Finnic on the old continent, as well as the *Algonquin-Lenape language and some others in America.*" ("New American Cyclopædia," art. *Basques.*)

Duponceau says of the Basque tongue:

"This language, preserved in a corner of Europe by a few thousand mountaineers, is the sole remaining fragment of, perhaps, a hundred dialects constructed on the same plan, which probably existed and were universally spoken at a remote period in that quarter of the world. Like the bones of the mammoth, it remains a monument of the destruction produced by a succession of ages. It stands single and alone of its kind, surrounded by idioms that have no affinity with it."

We have seen them settling, in the earliest ages, in Ireland. They also formed the base of the dark-haired population of England and Scotland. They seem to have race affinities with the Berbers, on the Mediterranean coast of Africa.

Dr. Bodichon, for fifteen years a surgeon in Algiers, says:

"Persons who have inhabited Brittany, and then go to Algeria, are struck with the resemblance between the ancient Armoricans (the *Brètons*) and the Cabyles (of Algiers). In fact, the moral and physical character is identical. The Breton of pure blood has a long head, light yellow complexion of bistre tinge, eyes black or brown, stature short, and the black hair of the Cabyle. Like him, he instinctively hates strangers; in both are the same perverseness and obstinacy, same endurance of fatigue, same love of independence, same inflexion of the voice, same expression of feelings. Listen to a Cabyle speaking his native tongue, and you will think you hear a Breton talking Celtic."

The Bretons, he tells us, form a strong contrast to the people around them, who are "Celts of tall stature, with blue eyes, white skins, and blond hair: they are communicative, impetuous, versatile; they pass rapidly from courage to despair. The Bretons are entirely different: they are taciturn, hold strongly to their ideas and usages, are persevering and melancholic; in a word, both in *morale* and *physique* they present the type of a southern race—of the *Atlanteans*."

By Atlanteans Dr. Bodichon refers to the inhabitants of the Barbary States—that being one of the names by which they were known to the Greeks and Romans. He adds:

"The Atlanteans, among the ancients, passed for the favorite children of Neptune; they made known the worship of this god to other nations—to the Egyptians, for example. In other words, the Atlanteans were the first known navigators. Like all navigators, they must have planted colonies at a distance. The Bretons, in our opinion, sprung from one of them."

Neptune was Poseidon, according to Plato, founder of Atlantis.

I could multiply proofs of the close relationship between the people of the Bronze Age of Europe and the ancient inhabitants of Northern Africa, which should be read remembering that "connecting ridge" which, according to the deep-sea soundings, united Africa and Atlantis.

CHAPTER V.

THE PERUVIAN COLONY.

IF we look at the map of Atlantis, as revealed by the deep-sea soundings, we will find that it approaches at one point, by its connecting ridge, quite closely to the shore of South America, above the mouth of the Amazon, and that probably it was originally connected with it.

If the population of Atlantis expanded westwardly, it naturally found its way in its ships up the magnificent valley of the Amazon and its tributaries; and, passing by the low and fever-stricken lands of Brazil, it rested not until it had reached the high, fertile, beautiful, and healthful regions of Bolivia, from which it would eventually cross the mountains into Peru.

Here it would establish its outlying colonies at the terminus of its western line of advance, arrested only by the Pacific Ocean, precisely as we have seen it advancing up the valley of the Mississippi, and carrying on its mining operations on the shores of Lake Superior; precisely as we have seen it going eastward up the Mediterranean, past the Dardanelles, and founding Aryan, Hamitic, and probably Turanian colonies on the farther shores of the Black Sea and on the Caspian. This is the universal empire over which, the Hindoo books tell us, Deva Nahusha was ruler; this was "the great and aggressive empire" to which Plato alludes; this was the mighty kingdom, embracing the whole of the then known world, from which the Greeks obtained their conception of the universal father of all men in King Zeus. And in this universal empire Señor Lopez must find an explanation of the similarity which, as we

shall show, exists between the speech of the South American
Pacific coast on the one hand, and the speech of Gaul, Ireland,
England, Italy, Greece, Bactria, and Hindostan on the other.

Montesino tells us that at some time near the date of the
Deluge, in other words, in the highest antiquity, America was
invaded by a people with four leaders, named Ayar - manco-
topa, Ayar-chaki, Ayar-aucca, and Ayar-uyssu. ' "Ayar," says
Señor Lopez, " is the Sanscrit *Ajar*, or *aje*, and means primitive chief ; and *manco, chaki, aucca*, and *uyssu*, mean believers,
wanderers, soldiers, husbandmen. We have here a tradition of
castes like that preserved in the four tribal names of Athens."
The laboring class (naturally enough in a new colony) obtained
the supremacy, and its leader was named Pirhua - manco, re-
vealer of *Pir*, light ($\pi\bar{v}\rho$, Umbrian *pir*). Do the laws which
control the changes of language, by which a labial succeeds a
labial, indicate that the Mero or Merou of Theopompus, the
name of Atlantis, was carried by the colonists of Atlantis to
South America (as the name of old York was transplanted in
a later age to New York), and became in time Pérou or Peru ?
Was not the Nubian "Island of Merou," with its pyramids
built by "red men," a similar transplantation ? And when the
Hindoo priest points to his sacred emblem with five projecting
points upon it, and tells us that they typify "Mero and the
four quarters of the world," does he not refer to Atlantis and
its ancient universal empire ?

Manco, in the names of the Peruvian colonists, it has been
urged, was the same as Mannus, Manu, and the Santhal Maniko.
It reminds us of Menes, Minos, etc., who are found at the beginning of so many of the Old World traditions.

The Quichuas—this invading people—were originally a fair-
skinned race, with blue eyes and light and even auburn hair ;
they had regular features, large heads, and large bodies. Their
descendants are to this day an olive-skinned people, much lighter
in color than the Indian tribes subjugated by them.

They were a great race. Peru, as it was known to the Spaniards, held very much the same relation to the ancient Quichua civilization as England in the sixteenth century held to the civilization of the empire of the Cæsars. The Incas were simply an offshoot, who, descending from the mountains, subdued the rude races of the sea-coast, and imposed their ancient civilization upon them.

The Quichua nation extended at one time over a region of country more than two thousand miles long. This whole region, when the Spaniards arrived, " was a populous and prosperous empire, complete in its civil organization, supported by an efficient system of industry, and presenting a notable development of some of the more important arts of civilized life." (Baldwin's "Ancient America," p. 222.)

The companions of Pizarro found everywhere the evidences of a civilization of vast antiquity. Cieça de Leon mentions "great edifices" that were in ruins at Tiahuanaca, "an artificial hill raised on a groundwork of stone," and "two stone idols, apparently made by skilful artificers," ten or twelve feet high, clothed in long robes. "In this place, also," says De Leon, "there are stones so large and so overgrown that our wonder is excited, it being incomprehensible how the power of man could have placed them where we see them. They are variously wrought, and some of them, having the form of men, must have been idols. Near the walls are many caves and excavations under the earth; but in another place, farther west, are other and greater monuments, such as large gate-ways with hinges, platforms, and porches, each made of a single stone. It surprised me to see these enormous gate-ways, made of great masses of stone, some of which were thirty feet long, fifteen high, and six thick."

The capital of the Chimus of Northern Peru at Gran-Chimu was conquered by the Incas after a long and bloody struggle, and the capital was given up to barbaric ravage and spoliation. " But its remains exist to-day, the marvel of the Southern Continent, *covering not less than twenty square miles.* Tombs, temples, and palaces arise on every hand, ruined but still trace-able. Immense pyramidal structures, some of them *half a mile in circuit;* vast areas shut in by massive walls, each con-taining its water-tank, its shops, municipal edifices, and the dwellings of its inhabitants, and each a branch of a larger or-ganization; prisons, furnaces for smelting metals, and almost every concomitant of civilization, existed in the ancient Chimu capital. One of the great pyramids, called the " Temple of the Sun," is 812 feet long by 470 wide, and 150 high. These vast structures have been ruined for centuries, but still the work of excavation is going on.

One of the centres of the ancient Quichua civilization was around Lake Titicaca. The buildings here, as throughout Peru, were all constructed of hewn stone, and had doors and win-dows with posts, sills, and thresholds of stone.

At Cuelap, in Northern Peru, remarkable ruins were found. " They consist of a wall of wrought stones 3600 feet long, 560 broad, and 150 high, constituting a solid mass with a level summit. On this mass was another 600 feet long, 500 broad, and 150 high," making *an aggregate height of three hundred feet!* In it were rooms and cells which were used as tombs.

Very ancient ruins, showing remains of large and remarkable edifices, were found near Huamanga, and described by Cieça de Leon. The native traditions said this city was built " by *beard-ed white men,* who came there long before the time of the Incas, and established a settlement."

" The Peruvians made large use of aqueducts, which they built with notable skill, using hewn stones and cement, and making them very substantial." One extended four hundred and fifty miles across sierras and over rivers. Think of a stone aqueduct reaching from the city of New York to the State of North Carolina!

The public roads of the Peruvians were most remarkable; they were built on masonry. One of these roads ran along the mountains through the whole length of the empire, from

Quito to Chili; another, starting from this at Cuzco, went down to the coast, and extended northward to the equator. These roads were from twenty to twenty-five feet wide, were macadamized with pulverized stone mixed with lime and bituminous cement, and were walled in by strong walls "more than a fathom in thickness." In many places these roads were cut for leagues through the rock; great ravines were filled up with solid masonry; rivers were crossed by suspension bridges, used here ages before their introduction into Europe. Says Baldwin, "The builders of our Pacific Railroad, with their superior engineering skill and mechanical appliances, might reasonably shrink from the cost and the difficulties of such a work as this. Extending from one degree north of Quito to Cuzco, and from Cuzco to Chili, *it was quite as long as the two Pacific railroads,* and its wild route among the mountains was far more difficult." Sarmiento, describing it, said, "It seems to me that if the emperor (Charles V.) should see fit to order the construction of another road like that which leads from Quito to Cuzco, or that which from Cuzco goes toward Chili, I certainly think he would not be able to make it, with all his power." Humboldt said, "This road was marvellous; none of the Roman roads I had seen in Italy, in the south of France, or in Spain, appeared to me more imposing than this work of the ancient Peruvians."

Along these great roads caravansaries were established for the accommodation of travellers.

These roads were ancient in the time of the Incas. They were the work of the white, auburn-haired, bearded men from Atlantis, thousands of years before the time of the Incas. When Huayna Capac marched his army over the main road to invade Quito, it was so old and decayed "that he found great difficulties in the passage," and he immediately ordered the necessary reconstructions.

It is not necessary, in a work of this kind, to give a detailed description of the arts and civilization of the Peruvians. They were simply marvellous. Their works in cotton and wool exceeded in fineness anything known in Europe at that time. They had carried irrigation, agriculture, and the cutting of gems to a point equal to that of the Old World. Their accumulations of the precious metals exceeded anything previously known in the history of the world. In the course of twenty-five years after the Conquest the Spaniards sent from Peru to Spain *more than eight hundred millions of dollars of gold*, nearly all of it taken from the Peruvians as "booty." In one of their palaces "they had an artificial garden, the soil of which was made of small pieces of fine gold, and this was artificially planted with different kinds of maize, which were of gold, their stems, leaves, and ears. Besides this, they had more than twenty sheep (llamas) with their lambs, attended by shepherds, all made of gold." In a description of one lot of golden articles, sent to Spain in 1534 by Pizarro, there is mention of " four llamas, ten statues of women of full size, and a cistern of gold, so curious that it excited the wonder of all."

Can any one read these details and declare Plato's description of Atlantis to be fabulous, simply because he tells us of the enormous quantities of gold and silver possessed by the people? Atlantis was the older country, the parent country, the more civilized country ; and, doubtless, like the Peruvians, its people regarded the precious metals as sacred to their gods ; and they had been accumulating them from all parts of the world for countless ages. If the story of Plato is true, there now lies beneath the waters of the Atlantic, covered, doubtless, by hundreds of feet of volcanic débris, an amount of gold and silver exceeding many times that brought to Europe from Peru, Mexico, and Central America since the time of Columbus ; a treasure which, if brought to light, would revolutionize the financial values of the world.

I have already shown, in the chapter upon the similarities between the civilizations of the Old and New Worlds, some of the remarkable coincidences which existed between the Peruvians and the ancient European races; I will again briefly refer to a few of them:

1. They worshipped the sun, moon, and planets.

2. They believed in the immortality of the soul.

3. They believed in the resurrection of the body, and accordingly embalmed their dead.

4. The priest examined the entrails of the animals offered in sacrifice, and, like the Roman augurs, divined the future from their appearance.

5. They had an order of women vowed to celibacy—vestal virgins—nuns; and a violation of their vow was punished, in both continents, by their being buried alive.

6. They divided the year into twelve months.

7. Their enumeration was by tens; the people were divided into decades and hundreds, like the Anglo-Saxons; and the whole nation into bodies of 500, 1000, and 10,000, with a governor over each.

8. They possessed castes; and the trade of the father descended to the son, as in India.

9. They had bards and minstrels, who sung at the great festivals.

10. Their weapons were the same as those of the Old World, and made after the same pattern.

11. They drank toasts and invoked blessings.

12. They built triumphal arches for their returning heroes, and strewed the road before them with leaves and flowers.

13. They used sedan-chairs.

14. They regarded agriculture as the principal interest of the nation, and held great agricultural fairs and festivals for the interchange of the productions of the farmers.

15. The king opened the agricultural season by a great celebration, and, like the kings of Egypt, he put his hand to the plough, and ploughed the first furrow.

16. They had an order of knighthood, in which the candidate knelt before the king; his sandals were put on by a no-

bleman, very much as the
spurs were buckled on the
European knight; he was
then allowed to use the
girdle or sash around the
loins, corresponding to the
toga virilis of the Romans;
he was then crowned with

CYCLOPEAN WALL, GREECE.

flowers. According to Fernandez, the candidates wore white
shirts, like the knights of the Middle Ages, with a cross em-
broidered in front.

17. There was a striking resemblance between the architecture of the Peruvians and that of some of the nations of the
Old World. It is enough for me to quote Mr. Ferguson's
words, that the coincidence between the buildings of the Incas

CYCLOPEAN MASONRY, PERU.

and the Cyclopean remains attributed to the Pelasgians in Italy and Greece, " is the most remarkable in the history of architecture."

The illustrations on page 397 strikingly confirm Mr. Ferguson's views.

" The sloping jambs, the window cornice, the polygonal masonry, and other forms so closely resemble what is found in the old Pelasgic cities of Greece and Italy, that it is difficult to resist the conclusion that there may be some relation between them."

Even the mode of decorating their palaces and temples finds a parallel in the Old World.   A recent writer says:

" We may end by observing, what seems to have escaped Señor Lopez, that the *interior* of an Inca palace, with its walls

OWL-HEADED VASE, TROY.   OWL-HEADED VASE, PERU.

covered with gold, as described by Spaniards, with its artificial golden flowers and golden beasts, must have been exactly like the interior of the house of Alkinous or Menelaus—

     " ' The doors were framed of gold,
Where underneath the brazen floor doth glass
Silver pilasters, which with grace uphold
Lintel of silver framed ; the ring was burnished gold,
And dogs on each side of the door there stand,
Silver and golden.' "

"I can personally testify" (says Winchell, "Preadamites," p. 387) "that a study of ancient Peruvian pottery has constantly reminded me of forms with which we are familiar in Egyptian archæology."

Dr. Schliemann, in his excavations of the ruins of Troy, found a number of what he calls "owl-headed idols" and vases. I give specimens on page 398 and page 400.

In Peru we find vases with very much the same style of face.

I might pursue those parallels much farther ; but it seems to me that these extraordinary coin-cidences must have arisen either from identity of origin or long-continued ancient intercourse. There can be little doubt that a fair-skinned, light-haired, bearded race, holding the religion which Plato says prevailed in Atlantis, carried an Atlantean civilization at an early day up the valley of the Amazon to the heights of Bolivia and Peru, precisely as a similar emigration of Aryans went westward to the shores of the Mediterranean and Caspian, and it is very likely that these diverse migrations habitually spoke the same language.

OWL-HEADED VASE, PERU.

Señor Vincente Lopez, a Spanish gentleman of Montevideo, in 1872 published a work entitled " Les Races Aryennes in Pérou," in which he attempts to prove that the great Quichua language, which the Incas imposed on their subjects over a vast extent of territory, and which is still a living tongue in Peru and Bolivia, is really a branch of the great Aryan or Indo-

OWL-HEADED VASE, TROY.

European speech. I quote Andrew Lang's summary of the proofs on this point:

"Señor Lopez's view, that the Peruvians were Aryans who left the parent stock long before the Teutonic or Hellenic races entered Europe, is supported by arguments drawn from language, from the traces of institutions, from religious beliefs, from legendary records, and artistic remains. The evidence from language is treated scientifically, and not as a kind of ingenious guessing. Señor Lopez first combats the idea that the living dialect of Peru is barbarous and fluctuating. It is not one of the casual and shifting forms of speech produced by nomad races. To which of the stages of language does this belong—the agglutinative, in which one root is fastened on to another, and a word is formed in which the constitutive elements are obviously distinct, or the inflexional, where the auxiliary roots get worn down and are only distinguishable by the philologist? As all known Aryan tongues are inflexional, Señor Lopez may appear to contradict himself when he says that Quichua is an *agglutinative Aryan language.* But he quotes Mr. Max Müller's opinion that there must have been a time when the germs of Aryan tongues had not yet reached the inflexional stage, and shows that while the form of Quichua is agglutinative, as in Turanian, the *roots of words* are Aryan. If this be so, Quichua may be a linguistic missing link.

" When we first look at Quichua, with its multitude of words beginning with *hu,* and its great preponderance of *q's,* it seems almost as odd as Mexican. But many of these forms are due to a scanty alphabet, and really express familiar sounds; and many, again, result from the casual spelling of the Spaniards. We must now examine some of the forms which Aryan roots are supposed to take in Quichua. In the first place, Quichua abhors the shock of two consonants. Thus, a word like πλέω in Greek would be unpleasant to the Peruvian's ear, and he says *pillui,* ' I sail.' The *plu,* again, in *pluma,* a feather, is said to be found in *pillu,* ' to fly.' Quichua has no *v,* any more than Greek has, and just as the Greeks had to spell Roman words beginning with *V* with *Ou,* like *Valerius*—Ούαλέριος—so, where Sanscrit has *v,* Quichua has sometimes *hu.* Here is a list of words in *hu :*

QUICHUA.	SANSCRIT.
Huakia, to call.	*Vacc,* to speak.
Huasi, a house.	*Vas,* to inhabit.
Huayra, air, αῦρα.	*Vâ,* to breathe.
Huasa, the back.	*Vas,* to be able (*pouvoir*).

" There is a Sanscrit root, *kr,* to act, to do : this root is found in more than three hundred names of peoples and places in

Southern America. Thus there are the Caribs, whose name may have the same origin as that of our old friends the Carians, and mean the Braves, and their land the home of the Braves, like Kaleva-la, in Finnish. The same root gives *kara*, the hand, the Greek χείρ, and *kkalli*, brave, which a person of fancy may connect with καλός. Again, Quichua has an 'alpha privative'—thus *A-stani* means 'I change a thing's place;' for *ni* or *mi* is the first person singular, and, added to the root of a verb, is the sign of the first person of the present indicative. For instance, *can* means being, and *Can-mi*, or *Cani*, is, 'I am.' In the same way *Munanmi*, or *Munani*, is 'I love,' and *Apan-mi*, or *Apani*, 'I carry.' So Lord Strangford was wrong when he supposed that the last verb in *mi* lived with the last patriot in Lithuania. Peru has stores of a grammatical form which has happily perished in Europe. It is impossible to do more than refer to the supposed Aryan roots contained in the glossary, but it may be noticed that the future of the Quichuan verb is formed in *s*—I love, *Munani;* I shall love, *Munasa*—and that the affixes denoting cases in the noun are curiously like the Greek prepositions."

The resemblance between the Quichua and Mandan words for I or me—*mi*—will here be observed.

Very recently Dr. Rudolf Falb has announced (*Neue Freie Presse*, of Vienna) that he has discovered that the relation of the Quichua and Aimara languages to the Aryan and Semitic tongues is very close; that, in fact, they "exhibit the most astounding affinities with the Semitic tongue, and particularly the Arabic, in which tongue Dr. Falb has been skilled from his boyhood. Following up the lines of this discovery, Dr. Falb has found (1) a connecting link with the Aryan roots, and (2) has ultimately arrived face to face with the surprising revelation that "the Semitic roots are universally Aryan." The common stems of all the variants are found in their purest condition in Quichua and Aimara, from which fact Dr. Falb derives the conclusion that the high plains of Peru and Bolivia must be regarded as the point of exit of the present human race.

[Since the above was written I have received a letter from Dr. Falb, dated Leipsic, April 5th, 1881. Scholars will be glad to learn that Dr. Falb's great work on the relationship of the Aryan and Semitic languages to the Quichua and Aimara tongues will be published in a year or two; the manuscript contains over two thousand pages, and Dr. Falb has devoted to it ten years of study. A work from such a source, upon so curious and important a subject, will be looked for with great interest.]

But it is impossible that the Quichuas and Aimaras could have passed across the wide Atlantic to Europe if there had been no stepping-stone in the shape of Atlantis with its bridge-like ridges connecting the two continents.

It is, however, more reasonable to suppose that the Quichuas and Aimaras were a race of emigrants from Plato's island than to think that Atlantis was populated from South America. The very traditions to which we have referred as existing among the Peruvians, that the civilized race were white and bearded, and that they entered or invaded the country, would show that civilization did not originate in Peru, but was a transplantation from abroad, and only in the direction of Atlantis can we look for a white and bearded race.

In fact, kindred races, with the same arts, and speaking the same tongue in an early age of the world, separated in Atlantis and went east and west—the one to repeat the civilization of the mother-country along the shores of the Mediterranean Sea, which, like a great river, may be said to flow out from the Black Sea, with the Nile as one of its tributaries, and along the shores of the Red Sea and the Persian Gulf; while the other emigration advanced up the Amazon, and created mighty nations upon its head-waters in the valleys of the Andes and on the shores of the Pacific.

Chapter VI.

THE AFRICAN COLONIES.

Africa, like Europe and America, evidences a commingling of different stocks: the blacks are not all black, nor all woolly-haired; the Africans pass through all shades, from that of the light Berber, no darker than the Spaniard, to the deep black of the Iolofs, between Senegal and Gambia.

The traces of red men or copper-colored races are found in many parts of the continent. Prichard divides the true negroes into four classes; his second class is thus described:

"2. Other tribes have forms and features like the European; their complexion is black, or a *deep olive*, or a *copper color* approaching to black, while their hair, though often crisp and frizzled, is not in the least woolly. Such are the Bishari and Danekil and Hazorta, and the darkest of the Abyssinians.

"The complexion and hair of the Abyssinians vary very much, their complexion ranging from almost white to dark brown or black, and their hair from straight to crisp, frizzled, and almost woolly." (Nott and Gliddon, "Types of Mankind," p. 194.)

"Some of the Nubians are copper-colored or black, with a tinge of red." (*Ibid.*, p. 198.)

Speaking of the Barbary States, these authors further say (*Ibid.*, p. 204):

"On the northern coast of Africa, between the Mediterranean and the Great Desert, including Morocco, Algiers, Tunis, Tripoli, and Benzazi, there is a continuous system of highlands, which have been included under the general term *Atlas* —*anciently Atlantis,* now the Barbary States. . . . Throughout

Barbary we encounter a peculiar group of races, subdivided into many tribes of various shades, now spread over a vast area, but which formerly had its principal and perhaps *aboriginal abode along the mountain slopes of Atlas.* . . . The real name of the Berbers is *Mazirgh,* with the article prefixed or suffixed—T-amazirgh or Amazirgh-T—meaning *free, dominant,* or *'noble* race.' . . . We have every reason to believe the Berbers existed in the remotest times, with all their essential moral and physical peculiarities. . . . They existed in the time of Menes in the same condition in which they were discovered by Phœnician navigators previously to the foundation of Carthage. They are an indomitable, nomadic people, who, since the introduction of camels, have penetrated in considerable numbers into the Desert, and even as far as Nigritia. . . . *Some of these clans are white,* others black, with woolly hair."

Speaking of the Barbary Moors, Prichard says:

"Their figure and stature are nearly the same as those of the southern Europeans, and their complexion, if darker, is only so in proportion to the higher temperature of the country. It displays great varieties."

Jackson says:

"The men of Temsena and Showiah are of a strong, robust make, *and of a copper color;* the women are beautiful. The women of Fez are fair as the Europeans, but hair and eyes always dark. The women of Mequinas are very beautiful, and *have the red-and-white complexion of English women.*"

Spix and Martius, the German travellers, depict the Moors as follows:

"A high forehead, an oval countenance, large, speaking, black eyes, shaded by arched and strong eyebrows, a thin, rather long, but not too pointed nose, rather broad lips, meeting in an acute angle, *brownish-yellow complexion,* thick, smooth, and black hair, and a stature greater than the middle height."

Hodgson states:

"The Tuarycks are a *white* people, of the Berber race; the Mozabiaks are a *remarkably white* people, and mixed with the Bedouin Arabs. The Wadreagans and Wargelans are of a *dark bronze,* with woolly hair."

The Foolahs, Fulbe (sing. *Pullo*), Fellani, or Fellatah, are a people of West and Central Africa. It is the opinion of modern travellers that the Foolahs are destined to become the dominant people of Negro-land. In language, appearance, and history they present striking differences from the neighboring tribes, to whom they are superior in intelligence, but inferior, according to Garth, in physical development. Golbery describes them as " robust and courageous, of a *reddish*-black color, with regular features, hair longer and less woolly than that of the common negroes, and high mental capacity." Dr. Barth found great local differences in their physical characteristics, as Bowen describes the Foolahs of Bomba as being some black, some almost white, and many of a mulatto color, varying from dark to very bright. Their features and skulls were cast in the European mould. They have a tradition that their ancestors were whites, and certain tribes call themselves white men. They came from Timbuctoo, which lies to the north of their present location.

The Nubians and Foolahs are classed as Mediterraneans. They are not black, but yellowish-brown, or *red*-brown. The hair is not woolly but curly, and sometimes quite straight; it is either dark-brown or black, with a fuller growth of beard than the negroes. The oval face gives them a Mediterranean type. Their noses are prominent, their lips not puffy, and their languages have no connection with the tongues of the negroes proper. ("American Cyclopædia," art. *Ethnology*, p. 759.)

" The Cromlechs (*dolmens*) of Algeria " was the subject of an address made by General Faidherbe at the Brussels International Congress. He considers these structures to be simply sepulchral monuments, and, after examining five or six thousand of them, maintains that the dolmens of Africa and of Europe were all constructed *by the same race*, during their emigration from the shores of the Baltic to the southern coast of the Mediterranean. The author does not, however, attempt to explain the existence of these monuments in other countries—

Hindostan, for instance, and America. " In Africa," he says, " cromlechs are called tombs of the idolaters"—the *idolaters* being neither Romans, nor Christians, nor Phœnicians, but some antique race. He regards the Berbers as the descendants of the primitive dolmen-builders. Certain Egyptian monuments tell of invasions of Lower Egypt one thousand five hundred years before our era by blond tribes from the West. The bones found in the cromlechs are those of a large and dolichocephalous race. General Faidherbe gives the average stature (including the women) at 1.65 or 1.74 metre, while the average stature of French carabineers is only 1.65 metre. He did not find a single brachycephalous skull. The profiles indicated great intelligence. The Egyptian documents already referred to call the invaders Tamahu, which must have come from the invaders' own language, as it is not Egyptian. The Tuaregs of the present day may be regarded as the best representatives of the Tamahus. They are of lofty stature, have blue eyes, and cling to the custom of bearing long swords, to be wielded by both hands. In Soudan, on the banks of the Niger, dwells a negro tribe ruled by a royal family (Masas), who are of rather fair complexion, and claim

TAMAHU, FROM THE EGYPTIAN MONUMENTS, 1500 B.C.

descent from white men. *Masas* is perhaps the same as *Mashash*, which occurs in the Egyptian documents applied to the Tamahus. The Masas wear the hair in the same fashion as the Tamahus, and General Faidherbe is inclined to think that they too are the descendants of the dolmen-builders.

These people, according to my theory, were colonists from Atlantis—colonists of three different races—white, yellow, and sunburnt or red.

CHAPTER VII.

THE IRISH COLONIES FROM ATLANTIS.

WE have seen that beyond question Spain and France owed a great part of their population to Atlantis. Let us turn now to Ireland.

We would naturally expect, in view of the geographical position of the country, to find Ireland colonized at an early day by the overflowing population of Atlantis. And, in fact, the Irish annals tell us that their island was settled *prior to the Flood*. In their oldest legends an account is given of three Spanish fishermen who were driven by contrary winds on the coast of Ireland before the Deluge. After these came the Formorians, who were led into the country prior to the Deluge by the *Lady Banbha*, or Kesair; her maiden name was h'Erni, or Berba; she was accompanied by fifty maidens and three men—Bith, Ladhra, and Fintain. Ladhra was their conductor, who was the first buried in Hibernia. That ancient book, the "Cin of Drom-Snechta," is quoted in the "Book of Ballymote" as authority for this legend.

The Irish annals speak of the Formorians as a warlike race, who, according to the "Annals of Clonmacnois," "were a sept descended from Cham, the son of Noeh, and lived by pyracie and spoile of other nations, and were in those days *very troublesome to the whole world*."

Were not these the inhabitants of Atlantis, who, according to Plato, carried their arms to Egypt and Athens, and whose subsequent destruction has been attributed to divine vengeance invoked by their arrogance and oppressions?

The Formorians were from Atlantis. They were called *Fomhoraicc, F"omoraig Afraic,* and *Formoragh,* which has been rendered into English as *Formorians.* They possessed ships, and the uniform representation is that they came, as the name *F"omoraig Afraic* indicated, from *Africa.* But in that day Africa did not mean the continent of Africa, as we now understand it. Major Wilford, in the eighth volume of the "Asiatic Researches," has pointed out that Africa comes from *Apar, Aphar, Apara,* or *Aparica,* terms used to signify "the West," just as we now speak of the Asiatic world as "the East." When, therefore, the Formorians claimed to come from Africa, they simply meant that they came from the West—in other words, from Atlantis—for there was no other country except America west of them.

They possessed Ireland from so early a period that by some of the historians they are spoken of as the aborigines of the country.

The first invasion of Ireland, subsequent to the coming of the Formorians, was led by a chief called Partholan: his people are known in the Irish annals as "Partholan's people." They were also probably Atlanteans. They were from Spain. A British prince, Gulguntius, or Gurmund, encountered off the Hebrides a fleet of thirty ships, filled with men and women, led by one Partholyan, who told him they were from *Spain,* and seeking some place to colonize. The British prince directed him to Ireland. ("De Antiq. et Orig. Cantab.")

Spain in that day was the land of the Iberians, the Basques; that is to say, the Atlanteans.

The Formorians defeated Partholan's people, killed Partholan, and drove the invaders out of the country.

The Formorians were a civilized race; they had "a fleet of sixty ships and a strong army."

The next invader of their dominions was Neimhidh; he captured one of their fortifications, but it was retaken by the Formorians under "Morc." Neimhidh was driven out of the country, and the Atlanteans continued in undisturbed possession of the island for four hundred years more. Then came the Fir-Bolgs. They conquered the whole island, and divided it into five provinces. They held possession of the country for only thirty-seven years, when they were overthrown by the Tuatha-de-Dananns, a people more advanced in civilization; so much so that when their king, Nuadha, lost his hand in battle, "Creidne, the artificer," we are told, "put a silver hand upon him, the fingers of which were capable of motion." This great race ruled the country for one hundred and ninety-seven years: they were overthrown by an immigration from Spain, probably of Basques, or Iberians, or Atlanteans, "the sons of Milidh," or Milesius, who "possessed a large fleet and a strong army." This last invasion took place about the year 1700 B.C.; so that the invasion of Neimhidh must have occurred about the year 2334 B.C.; while we will have to assign a still earlier date for the coming of Partholan's people, and an earlier still for the occupation of the country by the Formorians from the West.

In the Irish historic tales called "Catha; or Battles," as given by the learned O'Curry, a record is preserved of a great battle which was fought between the Tuatha-de-Dananns and the Fir-Bolgs, from which it appears that these two races spoke the same language, and that they were intimately connected with the Formorians. As the armies drew near together the Fir-Bolgs sent out Breas, one of their great chiefs, to reconnoitre the camp of the strangers; the Tuatha-de-Dananns appointed one of their champions, named Sreng, to meet the emissary of the enemy; the two warriors met and talked to one another over the tops of their shields, and each was delighted to find that *the other spoke the same language.* A battle followed, in which Nunda, king of the Fir-Bolgs, was slain; Breas succeeded him; he encountered the hostility of the bards, and was compelled to resign the crown. He went to the court of his father-in-law, Elathe, *a Formorian sea-king or pirate;* not being well received, he repaired to the camp of Balor of the Evil Eye, a *Formorian chief.* The Formorian head-quarters seem to have been in the Hebrides. Breas and Balor collected a vast army and navy and invaded Ireland, but were defeated in a great battle by the Tuatha-de-Dananns.

These particulars would show the race-identity of the Fir-Bolgs and Tuatha-de-Dananns; and also their intimate connection, if not identity with, the Formorians.

The Tuatha-de-Dananns seem to have been a civilized people; besides possessing ships and armies and working in the metals, they had an organized body of surgeons, whose duty it was to attend upon the wounded in battle; and they had also a bardic or Druid class, to preserve the history of the country and the deeds of kings and heroes.

According to the ancient books of Ireland the race known as "Partholan's people," the Nemedians, the Fir-Bolgs, the Tuatha-de-Dananns, and the Milesians were all descended from two brothers, sons of Magog, son of Japheth, son of Noah, who escaped from the catastrophe which destroyed his country. Thus all these races were Atlantean. They were connected with the African colonies of Atlantis, the Berbérs, and with the Egyptians. The Milesians lived in Egypt: they were expelled thence; they stopped a while in Crete, then in Scythia, then they settled in Africa (See MacGeoghegan's "History of Ireland," p. 57), at a place called Gæthulighe or Getulia, and lived there during eight generations, say two hundred and fifty years; "then they entered Spain, where they built Brigantia, or Briganza, named after their king Breogan: they dwelt in Spain a considerable time. Milesius, a descendant of Breogan, went on an expedition to Egypt, took part in a war against the Ethiopians, married the king's daughter, Scota: he died in Spain, but his people soon after conquered Ireland. On landing on the coast they offered sacrifices to Neptune or Poseidon"—the god of Atlantis. (*Ibid.*, p. 58.)

The Book of Genesis (chap. x.) gives us the descendants

of Noah's three sons, Shem, Ham, and Japheth. We are told that the sons of Japheth were Gomer, and Magog, and Madai, and Javan, and Tubal, and Meshech, and Tiras. We are then given the names of the descendants of Gomer and Javan, but not of Magog. Josephus says the sons of Magog were the Scythians. The Irish annals take up the genealogy of Magog's family where the Bible leaves it. The Book of Invasions, the "Cin of Drom-Snechta," claims that these Scythians were the Phœnicians; and we are told that a branch of this family were driven out of Egypt in the time of Moses.: "He wandered through Africa for forty-two years, and passed by the lake of Salivœ to the altars of the Philistines, and between Rusicada and the mountains Azure, and he came by the river Monlon, and by the sea to the Pillars of Hercules, and through the Tuscan sea, and he made for Spain, and dwelt there many years, and he increased and multiplied, and his people were multiplied."

From all these facts it appears that the population of Ireland *came from the West*, and not from Asia—that it was one of the many waves of population flowing out from the Island of Atlantis—and herein we find the explanation of that problem which has puzzled the Aryan scholars. As Ireland is farther from the Punjab than Persia, Greece, Rome, or Scandinavia, it would follow that the Celtic wave of migration must have been the earliest sent out from the Sanscrit centre; but it is now asserted by Professor Schleicher and others that the Celtic tongue shows that it separated from the Sanscrit original tongue *later* than the others, and that it is more closely allied to the Latin than any other Aryan tongue. This is entirely inexplicable upon any theory of an Eastern origin of the Indo-European races, but very easily understood if we recognize the Aryan and Celtic migrations as going out about the same time from the Atlantean fountain-head.

There are many points confirmatory of this belief. In the first place, the civilization of the Irish dates back to a vast

antiquity. We have seen their annals laying claim to an immigration from the direction of Atlantis prior to the Deluge,
with no record that the people of Ireland were subsequently
destroyed by the Deluge. From the Formorians, who came before the Deluge, to the Milesians, who came from Spain in the
Historic Period, the island was continuously inhabited. This
demonstrates (1) that these legends did not come from Christian sources, as the Bible record was understood in the old
time to imply a destruction of all who lived before the Flood
except Noah and his family; (2) it confirms our view that the
Deluge was a local catastrophe, and did not drown the whole
human family; (3) that the coming of the Formorians having
been before the Deluge, that great cataclysm was of comparatively recent date, to wit, since the settlement of Ireland; and
(4) that as the Deluge was a local catastrophe, it must have
occurred somewhere not far from Ireland to have come to
their knowledge. A rude people could scarcely have heard
in that day of a local catastrophe occurring in the heart of
Asia.

There are many evidences that the Old World recognized Ireland as possessing a very ancient civilization. In the Sanscrit
books it is referred to as Hiranya, the "Island of the Sun," to
wit, of sun-worship; in other words, as pre-eminently the centre of that religion which was shared by all the ancient races
of Europe, Asia, Africa, and America. It is believed that Ireland was the "Garden of Phœbus" of the Western mythologists.

The Greeks called Ireland the "Sacred Isle" and "Ogygia."
"Nor can any one," says Camden, "conceive why they should
call it Ogygia, unless, perhaps, from its antiquity; for the
Greeks called nothing Ogygia unless what was extremely ancient." We have seen that Ogyges was connected by the
Greek legends with a first deluge, and that Ogyges was "a
quite mythical personage, lost in the night of ages."

It appears, as another confirmation of the theory of the
Atlantis origin of these colonies, that their original religion

was sun-worship; this, as was the case in other countries, became subsequently overlaid with idol-worship. In the reign of
King Tighernmas the worship of idols was introduced. The
priests constituted the Order of Druids. Naturally many analogies have been found to exist between the beliefs and customs of the Druids and the other religions which were drawn
from Atlantis. We have seen in the chapter on sun-worship
how extensive this form of religion was in the Atlantean days,
both in Europe and America.

It would appear probable that the religion of the Druids
passed from Ireland to England and France. The metemp-
sychosis or transmigration of souls was one of the articles of
their belief long before the time of Pythagoras; it had probably been drawn from the storehouse of Atlantis, whence it
passed to the Druids, the Greeks, and the Hindoos. The Druids
had a *pontifex maximus* to whom they yielded entire obedience. Here again we see a practice which extended to the
Phœnicians, Egyptians, Hindoos, Peruvians, and Mexicans.

The Druids of Gaul and Britain offered human sacrifices,
while it is claimed that the Irish Druids did not. This would
appear to have been a corrupt after-growth imposed upon the
earlier and purer sacrifice of fruits and flowers known in Atlantis, and due in part to greater cruelty and barbarism in their
descendants. Hence we find it practised in degenerate ages
on both sides of the Atlantic.

The Irish Druidical rites manifested themselves principally
in sun-worship. Their chief god was Bel or Baal—the same
worshipped by the Phœnicians—the god of the sun. The Irish
name for the sun, *Grian*, is, according to Virgil, one of the
names of Apollo — another sun-god, Gryneus. Sun-worship
continued in Ireland down to the time of St. Patrick, and some
of its customs exist among the peasantry of that country to
this day. We have seen that among the Peruvians, Romans,
and other nations, on a certain day all fires were extinguished throughout the kingdom, and a new fire kindled at the

chief temple by the sun's rays, from which the people obtained their fire for the coming year. In Ireland the same practice was found to exist. A piece of land was set apart, where the four provinces met, in the present county of Meath; here, at a palace called Tlachta, the divine fire was kindled. Upon the night of what is now All-Saints-day the Druids assembled at this place to offer sacrifice, and it was established, under heavy penalties, that no fire should be kindled except from this source. On the first of May a convocation of Druids was held in the royal palace of the King of Connaught, and two fires were lit, between which cattle were driven, as a preventive of murrain and other pestilential disorders. This was called Beltinne, or the day of Bel's fire. And unto this day the Irish call the first day of May "Lha-Beul-tinne," which signifies "the day of Bel's fire." The celebration in Ireland of St. John's-eve by watch-fires is a relic of the ancient sun-worship of Atlantis. The practice of driving cattle through the fire continued for a long time, and Kelly mentions in his "Folk-lore" that in Northampton-shire, in England, a calf was sacrificed in one of these fires to "stop the murrain" *during the present century.* Fires are still lighted in England and Scotland as well as Ireland for super-stitious purposes; so that the people of Great Britain, it may be said, are still in some sense in the midst of the ancient sun-worship of Atlantis.

We find among the Irish of to-day many Oriental customs. The game of "jacks," or throwing up five pebbles and catch-ing them on the back of the hand, was known in Rome. "The Irish *keen* (caoine), or the lament over the dead, may still be heard in Algeria and Upper Egypt, even as Herodotus heard it chanted by the Libyan women." The same practice exist-ed among the Egyptians, Etruscans, and Romans. The Irish *wakes* are identical with the funeral feasts of the Greeks, Etrus-cans, and Romans. (Cusack's "History of Ireland," p. 141.) The Irish custom of saying "God bless you!" when one sneezes, is a very ancient practice; it was known to the Romans, and referred, it is said, to a plague in the remote past, whose first symptom was sneezing.

We find many points of resemblance between the customs of the Irish and those of the Hindoo. The practice of the creditor fasting at the door-step of his debtor until he is paid, is known to both countries; the kindly "God save you!" is the same as the Eastern "God be gracious to you, my son!" The reverence for the wren in Ireland and Scotland reminds us of the Oriental and Greek respect for that bird. The practice of pilgrimages, fasting, bodily macerations, and devotion to holy wells and particular places, extends from Ireland to India.

All these things speak of a common origin; this fact has been generally recognized, but it has always been interpreted that the Irish came from the East, and were in fact a migration of Hindoos. There is not the slightest evidence to sustain this theory. The Hindoos have never within the knowledge of man sent out colonies or fleets for exploration; but there is abundant evidence, on the other hand, of migrations from Atlantis eastward. And how could the Sanscrit writings have preserved maps of Ireland, England, and Spain, giving the shape and outline of their coasts, and their very names, and yet have preserved no memory of the expeditions or colonizations by which they acquired that knowledge? †

Another proof of our theory is found in "the round-towers" of Ireland. Attempts have been made to show, by Dr. Petrie and others, that these extraordinary structures are of modern origin, and were built by the Christian priests, in which to keep their church-plate. But it is shown that the "Annals of Ulster" mention the destruction of fifty-seven of them by an earthquake in A.D. 448; and Giraldus Cambrensis shows that Lough Neagh was created by an inundation, or sinking of the land, in A.D. 65, and that in his day the fishermen could

> "See the round-towers of other days
> In the waves beneath them shining."

---

† One wonders what maps Donnelly is referring to.—E.F.B.

Moreover, we find Diodorus Siculus, in a well-known passage, referring to Ireland, and describing it as " an island in the ocean over against Gaul, to the north, and not inferior in size to Sicily, the soil of which is so fruitful that they mow there twice in the year." He mentions the skill of their harpers, their sacred groves, *and their singular temples of round form.*

We find similar structures in America, Sardinia, and India. The remains of similar round-towers are very abundant in the Orkneys and Shetlands. "They have been supposed by some," says Sir John Lubbock, "to be Scandinavian, but no similar buildings exist in Norway, Sweden, or Denmark, so that this style of architecture is no doubt anterior to the arrival of the

THE BURGH OF MOUSSA, IN THE SHETLANDS.

Northmen." I give above a picture of the Burgh or Broch of the little island of Moussa, in the Shetlands. It is circular in form, forty-one feet in height, open at the top; the central

space is twenty feet in diameter, the walls about fourteen feet
thick at the base, and eight feet at the top.   They contain
a staircase, which leads to the top of the building.   Similar
structures are found in the Island of Sardinia.

In New Mexico and Colorado the remains of round-towers
are very abundant.   The illustration below represents one

ROUND-TOWER OF THE CAÑON OF THE MANCOS, COLORADO, U. S.

of these in the valley of the Mancos, in the south-western
corner of Colorado.   A model of it is to be found in the
Smithsonian collection at Washington.   The tower stands at
present, in its ruined condition, twenty feet high.   It will be
seen that it resembles the towers of Ireland, not only in its
circular form but also in the fact that its door-way is situated
at some distance from the ground.

It will not do to say that the resemblance between these
prehistoric and singular towers, in countries so far apart as
Sardinia, Ireland, Colorado, and India, is due to an accidental
coincidence.   It might as well be argued that the resemblance

between the roots of the various Indo-European languages was also due to accidental coincidence, and did not establish any similarity of origin. In fact, we might just as well go back to the theory of the philosophers of one hundred and fifty years ago, and say that the resemblance between the fossil forms in the rocks and the living forms upon them did not indicate relationship, or prove that the fossils were the remains of creatures that had once lived, but that it was simply a way nature had of working out extraordinary coincidences in a kind of joke; a sort of "plastic power in nature," as it was called.

We find another proof that Ireland was settled by the people of Atlantis in the fact that traditions long existed among the Irish peasantry of a land in the "Far West," and that this belief was especially found among the posterity of the Tuatha-de-Dananns, whose connection with the Formorians we have shown.

The Abbé Brasseur de Bourbourg, in a note to his translation of the "Popol Vuh," says:

"There is an abundance of legends and traditions concerning the passage of the Irish into America, and their habitual communication with that continent many centuries before the time of Columbus. We should bear in mind that Ireland was colonized by the Phœnicians (or by people of that race). An Irish saint named Vigile, who lived in the eighth century, was accused to Pope Zachary of having taught heresies on the subject of the antipodes. At first he wrote to the pope in reply to the charge, but afterward he went to Rome in person to justify himself, and there he proved to the pope that the Irish had been *accustomed to communicate with a transatlantic world.*"

"This fact," says Baldwin, "seems to have been preserved in the records of the Vatican."

The Irish annals preserve the memory of St. Brendan of Clonfert, and his remarkable voyage to a land in the West, made A.D. 545. His early youth was passed under the care of St. Ita, a lady of the princely family of the Desii. When he was five years old he was placed under the care of Bishop Ercus. Kerry was his native home; the blue waves of the Atlantic washed its shores; the coast was full of traditions of a wonderful land in the West. He went to see the venerable St. Enda, the first abbot of Arran, for counsel. He was probably encouraged in the plan he had formed of carrying the Gospel to this distant land. "He proceeded along the coast of Mayo, inquiring as he went for *traditions of the Western continent.* On his return to Kerry he decided to set out on the important expedition. St. Brendan's Hill still bears his name; and from the bay at the foot of this lofty eminence he sailed for the ' Far West.' Directing his course *toward the south-west,* with a few faithful companions, in a well-provisioned bark, he came, after some rough and dangerous navigation, to calm seas, where, without aid of oar or sail, he was borne along for many weeks." He had probably entered upon the same great current which Columbus travelled nearly one thousand years later, and which extends from the shores of Africa and Europe to America. He finally reached land; he proceeded inland until he came to a large river flowing from east to west, supposed by some to be the Ohio. "After an absence of seven years he returned to Ireland, and lived not only to tell of the marvels he had seen, but to found a college of three thousand monks at Clonfert." There are eleven Latin MSS. in the *Bibliothèque Impériale* at Paris of this legend, the dates of which vary from the eleventh to the fourteenth century, but all of them anterior to the time of Columbus.

The fact that St. Brendan sailed in search of a country in the west cannot be doubted; and the legends which guided him were probably the traditions of Atlantis among a people whose ancestors had been derived directly or at second-hand from that country.

This land was associated in the minds of the peasantry with traditions of Edenic happiness and beauty. Miss Eleanor C. Donnelly, of Philadelphia, has referred to it in her poem, "The

Sleeper's Sail," where the starving boy dreams of the pleasant and plentiful land:

> " ' Mother, I've been on the cliffs out yonder,
>   Straining my eyes o'er the breakers free
>   To the lovely spot where the sun was setting,
>   Setting and sinking into the sea.
>
> " ' The sky was full of the fairest colors---
>   Pink and purple and paly green,
>   With great soft masses of gray and amber,
>   And great bright rifts of gold between.
>
> " ' And all the birds that way were flying,
>   Heron and curlew overhead,
>   With a mighty eagle westward floating,
>   Every plume in their pinions red.
>
> " ' And then I saw it, the fairy city,
>   Far away o'er the waters deep;
>   Towers and castles and chapels glowing,
>   Like blessèd dreams that we see in sleep.
>
> " ' What is its name?'   ' Be still, *acushla*
>   (Thy hair is wet with the mists, my boy);
>   Thou hast looked perchance on the Tir-na-n'oge,
>   Land of eternal youth and joy!
>
> " ' Out of the sea, when the sun is setting,
>   It rises, golden and fair to view;
>   No trace of ruin, or change of sorrow,
>   No sign of age where all is new.
>
> " ' Forever sunny, forever blooming,
>   Nor cloud nor frost can touch that spot,
>   Where the happy people are ever roaming,
>   The bitter pangs of the past forgot.'

This is the Greek story of Elysion; these are the Elysian Fields of the Egyptians; these are the Gardens of the Hesperides; this is the region in the West to which the peasant of Brittany looks from the shores of Cape Raz; this is Atlantis.

'The starving child seeks to reach this blessed land in a boat
and is drowned.

> " High on the cliffs the light-house keeper
>   Caught the sound of a piercing scream;
> Low in her hut the lonely widow
>   Moaned in the maze of a troubled dream;
>
> " And saw in her sleep a seaman ghostly,
>   With sea-weeds clinging in his hair,
> Into her room, all wet and dripping,
>   A drownèd boy on his bosom bear.
>
> " Over Death Sea on a bridge of silver
>   The child to his Father's arms had passed;
> Heaven was nearer than Tir-na-n'oge,
>   And the golden city was reached at last."

CHAPTER VIII.

THE OLDEST SON OF NOAH.

THAT eminent authority, Dr. Max Müller, says, in his "Lectures on the Science of Religion,"

"If we confine ourselves to the Asiatic continent, with its important peninsula of Europe, we find that in the vast desert of drifting human speech three, and only three, oases have been formed in which, *before the beginning of all history,* language became permanent and traditional—assumed, in fact, a new character, a character totally different from the original character of the floating and constantly varying speech of human beings. These three oases of language are known by the name of *Turanian, Aryan,* and *Semitic.* In these three centres, more particularly in the *Aryan* and *Semitic,* language ceased to be natural; its growth was arrested, and it became permanent, solid, petrified, or, if you like, historical speech. I have always maintained that this centralization and traditional conservation of language could only have been the result of religious and political influences, and I now mean to show that we really have clear evidence of three independent settlements of religion — the *Turanian,* the *Aryan,* and the *Semitic*—concomitantly with the three great settlements of language."

There can be no doubt that the Aryan and another branch, which Müller calls Semitic, but which may more properly be called Hamitic, radiated from Noah; it is a question yet to be decided whether the Turanian or Mongolian is also a branch of the Noachic or Atlantean stock.

To quote again from Max Müller:

"If it can only be proved that the religions of the Aryan nations are united by the same bonds of a real relationship

which have enabled us to treat their languages as so many
varieties of the same type—and so also of the Semitic—the
field thus opened is vast enough, and its careful clearing and
cultivation will occupy several generations of scholars.   And
this original relationship, I believe, can be proved.   Names of
the principal deities, words also expressive of the most essential
elements of religion, such as *prayer, sacrifice, altar, spirit, law,*
and *faith,* have been preserved among the Aryan and among
the Semitic nations, and these relics admit of one explanation
only.   After that, a comparative study of the Turanian religions may be approached with better hope of success; for that
there was not only a primitive Aryan and a primitive Semitic
religion, *but likewise a primitive Turanian religion, before each
of these primeval races was broken up and became separated in
language, worship, and national sentiment, admits, I believe, of little doubt.* . . . . There was a period during which the ancestors of
the Semitic family had not yet been divided, whether in language or in religion.   That period transcends the recollection
of every one of the Semitic races, in the same way as neither
Hindoos, Greeks, nor Romans have any recollection of the time
when they spoke a common language, and worshipped their
Father in heaven by a name that was as yet neither Sanscrit,
nor Greek, nor Latin.   But I do not hesitate to call this Prehistoric Period historical in the best sense of the word.   It was
a real period, because, unless it was real, all the realities of the
Semitic languages and the Semitic religions, such as we find
them after their separation, would be unintelligible.   Hebrew,
Syriac, and Arabic point to a common source as much as Sanscrit, Greek, and Latin; and unless we can bring ourselves to
doubt that the Hindoos, the Greeks, the Romans, and the Teu-
tons derived the worship of their principal deity from their
common Aryan sanctuary, we shall not be able to deny that
there was likewise a primitive religion of the whole Semitic
race, and that *El,* the Strong One in heaven, was invoked by
the ancestors of all the Semitic races before there were Babylonians in Babylon, Phœnicians in Sidon and Tyrus—before
there were Jews in Mesopotamia or Jerusalem.   The evidence
of the Semitic is the same as that of the Aryan languages: the
conclusion cannot be different. . . .

   " These three classes of religion are not to be mistaken—as
little as the three classes of language, the Turanian, the Semitic,

and the Aryan. They mark three events in the most ancient history of the world, events which have determined the whole fate of the human race, and of which we ourselves still feel the consequences in our language, in our thoughts, and in our religion."

We have seen that all the evidence points to the fact that this original seat of the Phœnician-Hebrew family was in Atlantis.

The great god of the so-called Semites was El, the Strong One, from whose name comes the Biblical names *Beth-el*, the house of God; *Ha-el*, the strong one; *El-ohim*, the gods; *El-oah*, God; and from the same name is derived the Arabian name of God, Al-lah.

Another evidence of the connection between the Greeks, Phœnicians, Hebrews, and Atlanteans is shown in the name of Adonis.

The Greeks tell us that Adonis was the lover of Aphrodite, or Venus, who was the offspring of Uranus—"she came out of the sea;" Uranus was the father of Chronos, and the grandfather of Poseidon, king of Atlantis.

Now we find *Adonâi* in the Old Testament used exclusively as the name of Jehovah, while among the Phœnicians Adonâi was the supreme deity. In both cases the root *Ad* is probably a reminiscence of *Ad*-lantis.

There seem to exist similar connections between the Egyptian and the Turanian mythology. The great god of Egypt was Neph or Num; the chief god of the Samoyedes is Num; and Max Müller established an identity between the *Num* of the Samoyedes and the god *Yum-ala* of the Finns, and probably with the name of the god *Nam* of the Thibetians.

That mysterious people, the Etruscans, who inhabited part of Italy, and whose bronze implements agreed exactly in style and workmanship with those which we think were derived from Atlantis, were, it is now claimed, a branch of the Turanian family.

"At a recent meeting of the English Philological Society great interest was excited by a paper on Etruscan Numerals, by the Rev. Isaac Taylor. He stated that the long-sought key to the Etruscan language had at last been discovered. Two dice had been found in a tomb, with their six faces marked with words instead of pips. He showed that these words were identical with the first six digits in the Altaic branch of the Turanian family of speech. Guided by this clew, it was easy to prove that the grammar and vocabulary of the 3000 Etruscan inscriptions were also Altaic. The words denoting kindred, the pronouns, the conjugations, and the declensions, corresponded closely to those of the Tartar tribes of Siberia. The Etruscan mythology proved to be essentially the same as that of the Kalevala, the great Finnic epic."

According to Lenormant ("Ancient History of the East," vol. i., p. 62; vol. ii., p. 23), the early contests between the Aryans and the Turanians are represented in the Iranian traditions as "contests between hostile *brothers* . . . the Ugro-Finnish races must, according to all appearances, be looked upon as *a branch, earlier detached than the others from the Japhetic stem.*"

If it be true that the first branch originating from Atlantis was the Turanian, which includes the Chinese and Japanese, then we have derived from Atlantis all the building and metal-working races of men who have proved themselves capable of civilization; and we may, therefore, divide mankind into two great classes: those capable of civilization, derived from Atlantis, and those essentially and at all times barbarian, who hold no blood relationship with the people of Atlantis.

Humboldt is sure "that some connection existed between ancient Ethiopia and the elevated plain of Central Asia." There were invasions which reached from the shores of Arabia into China. "An Arabian sovereign, Schamar-Iarasch (Abou Karib), is described by Hamza, Nuwayri, and others as a powerful ruler and conqueror, who carried his arms successfully far into Central Asia; he occupied Samarcand and invaded China. He erected an edifice at Samarcand, bearing an inscription, in

Himyarite or Cushite characters, 'In the name of God, Scha-mar-Iarasch has erected this edifice to the sun, his Lord.'" (Baldwin's "Prehistoric Nations," p. 110.) These invasions must have been prior to 1518 B.C.

Charles Walcott Brooks read a paper before the California Academy of Sciences, in which he says:

"According to Chinese annals, Tai-Ko-Fokee, the great stranger king, ruled the kingdom of China. In pictures he is represented with two small horns, like those associated with the representations of Moses. He and his successor are said to have introduced into China 'picture-writing,' like that in use in Central America at the time of the Spanish conquest. He taught the motions of the heavenly bodies, and divided time into years and months; he also introduced many other useful arts and sciences.

"Now, there has been found at Copan, in Central America, a figure strikingly like the Chinese symbol of Fokee, with his two horns; and, in like manner, there is a close resemblance between the Central American and the Chinese figures repre-senting earth and heaven. Either one people learned from the other, or both acquired these forms from a common source. Many physico-geographical facts favor the hypothesis that they were derived in very remote ages from America, and that from China they passed to Egypt. Chinese records say that the progenitors of the Chinese race came from across the sea."

COW-HEADED IDOL, MYCENÆ
(FROM SCHLIEMANN).

The two small horns of Tai-Ko-Fokee and Moses are probably a reminiscence of Baal. We find the horns of Baal rep-resented in the remains of the Bronze Age of Europe. Bel sometimes wore a tiara with his bull's horns; the tiara was the crown subsequently worn by the Persian kings, and it be-came, in time, the symbol of Papal authority.

The Atlanteans having domesticated cattle, and discovered

their vast importance to humanity, associated the bull and cow
with religious ideas, as revealed in the oldest hymns of the
Aryans and the cow-headed idols of Troy, a representation of
one of which is shown on the preceding page. Upon the head
of their great god Baal they placed the horns of the bull; and
these have descended in popular imagination to the spirit of
evil of our day. Burns says:

> "O thou! whatever title suit thee,
> Auld *Hornie*, Satan, Nick, or Clootie."

"Clootie" is derived from the cleft hoof of a cow; while the
Scotch name for a bull is *Bill*, a corruption, probably, of Bel.
Less than two hundred years ago it was customary to sacrifice
a bull on the 25th of August to the "God Mowrie" and "his
devilans" on the island of Inis Maree, Scotland. ("The Past

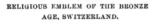

RELIGIOUS EMBLEM OF THE BRONZE   BAAL, THE PHŒNICIAN GOD.
AGE, SWITZERLAND.

in the Present," p. 165.) The trident of Poseidon has degener-
ated into the pitchfork of Beelzebub!

And when we cross the Atlantic, we find in America the
horns of Baal reappearing in a singular manner. The first cut
on page 429 represents an idol of the Moquis of New Mexico:
the head is very bull-like. In the next figure we have a representation of the war-god of the Dakotas, with something like a

trident in his hand; while the next illustration is taken from
Zarate's "Peru," and depicts "the god of a degrading worship."
He is very much like the traditional conception of the European devil—horns, pointed ears, wings, and poker. Compare
this last figure, from Peru, with the representation on page
430 of a Greek siren, one of those cruel monsters who, according to Grecian mythology, sat in the midst of bones and blood,
tempting men to ruin by their sweet music. Here we have
the same bird-like legs and claws as in the Peruvian demon.

Heeren shows that a great overland commerce extended in

MOQUI IDOL.   DAKOTA IDOL.   PERUVIAN DEVIL.

ancient times between the Black Sea and "Great Mongolia;"
he mentions a "Temple of the Sun," and a great caravansary
in the desert of Gobi. Arminius Vámbéry, in his "Travels
in Central Asia," describes very important ruins near the eastern shore of the Caspian Sea, at a place called Gömüshtepe;
and connected with these are the remains of a great wall
which he followed "ten geographical miles." He found a vast
aqueduct one hundred and fifty miles long, extending to the
Persian mountains. He reports abundant ruins in all that
country, *extending even to China.*

The early history of China indicates contact with a superior race. "Fuh-hi, who is regarded as a demi-god, founded the Chinese Empire 2852 B.C. He introduced cattle, taught the people how to raise them, and taught the art of writing." ("American Cyclopædia," art. *China.*) He might have invented his alphabet, but he did not invent the cattle; he must have got them from some nation who, during many centuries of civilization, had domesticated them; and from what nation was he more likely to have obtained them than from the Atlanteans, whose colonies we have seen reached his borders, and whose armies invaded his territory? "He instituted the ceremony of marriage." (*Ibid.*) This also was an importation from a civilized land. "His successor, Shin-nung, during a reign of one hundred and forty years, introduced agriculture and medical science. The next emperor, Hwang-ti, is believed to have invented weapons, wagons, ships, clocks, and musical instruments, and to have introduced coins, weights, and measures." (*Ibid.*) As these various inventions in all other countries have been the result of slow development, running through many centuries, or are borrowed from some other more civilized people, it is certain that no emperor of China ever invented them all during a period of one hundred and sixty-four

GREEK SIREN.

years. These, then, were also importations from the West. In fact, the Chinese themselves claim to have invaded China in the early days *from the north-west;* and their first location is placed by Winchell near Lake Balkat, a short distance east of the Caspian, where we have already seen Aryan Atlantean colonies planted at an early day. "The third successor of Fuh-hi, Ti-ku, established schools, and was the first to practise polygamy. In 2357 his son Yau ascended the throne, and it is from his reign that the regular historical records begin. A great flood, which occurred in his reign, has been considered synchronous and identical with the Noachic Deluge, and to Yau is attributed the merit of having successfully battled against the waters."

There can be no question that the Chinese themselves, in their early legends, connected their origin with a people who were destroyed by water in a tremendous convulsion of the earth. Associated with this event was a divine personage called Niu-va (Noah?).

Sir William Jones says:

"The Chinese believe the earth to have been wholly covered with water, which, in works of undisputed authenticity, they describe as flowing abundantly, then subsiding and *separating the higher from the lower ages of mankind;* that this division of time, from which their poetical history begins, just preceded the appearance of Fo-hi on the mountains of Chin. ("Discourse on the Chinese; Asiatic Researches," vol. ii., p. 376.)

The following history of this destruction of their ancestors vividly recalls to us the convulsion depicted in the Chaldean and American legends:

"The pillars of heaven were broken; the earth shook to its very foundations; the heavens sunk lower toward the north; the sun, the moon, and the stars changed their motions; the earth fell to pieces, and the waters enclosed within its bosom *burst forth with violence and overflowed it.* Man having rebelled against Heaven, the system of the universe was totally disordered. The sun was eclipsed, the planets altered their course, and the grand harmony of nature was disturbed."

A learned Frenchman, M. Terrien de la Couperie, member of the Asiatic Society of Paris, has just published a work (1880) in which he demonstrates the astonishing fact that the Chinese language is clearly related to the Chaldean, and that both the Chinese characters and the cuneiform alphabet are degenerate descendants of an original hieroglyphical alphabet. The same signs exist for many words, while numerous words are very much alike. M. de la Couperie gives a table of some of these similarities, from which I quote as follows:

English.	Chinese.	Chaldee.
To shine	Mut	Mul.
To die	Mut	Mit.
Book	King	Kin.
Cloth	Sik	Sik.
Right hand	Dzek	Zag.
Hero	Tan	Dun.
Earth	Kien-kai	Kiengi.
Cow	Lub	Lu, lup.
Brick	Ku	Ku.

This surprising discovery brings the Chinese civilization still nearer to the Mediterranean head-quarters of the races, and increases the probability that the arts of China were of Atlantean origin; and that the name of Nai Hoang-ti, or Nai Korti, the founder of Chinese civilization, may be a reminiscence of Nakhunta, the chief of the gods, as recorded in the Susian texts, and this, in turn, a recollection of the Deva-Nahusha of the Hindoos, the Dionysos of the Greeks, the king of Atlantis, whose great empire reached to the "farther parts of India," and embraced, according to Plato, "parts of the continent of America."

Linguistic science achieved a great discovery when it established the fact that there was a continuous belt of languages from Iceland to Ceylon which were the variant forms of one mother-tongue, the Indo-European; but it must prepare itself for a still wider generalization. There is abundant proof—proof with which pages might be filled—that there was a still older mother-tongue, from which Aryan, Semitic, and Hamitic were all derived—the language of Noah, the language of Atlantis, the language of the great "aggressive empire" of Plato, the language of the empire of the Titans.

The Arabic word *bin,*[†]within, becomes, when it means interval, space, *binnon;* this is the German and Dutch *binnen* and Saxon *binnon,* signifying within. The Ethiopian word *aorf,* to fall asleep, is the root of the word *Morpheus,* the god of sleep. The Hebrew word *chanah,* to dwell, is the parent of the Anglo-Saxon *inne* and Icelandic *inni,* a house, and of our word *inn,* a hotel. The Hebrew word *naval* or *nafal* signifies to fall; from it is derived our word fall and fool (one who falls); the Chaldee word is *nabal,* to make foul, and the Arabic word *nabala* means to die, that is, to fall. From the last syllable of the Chaldee *nasar,* to saw, we can derive the Latin *serra,* the High German *sagen,* the Danish *sauga,* and our word *to saw.* The Arabic *nafida,* to fade, is the same as the Italian *fado,* the Latin *fatuus* (foolish, tasteless), the Dutch *vadden,* and our *to fade.* The Ethiopic word *gaber,* to make, to do, and the Arabic word *jabara,* to make strong, becomes the Welsh word *goberu,* to work, to operate, the Latin *operor,* and the English *operate.* The Arabic word *abara* signifies to prick, to sting; we see this root in the Welsh *bar,* a summit, and *pâr,* a spear, and *per,* a spit; whence our word *spear.* In the Chaldee, Syriac, and Arabic *zug* means to join, to couple; from this the Greeks obtained *ζυγος,* the Romans *jugum,* and we the word *yoke;* while the Germans obtained *jok* or *jog,* the Dutch *juk,* the Swedes *ok.* The Sanscrit is *juga.* The Arabic *sanna,* to be old, reappears in the Latin *senex,* the Welsh *hen,* and our *senile.* The Hebrew *banah,* to build, is the Irish *bun,* foundation, and the Latin *fundo, fundare,* to found. The Arabic *baraka,* to bend the knee, to fall on the breast, is probably the

[†] The following is all fanciful.—E.F.B.

Saxon *brecau*, the Danish *bräkke*, the Swedish *bräcka*, Welsh *bregu*, and our word *to break*. The Arabic *baraka* also signifies to rain violently; and from this we get the Saxon *rægn*, to rain, Dutch *regen*, to rain, Cimbric *rækia*, rain, Welsh *rheg*, rain. The Chaldee word *braic*, a branch, is the Irish *braic* or *raigh*, an arm, the Welsh *braic*, the Latin *brachium*, and the English *brace*, something which supports like an arm. The Chaldee *frak*, to rub, to tread out grain, is the same as the Latin *frico, frio*, and our word *rake*. The Arabic word to rub is *fraka*. The Chaldee *rag, ragag*, means to desire, to long for; it is the same as the Greek ορεγω, the Latin *porrigere*, the Saxon *ræccan*, the Icelandic *rakna*, the German *reichen*, and our *to reach*, to rage. The Arabic *rauka*, to strain or purify, as wine, is precisely our English word *rack*, to rack wine. The Hebrew word *bara*, to create, is our word *to bear*, as to bear children: a great number of words in all the European languages contain this root in its various modifications. The Hebrew word *kafar*, to cover, is our word *to cover*, and *coffer*, something which covers, and *covert*, a secret place; from this root also comes the Latin *cooperio* and the French *couvrir*, to cover. The Arabic word *shakala*, to bind under the belly, is our word *to shackle*. From the Arabic *walada* and Ethiopian *walad*, to beget, to bring forth, we get the Welsh *llawd*, a shooting out; and hence our word *lad*. Our word *matter*, or *pus*, is from the Arabic *madda;* our word *mature* is originally from the Chaldee *mita*. The Arabic word *amida* signifies to end, and from this comes the noun, a limit, a termination, Latin *meta*, and our words *meet* and *mete*.

I might continue this list, but I have given enough to show that all the Atlantean races once spoke the same language, and that the dispersion on the plains of Shinar signifies that breaking up of the tongues of one people under the operation of vast spaces of time. Philology is yet in its infancy, and the time is not far distant when the identity of the languages of all the Noachic races will be as clearly established and as uni-

versally acknowledged as is now the identity of the languages
of the Aryan family of nations.

And precisely as recent research has demonstrated the relationship between Pekin and Babylon, so investigation in Central America has proved that there is a mysterious bond of
union connecting the Chinese and one of the races of Mexico.
The resemblances are so great that Mr. Short ("North Americans of Antiquity," p. 494) says, "There is no doubt that
strong analogies exist between the Otomi and the Chinese."
Señor Najera ("Dissertacion Sobre la lingua Othomi, Mexico," pp. 87, 88) gives a list of words from which I quote the
following:

Chinese.	Othomi.	English.	Chinese.	Othomi.	English.
Cho	To	The, that.	Pa	Da	To give.
Y	N-y	A wound.	Tsun	Nsu	Honor.
Ten	Gu, mu	Head.	Hu	Hmu	Sir, Lord.
Siao	Sui	Night.	Na	Na	That.
Tien	Tsi	Tooth.	Hu	He	Cold.
Ye	Yo	Shining.	Ye	He	And.
Ky	Hy (ji)	Happiness.	Hoa	Hia	Word.
Ku	Du	Death.	Nugo	Nga	I.
Po	Yo	No.	Ni	Nuy	Thou.
Na	Ta	Man.	Hao	Nho	The good.
Nin	Nsu	Female.	Ta	Da	The great.
Tseu	Tsi, ti	Son.	Li	Ti	Gain.
Tso	Tsa	To perfect.	Ho	To	Who.
Kuan	Khuani	True.	Pa	Pa	To leave.
Siao	Sa	To mock.	Mu, mo	Me	Mother.

Recently Herr Forchhammer, of Leipsic, has published a
truly scientific comparison of the grammatical structure of the
Choctaw, Chickasaw, Muscogee, and Seminole languages with
the Ural-Altaic tongues, in which he has developed many interesting points of resemblance.

It has been the custom to ascribe the recognized similarities
between the Indians of America and the Chinese and Japanese to a migration by way of Behring's Strait from Asia into
America; but when we find that the Chinese themselves only

reached the Pacific coast within the Historical Period, and that they came to it from the direction of the Mediterranean and Atlantis, and when we find so many and such distinct recollections of the destruction of Atlantis in the Flood legends of the American races, it seems more reasonable to conclude that the resemblances between the Othomi and the Chinese are to be accounted for by intercourse through Atlantis.

We find a confirmation in all these facts of the order in which Genesis names the sons of Noah:

" Now these are the generations of the sons of Noah: Shem, Ham, and Japheth, and unto them were sons born after the flood."

Can we not suppose that these three sons represent three great races in the order of their precedence?

The record of Genesis claims that the Phœnicians were descended from Ham, while the Hebrews were descended from Shem; yet we find the Hebrews and Phœnicians united by the ties of a common language, common traditions, and common race characteristics. The Jews are the great merchants of the world eighteen centuries after Christ, just as the Phœnicians were the great merchants of the world fifteen centuries before Christ.

Moreover, the Arabians, who are popularly classed as Semites, or sons of Shem, admit in their traditions that they are descended from "Ad, *the son of Ham;*" and the tenth chapter of Genesis classes them among the descendants of Ham, calling them Seba, Havilah, Raamah, etc. If the two great so-called Semitic stocks—the Phœnicians and Arabians—are Hamites, surely the third member of the group belongs to the same " sunburnt" race.

If we concede that the Jews were also a branch of the Hamitic stock, then we have, firstly, a Semitic stock, the Turanian, embracing the Etruscans, the Finns, the Tartars, the Mongols, the Chinese, and Japanese; secondly, a Hamitic family, "the sunburnt" race — a red race — including the Cushites, Phœnicians, Egyptians, Hebrews, Berbers, etc.; and, thirdly, a Japhetic or whiter stock, embracing the Greeks, Italians, Celts, Goths, and the men who wrote Sanscrit—in other words, the entire Aryan family.

If we add to these three races the negro race—which cannot be traced back to Atlantis, and is not included, according to Genesis, among the descendants of Noah—we have the four races, the *white, red, yellow,* and *black,* recognized by the Egyptians as embracing all the people known to them.

There seems to be some confusion in Genesis as to the Semitic stock. It classes different races as both Semites and Hamites; as, for instance, Sheba and Havilah; while the race of Mash, or Meshech, is classed among the sons of Shem and the sons of Japheth. In fact, there seems to be a confusion of Hamitic and Semitic stocks. "This is shown in the blending of Hamitic and Semitic in some of the most ancient inscriptions; in the facility of intercourse between the Semites of Asia and the Hamites of Egypt; in the peaceful and unobserved absorption of all the Asiatic Hamites, and the Semitic adoption of the Hamitic gods and religious system. It is manifest that, at a period not long previous, *the two families* had dwelt together and spoken the same language." (Winchell's "Pre-Adamites," p. 36.) Is it not more reasonable to suppose that the so-called Semitic races of Genesis were a mere division of the Hamitic stock, and that we are to look for the third great division of the sons of Noah among the Turanians?

Francis Lenormant, high authority, is of the opinion that the Turanian races are descended from Magog, the son of Japheth. He regards the Turanians as intermediate between the white and yellow races, graduating insensibly into each. "The Uzbecs, the Osmanli Turks, and the Hungarians are not to be distinguished in appearance from the most perfect branches of the white race; on the other hand, the Tchondes almost exactly resemble the Tongouses, who belong to the yellow race.

The Turanian languages are marked by the same agglutinative character found in the American races.

The Mongolian and the Indian are alike in the absence of a heavy beard. The royal color of the Incas was yellow; yellow is the color of the imperial family in China. The religion of the Peruvians was sun-worship; "the sun was the peculiar god of the Mongols from the earliest times." The Peruvians regarded Pachacamac as the sovereign creator. Camac-Hya was the name of a Hindoo goddess. *Haylli* was the burden of every verse of the song composed in praise of the sun and the Incas. Mr. John Ranking derives the word *Allah* from the word *Haylli*, also the word *Halle*-lujah. In the city of Cuzco was a portion of land which none were permitted to cultivate except those of the royal blood. At certain seasons the Incas turned up the sod here, amid much rejoicing and many ceremonies. A similar custom prevails in China: The emperor ploughs a few furrows, and twelve illustrious persons attend the plough after him. (Du Halde, "Empire of China," vol. i., p. 275.) The cycle of sixty years was in use among most of the nations of Eastern Asia, and among the Muyscas of the elevated plains of Bogota. *The "quipu," a knotted reckoning-cord, was in use in Peru and in China.* (Bancroft's "Native Races," vol. v., p. 48.) In Peru and China "both use hieroglyphics, which are read from above downward." † (*Ibid.*)

"It appears most evident to me," says Humboldt, "that the monuments, methods of computing time, systems of cosmogony, and many myths of America, offer striking analogies with the ideas of Eastern Asia—*analogies which indicate an ancient communication,* and are not simply the result of that uniform condition in which all nations are found in the dawn of civilization." ("Exam. Crit.," tom. ii., p. 68.)

"In the ruined cities of Cambodia, which lies farther to the east of Burmah, recent research has discovered teocallis like those in Mexico, and the remains of temples of the same type and pattern as those of Yucatan. And when we reach the sea

---

† The Peruvians probably did not have a writing system, although recently the great linguist Barthel has interpreted elements in Mochica pottery as glyphs.—E.F.B.

we encounter at Suku, in Java, a teocalli which is absolutely identical with that of Tehuantepec. Mr. Ferguson said, ' as we advance eastward from the valley of the Euphrates, at every step we meet with forms of art becoming more and more like those of Central America.' " ("Builders of Babel," p. 88.)

Prescott says:

" The coincidences are sufficiently strong to authorize a belief that the civilization of Anahuac was in some degree influenced by that of Eastern Asia; and, secondly, that the discrepancies are such *as to carry back the communication to a very remote period.*" ("Mexico," vol. iii., p. 418.)

"All appearances," continues Lenormant ("Ancient History of the East," vol. i., p. 64), "would lead us to regard the Turanian race as the first branch of the family of Japheth which went forth into the world; and by that premature separation, by an isolated and antagonistic existence, took, or rather preserved, a completely distinct physiognomy. . . . It is a type of the white race imperfectly developed."

We may regard this yellow race as the first and oldest wave from Atlantis, and, therefore, reaching farthest away from the common source; then came the Hamitic race; then the Japhetic.

Chapter IX.

THE ANTIQUITY OF SOME OF OUR GREAT INVEN-TIONS. †

It may seem like a flight of the imagination to suppose that the mariner's compass was known to the inhabitants of Atlantis. And yet, if my readers are satisfied that the Atlanteans were a highly civilized maritime people, carrying on commerce with regions as far apart as Peru and Syria, we must conclude that they possessed some means of tracing their course in the great seas they traversed; and accordingly, when we proceed to investigate this subject, we find that as far back as we may go in the study of the ancient races of the world, we find them possessed of a knowledge of the virtues of the magnetic stone, and in the habit of utilizing it. The people of Europe, rising a few centuries since out of a state of semi-barbarism, have been in the habit of claiming the invention of many things which they simply borrowed from the older nations. This was the case with the mariner's compass. It was believed for many years that it was first invented by an Italian named Amalfi, A.D. 1302. In that interesting work, Goodrich's " Life of Columbus," we find a curious history of the magnetic compass prior to that time, from which we collate the following points :

" In A.D. 868 it was employed by the Northmen." (" The Landnamabok," vol. i., chap. 2.) An Italian poem of A.D. 1190 refers to it as in use among the Italian sailors at that date. In the ancient language of the Hindoos, the Sanscrit—which has been a dead language for twenty-two hundred years—the

---

† Much of the material in this chapter is incorrect. Donnelly should have known better and presumably was carried away by his own rhetoric.—E.F.B.

magnet was called " the precious stone beloved of Iron." The Talmud speaks of it as " the stone of attraction ;" and it is alluded to in the early Hebrew prayers as *Kalamitah*, the same name given it by the Greeks, from the reed upon which the compass floated. The Phœnicians were familiar with the use of the magnet. At the prow of their vessels stood the figure of a woman (Astarte) holding a cross in one hand and pointing the way with the other; the cross represented the compass, which was a magnetized needle, floating in water crosswise upon a piece of reed or wood. The cross became the coat of arms of the Phœnicians—not only, possibly, as we have shown, as a recollection of the four rivers of Atlantis, but because it represented the secret of their great sea-voyages, to which they owed their national greatness. The hyperborean magician, Abaras, carried " a guiding arrow," which Pythagoras gave him, " in order that it may be useful to him in all difficulties in his long journey." (" Herodotus," vol. iv., p. 36.)

The magnet was called the " Stone of Hercules." Hercules was the patron divinity of the Phœnicians. He was, as we have shown elsewhere, one of the gods of Atlantis—probably one of its great kings and navigators. The Atlanteans were, as Plato tells us, a maritime, commercial people, trading up the Mediterranean as far as Egypt and Syria, and across the Atlantic to " the whole opposite continent that surrounds the sea ;" the Phœnicians, as their successors and descendants, and colonized on the shores of the Mediterranean, inherited their civilization and their maritime habits, and with these that invention without which their great voyages were impossible. From them the magnet passed to the Hindoos, and from them to the Chinese, who certainly possessed it at an early date. In the year 2700 B.C. the Emperor Wang-ti placed a magnetic figure with an extended arm, like the Astarte of the Phœnicians, on the front of carriages, the arm always turning and pointing to the south, which the Chinese regarded as the

principal pole. (See Goodrich's " Columbus," p. 31, etc.)   This
illustration represents one of these chariots :

CHINESE MAGNETIC CAR.

In the seventh century it was used by the navigators of the
Baltic Sea and the German Ocean.

The ancient Egyptians called the loadstone the bone of
Haroeri, and iron the bone of Typhon.   Haroeri was the son
of Osiris and grandson of Rhea, a goddess of *the earth*, a queen
of Atlantis, and *mother of Poseidon;* Typhon was a wind-god
and an evil genius, but also a son of Rhea, the earth goddess.
Do we find in this curious designation of iron and loadstone as
"bones of the descendants of the earth," an explanation of that
otherwise inexplicable Greek legend about Deucalion " throwing the bones of the earth behind him, when instantly men
rose from the ground, and the world was repeopled ?"   Does it
mean that by means of the magnet he sailed, after the Flood,
to the European colonies of Atlantis, already thickly inhabited ?

A late writer, speaking upon the subject of the loadstone, tells us:

"Hercules, it was said, being once overpowered by the heat of the sun, drew his bow against that luminary; whereupon the god Phœbus, admiring his intrepidity, gave him a golden cup, with which he sailed over the ocean. This cup was the compass, which old writers have called *Lapis Heracleus.* Pisander says *Oceanus lent him the cup,* and Lucian says it was a sea-shell. Tradition affirms that the magnet originally was not on a pivot, but set to float on water in a cup. The old antiquarian is wildly theoretical on this point, and sees a compass in the Golden Fleece of Argos, in the oracular needle which Nero worshipped, and in everything else. Yet undoubtedly there are some curious facts connected with the matter. Osonius says that Gama and the Portuguese got the compass from some pirates at the Cape of Good Hope, A.D. 1260. M. Fauchet, the French antiquarian, finds it plainly alluded to in some old poem of Brittany belonging to the year A.D. 1180. Paulo Venetus brought it in the thirteenth century from China, where it was regarded as oracular. Genebrand says Melvius, a Neapolitan, brought it to Europe in A.D. 1303. Costa says Gama got it from Mohammedan seamen. But all nations with whom it was found *associate it with regions where Heraclean myths prevailed.* And one of the most curious facts is that the ancient Britons, as the Welsh do to-day, call a pilot *llywydd* (lode). Lodemanage, in Skinner's 'Etymology,' is the word for the price paid to a pilot. But whether this famous, and afterward deified, mariner (Hercules) had a compass or not, we can hardly regard the association of his name with so many Western monuments as accidental."

Hercules was, as we know, a god of Atlantis, and Oceanos, who lent the magnetic cup to Hercules, was the name by which the Greeks designated the Atlantic Ocean. And this may be the explanation of the recurrence of a cup in many antique paintings and statues. Hercules is often represented with a cup in his hand; we even find the cup upon the handle of the bronze dagger found in Denmark, and represented in the chapter on the Bronze Age, in this work. (See p. 254 *ante.*)

So "oracular" an object as this self-moving needle, always pointing to the north, would doubtless affect vividly the minds of the people, and appear in their works of art. When Hercules left the coast of Europe to sail to the island of Erythea in the Atlantic, in the remote west, we are told, in Greek mythology (Murray, p. 257), that he borrowed "the cup" of Helios, in (with) which "he was accustomed to sail every *night*." Here we seem to have a reference to the magnetic cup used in

ANCIENT COINS OF TYRE.

night sailing; and this is another proof that the use of the magnetic needle in sea-voyages was associated with the Atlantean gods.

Lucian tells us that a sea-shell often took the place of the cup, as a vessel in which to hold the water where the needle floated, and hence upon the ancient coins of Tyre we find a sea-shell represented.

Here, too, we have the Pillars of Hercules, supposed to have been placed at the mouth of the Mediterranean, and the tree of life or knowledge, with the serpent twined around it, which appears in Genesis; and in the combination of the two pillars and the serpent we have, it is said, the original source of our dollar mark [$].

Compare these Phœnician coins with the following representation of a copper coin, two inches in diameter and three lines thick, found nearly a century ago by Ordonez, at the city of Guatemala. " M. Dupaix noticed an indication of the use of the compass in the centre of one of the sides, the figures on the same side representing a kneeling, bearded, turbaned man between two fierce heads, perhaps of crocodiles, which appear to defend the entrance to a mountainous and wooded country. The reverse presents a serpent coiled around a fruit-tree, and an eagle on a hill." (Bancroft's " Native Races," vol. iv., p. 118.) The mountain leans to one side: it is a "culhuacan," or crooked mountain.

We find in Sanchoniathon's "Legends of the Phœnicians" that Ouranus, the first god of the people of Atlantis, " devised

COIN FROM CENTRAL AMERICA.

Bætulia, *contriving stones that moved as having life,* which were supposed to fall from heaven." These stones were probably magnetic loadstones; in other words, Ouranus, the first god of Atlantis, devised the mariner's compass.

I find in the "Report of United States Explorations for a Route for a Pacific Railroad " a description of a New Mexican Indian priest, who foretells the result of a proposed war by placing a piece of wood in a bowl of water, and causing it to turn to the right or left, or sink or rise, as he directs it.   This is incomprehensible, unless the wood, like the ancient Chinese compass, contained a piece of magnetic iron hidden in it, which would be attracted or repulsed, or even drawn downward, by a piece of iron held in the hand of the priest, on the outside of the bowl.   If so, this trick was a remembrance of the mariner's compass transmitted from age to age by the medicine men.   The reclining statue of Chac-Mol, of Central America, holds a bowl or dish upon its breast.

Divination was the *ars Etrusca.*   The Etruscans set their temples squarely with the cardinal points of the compass; so did the Egyptians, the Mexicans, and *the Mound Builders of America.*   Could they have done this without the magnetic compass?

The Romans and the Persians called the line of the axis of the globe *cardo,* and it was to *cardo* the needle pointed.   Now "*Cardo* was the name of the mountain on which the human race took refuge from the Deluge . . . the primitive geographic point for the countries which were the cradle of the human race." (Urquhart's "Pillars of Hercules," vol. i., p. 145.)   From this comes our word "cardinal," as the cardinal points.

Navigation.—Navigation was not by any means in a rude state in the earliest times:

"In the wanderings of the heroes returning from Troy, Aristoricus makes Menelaus circumnavigate Africa more than 500 years before Neco sailed from Gadeira to India." ("Cosmos," vol. ii., p. 144.)

"In the tomb of Rameses the Great is a representation of a naval combat between the Egyptians and some other people, supposed to be the Phœnicians, whose huge ships are propelled by sails." (Goodrich's "Columbus," p. 29.)

The proportions of the fastest sailing-vessels of the present day are about 300 feet long to 50 wide and 30 high; these were precisely the proportions of Noah's ark—300 cubits long, 50 broad, and 30 high.

"Hiero of Syracuse built, under the superintendence of Archimedes, a vessel which consumed in its construction the material for fifty galleys; it contained galleries, gardens, stables, fish-ponds, mills, baths, a temple of Venus, and an engine to throw stones three hundred pounds in weight, and arrows thirty-six feet long. The floors of this monstrous vessel were inlaid with scenes from Homer's 'Iliad.'" (*Ibid.*, p. 30.)

The fleet of Sesostris consisted of four hundred ships; and when Semiramis invaded India she was opposed by four thousand vessels.

It is probable that in the earliest times the vessels were sheeted with metal. A Roman ship of the time of Trajan has been recovered from Lake Ricciole after 1300 years. The outside was covered with sheets of lead fastened with small copper nails. Even the use of iron chains in place of ropes for the anchors was known at an early period. Julius Cæsar tells us that the galleys of the Veneti were thus equipped. (Goodrich's "Columbus," p. 31.)

Gunpowder.—It is not impossible that even the invention of gunpowder may date back to Atlantis. It was certainly known in Europe long before the time of the German monk, Berthold Schwarz, who is commonly credited with the invention of it. It was employed in 1257 at the siege of Niebla, in Spain. It was described in an Arab treatise of the thirteenth century. In A.D. 811 the Emperor Leo employed fire-arms. "Greek-fire" is supposed to have been gunpowder mixed with resin or petroleum, and thrown in the form of fuses and explosive shells. It was introduced from Egypt A.D. 668. In A.D. 690 the Arabs used fire-arms against Mecca, bringing the knowledge of them from India. *In A.D. 80 the Chinese obtained from India a knowledge of gunpowder.* There is reason to believe that the Carthaginian (Phœnician) general, Hannibal, used gunpowder in breaking a way for his army over the Alps. The Romans, who were ignorant of its use, said that Hannibal made his way by making fires against the rocks, and pouring vinegar and water over the ashes. It is evident that fire and vinegar would have no effect on masses of the Alps great enough to arrest the march of an army. Dr. William Maginn has suggested that the wood was probably burnt by Hannibal to obtain charcoal; and the word which has been translated "vinegar" probably signified some preparation of nitre and sulphur, and that Hannibal made gunpowder and blew up the rocks. The same author suggests that the story of Hannibal breaking loose from the mountains where he was surrounded on all sides by the Romans, and in danger of starvation, by fastening firebrands to the horns of two thousand oxen, and sending them rushing at night among the terrified Romans, simply refers to the use of rockets. As Maginn well asks, how could Hannibal be in danger of starvation when he had two thousand oxen to spare for such an experiment? And why should the veteran Roman troops have been so terrified and panic-stricken by a lot of cattle with firebrands on their horns? At the battle of Lake Trasymene, between Hannibal and Flaminius, we have another curious piece of information which goes far to confirm the belief that Hannibal was familiar with the use of gunpowder. In the midst of the battle there was, say the Roman historians, an "earthquake;" the earth reeled under the feet of the soldiers, a tremendous crash was heard, a fog or smoke covered the scene, the earth broke open, and the rocks fell upon the heads of the Romans. This reads very much as if the Carthaginians had decoyed the Romans into a pass where they had already planted a mine, and had exploded it at the proper moment to throw them into a panic. Earthquakes do not cast rocks up in the air to fall on men's heads!

And that this is not all surmise is shown by the fact that a city of India, in the time of Alexander the Great, defended itself by the use of gunpowder: it was said to be a favorite of the gods, because thunder and lightning came from its walls to resist the attacks of its assailants.

As the Hebrews were a branch of the Phœnician race, it is not surprising that we find some things in their history which look very much like legends of gunpowder.

When Korah, Dathan, and Abiram led a rebellion against Moses, Moses separated the faithful from the unfaithful, and thereupon "the ground clave asundei that was under them: and the earth opened her mouth, and swallowed them up, and their houses, and all the men that appertained unto Korah, and all their goods. . . . And there came out a fire from the Lord, and consumed the two hundred and fifty men that offered incense. . . . But on the morrow all the congregation of the children of Israel murmured against Moses and against Aaron, saying, Ye have killed the people of the Lord." (Numb. xvi., 31–41.)

This looks very much as if Moses had blown up the rebels with gunpowder.

Roger Bacon, who himself rediscovered gunpowder, was of opinion that the event described in Judges vii., where Gideon captured the camp of the Midianites with the roar of trumpets, the crash caused by the breaking of innumerable pitchers, and the flash of a multitude of lanterns, had reference to the use of gunpowder; that the noise made by the breaking of the pitchers represented the detonation of an explosion, the flame of the lights the blaze, and the noise of the trumpets the thunder of the gunpowder. We can understand, in this wise, the results that followed; but we cannot otherwise understand how the breaking of pitchers, the flashing of lamps, and the clangor of trumpets would throw an army into panic, until "every man's sword was set against his fellow, and the host fled to Beth-shittah;" and this, too, without any attack upon the part of the Israelites, for "they stood every man in his place around the camp; and all the host ran and cried and fled."

If it was a miraculous interposition in behalf of the Jews, the Lord could have scared the Midianites out of their wits without the smashed pitchers and lanterns; and certain it is the pitchers and lanterns would not have done the work with-out a miraculous interposition.

Having traced the knowledge of gunpowder back to the most remote times, and to the different races which were de-scended from Atlantis, we are not surprised to find in the legends of Greek mythology events described which are only explicable by supposing that the Atlanteans possessed the secret of this powerful explosive.

A rebellion sprang up in Atlantis (see Murray's "Manual of Mythology," p. 30) against Zeus; it is known in mythology as the "War of the Titans:"

"The struggle lasted many years, all the might which the Olympians could bring to bear being useless, until, on the ad-vice of Gæa, Zeus set free the Kyklopes and the Hekaton-cheires" (that is, brought the ships into play), "of whom the former fashioned *thunder-bolts* for him, while the latter ad-vanced on his side with *force equal to the shock of an earth-quake. The earth trembled down to lowest Tartarus* as Zeus now appeared with his *terrible weapon* and new allies. Old Chaos thought his hour had come, as from a *continuous blaze of thunder-bolts the earth took fire,* and the waters seethed in the sea. The rebels were partly slain or consumed, and partly hurled into *deep chasms, with rocks and hills reeling after them.*"

Do not these words picture the explosion of a mine with a "force equal to the shock of an earthquake?"

We have already shown that the Kyklopes and Hekaton-cheires were probably great war-ships, armed with some ex-plosive material in the nature of gunpowder.

Zeus, the king of Atlantis, was known as "the thunderer," and was represented armed with thunder-bolts.

Some ancient nation must, in the most remote ages, have invented gunpowder; and is it unreasonable to attribute it to that "great original race" rather than to any one people of their posterity, who seem to have borrowed all the other arts from them; and who, during many thousands of years, did not add a single new invention to the list they received from Atlantis?

Iron.—We have seen that the Greek mythological legends asserted that before the submergence of the great race over whom their gods reigned there had been not only an Age of Bronze but an Age of Iron. This metal was known to the Egyptians in the earliest ages; fragments of iron have been found in the oldest pyramids. The Iron Age in Northern Europe far antedated intercourse with the Greeks or Romans. In the mounds of the Mississippi Valley, as I have shown, the remains of iron implements have been found. In the "Mercurio Peruano" (tom. i., p. 201, 1791) it is stated that "anciently the Peruvian sovereigns worked magnificent iron mines at Ancoriames, on the west shore of Lake Titicaca." "It is remarkable," says Molina, "that iron, which has been thought unknown to the ancient Americans, had particular names in some of their tongues." In official Peruvian it was called *quillay*, and in Chilian *panilic*. The Mound Builders fashioned implements out of meteoric iron. (Foster's "Prehistoric Races," p. 333.)

As we find this metal known to man in the earliest ages on both sides of the Atlantic, the presumption is very strong that it was borrowed by the nations, east and west, from Atlantis.

Paper.—The same argument holds good as to paper. The oldest Egyptian monuments contain pictures of the papyrus roll; while in Mexico, as I have shown, a beautiful paper was manufactured and formed into books shaped like our own. In Peru a paper was made of plantain leaves, and books were common in the earlier ages. Humboldt mentions books of hieroglyphical writings among the Panoes, which were "bundles of their paper resembling our volumes in quarto."

Silk Manufacture.—The manufacture of a woven fabric of great beauty out of the delicate fibre of the egg-cocoon of a worm could only have originated among a people who had attained the highest degree of civilization; it implies the art of weaving by delicate instruments, a dense population, a patient, skilful, artistic people, a sense of the beautiful, and a wealthy and luxurious class to purchase such costly fabrics.

We trace it back to the most remote ages. In the introduction to the "History of Hindostan," or rather of the Mohammedan Dynasties, by Mohammed Cassim, it is stated that in the year 3870 B.C. an Indian king sent various silk stuffs as a present to the King of Persia. The art of making silk was known in China more than two thousand six hundred years before the Christian era, at the time when we find them first possessed of civilization. The Phœnicians dealt in silks in the most remote past; they imported them from India and sold them along the shores of the Mediterranean. It is probable that the Egyptians understood and practised the art of manufacturing silk. It was woven in the island of Cos in the time of Aristotle. The "Babylonish garment" referred to in Joshua (chap. vii., 21), and for secreting which Achan lost his life, was probably a garment of silk; it was rated above silver and gold in value.

It is not a violent presumption to suppose that an art known to the Hindoos 3870 B.C., and to the Chinese and Phœnicians at the very beginning of their history — an art so curious, so extraordinary—may have dated back to Atlantean times.

Civil Government.—Mr. Baldwin shows ("Prehistoric Nations," p. 114) that the Cushites, the successors of the Atlanteans, whose very ancient empire extended from Spain to Syria, were the first to establish independent municipal republics, with the right of the people to govern themselves; and that this system was perpetuated in the great Phœnician communities; in "the fierce democracies" of ancient Greece; in the "village republics" of the African Berbers and the Hindoos; in the "free cities" of the Middle Ages in Europe; and in the independent governments of the Basques, which continued down to our own day. The Cushite state was an aggregation of municipalities, each possessing the right of self-government, but subject within prescribed limits to a general authority; in other words, it was precisely the form of government possessed to-day by the United States. It is a surprising thought that the perfection of modern government may be another perpetuation of Atlantean civilization.

Agriculture.—The Greek traditions of "the golden apples of the Hesperides" and "the golden fleece" point to Atlantis. The allusions to the golden apples indicate that tradition regarded the "Islands of the Blessed" in the Atlantic Ocean as a place of orchards. And when we turn to Egypt we find that in the remotest times many of our modern garden and field plants were there cultivated. When the Israelites murmured in the wilderness against Moses, they cried out (Numb., chap. xi., 4, 5), "Who shall give us flesh to eat? We remember the fish which we did eat in Egypt freely; the cucumbers, and the melons, and the leeks, and the onions, and the garlic." The Egyptians also cultivated wheat, barley, oats, flax, hemp, etc. In fact, if we were to take away from civilized man the domestic animals, the cereals, and the field and garden vegetables possessed by the Egyptians at the very dawn of history, there would be very little left for the granaries or the tables of the world.

Astronomy.—The knowledge of the ancients as to astronomy was great and accurate. Callisthenes, who accompanied Alexander the Great to Babylon, sent to Aristotle a series of Chaldean astronomical observations which he found preserved there, recorded on tablets of baked clay, and extending back as far as 2234 B.C. Humboldt says, "The Chaldeans knew the mean motions of the moon with an exactness which induced the Greek astronomers to use their calculations for the foundation of a lunar theory." The Chaldeans knew the true nature of comets, and could foretell their reappearance. "A lens of considerable power was found in the ruins of Babylon; it was an inch and a half in diameter and nine-tenths of an inch thick." (Layard's "Nineveh and Babylon," pp. 16, 17.) Nero used optical glasses when he watched the fights of the gladiators; they are supposed to have come from Egypt and the East. Plutarch speaks of optical instruments used by Archimedes "to manifest to the eye the largeness of the sun." "There are actual astronomical calculations in existence, with calendars formed upon them, which eminent astronomers of England and France admit to be genuine and true, and which carry back the antiquity of the science of astronomy, together with the constellations, to within a few years of the Deluge, even on the longer chronology of the Septuagint." ("The Miracle in Stone," p. 142.) Josephus attributes the invention of the constellations to the family of the antediluvian Seth, the son of Adam, while Origen affirms that it was asserted in the Book of Enoch that in the time of that patriarch the constellations were already divided and named. The Greeks associated the origin of astronomy with Atlas and Hercules, Atlantean kings or heroes. The Egyptians regarded Taut (At?) or Thoth, or _At_-hotes, as the originator of both astronomy and the alphabet; doubtless he represented a civilized people, by whom their country was originally colonized. Bailly and others assert that astronomy "must have been established when the summer solstice was in the first degree of Virgo, and that the solar and lunar zodiacs were of similar antiquity, which would be about four thousand years before the Christian era. They suppose the originators to have lived in about the _fortieth degree of north latitude_, and to have been a highly-civilized people." It will be remembered that the fortieth degree of north latitude passed through Atlantis. Plato knew ("Dialogues, Phædo," 108) that the earth "is a body in the centre of the heavens" held in equipoise. He speaks of it as a "round body," a "globe;" he even understood that it revolved on its axis, and that these revolutions produced day and night. He says—"Dialogues, Timæus"—"The earth circling around the pole (which is extended through the universe) he made to be the artificer of night and day." All this Greek learning was probably drawn from the Egyptians.

Only among the Atlanteans in Europe and America do we find traditions preserved as to the origin of all the principal inventions which have raised man from a savage to a civilized condition. We can give in part the very names of the inventors.

Starting with the Chippeway legends, and following with the Bible and Phœnician records, we make a table like the appended :

The Invention or Discovery.	The Race.	The Inventors.
Fire..................	Atlantean.....	Phos, Phur, and Phlox.
The bow and arrow......	Chippeway....	Manaboshu.
The use of flint.........	"	"
The use of copper.......		
The manufacture of bricks	Atlantean.....	Autochthon and Technites.
Agriculture and hunting..	"	Argos and Agrotes.
Village life, and the rearing of flocks....	"	Amynos and Magos.
The use of salt	"	Misor and Sydyk.
The use of letters.......	"	Taautos, or Taut.
Navigation.............	"	The Cabiri, or Corybantes.
The art of music........	Hebrew......	Jubal.
Metallurgy, and the use of iron.............	"	Tubal-cain.
The syrinx.............	Greek........	Pan.
The lyre..............	"	Hermes.

We cannot consider all these evidences of the vast antiquity of the great inventions upon which our civilization mainly rests, including the art of writing, which, as I have shown, dates back far beyond the beginning of history ; we cannot remember that the origin of all the great food-plants, such as wheat, oats, barley, rye, and maize, is lost in the remote past; and that all the domesticated animals, the horse, the ass, the ox, the sheep, the goat, and the hog had been reduced to subjection to man in ages long previous to written history, without having the conclusion forced upon us irresistibly that beyond Egypt and Greece, beyond Chaldea and China, there existed a mighty civilization, of which these states were but the broken fragments.

Chapter X.

THE ARYAN COLONIES FROM ATLANTIS.

We come now to another question: "Did the Aryan or Japhetic race come from Atlantis?"

If the Aryans *are* the Japhetic race, and if Japheth was one of the sons of the patriarch who escaped from the Deluge, then assuredly, if the tradition of Genesis be true, the Aryans came from the drowned land, to wit, Atlantis. According to Genesis, the descendants of the Japheth who escaped out of the Flood with Noah are the Ionians, the inhabitants of the Morea, the dwellers on the Cilician coast of Asia Minor, the Cyprians, the Dodoneans of Macedonia, the Iberians, and the Thracians. These are all now recognized as Aryans, except the Iberians.

"From non-Biblical sources," says Winchell, "we obtain further information respecting the early dispersion of the Japheth-ites or Indo - Europeans — called also Aryans. *All determinations confirm the Biblical account of their primitive residence in the same country with the Hamites and Semites.* Rawlinson informs us that even Aryan roots are mingled with Presemitic in some of the old inscriptions of Assyria. The precise region where these three families dwelt *in a common home* has not been pointed out." ("Preadamites," p. 43.)

I have shown in the chapter in relation to Peru that all the languages of the Hamites, Semites, and Japhethites are varieties of one aboriginal speech.

The centre of the Aryan migrations (according to popular opinion) within the Historical Period was Armenia. Here too

is Mount Ararat, where it is said the ark rested—another identification with the Flood regions, as it represents the usual trans-
fer of the Atlantis legend by an Atlantean people to a high
mountain in their new home.

Now turn to a map: Suppose the ships of Atlantis to have
reached the shores of Syria, at the eastern end of the Mediterranean, where dwelt a people who, as we have seen, used the
Central American Maya alphabet; the Atlantis ships are then
but two hundred miles distant from Armenia. But these ships
need not stop at Syria, they can go by the Dardanelles and the
Black Sea, by uninterrupted water communication, to the shores
of Armenia itself. If we admit, then, that it was from Armenia the Aryans stocked Europe and India, there is no reason
why the original population of Armenia should not have been
themselves colonists from Atlantis.

But we have seen that in the earliest ages, before the first
Armenian migration of the historical Aryans, a people went
from Iberian Spain and settled in Ireland, and the language of
this people, it is now admitted, is Aryan. And these Iberians
were originally, according to tradition, from the *West*.

The Mediterranean Aryans are known to have been in South-
eastern Europe, along the shores of the Mediterranean, 2000 B.C.
They at that early date possessed the plough; also wheat, rye,
barley, gold, silver, and bronze. Aryan faces are found depicted upon the monuments of Egypt, painted four thousand years
before the time of Christ. "The conflicts between the Kelts
(an Aryan race) and the Iberians were far anterior in date to
the settlements of the Phœnicians, Greeks, Carthaginians, and
Noachites on the coasts of the Mediterranean Sea." ("American Cyclopædia," art. *Basques*.) There is reason to believe
that these Kelts were originally part of the population and
Empire of Atlantis. We are told (Rees's "British Encyclopædia," art. *Titans*) that "Mercury, one of the Atlantean gods,
was placed as ruler over the Celtæ, and became their great
divinity." F. Pezron, in his "Antiquity of the Celtæ," makes

out that the Celtæ were the same as the Titans, the giant race
who rebelled in Atlantis, and "that their princes were the
same with the giants of Scripture." He adds that the word
Titan "is perfect Celtic, and comes from *tit*, the earth, and
ten or *den*, man, and hence the Greeks very properly also called
them *terriginæ*, or earth-born." And it will be remembered
that Plato uses the same phrase when he speaks of the race
into which Poseidon intermarried as "the earth-born primeval
men of that country."

The Greeks, who are Aryans, traced their descent from the
people who were destroyed by the Flood, as did other races
clearly Aryan.

"The nations who are comprehended under the common
appellation of Indo-European," says Max Müller—"the Hindoos, the Persians, the Celts, Germans, Romans, Greeks, and
Slavs—do not only share the same words and the same grammar, slightly modified in each country, but they seem to have
likewise preserved a mass of popular traditions which had
grown up before they left their common home."

"Bonfey, L. Geiger, and other students of the ancient Indo-
European languages, have recently advanced the opinion that
the original home of the Indo-European races must be sought
in Europe, because their stock of words is rich in the names of
plants and animals, and contains names of seasons that are not
found in tropical countries or anywhere in Asia." ("American
Cyclopædia," art. *Ethnology*.)

By the study of comparative philology, or the seeking out
of the words common to the various branches of the Aryan
race before they separated, we are able to reconstruct an outline of the civilization of that ancient people. Max Müller
has given this subject great study, and availing ourselves of
his researches we can determine the following facts as to
the progenitors of the Aryan stock: They were a civilized
race; they possessed the institution of marriage; they recognized the relationship of father, mother, son, daughter, grand-

son, brother, sister, mother-in-law, father-in-law, son-in-law, daughter-in-law, brother-in-law, and sister-in-law, and had separate words for each of these relationships, which we are only able to express by adding the words "in-law." They recognized also the condition of widows, or "the husband-less." They lived in an organized society, governed by a king. They possessed houses with doors and solid walls. They had wagons and carriages. They possessed family names. They dwelt in towns and cities, on highways. *They were not hunters or nomads.* They were a peaceful people; the warlike words in the different Aryan languages cannot be traced back to this original race. They lived in a country having few wild beasts; the only wild animals whose names can be assigned to this parent stock being the bear, the wolf, and the serpent. The name of the elephant, "the beast with a hand," occurs only twice in the "Rig-Veda;" a singular omission if the Aryans were from time immemorial an Asiatic race; and " when it does occur, it is in such a way as to show that he was still an object of wonder and terror to them." (Whitney's "Oriental and Linguistic Studies," p. 26.) They possessed nearly all the domestic animals we now have—the ox and the cow, the horse, the dog, the sheep, the goat, the hog, the donkey, and the goose. They divided the year into twelve months. They were farmers; they used the plough; their name as a race (Aryan) was derived from it; they were, *par excellence*, ploughmen; they raised various kinds of grain, including flax, barley, hemp, and wheat; they had mills and millers, and ground their corn. The presence of millers shows that they had proceeded beyond the primitive condition where each family ground its corn in its own mill. They used fire, and cooked and baked their food; they wove cloth and wore clothing; they spun wool; they possessed the different metals, *even iron:* they had gold. The word for "water" also meant "salt made from water," from which it might be inferred that the water with which they were familiar was salt-water. It is evident they manufactured salt by evaporating salt-

water. They possessed boats and ships. They had progressed
so far as to perfect "a decimal system of enumeration, in itself," says Max Müller, "one of the most marvellous achievements of the human mind, based on an abstract conception of

ANCIENT EGYPTIAN PLOUGH.

quantity, regulated by a philosophical classification, and yet
conceived, nurtured, and finished before the soil of Europe was
trodden by Greek, Roman, Slav, or Teuton."

And herein we find another evidence of relationship between
the Aryans and the people of Atlantis. Although Plato does
not tell us that the Atlanteans possessed the decimal system of
numeration, nevertheless there are many things in his narrative
which point to that conclusion: "There were ten kings ruling
over ten provinces; the whole country was divided into military districts or squares ten stadia each way; the total force of
chariots was ten thousand; the great ditch or canal was one
hundred feet deep and ten thousand stadia long; there were
one hundred Nereids," etc. In the Peruvian colony the decimal
system clearly obtained: "The army had heads of ten, fifty, a
hundred, five hundred, a thousand, ten thousand. . . . The community at large was registered in groups, under the control of
officers over tens, fifties, hundreds, and so on." (Herbert Spencer, "Development of Political Institutions," chap. x.)   The
same division into tens and hundreds obtained among the Anglo-Saxons.

Where, we ask, could this ancient nation, which existed before Greek was Greek, Celt was Celt, Hindoo was Hindoo, or Goth was Goth, have been located? The common opinion says, in Armenia or Bactria, in Asia. But where in Asia could they have found a country so peaceful as to know no terms for war or bloodshed;—a country so civilized as to possess no wild beasts save the bear, wolf, and serpent? No people could have been developed in Asia without bearing in its language traces of century-long battles for life with the rude and barbarous races around them; no nation could have fought for ages for existence against "man-eating" tigers, lions, elephants, and hyenas, without bearing the memory of these things in their tongue. A tiger, identical with that of Bengal, still exists around Lake Aral, in Asia; from time to time it is seen in Siberia. "The last tiger killed in 1828 was on the Lena, in latitude fifty-two degrees thirty minutes, in a climate colder than that of St. Petersburg and Stockholm."

The fathers of the Aryan race must have dwelt for many thousand years so completely protected from barbarians and wild beasts that they at last lost all memory of them, and all words descriptive of them; and where could this have been possible save in some great, long-civilized land, surrounded by the sea, and isolated from the attack of the savage tribes that occupied the rest of the world? And if such a great civilized nation had dwelt for centuries in Asia, Europe, or Africa, why have not their monuments long ago been discovered and identified? Where is the race who are their natural successors, and who must have continued to live after them in that sheltered and happy land, where they knew no human and scarcely any animal enemies? Why would any people have altogether left such a home? Why, when their civilization had spread to the ends of the earth, did it cease to exist in the peaceful region where it originated?

Savage nations cannot usually count beyond five. This people had names for the numerals up to one hundred, and the power, doubtless, of combining these to still higher powers, as three hundred, five hundred, ten hundred, etc. Says a high authority, "If any more proof were wanted as to the reality of that period which must have preceded the dispersion of the Aryan race, we might appeal to the Aryan numerals as irrefragable evidence of that long-continued intellectual life which characterizes that period." Such a degree of progress implies necessarily an alphabet, writing, commerce, and trade, even as the existence of words for boats and ships has already implied navigation.

In what have we added to the civilization of this ancient people? Their domestic animals were the same as our own, except one fowl adopted from America. In the past ten thousand years we have added one bird to their list of domesticated animals! They raised wheat and wool, and spun and wove as we do, except that we have added some mechanical contrivances to produce the same results. Their metals are ours. Even iron, the triumph, as we had supposed, of more modern times, they had already discovered. And it must not be forgotten that Greek mythology tells us that the god-like race who dwelt on Olympus, that great island "in the midst of the Atlantic," in the remote west, wrought in iron; and we find the remains of an iron sword and meteoric iron weapons in the mounds of the Mississippi Valley, while the name of the metal is found in the ancient languages of Peru and Chili, and the Incas worked in iron on the shores of Lake Titicaca.

A still further evidence of the civilization of this ancient race is found in the fact that, before the dispersion from their original home, the Aryans had reached such a degree of development that they possessed a regularly organized religion: they worshipped God, they believed in an evil spirit, they believed in a heaven for the just. All this presupposes temples, priests, sacrifices, and an orderly state of society.

We have seen that Greek mythology is really a history of the kings and queens of Atlantis.

When we turn to that other branch of the great Aryan

family, the Hindoos, we find that their gods are also the kings of Atlantis. The Hindoo god Varuna is conceded to be the Greek god Uranos, who was the founder of the royal family of Atlantis.

In the Veda we find a hymn to "King Varuna," in which occurs this passage:

"This earth, too, belongs to Varuna, *the king*, and this wide sky, with its ends far apart. *The two seas are Varuna's loins;* he is contained also in this drop of water."

Again in the Veda we find another hymn to King Varuna:

"He who knows the place of the birds that fly through the sky; who on the waters knows *the ships*. He, the upholder of order, who knows *the twelve months with the offspring of each*, and knows *the month that is engendered afterward.*"

This verse would seem to furnish additional proof that the Vedas were written by a maritime people; and in the allusion to the twelve months we are reminded of the Peruvians, who also divided the year into twelve parts of thirty days each, and afterward added six days to complete the year. The Egyptians and Mexicans also had intercalary days for the same purpose.

But, above all, it must be remembered that the Greeks, an Aryan race, in their mythological traditions, show the closest relationship to Atlantis. *At*-tika and *At*-hens are reminiscences of *Ad*, and we are told that Poseidon, god and founder of Atlantis, founded Athens. We find in the "Eleusinian mysteries" an Atlantean institution; their influence during the whole period of Greek history down to the coming of Christianity was extraordinary; and even then this masonry of Pre-Christian days, in which kings and emperors begged to be initiated, was, it is claimed, continued to our own times in our own Freemasons, who trace their descent back to "a Dionysiac fraternity which originated in Attika." And just as we have seen the Saturnalian festivities of Italy descending from Atlantean harvest-feasts, so these Eleusinian mysteries can be traced back to Plato's island. Poseidon was at the base of them; the first hierophant, Eumolpus, was "a son of Posei-don," and all the ceremonies were associated with seed-time and harvest, and with Demeter or Ceres, an Atlantean goddess, daughter of Chronos, who first taught the Greeks to use the plough and to plant barley. And, as the "Carnival" is a sur-vival of the "Saturnalia," so Masonry is a survival of the Eleu-sinian mysteries. The roots of the institutions of to-day reach back to the Miocene Age.

We have seen that Zeus, the king of Atlantis, whose tomb was shown at Crete, was transformed into the Greek god Zeus; and in like manner we find him reappearing among the Hin-doos as Dyaus. He is called "Dyaus-pitar," or God the Fa-ther, as among the Greeks we have "Zeus-pater," which be-came among the Romans "Jupiter."

The strongest connection, however, with the Atlantean sys-tem is shown in the case of the Hindoo god Deva-Nahusha.

We have seen in the chapter on Greek mythology that Dionysos was a son of Zeus and grandson of Poseidon, being thus identified with Atlantis. "When he arrived at manhood," said the Greeks, "he set out on a journey through all known countries, even into the remotest parts of *India,* instructing the people, as he proceeded, how to tend the vine, and how to practise many other arts of peace, besides teaching them the value of just and honorable dealings. He was praised every-where as the greatest benefactor of mankind." (Murray's "My-thology," p. 119.)

In other words, he represented the great Atlantean civiliza-tion, reaching into "the remotest parts of India," and "to all parts of the known world," from America to Asia. In conse-quence of the connection of this king with the vine, he was converted in later times into the dissolute god Bacchus. But everywhere the traditions concerning him refer us back to Atlantis. "All the legends of Egypt, India, Asia Minor, and the older Greeks describe him as a king very great during his life, and deified after death. . : . Amon, king of Arabia or Ethiopia, married Rhea, sister of Chronos, who reigned over Italy, Sicily, and *certain countries of Northern Africa.*" Dionysos, according to the Egyptians, was the son of Amon by the beautiful Amalthea. Chronos and Amon had a prolonged war; Dionysos defeated Chronos and captured his capital, dethroned him, and put his son Zeus in his place; Zeus reigned nobly, and won a great fame. Dionysos succeeded his father Amon, and "became the greatest of sovereigns. He extended his sway in all the neighboring countries, and completed the conquest of India. . . . He gave much attention to the Cushite colonies in Egypt, greatly increasing their strength, intelligence, and prosperity." (Baldwin's "Prehistoric Nations," p. 283.)

When we turn to the Hindoo we still find this Atlantean king.

In the Sanscrit books we find reference to a god called Deva-Nahusha, who has been identified by scholars with Dionysos. He is connected " with *the oldest history and mythology in the world.*" He is said to have been a contemporary with Indra, king of *Meru,* who was also deified, and who appears in the Veda as a principal form of representation of the Supreme Being.

" The warmest colors of imagination are used in portraying the greatness of Deva-Nahusha. For a time he had sovereign control of affairs in Meru; he conquered the seven dwipas, and led his armies *through all the known countries of the world;* by means of matchless wisdom and miraculous heroism *he made his empire universal.*" (*Ibid.,* p. 287.)

Here we see that the great god Indra, chief god of the Hindoos, was formerly king of Meru, and that Deva-Nahusha (De(va)nushas — De-onyshas) had also been king of Meru; and we must remember that Theopompus tell us that the island of Atlantis was inhabited by the " Meropes;" and Lenormant has reached the conclusion that the first people of the ancient world were "the men of Mero."

We can well believe, when we see traces of the same civilization extending from Peru and Lake Superior to Armenia and the frontiers of China, that this Atlantean kingdom was indeed "universal," and extended through all the "known countries of the world."

"We can see in the legends that Pŭrūrăvas, Nahusha, and others had no connection with Sanscrit history. They are referred to ages very long anterior to the Sanscrit immigration, and must have been great personages celebrated in the traditions of the natives or Dasyus. . . . Pŭrūrăvas was a king of great renown, *who ruled over thirteen islands of the ocean*, altogether surrounded by inhuman (or superhuman) personages; he engaged in a contest with Brahmans, and perished. Nahusha, mentioned by Maull, and in many legends, as famous for hostility to the Brahmans, lived at the time when Indra ruled on earth. He was a very great king, who ruled with justice a mighty empire, and *attained the sovereignty of three worlds.*" (Europe, Africa, and America?) "Being intoxicated with pride, he was arrogant to Brahmans, compelled them to bear his palanquin, and even dared to touch one of them with his foot" (kicked him?), "whereupon he was transformed into a serpent." (Baldwin's "Prehistoric Nations," p. 291.)

The Egyptians placed Dionysos (Osiris) at the close of the period of their history which was assigned to the gods, that is, toward the close of the great empire of Atlantis.

When we remember that the hymns of the "Rig-Veda" are admitted to date back to a vast antiquity, and are written in a language that had ceased to be a living tongue thousands of years ago, we can almost fancy those hymns preserve some part of the songs of praise uttered of old upon the island of Atlantis. Many of them seem to belong to sun-worship, and might have been sung with propriety upon the high places of Peru:

"In the beginning there arose *the golden child*. He was the one born Lord of all that is. He established the earth and the sky. Who is the god to whom we shall offer sacrifice?

" He who gives life; He who gives strength; whose command all the bright gods " (the stars ?) " revere; whose light is immortality; whose shadow is death. . . . He who through his power is the one God of the breathing *and awakening world.* He who governs all, man and beast. He whose greatness these snowy mountains, whose greatness the sea proclaims, with the distant river. *He through whom the sky is bright and the earth firm.* . . . He who measured out the light in the air. . . . Wherever the mighty water-clouds went, where they placed the seed and lit the fire, thence arose He who is the sole life of the bright gods. . . . He to whom heaven and earth, standing firm by His will, look up, trembling inwardly. . . . *May he not destroy us;* He, the creator of the earth; He, the righteous, who created heaven. He also created *the bright and mighty waters.*"

This is plainly a hymn to the sun, or to a god whose most glorious representative was the sun. It is the hymn of a people near the sea; it was not written by a people living in the heart of Asia. It was the hymn of a people living in a volcanic country, who call upon their god to keep the earth "firm" and not to destroy them. It was sung at daybreak, as the sun rolled up the sky over an "awakening world."

The fire (Agni) upon the altar was regarded as a messenger rising from the earth to the sun:

" Youngest of the gods, their messenger, their invoker. . . . For thou, O sage, goest wisely between these two creations (heaven and earth, God and man) like a friendly messenger between two hamlets."

The dawn of the day (Ushas), part of the sun-worship, became also a god:

" She shines upon us like a young wife, rousing every living being to go to his work. When the fire had to be kindled by man, she made the light by striking down the darkness."

As the Egyptians and the Greeks looked to a happy abode (an under-world) in the west, beyond the waters, so the Aryan's paradise was the other side of some body of water. In the

Veda (vii. 56, 24) we find a prayer to the Maruts, the storm-gods: "O, Maruts, may there be to us a strong son, who is a living ruler of men; through whom we may *cross the waters on our way to the happy abode.*" This happy abode is described as "where King Vaivasvata reigns; where the secret place of heaven is; *where the mighty waters are . . .* where there is food and rejoicing . . . where there is happiness and delight; where joy and pleasure reside." (Rig-Veda ix. 113, 7.) This is the paradise beyond the seas; the Elysion; the Elysian Fields of the Greek and the Egyptian, located upon an island in the Atlantic which was destroyed by water. One great chain of tradition binds together these widely separated races.

"The religion of the Veda knows no idols," says Max Müller; "the worship of idols in India is a secondary formation, a degradation of the more primitive worship of ideal gods."

It was pure sun-worship, such as prevailed in Peru on the arrival of the Spaniards. It accords with Plato's description of the religion of Atlantis.

"The Dolphin's Ridge," at the bottom of the Atlantic, or the high land revealed by the soundings taken by the ship *Challenger*, is, as will be seen, of a three-pronged form—one prong pointing toward the west coast of Ireland, another connecting with the north-east coast of South America, and a third near or on the west coast of Africa. It does not follow that the island of Atlantis, at any time while inhabited by civilized people, actually reached these coasts; there is a strong probability that races of men may have found their way there from the three continents of Europe, America, and Africa; or the great continent which once filled the whole bed of the present Atlantic Ocean, and from whose débris geology tells us the Old and New Worlds were constructed, may have been the scene of the development, during immense periods of time, of diverse races of men, occupying different zones of climate.

There are many indications that there were three races of men dwelling on Atlantis. Noah, according to Genesis, had three sons —Shem, Ham, and Japheth—who represented three different races of men of different colors. The Greek legends tell us of the rebellions inaugurated at different times in Olympus. One of these was a rebellion of the Giants, "a race of beings sprung from the blood of Uranos," the great original progenitor of the stock. "Their king or leader was Porphyrion, their most powerful champion Alkyoneus." Their mother was the earth: this probably meant that they represented the common people of a darker hue. They made a desperate struggle for supremacy, but were conquered by Zeus. There were also two rebellions of the Titans. The Titans seem to have had a government of their own, and the names of twelve of their kings are given in the Greek mythology (see Murray, p. 27). They also were of "the blood of Uranos," the Adam of the people. We read, in fact, that Uranos married Gæa (the earth), and had three families: 1, the Titans; 2, the Hekatoncheires; and 3, the Kyklopes. We should conclude that the last two were maritime peoples, and I have shown that their mythical characteristics were probably derived from the appearance of their ships. Here we have, I think, a reference to the three races: 1, the red or sunburnt men, like the Egyptians, the Phœnicians, the Basques, and the Berber and Cushite stocks; 2, the sons of Shem, possibly the yellow or Turanian race; and 3, the whiter men, the Aryans, the Greeks, Kelts, Goths, Slavs, etc. If this view is correct, then we may suppose that colonies of the pale-faced stock may have been sent out from Atlantis to the northern coasts of Europe at different and perhaps widely separated periods of time, from some of which the Aryan families of Europe proceeded; hence the legend, which is found among them, that they were once forced to dwell in a country where the summers were only two months long.

From the earliest times two grand divisions are recognized in the Aryan family: "to the east those who specially called themselves *Arians,* whose descendants inhabited Persia, India,

etc.; to the west, the *Yavana*, or the Young Ones, who first emi·
grated westward, and from whom have descended the various
nations that have populated Europe. This is the name (Javan)
found in the tenth chapter of Genesis." (Lenormant and
Chevallier, "Ancient History of the East," vol. ii., p. 2.) But
surely those who "first emigrated westward," the earliest to
leave the parent stock, could not be the "Young Ones;" they
would be rather the elder brothers. But if we can suppose
the Bactrian population to have left Atlantis at an early date,
and the Greeks, Latins, and Celts to have left it at a later
period, then they would indeed be the "Young Ones" of the
family, following on the heels of the earlier migrations, and
herein we would find the explanation of the resemblance between the Latin and Celtic tongues. Lenormant says the name
of Erin (Ireland) is derived from Aryan; and yet we have seen
this island populated and named Erin by races distinctly connected with Spain, Iberia, Africa, and Atlantis.

There is another reason for supposing that the Aryan nations came from Atlantis.

We find all Europe, except a small corner of Spain and a
strip along the Arctic Circle, occupied by nations recognized as
Aryan; but when we turn to Asia, there is but a corner of it,
and that corner in the part *nearest Europe*, occupied by the
Aryans. All the rest of that great continent has been filled
from immemorial ages by non-Aryan races. There are seven
branches of the Aryan family: 1. Germanic or Teutonic; 2.
Slavo-Lithuanic; 3. Celtic; 4. Italic; 5. Greek; 6. Iranian or
Persian; 7. Sanscritic or Indian; and of these seven branches
five dwell on the soil of Europe, and the other two are intrusive races in Asia *from the direction of Europe*. The Aryans
in Europe have dwelt there apparently since the close of the
Stone Age, if not before it, while the movements of the Aryans
in Asia are within the Historical Period, and they appear as
intrusive stocks, forming a high caste amid a vast population
of a different race. The Vedas are supposed to date back to

2000 B.C., while there is every reason to believe that the Celt inhabited Western Europe 5000 B.C. If the Aryan race had originated in the heart of Asia, why would not its ramifications have extended into Siberia, China, and Japan, and all over Asia? And if the Aryans moved at a comparatively recent date into Europe from Bactria, where are the populations that then inhabited Europe—the men of the ages of stone and bronze? We should expect to find the western coasts of Europe filled with them, just as the eastern coasts of Asia and India are filled with Turanian populations. On the contrary, we know that the Aryans descended upon India from the Punjab, which lies to the *north-west* of that region; and that their traditions represent that they came there from the *west*, to wit, from the direction of Europe and Atlantis.

Chapter XI.

ATLANTIS RECONSTRUCTED.

The farther we go back in time toward the era of Atlantis, the more the evidences multiply that we are approaching the presence of a great, wise, civilized race. For instance, we find the Egyptians, Ethiopians, and Israelites, from the earliest ages, refusing to eat the flesh of swine. The Western nations departed from this rule, and in these modern days we are beginning to realize the dangers of this article of food, on account of the *trichina* contained in it; and when we turn to the Talmud, we are told that it was forbidden to the Jews, "because of a small insect which infests it."

The Egyptians, the Ethiopians, the Phœnicians, the Hebrews, and others of the ancient races, practised circumcision. It was probably resorted to in Atlantean days, and imposed as a religious duty, to arrest one of the most dreadful scourges of the human race—a scourge which continued to decimate the people of America, arrested their growth, and paralyzed their civilization. Circumcision stamped out the disease in Atlantis; we read of one Atlantean king, the Greek god Ouranos, who, in a time of plague, compelled his whole army and the armies of his allies to undergo the rite. The colonies that went out to Europe carried the practice but not the disease out of which it originated with them; and it was not until Columbus reopened communication with the infected people of the West India Islands that the scourge crossed the Atlantic and "turned Europe," as one has expressed it, "into a charnal-house."

Life-insurance statistics show, nowadays, that the average

life and health of the Hebrew is much greater than that of other men; and he owes this to the retention of practices and beliefs imposed ten thousand years ago by the great, wise race of Atlantis.

Let us now, with all the facts before us, gleaned from various sources, reconstruct, as near as may be, the condition of the antediluvians.

They dwelt upon a great island, near which were other smaller islands, probably east and west of them, forming stepping-stones, as it were, toward Europe and Africa in one direction, and the West India Islands and America in the other. There were volcanic mountains upon the main island, rising to a height of fifteen hundred feet, with their tops covered with perpetual snow. Below these were elevated table-lands, upon which were the royal establishments. Below these, again, was "the great plain of Atlantis." There were four rivers flowing north, south, east, and west from a central point. The climate was like that of the Azores, mild and pleasant; the soil volcanic and fertile, and suitable at its different elevations for the growth of the productions of the tropical and temperate zones.

The people represented at least two different races: a dark brown reddish race, akin to the Central Americans, the Berbers and the Egyptians; and a white race, like the Greeks, Goths, Celts, and Scandinavians. Various battles and struggles followed between the different peoples for supremacy. The darker race seems to have been, physically, a smaller race, with small hands; the lighter-colored race was much larger—hence the legends of the Titans and Giants. The Guanches of the Canary Islands were men of very great stature. As the works of the Bronze Age represent a small-handed race, and as the races who possessed the ships and gunpowder joined in the war against the Giants, we might conclude that the dark races were the more civilized, that they were the metal-workers and navigators.

The fact that the same opinions and customs exist on both sides of the ocean implies identity of origin; it might be argued that the fact that the explanation of many customs existing on both hemispheres is to be found only in America, implies that the primeval stock existed in America, the emigrating portion of the population carrying away the custom, but forgetting the reason for it. The fact that domestic cattle and the great cereals, wheat, oats, barley, and rye, are found in Europe and not in America, would imply that after population moved to Atlantis from America civilization was developed in Atlantis, and that in the later ages communication was closer and more constant between Atlantis and Europe than between Atlantis and America. In the case of the bulky domestic animals, it would be more difficult to transport them, in the open vessels of that day, from Atlantis across the wider expanse of sea to America, than it would be to carry them by way of the now submerged islands in front of the Mediterranean Sea to the coast of Spain. It may be, too, that the climate of Spain and Italy was better adapted to the growth of wheat, barley, oats and rye, than maize; while the drier atmosphere of America was better suited to the latter plant. Even now comparatively little wheat or barley is raised in Central America, Mexico, or Peru, and none on the low coasts of those countries; while a smaller quantity of maize, proportionately, is grown in Italy, Spain, and the rest of Western Europe, the rainy climate being unsuited to it. We have seen (p. 60, *ante*) that there is reason to believe that maize was known in a remote period in the drier regions of the Egyptians and Chinese.

As science has been able to reconstruct the history of the migrations of the Aryan race, by the words that exist or fail to appear in the kindred branches of that tongue, so the time will come when a careful comparison of words, customs, opinions, arts existing on the opposite sides of the Atlantic will furnish an approximate sketch of Atlantean history.

The people had attained a high position as agriculturists.

The presence of the plough in Egypt and Peru implies that they possessed that implement. And as the horns and ox-head of Baal show the esteem in which cattle were held among them, we may suppose that they had passed the stage in which the plough was drawn by men, as in Peru and Egypt in ancient times, and in Sweden during the Historical Period, and that it was drawn by oxen or horses. They first domesticated the horse, hence the association of Poseidon or Neptune, a sea-god, with horses; hence the race-courses for horses described by Plato. They possessed sheep, and manufactured woollen goods; they also had goats, dogs, and swine. They raised cotton and made cotton goods; they probably cultivated maize, wheat, oats, barley, rye, tobacco, hemp, and flax, and possibly potatoes; they built aqueducts and practised irrigation; they were architects, sculptors, and engravers; they possessed an alphabet; they worked in tin, copper, bronze, silver, gold, and iron.

During the vast period of their duration, as peace and agriculture caused their population to increase to overflowing, they spread out in colonies east and west to the ends of the earth. This was not the work of a few years, but of many centuries; and the relations between these colonies may have been something like the relation between the different colonies that in a later age were established by the Phœnicians, the Greeks, and the Romans; there was an intermingling with the more ancient races, the *autochthones* of the different lands where they settled; and the same crossing of stocks, which we know to have been continued all through the Historical Period, must have been going on for thousands of years, whereby new races and new dialects were formed; and the result of all this has been that the smaller races of antiquity have grown larger, while all the complexions shade into each other, so that we can pass from the whitest to the darkest by insensible degrees.

In some respects the Atlanteans exhibited conditions similar to those of the British Islands: there were the same, and even greater, race differences in the population; the same plantation of colonies in Europe, Asia, and America; the same carrying of civilization to the ends of the earth. We have seen colonies from Great Britain going out in the third and fifth centuries to settle on the shores of France, in Brittany, representing one of the nationalities and languages of the mother-country—a race Atlantean in origin. In the same way we may suppose Hamitic emigrations to have gone out from Atlantis to Syria, Egypt, and the Barbary States. If we could imagine Highland Scotch, Welsh, Cornish, and Irish populations emigrating *en masse* from England in later times, and carrying to their new lands the civilization of England, with peculiar languages not English, we would have a state of things probably more like the migrations which took place from Atlantis. England, with a civilization Atlantean in origin, peopled by races from the same source, is repeating in these modern times the empire of Zeus and Chronos; and, just as we have seen Troy, Egypt, and Greece warring against the parent race, so in later days we have seen Brittany and the United States separating themselves from England, the race characteristics remaining after the governmental connection had ceased.

In religion the Atlanteans had reached all the great thoughts which underlie our modern creeds. They had attained to the conception of one universal, omnipotent, great First Cause. We find the worship of this One God in Peru and in early Egypt. They looked upon the sun as the mighty emblem, type, and instrumentality of this One God. Such a conception could only have come with civilization. It is not until these later days that science has realized the utter dependence of all earthly life upon the sun's rays:

" All applications of animal power may be regarded as derived directly or indirectly from the static chemical power of the vegetable substance by which the various organisms and their capabilities are sustained; and this power, in turn, from the kinetic action of the sun's rays.

" Winds and ocean currents, hailstorms and rain, sliding

glaciers, flowing rivers, and falling cascades are the direct off-spring of solar heat. All our machinery, therefore, whether driven by the windmill or the water-wheel, by horse-power or by steam—all the results of electrical and electro-magnetic changes—our telegraphs, our clocks, and our watches, all are wound up primarily by the sun.

"The sun is the great source of energy in almost all terrestrial phenomena. From the meteorological to the geographical, from the geological to the biological, in the expenditure and conversion of molecular movements, derived from the sun's rays, must be sought the motive power of all this infinitely varied phantasmagoria."

But the people of Atlantis had gone farther; they believed that the soul of man was immortal, and that he would live again in his material body; in other words, they believed in "the resurrection of the body and the life everlasting." They accordingly embalmed their dead.

The Duke of Argyll ("The Unity of Nature") says:

"We have found in the most ancient records of the Aryan language proof that the indications of religious thought are higher, simpler, and purer as we go back in time, until at last, in the very oldest compositions of human speech which have come down to us, we find the Divine Being spoken of in the sublime language which forms the opening of the Lord's Prayer. The date in absolute chronology of the oldest Vedic literature does not seem to be known. Professor Max Müller, however, considers that it may possibly take us back 5000 years. . . . All we can see with certainty is that the earliest inventions of mankind are the most wonderful that the race has ever made. . . . The first use of fire, and the discovery of the methods by which it can be kindled; the domestication of wild animals; and, above all, the processes by which the various cereals were first developed out of some wild grasses—these are all discoveries with which, in ingenuity and in importance, no subsequent discoveries may compare. They are all unknown to history—all lost in the light of an effulgent dawn."

The Atlanteans possessed an established order of priests; their religious worship was pure and simple. They lived under a kingly government; they had their courts, their judges, their records, their monuments covered with inscriptions, their mines, their founderies, their workshops, their looms, their grist-mills, their boats and sailing-vessels, their highways, aqueducts, wharves, docks, and canals. They had processions, banners, and triumphal arches for their kings and heroes; they built pyramids, temples, round-towers, and obelisks; they practised religious ablutions; they knew the use of the magnet and of gunpowder. In short, they were in the enjoyment of a civilization nearly as high as our own, lacking only the printing-press, and those inventions in which steam, electricity, and magnetism are used. We are told that Deva-Nahusha visited his colonies in Farther India. An empire which reached from the Andes to Hindostan, if not to China, must have been magnificent indeed. In its markets must have met the maize of the Mississippi Valley, the copper of Lake Superior, the gold and silver of Peru and Mexico, the spices of India, the tin of Wales and Cornwall, the bronze of Iberia, the amber of the Baltic, the wheat and barley of Greece, Italy, and Switzerland.

It is not surprising that when this mighty nation sank beneath the waves, in the midst of terrible convulsions, with all its millions of people, the event left an everlasting impression upon the imagination of mankind. Let us suppose that Great Britain should to-morrow meet with a similar fate. What a wild consternation would fall upon her colonies and upon the whole human family! The world might relapse into barbarism, deep and almost universal. William the Conqueror, Richard Cœur de Lion, Alfred the Great, Cromwell, and Victoria might survive only as the gods or demons of later races; but the memory of the cataclysm in which the centre of a universal empire instantaneously went down to death would never be forgotten; it would survive in fragments, more or less complete, in every land on earth; it would outlive the memory of a thousand lesser convulsions of nature; it would survive dynasties, nations, creeds, and languages; it would never be forgotten while man continued to inhabit the face of the globe.

Science has but commenced its work of reconstructing the past and rehabilitating the ancient peoples, and surely there is no study which appeals more strongly to the imagination than that of this drowned nation, the true antediluvians. They were the founders of nearly all our arts and sciences; they were the parents of our fundamental beliefs; they were the first civilizers, the first navigators, the first merchants, the first colonizers of the earth; their civilization was old when Egypt was young, and they had passed away thousands of years before Babylon, Rome, or London were dreamed of. This lost people were our ancestors, their blood flows in our veins; the words we use every day were heard, in their primitive form, in their cities, courts, and temples. Every line of race and thought, of blood and belief, leads back to them.

Nor is it impossible that the nations of the earth may yet employ their idle navies in bringing to the light of day some of the relics of this buried people. Portions of the island lie but a few hundred fathoms beneath the sea; and if expeditions have been sent out from time to time in the past, to resurrect from the depths of the ocean sunken treasure-ships with a few thousand doubloons hidden in their cabins, why should not an attempt be made to reach the buried wonders of Atlantis? A single engraved tablet dredged up from Plato's island would be worth more to science, would more strike the imagination of mankind, than all the gold of Peru, all the monuments of Egypt, and all the terra-cotta fragments gathered from the great libraries of Chaldea.

May not the so-called "Phœnician coins" found on Corvo, one of the Azores, be of Atlantean origin? Is it probable that that great race, pre-eminent as a founder of colonies, could have visited those islands within the Historical Period, and have left them unpeopled, as they were when discovered by the Portuguese?

We are but beginning to understand the past: one hundred years ago the world knew nothing of Pompeii or Herculaneum; nothing of the lingual tie that binds together the Indo-European nations; nothing of the significance of the vast volume of inscriptions upon the tombs and temples of Egypt; nothing of the meaning of the arrow-headed inscriptions of Babylon; nothing of the marvellous civilizations revealed in the remains of Yucatan, Mexico, and Peru. We are on the threshold. Scientific investigation is advancing with giant strides. Who shall say that one hundred years from now the great museums of the world may not be adorned with gems, statues, arms, and implements from Atlantis, while the libraries of the world shall contain translations of its inscriptions, throwing new light upon all the past history of the human race, and all the great problems which now perplex the thinkers of our day?

INDEX.

A.

Abaras, 441.
Acla, 171.
Ad, the people of, 236; "as old as Ad," 277; people of, colonized Arabia, 277; empire of, 278; language of, 278; at base of many races, 282.
Adah, sons of, 280.
Adam, 72; a red man, 193; composed books in Paradise, 236; author of arts and letters, 236, 329.
Ad-amah, 279.
Ad-ami, the, 236, 281.
Ad-im, 279.
Ad-ima, 279.
Adites, ancient people of Arabia, 27, 276; sun-worshippers, 277; red-men, 278.
Aditi, the, 280.
Aditya, the, 280.
Ad, Mashab, 279.
Ad-mi, 281.
Adon, 279.
Adonâi, 425.
Adonis, 425.
Ad; Shed-Ad, ben, 276.
Ægean Sea, 25.
Ælian, 27.
Afghans, 185.
Africa, Egyptian circumnavigation of, 3.
Africans not all negroes, 404; red and white races among, 404, 405; origin of these, 407.
Agatharcides, 278.
Agni, the god, 467.
Agriculture, 141; origin of, 453.
Agros, 329.
Ahuramazda, 89.
Alcinous, Gardens of, 2, 323.
Alexander the Great, 136.
Allah, 425.
Alphabet, the, origin of, 214; Egyptians did not invent the, 214; slow growth of ages, 215; letters added by Greeks and Romans, 216; the Phœnician letters, 216; the Maya alphabet, 216; analyzed, 218; table of alphabets, 219; relation of Phœnician and Egyptian alphabets, 232; antiquity of, 235.
Amasis, King of Egypt, 7.
Ambrosia, 287.
America, Deluge legends of, 98.
American continent described by priests of Egypt, 10; ruled over by Atlantis, 11; Eastern origin of the races, 165, 167, 168; not all red men, 184; not all of same type, 190.
Amon, 465.
Ampheres, son of Poseidon, 13.
Amyander, 7.
Amynos, 329.
Ancestor-worship, 155.
Ancient ships, of Troy, 446; of Rameses the Great, 446; of Sesostris, 447; of Syracuse, 447; of the Romans, 447; of the Veneti, 447.
Animal-worship, 148.
Antediluvian patriarchs, 27; kings of Chaldea, 27.
Antediluvians, the, possessed an alphabet, 235.
Antlan, 168, 171.
Anubis, 236.
Apache, the, Flood legends, 117.
Apar, Aphar, Apara, 409.
Apaturia, 7.
Apis, 147.
Aqueducts, the, of Peru, 141.
Arabs, 27; red men, 193.
Ar-Ad, 279.
Arameans, their Deluge legend, 85.
Arch, the, 140; of Central America, 353, 354; of ancient Greece, 357; of the Etruscans, 357.
Architecture of Europe and America compared, 136.
Ark, the, venerated by different nations, 207; of the Mandans, 111; of the Egyptians, 359.
Armenia Major, list of cities in, 178.
Aryans, the, from Europe and Atlantis, 177, 423, 426, 456; not from Asia, 457; their civilization, 459; their religion, 462; the two great divisions of, 469.
Ascension, the island of, 43.
Asgard, 313, 324.
Asshurbanapal, 77.
Assyrian cycles, 29; exorcisms, 211.
Astronomy, perfection of, among ancient Egyptians, 364; origin of, 453.
Astynome, 330.
Atargatis, 86.
Athene, 7, 304.
Athens, ancient pre-eminence of, 9; led the forces opposed to Atlantis, 11; founded by Poseidon, 304.
At-hotes, the Egyptian god, 278.

Atlantes described by Herodotus, 172.
Atlantic Ocean impenetrable, 11; origin of name, 13, 171.
Atlantids, the, 306.
Atlantis, Plato's history of, was true, 1; was the birthplace of civilization, 1; was colonized by Europe and America, 1; was the Garden of Eden, 1; its kings became the gods of Greece, 2; founded Egypt, 2; its Bronze Age, 2; originated one alphabet, 2; original seat of Aryans and Semites, 2; sunk in the ocean, 2; Deluge legends refer to destruction of, 2; Solon's account of, 5; described by priests of Sais, 10; size of, 10; extent of its empire, 11; its invasion of Greece, 11; its destruction, 11; described in detail by Plato, 13; its fruits and flowers, 14; its kings, 14; its animals, 14; its temples, harbors, and docks, 15; its great canal, 15; its architecture, 15; its walls, 15; its baths and race-courses, 16; its docks, 17; its mountains, 17; its ships and merchants, 17; its great plain, 18; its military service, 18; the arrangement of its government, 19; its columns covered with inscriptions, 19; the administration of justice in, 19; its records, 20; its golden age, 20; its wickedness, 20; traditions of, 276; sun-worship in, 284; its kings become the gods of the Greeks, 283, 285; and of the Phœnicians, 309; original seat of Phœnicians, 310; the Garden of Eden, 323; the colonies of, 348; the inventions derived from, 440; reconstructed, 472; interdiction of swine-flesh in, 472; practice of circumcision in, 472; its religion, 476; its destruction, 478.
Atlas, oldest son of Poseidon, 13; supreme ruler of Atlantis, 14, 20, 149; origin of name, 171; mountains of, 172, 308; he lived in the Hesperides, 288, 289.
Atl-tona-ti-uh, 282.
At-otarho, 149.
Atreus, Mycenæ, treasure house at, 265.
Attika, 304, 308.
At-tit, 282.
Augurs, 144, 148.
Australian Archipelago, 32.
Autochthon, son of Poseidon, 13, 308, 309, 329.
Ayar, 391.
Aymaras, 189.
Azaes, son of Poseidon, 14.
Azores, black rocks of, 24; the islands of, are surviving fragments of Atlantis, 26; earthquakes in, 43; revealed by deep-sea soundings, 46; covered with volcanic débris, 46, 50; climate of, 473.
Aztlan, 97, 105, 326, 327.
Aztecs, the, were from Aztlan, 106; their civilization, 350; their religion, 351; their customs, 351.

B.

Baal, 83; in Ireland, 414; the horns of, 427, 428.
Baalim, 182.
Babel, Tower of, American legend, 200, 202.
Babylon, 76.
Bacchus, 149, 305, 306, 464.
Bacon, "New Atlantis," 23; his opinion of Greek mythology, 283.
Balam Agab, 182.
Balam Quitze, 176, 182.
Balboa, 176.
Banana, carried by man in ancient times across the Atlantic, 57.
Banbha, the Lady, 408.
Baptism, Mexican, described, 158, 208.
Barbarians of Homer, 179.
Barbary States, 172.
Basques, the, described, 388; their language, 172; their American affinities, 173.
Baths, hot and cold, in Atlantis, 16.
Baukis, 302.
Bearded men in America, 165, 166.
Bel, 83.
Belus, temple of, 335, 341.
Berber languages, 196, 407.
Berosus, 27; his version of the Chaldean Deluge legend, 75.
Beth-el, 308, 425.
Bhâgavata-Purâna, 88, 126.
Bilma, 172.
Bind Madhu, temple of, 334.
Black Caribbees, 176.
Black Celts, 183.
Black Indians of California, 185.
Black Sea, 311.
Bochica, 105.
Boeckh, 27, 91.
Brahma, 27, 323.
Brahmadikas, the, 27.
Brasseur de Bourbourg, 100, 167, 179; his description of Indians, 196; he discovers Landa's MS. in Madrid library, 217, 419.
Brazil, fauna of, 53.
Bretons, the, 389.
Bricks, use of, on both continents, 140.
Bride-cake, 158.
Brigantia, 411.
British Islands, formerly submerged, 34.
Britons, a civilized race, 134; ancient, horror of hares, 147.
Bronze Age, its origin, 2; Flood occurred during, 90; in Europe, 237; a perplexing problem, 237; preceded by an age of copper and tin, 237; was imported into Europe, 238, 245; not attributable to Romans, 241; nor Phœnicians, 241; represents new people, 248; in Iceland, 249; came from common centre, 250; in Olympus, 290.
Bronze celts, 250, 253; one with inscription, 258.

Bronze hut-urn, Albano, 255.
Bronze knives, 254.
Bronze lake-village, 255.
Bronze ornaments, 258, 259, 260.
Bronze razor-knives, 256.
Bronze swords, 251.
Bronze was known to the ancient Americans, 140.
Buckle, his opinion of Herodotus, 3.
Buddha, 195, 316.
Buddhists, 323, 332.
Burial rites, 154, 155.
Burnt offerings, 148.

C.

Cabiri, the, 309.
Cabyles, the, 389.
Cadiz, 172.
Cain's migrations, 281; his race did not perish in the Deluge, 281.
Calaveras, fossil skull of, 29.
Caledonians, the ancient, flattened the skull, 270.
Calendar, Náhua, same as Asian, 151.
Calendar stone of Mexico, 107.
Calmucks' fear of the rabbit, 147.
Calypso, 298.
Camel, the, fossil remains of, found in Kansas, 55.
Canary Islands, 28; earthquakes in, 36, 178.
Canoes of bark, 156; of skin, 156.
Cara Gigantesca, 140.
Cardo, the mountain, 446.
Carians, the, 179.
Caribs, the, 179.
Castes date back to great antiquity in Egypt, 10, 151.
Çatapatha Brâhmana, 87.
Catlin, Flood legends of Mandans, 111; complexion of Mandans, 185.
Cattle, ancient domestication of, 55.
Caxapa, 175.
Celibacy of Mexican priests, 160.
Celts, the, 389.
Cement, the use of, 140.
Central America ruled over by Atlantis, 23; bronze chisel, 262.
Central American colonies from Atlantis, 348; arch of, 353.
Cerambos, 91.
Cereals, origin of great, unknown, 177.
Ceres, 305.
Ceridwen, 235.
Chacmol, 178, 446.
Chaldea, 27.
Chaldeans, their Deluge legends, 75; Berosus's version of, 75; the Nineveh legend, 76; their language, its relations to Chinese, 432.
Challenger, British ship, its deep-sea explorations, 24, 46.
Challenger Ridge, the, 49.
Chanes, 314.
Charanzanis, the, 196.
Chariots of war in Egypt and Britain, 25.

Charruas of Brazil, they were negroes, 176.
Cheops, the pyramid of, 335, 338.
Cherokees, the ark of the, 207.
Chiapas, 26.
Chiapenecs, similarity of language to Hebrew, 234.
Chiapense, the, hero Votan, 313.
Chibchacum, 149.
Chibchas, their Flood legend, 105.
Chichen Itza, 166, 175, 178.
Chickasaws, the, Deluge legends of, 117.
Chili, plants of, 61.
Chinese, their kings, 27; an Atlantean race, 426; their original location, 431; Deluge of, 431; their language, its relations to Chaldean, 432; to the Otomi of Mexico, 435.
Chinooks, the, 271.
Chippeways, the, Deluge legends of, 108.
Chiquimala, 314.
Chiriqui, rock carvings of, 178.
Chivim, 314.
Cholula, legend of pyramid of, 200, 202, 335, 341.
Chronian Sea, the, 289, 301.
Chronos, 75, 82, 288, 300, 301, 308, 309, 465.
Chua, 309.
Circumcision, practised in Europe, Asia, Africa, and America, 151; antiquity of, 210; origin of, 472; effects of, on races of Europe and America, 472; practised by Uranos, King of Atlantis, 472.
Citlalatonac, 101.
Citlallinicué, 101.
Civilization, in what it consists, 129; inherited, 133; not communicable to all races, 133; European and American compared, 136.
Cleito, wife of Poseidon, 13; her temple, 16.
Clement, St., refers to worlds beyond the ocean, 28.
Coal measures of Pennsylvania, 31.
Coins, of Mexico, 345; of Palenque, 345, 350; of Tyre, 444; of Central America, 445; of Corvo, 479.
Codex Chimalpopoca, 100, 145.
Colhuas, the, 217.
Colonies from Atlantis, 348; to Central America, 348; to Egypt, 358; to Mississippi Valley, 370; to Spain, 387; to Peru, 390; to Africa, 404; to Ireland, 408.
Columbus, 311, 472.
Complexion of the races of men, 183.
Confession of sins practised in Mexico, 144.
Connecting ridges of Atlantis, 49.
Copper Age, the, found in America, 140, 238.
Copper axes, Ireland and Indiana, 266.
Cornwall, ancient land to west of, 49.
Cosmos, the monk, his map of the world, 95.
Cotton, manufacture of, known to ancient America and Europe, 59.

Couvade, the, 152.
Cow-headed idols, 427.
Coxcox, the Mexican Noah, 99.
Cremation practised on both continents, 152.
Critias, 6, 7.
Cro-Magnon, the man of, 273.
Cromlechs of Africa and Europe, 406.
Cross, the, 24, 317 ; St. George's, 318 ; St. Andrew's, 318, 334; Maltese, 318, 333 ; Greek, 318; Latin, 318; of the Nile, 318, 319 ; of Central America, 319 ; a symbol of the Garden of Eden, 320; the "key of the Nile," 321 ; of Nineveh, 321 ; of Britain, 321; of India, 321 ; of China, 321 ; of Scandinavia, 321.
Cross-cake of Egyptians, 322.
Crow Indians, the, 189.
Crux-ansata, the, 332.
Çúdúq, 330.
Culebres, the, 314.
Culhuacan, 97, 326.
Cukulcan, 166.
Cushites, red men, 194.
Customs, similarities of, in Europe and America, 150.
Cycles of sixty years, 151.
Cyclops, 294.

D.

Dagon, 308, 309.
Dakota legends of Atlantis, 114.
Dances: the buffalo dance, 156; the "mummers," 156; dog dances, 156; Dyonisiac dances, 156.
Danes' pipes in Ireland, 63.
Dark-whites, the, 195.
Darwin, Charles, submarine phenomena, 44 ; origin of our domestic animals, 55 ; of our domestic plants, 61.
Deformation of skull, 268.
Deluge, herdsmen and shepherds only survive in the, 8 : there were several deluges, 9 ; the Bible record, 68 ; describes destruction of Atlantis, 72, 290.
Deluge legends relate to destruction of Atlantis, 2, 65 ; tradition universal, 66 ; of the Chaldeans, 75 ; of America, 98.
Demeter, 305.
Deucalion, Deluge of, 8, 85, 89, 291.
Deva Nahusha, 24, 464.
Diaprepes, son of Poseidon, 14.
Diodorus Siculus describes Atlantis, 28.
Dionysus, 149, 305, 306, 465.
Dolphin, U. S. ship, 46.
Dolphin's Ridge, 26, 50, 468.
Dominica, earthquake in, 119.
Donnelly, Miss Eleanor C., poem of, 421.
Dropidas, 6, 12.
Druids, their books, 235.
Dwyfach, 93.
Dwyfan, 93.

E.

Ea, Chaldean god of the Flood, 75, 83, 125.

Earth, 9; submergences of, 31, 83.
Eastern origin of American races, 165, 167, 168.
Egypt, its mythology from Atlantis, 2; was the oldest colony of Atlantis, 2 ; founded by Athene, 9 ; no Flood legends in, 94 ; vast antiquity of, 131 ; people came from Atlantis, 132 ; given by Chronos to Taant, 309 ; the pyramids of, 329 ; colonized by Atlantis, 358 ; burial rites of, 359 ; great antiquity of, 360 ; vast monuments of, 362 ; laws of ancient, 363 ; their arts, 364.
Egyptian cross, 320 ; cross-cake, 322.
Egyptian plants found in lake dwellings of Switzerland, 62.
Egyptian priests gave Solon traditions of Atlantis, 6.
Egyptians, circumnavigation of Africa, 3 ; cycles, 29 ; red men, 194 ; their early religion monotheism, 211 ; aristocratic classes had receding foreheads, 274.
El, 182, 425.
Elasippus, son of Poseidon, 14.
Elephants, in Atlantis, 14 ; in America, 168 ; elephant mound, Wisconsin, 169 ; elephant pipe, Iowa, 169 ; elephant helmet, 170 ; Mexican representation of elephant, 170 ; elephant trunks, 170.
Eleusinian Mysteries, the, 463.
Eloah, 425.
Elohim, 425.
Elysian Fields, 1, 288, 359.
Elysion, 359.
Embalming the dead, 144, 179.
England, rock carvings in, 178.
Engraving, the art of, very ancient, 141.
Epilepsy, 148.
Erichthonus, 91.
Erythea, 307.
Erythræan Sea, 310.
Ethiopians, 28; were red men, 194.
Etruscans not the authors of the Bronze Age of Europe, 243, 426 ; they probably possessed the mariner's compass, 446.
Eumelus, 13.
Evæmon, son of Poseidon, 13.
Eve, in Toltec legends, 199.
Evenor, 13.
Exorcism of demons, 147.

F.

Fairies of America and Europe, 157.
Fauna of Europe and America compared, 54.
Fayal, 24.
Fezzan, 3.
Fir-Bolgs, the, 409.
Fire, sacred, of Mexicans, 146 ; of Asia Minor, 146 ; of India, 146 ; of Sweden, 146 ; of Romans, 146, 151 ; of Peru, 151.
Flat-head Indians, 271.
Flood of Deucalion, 291.

Flood tablet, Calendar stone, Mexico, 107.
Flora of Europe and America compared, 54.
Flora of Pacific States of America, 59.
Fogo, 43.
Folk-lore, 150, 160.
Foolahs, the, 406.
Formorians, the, 408.
Frog Indians, 272.

G.

Gadeirus, 13.
Gades, part of empire of Atlantis, 13; why so named, 13, 172.
Gæa, 308.
Gæthulighe, 411.
Galley, of Bronze Age, 256; of Romans, 257; of William the Conqueror, 257.
Gama, Vasquez de, discovery of the Cape of Good Hope, 3.
Games the same on both continents, 162.
Garden of Eden, 1, 24; cross a symbol of, 320; described, 324, 325, 326.
Gauls, possessed traditions of Atlantis, 28; a civilized race, 134.
Ge, 308.
Genea, 329.
Genesis, 27; contains a history of Atlantis, 198; similarities to American legends, 199; its great antiquity, 212.
Genos, 329.
Geological formation of United States, 32; of Europe, 33.
Germans, ancient, a civilized race, 134.
Gettysburg, U. S. ship, explorations by, 53.
Geryon, 307.
Ghosts, belief in, on both continents, 146.
Gihon, the river, 312, 325.
Glacial Period, the, causes of, 50.
Gobi, 429.
Gold sacred in Assyria and Peru to the sun; 347.
Gold, a sacred metal of Atlantis, 343; a sacred metal of Peruvians, 345.
Golden Age, the, 290, 301.
Gomer, 412.
Gömüshtepe, 429.
Goths, ancient writings of, 236; their mythology, 313, 316.
Graham's island, 36.
Grave-cists, 139.
Gray, Professor Asa, on flora of the Pacific coast, 59.
Greeks, no history of antiquity, 6; their legends of the Deluge, 89; their divinities the rulers of Atlantis, 283.
Gunpowder, its antiquity, 447; known to ancient Chinese, 447; to the Phœnicians, 448; to Hindoos, 448; to Moses, 449; to Atlantis, 450.
Guanaani, inhabitants of, 196.
Guanches, 178, 179, 180, 473.
Guatemala, 26.
Gucumatz, 199.

Gulf Stream, 50.
Gulguntius, 409.
Gurani, 179.

H.

Haadam, 281.
Hades, 288.
Ham, what races descended from, 436.
Hare, superstitious fear of, 147.
Harlequin, 210.
Haroeri, 442.
Havilah, 325.
Hayagriva, 88, 236.
Heads, hanging up of enemies', 208.
Hebrew language, similarity to Chiapenec, 234.
Hebrews, greater health of, 472.
Hecla, 43.
Hekatoncheires, 294; described, 299.
Hellenes, 8.
Hera, 86, 303.
Herculaneum and Pompeii, once called "the fabulous cities," 3.
Hercules, 306; Columns of, 10, 11, 27, 28; the stone of, 441, 443.
Hermes Trismegistus, 125.
Herodotus, increased respect for, 3; quotation from, 23; burial rites of Scythians, 136; describes the Maxyans, 196; describes Scythian mode of scalping enemies, 209, 333, 362.
Hesiod, 7.
Hesperides, the gardens of the, were in Atlantis, 288; golden apples of, 306.
Hesperis, 306.
Hiawatha, 149.
Hierapolis, 85; chasm of, 86.
Hieroglyphics, 214, 216, 233.
Himyaritic-Arabians, 194.
Hindoo legends of Deluge, 24, 86, 87, 181.
Hivim, 314.
Hivites, 314.
Homa, water of life, 27.
Homer, 7, 181, 297, 324.
Hood, Robin, 210.
Horse, race-courses and baths for, in Atlantis, 17; associated with Atlantis and Poseidon, 25; originated in North America, 54; domesticated in very ancient times, 55.
Hu, 93, 182; the writings of, 235.
Hu-hu-nap-hu, 182.
Hunaphu, 149, 182.
Hunbatz, 182.
Huncam, 182.
Hue Hue Tlapalan, 165, 384.
Humboldt, 151, 327, 335, 341, 426, 438.
Huns, the ancient, flattened the skull, 272.
Hurakan, a Central American god, 102.
Hurricane, origin of word, 103.
Hydrophoria, Greek ceremony having reference to Deluge, 90.
Hyksos, the, 333.
Hyperboreans, people from Atlantis visited the, 27.

I.

Iberians, the, a colony from Atlantis, 387.
Iceland, great convulsions in, 35; volcanoes of, 43.
Igh, 313.
Inox, 313.
Incarnation of gods, 149.
Incense burnt by Peruvians, 144.
India, visit of Dionysos to, 465.
Indian Deluge legends, 87, 107, 108, 109.
Intoxicating beverages, 150.
Inventions, no new ones for 6000 years, 130; the great antiquity of, 440; mariner's compass, 440; gunpowder, 447; iron, 451; paper, 451; silk, 451; order of, 455.
Iqui-Balam, 182.
Iranians, 27; their Deluge legend, 89.
Ireland, earthquakes in, 40; tobacco known to the ancient people of, 63; originally colonized from Atlantis, 408; different races of, 409; relations to Deluge, 412; was the "Island of the Sun," 413; the "Garden of Phœbus," 413; called "Ogygia," 413; great antiquity of people of, 413; ancient religion of, 414; ancient customs of, 415; round towers of, 416; traditions of America in, 419; St. Brendan's visit to America from, 419; the name of, Aryan, 470.
Irish, ancient, dread of hares, 147.
Iron, mined by Incas, 140; antiquity of manufacture of, 451; known in earliest ages to the Egyptians, 451; to the Peruvians, 451; to the Mound Builders, 377, 451.
Iron Age, 290.
Iroquois, Deluge legends of, 117.
Isiris, Egyptian god, 309.
Islands of the Blessed, 287.
Islands of the Sea, referred to in Bible, 28.
Islands, sunken, west of Spain, 53.
Isle Royal, Lake Superior, ancient copper mines on, 247.
Ixtlilxochitl, 103.
Izcalli, 127.

J.

Jamassi of Florida, negroes, 176.
Jambadwipa, 325.
Jamaica, earthquake in, 43.
Janus, 301.
Java, great convulsions in, 35, 38.
Jews, the, their customs similar to those of the Mexicans, 204; the miracle of their continued existence as a race, 213.
Josephus, 325.
Juno, 303.
Jupiter, 464.

K.

Kaimeni, Old, 37.
Karnac, the temple of, 362.

Kaws of Kansas, 184.
Kesair, 408.
Khasisatra, 75, 78, 81, 84.
Koran, Deluge legends of, 86.
Krodo, a Gothic god, 316.
Kronion, Father, 29.
Kuntze, Professor Otto, views of, 56, 57.
Kshatriyas, the, 194.
Kyklopes, 294; described, 299.

L.

Labyrinth, the, 362.
Laertas, gardens of, 323.
Lake-dwellings, animals of, 55; plants of, 62; bronze representation of, 255.
Lake Superior, metallurgy originated on shores of, 130; great extent of ancient copper mining on, 246.
Lancerota, island of, 36.
Landa, Bishop Diego de, his destruction of Maya books, 217; his preservation of Maya alphabet, 217.
Language of Noah, 433; of Chinese, 432; of Chaldeans, 432; of Otomi, 435; of North American Indians, 435; of Ural-Altaic races, 435.
Laying on of hands, 147.
Lemuria, the drowned continent of the Pacific, 32.
Lenni-Lenapi Deluge legends, 109.
Lenormant, François, 66, 74, 76, 82, 86, 87, 88, 94.
Le Plongeon, Dr., describes negroes, 175.
Libyans, the, 195.
Lisbon, great earthquake of, 40.
Livingstone, Dr., 315.
Lost tribes of Jews, 209.
Lycanthropy, 147.
Lyktonia, 29.
Lynd, Major J. W., 186; description of Dakotas, 189.

M.

Madeira, 43.
Magnetic cup, 254.
Magnetic needle, 254; known to ancients, 440.
Magog, 412, 437.
Maia, wife of Pan, 145.
Maize known to ancient Chinese and Egyptians, 60.
Man, antiquity of, 29.
Mandan Indians, Flood legends of, 110; tradition as to the origin of man, 114.
Mautchoos, the, 209.
Manu, 87, 181.
Manu Vaivasata, 87.
Manufactures, ancient, 142.
Mariner's compass, 254; probably known to Egyptians, Mexicans, and the Mound Builders of America, 446; antiquity of, 440; known to Phœnicians, 441; known to Chinese, 441; in New Mexico, 445; in Atlantis, 445.
Maruts, the, 468.

Marriage, 150; to one of same clan interdicted, 155; made but once a year in Peru and Babylonia, 158; in ancient Mexico, 159, 351; in ancient Egypt, 363.
Mashab-Ad, 279.
Masonry, Free, its origin, 463.
Maxyans, the, were red men, 196.
Mayapan, city of, 145, 314.
Mayas, their alphabet, 216; their conservatism, 218.
Medicine, knowledge of, received by Egypt from Atlantis, 101.
Mediterranean Sea, 10; a *cul de sac*, 176.
Medusa, 149.
Megaros, 90.
Meidoun Dachhour, 341.
Melicertes, 284.
Menaboshu, 108.
Menes, 360, 366.
Menominees, 184.
Men with tails, legends of, 148.
Men-wolves, 147.
Mermaids in America, 149.
Meropes, people of Atlantis, 27, 171.
Merops, the hero of the Deluge, 91, 92.
Merou, human race issued from, 171, 391.
Meru, 325, 465.
Mesomphalos, 323.
Mestor, son of Poseidon, 14, 309.
Metallurgy in Atlantis, 140.
Mexico, 26; plants of, 61; Flood legends of, 99; ancient, described, 350; marriage in, 351; slavery in, 351; religion in, 351.
Michoacan Indians, ark of, 207.
Midas, 27.
Milidh or Milesius, 410.
Miocene Age, flora of the, 56, 59.
Miztecs, Deluge legend of, 327.
Mneseus, son of Poseidon, 13, 309.
Mœris, the lake of, 362.
Mohammed, allusion to Deluge, 86, 92.
Money, origin of, 343; articles used for, 343, 344; of Mexico, 345; of Palenque, 345.
Mongoloids in Europe, 28.
Monte da Guia, 24.
Monte Queimada, 24.
Montezuma, 326.
Months, twelve, used by Peruvians, Egyptians, and Chaldeans, 151, 211; derived remotely from Atlantis, 287, 463.
Moon, silver sacred to, 346, 347.
Moon-worship, 347.
Moses, 412.
Mound Builders of America, 23; their leaf-shaped swords, 251; their stone celts, 253; their pottery, 260, 261, 263; their copper implements, 262, 263; from Atlantis, 370; a river people, 370; their works, 371; their civilization, 372; their system of weights and measures, 372; their pyramids, 372; they used the emblem of the cross, 375; their metallurgy, 376; their sculptures, 380; their manufactures, 380; their antiquity, 383; possessed an alphabet, 386; probably had mariner's compass, 446.
Mound, great, at Miamisburg, Ohio, 339.
Mounds, 136; of England, 341; of Mississippi Valley, 342; of Ireland, 342.
Municipal republics, origin of, 452.
Music, Highland Scotch and Chinese alike, 142.
Mythology of Greeks derived from Atlantis, 283, 308.

N.

Nachan, the city of, 313.
Nahsu, 194.
Nahua, calendar same as that of Asia, 151.
Nahuatl, 167, 171.
Nata, 100.
Navigation, ancient, 446.
Nectar, 287.
Negro, granite-head, 175.
Negroes, no tradition of Deluge among, 66; in ancient America, 174; idols, 174; figure of, at Palenque, 175.
Neimhidh, 409.
Neith, Egyptian goddess, 7.
Nemaun, 330.
Nena, 100.
Neph or Num, 425.
Nereids in Atlantis, 16, 181.
Nicaraguans, Flood legends, 117.
Nineveh, Deluge legend dug up at, 76; the library of the palace of, 77.
Nirumbees, the, 157.
Noah and the Deluge, 68; his name Aryan, 102.
Nod, the land of, 326.
Noronha, Fernando de, 43.
Nubians, the, 406.
Nymphs, the, 306.
Nyöe, the new island, 35.

O.

Oannes, 236.
Obartes Elbaratutu, 75.
Obelisks of Egypt and America, 367.
Ocean, source of gods and men, 181.
Odin, 271, 210; an American hero, 313.
Oerafa, 43.
Ogyges, Deluge of, 89.
Ojibbeways, their vine legend, 207.
Okanagaus, Deluge legends of, 117.
Okeanos, 323.
Olmecs, the, 167.
Olympus, 2; described, 286; it was in Atlantis, 286; a corruption of the word Atlantis, 291, 303.
Origin of American races, 165, 167, 168.
Orphic Argonaut, 29.
Osiris, 309, 466.
Otomi, the, of Mexico, relations of their language to Chinese, 435.
Ouranos, 308, 309; invented mariner's compass, 445.

P.

Painting, antiquity of the art of, 141.
Palenque, negroid figure from, 175, 313.
Pan adored in Europe and America, 145.
Panathenæa, 91.
Panuco, city of, 145.
Paper, antiquity of, 451 ; of Egypt, 451 ; of Mexico, 451 ; of Peru, 451.
Parian Gulf, Indians of, 196.
Partholan, 409.
Passage, west, from Atlantis to America, 172.
Peisdadien, the, kings, 27.
Penance, 144.
Penn, William, letter of, describing Indians, 185.
Perirrhoos, 91.
Persian Gulf, 310, 311.
Persian Magi, Flood legend, 92.
Peru, description of temple of Cuzco, 22 ; ruled over by Atlantis, 23 ; great public roads of, 141 ; aqueducts, 141 ; posts, 141 ; mile-stones, 141.
Peruvians, ancient, their color, 189 ; colonized from Atlantis, 390 ; their civilization, 392 ; its antiquity, 392 ; their great monuments, 393 ; their pyramids, 393 ; roads, 394 ; customs, 396 ; language, 402.
Petecatl, 145.
Petris, the ten, 27.
Phæacians, the, 298.
Phaëton, 8 ; the myth of, found in America, 145.
Phallus worship, 136.
Pharaoh Necho, circumnavigation of Africa, 3.
Pheryllt, books of, 235.
Philemon, 302.
Phison, 326.
Phœnicians, their gods derived from Atlantis, 2 ; letters, 2 ; red men, 194; origin of their alphabet, 214 ; not the authors of the Bronze Age of Europe, 241, 243 ; their mythology from Atlantis, 308; they came from the Erythræan Sea, 310 ; from Atlantis, 310 ; human sacrifices among, 311 ; extent of their commerce, 311 ; association with Bible records, 328.
Phoroneus, 8.
Phos, Phur, and Phlox, 329.
Pico, 43.
Pimas, Flood legends of, 118.
Pimerital, Señor, 218.
Pineapple known to ancient Assyrians, 63.
Pipes, tobacco, prehistoric in Ireland, 63 ; Indian, 64 ; African, (●
Phlebotomy in America, 160.
Plants, ancient, domesticated in Europe and America, 56 ; origin of, 61.
Platicnemism of ancient races, 273.
Plato, his story true, 1 ; his history of

Atlantis, 5 ; probabilities of his history of Atlantis, 22, 177, 235.
Plough festivals of Peru and Egypt, 141, 438.
Plutarch, opinion of Herodotus, 3 ; mentions islands in Atlantic, 28.
Pluto, 294, 297, 300.
Poisoned arrows, 156.
Pompeii and Herculaneum once called "the fabulous cities," 3 ; their discovery, 124.
Popul Vuh, 167 ; Deluge legend of, 102 ; it describes Atlantis, 175, 419.
Port Royal, earthquake at, 43.
Porto Praya, 44.
Poseidon, receives Atlantis as his share of the world, 13 ; marries Cleito, 13 ; builds a city, 13 ; his temple, 16 ; his chariot, 16, 25 ; his grove, 17 ; ancient worship of, in Europe, 24 ; called Neptune, 25 ; associated with the horse, 25 ; horses sacrificed to, 25 ; his trident, 26, 196, 294, 297, 300 ; described, 304, 308, 309, 428.
Potato known to ancient Chinese, 60.
Pottery of Bronze Age and mounds of United States compared, 261 ; of Colorado, 262 ; of Zunis, 262 ; Switzerland and Mexico, 266.
Poulle-i-feron (Hell-hole), 122.
Priapus worship, 136.
Priesthood, in Mexico, 159 ; celibacy of, 160.
Proclus, his allusion to Atlantis, 27.
Protogonos, 329.
Ptah-hotep, 212, 213.
Ptolemy's list of ancient cities, 178.
Public roads of Peru, 141.
Pyramid, the, 139, 317 ; a transcript of the holy mountain, 330; Arabian traditions as to, 331 ; of India, 330, 334 ; of Mexico, 335, 336 ; of Egypt, 835, 336.
Pyrrha, 8.

Q.

Qên, 329.
Qênath, 329.
Quetzalcoatl, 165.
Quiches, 106, 175 ; their gods, 149 ; their legends of the creation, 198.
Quichuas, the, 391.
Quinames, the giants, 204.
Quipu, the, 438.

R.

Ra, 284.
Races, the four, known to the Egyptians, 194 ; to the Aryans, 194.
Rainbow, the, 105 ; sign of promise to Peruvians, 207.
Rama, 284.
Rana, 359.
Rauda Kamba, 43.
Rayam, 359.
Raymi, 284.
Raz, Cape, 297, 359.

Reaping-machine, on wheels, of the ancient Gauls, 134.
Red men, ancient Egyptians, 174.
Red a sacred color, 194; Cushites and Ethiopians red men, 194.
Religion of ancient races, 143; the great religions derived from red men, 195; the essence of is conservatism, 210.
Republican form of government, origin of, 452.
Retzius, Anders, Professor, 179.
Rhea, 300.
Round-towers, of Ireland, 416; of India, 417; of Sardinia, 417; of the Shetlands, 417; of New Mexico and Colorado, 418.
Rua, 314.
Ru-Ad, 279.

S.

Sabæans, the, 278.
Sabian worship, 333.
Sailing-vessels known in ancient America, 142.
St. Brendan, of Ireland, visits America, 419.
St. Helena, 43.
St. Paul's Rocks, 49.
Sahara, sands of Desert of, 34.
Sais, city and district of, in Egypt, 7; priests of told Solon of Atlantis, 5, 7; description of, 7.
Sakkarah, 341.
Samé, 168.
Samson, 204.
Sanchoniathon, 308, 309, 310, 312, 329, 330, 445.
Sanscrit maps of Western Europe, 211.
Santorin, Gulf of, 37.
Sarku, the, 281.
Satar, a Gothic god, 316.
Saturn, 301.
Saturnalia, the Roman, 302, 464.
Saturnia, 301.
Saturnian continent, the, 289.
Satyravata, 88.
Satyrs, 148.
Savonarola, 190.
Scalping practised in Europe and America, 209.
Scandinavia, mythology of, 313, 324.
Scandinavian Flood legends, 93.
Scandinavians, 209; ancient, flattened the skull, 270.
Schlegel, Frederick, opinion of Herodotus, 3.
Schott, Dr. Arthur, 26, 140.
Scots, ancient, used iron swords, 134.
Sculpture, the art of, 140.
Scomalt, 117.
Scythians, their burial rites, 136, 412.
Seedless plants, 58.
Semiramis, 139.
Semitic, the, races, 177; from Atlantis, 423.
Serpent-mounds, 205.
Serpent-worship, 204.
Seth, the patriarch, 125.

Shedd-Ad-ben-Ad, 276.
Sheep, ancient, domestication of, 55.
Shem, the oldest son of Noah, 423; what races descended from, 436, 437.
Sicanes, an Iberian colony, 387.
Sicily, formerly submerged, 34.
Sidon, 25.
Silenus describes Altantis, 27, 28.
Silk, antiquity of manufacture of, 451; known to ancient Hindoos, 452; to ancient Chinese, 452; to Phœnicians, 452.
Silsbury Hill, England, 341.
Silver Age, the, 290.
Silver, a sacred metal of Atlantis, 343; sacred in Assyria to the moon, 347.
Similarities of customs, 150; of languages of Mandans and Welsh, 115; Dakota and European tongues, 116.
Sindree, submergence of, 38.
Sippara, City of the Sun, 75; antediluvian records buried there, 76.
Sirens, the Greek, 428.
Sithnides, 90.
Skull, artificial deformation of, 268; found in Europe, Asia, and America, 268; still practised in Normandy, 269; ancient Swiss skull, 270; Peruvian, 271; shape of in different races, 273; boring holes in by ancient nations, 273.
Slieve-donart, 122.
Solon wrote an account of Atlantis, 5; he visited Egypt, 5; verses by, 5; his poems recited, 7; his reception at Sais, 8.
Soma, 287.
Sorcerers who produce fair and foul weather, 148.
Spiral, the double, peculiar to Bronze Age, 262.
Stone Age in America and Europe, 206.
Stone Age of Europe, animals of, 55; its two divisions, 237.
Stone-beer, 156.
Strabo, 311, 387.
Submergences of the earth, 31, 34.
Suchiquecal, 199.
Sumbawa, convulsions in, 38.
Sun-worship, 143; Peru, 283; Egypt, 283; Babylonia, 283; Phœnicia, 283; Atlantis, 284; Samoyeds, 284; American races, 284.
Sutteeism, 155.
Swine-flesh, use of, 472.
Swiss, ancient, pottery of, 261; bronze implements of, 262.
Switzerland, fossil beds of, 56.
Sydyk, 329, 330.

T.

Taaut, the Phœnician god who invented the alphabet, 309.
Taautos, 125.
Tai-Ko-Fokee, 427.
Tamahu, the, 407.
Tamhu, 194.
Tartars, the, 209.

Tattooing practised on both continents, 156.
Tell, William, 210.
Ten, sacred character of the number, 27.
Teneriffe, 43, 178.
Tennessee, mummies found in, 190.
Teotihuacan, pyramids of, 174, 335.
Tethys, 181.
Theopompus describes Atlantis, 27.
Thia, island of, 37.
Thoth, 125.
Thrace, 25.
Three, sacred character of the number, 26.
Tien-Chan, 324.
Timagenes, 28.
Tin known to ancient Americans, 140.
Tir-na-n'oge, description of, 421.
Titæa, 306.
Titans, the empire of, 294, 297; beaten at Tartessus, 298, 469, 473.
Titicaca, Lake, 333.
Titlacahuan, 101.
Tlaloc, Mexican god of rain, 100.
Tobacco known to ancient inhabitants of China and Europe, 60; of Ireland, 64; used originally as incense, 64.
Tokhari, the, a Celtic race, 243; invaded Egypt, 243; and Assyria, 244.
Toltecs, their Flood legend, 103; came from the East, 165; their religion, 350.
Tortoise legends, 113, 115.
Totem, the, 155.
Tower of Babel, American legend, 200, 202.
Transmigration of souls, belief in, in America, 147.
Tree-worship, 157.
Tristan d'Acunha, 43.
Troy, 196; founded by Poseidon, 304.
Tsabaism, 215.
Tuareg, of Sahara, 185.
Tuatha-de-Danauns, 410.
Tubal, 412.
Tula, 109, 165.
Tulan, 106, 166, 314.
Tumuli, 139.
Turanian, the, races from Atlantis, 423, 426, 437.
Turdetani, the, 387.
Turduli, the, 387.
Tuxtla, 175.
Twelve gods, the, 287.
Typhon, 442.
Tyrrhenia governed by Atlantis, 11, 14.
Tzequil nation, 314.

U.

Uranos, 280, 294, 300, 425, 463, 469.
Uruk, 77.
Ushas, 467.

V.

Vaivasvata, the king, 468.
Valentini, 231.
Valum-Votan, 314.
Varuna, 280, 463.
Verde, Cape de, islands, 43.
Vestal virgins, 144.
Vigile, an Irish saint, 419.
Viracocha, 189.
Vishnu, 236.
Vocal statues in Peru, 149.
Volney, 152.
Votan, a Chiapenic hero, 210, 313.

W.

Wales, Flood legends of, 93.
War-paint, 157.
Weapons of Old and New World the same, 143.
Weeks and months, origin of, 211.
West India Islands, described by Egyptian priests, 10; earthquakes in, 43, 172.
Wheel of Kronos, 140.
Wheel symbol found in America, 140.
White deer, 147.
Wife-capture, 158.
Wild Huntsman, the, 210.
Winchell, Professor, changes of the earth's surface, 34.
Witchcraft in America, 149, 150.
Woden or Wuotan, 313.

X.

Xblanque, 149.
Xibalbay described, 166.
Xicalancans, the, 167.
Xisuthros, 75.
Xochiquetzal, wife of the Mexican Noah, 99, 107.
Xolotl, 149.

Y.

Yama, 281.
Yavana, the, 470.
Year, same number of days in both Europe and America, 151.
Yima, the father of men, 89, 281.
Yirad, 329.
Yucatan, 26; legends of, 167.
Yum-ala, 425.

Z.

Zalmat-Qaqadi, 281.
Zamna, the culture-hero, 167.
Zeus, resolves to destroy Atlantis, 21; his tomb in Crete, 285, 300, 301, 303, 304, 306, 309, 464, 465.
Zipanca, 204.
Zontem-que, 200.
Zuavas, the, 196.
Zunis, 184; their color, 184.

THE END.

A CATALOG OF SELECTED
DOVER BOOKS
IN ALL FIELDS OF INTEREST

A CATALOG OF SELECTED DOVER
BOOKS IN ALL FIELDS OF INTEREST

CONCERNING THE SPIRITUAL IN ART, Wassily Kandinsky. Pioneering work by father of abstract art. Thoughts on color theory, nature of art. Analysis of earlier masters. 12 illustrations. 80pp. of text. 5⅜ x 8½. 23411-8

ANIMALS: 1,419 Copyright-Free Illustrations of Mammals, Birds, Fish, Insects, etc., Jim Harter (ed.). Clear wood engravings present, in extremely lifelike poses, over 1,000 species of animals. One of the most extensive pictorial sourcebooks of its kind. Captions. Index. 284pp. 9 x 12. 23766-4

CELTIC ART: The Methods of Construction, George Bain. Simple geometric techniques for making Celtic interlacements, spirals, Kells-type initials, animals, humans, etc. Over 500 illustrations. 160pp. 9 x 12. (Available in U.S. only.) 22923-8

AN ATLAS OF ANATOMY FOR ARTISTS, Fritz Schider. Most thorough reference work on art anatomy in the world. Hundreds of illustrations, including selections from works by Vesalius, Leonardo, Goya, Ingres, Michelangelo, others. 593 illustrations. 192pp. 7⅛ x 10¼. 20241-0

CELTIC HAND STROKE-BY-STROKE (Irish Half-Uncial from "The Book of Kells"): An Arthur Baker Calligraphy Manual, Arthur Baker. Complete guide to creating each letter of the alphabet in distinctive Celtic manner. Covers hand position, strokes, pens, inks, paper, more. Illustrated. 48pp. 8¼ x 11. 24336-2

EASY ORIGAMI, John Montroll. Charming collection of 32 projects (hat, cup, pelican, piano, swan, many more) specially designed for the novice origami hobbyist. Clearly illustrated easy-to-follow instructions insure that even beginning papercrafters will achieve successful results. 48pp. 8¼ x 11. 27298-2

THE COMPLETE BOOK OF BIRDHOUSE CONSTRUCTION FOR WOOD-WORKERS, Scott D. Campbell. Detailed instructions, illustrations, tables. Also data on bird habitat and instinct patterns. Bibliography. 3 tables. 63 illustrations in 15 figures. 48pp. 5¼ x 8½. 24407-5

BLOOMINGDALE'S ILLUSTRATED 1886 CATALOG: Fashions, Dry Goods and Housewares, Bloomingdale Brothers. Famed merchants' extremely rare catalog depicting about 1,700 products: clothing, housewares, firearms, dry goods, jewelry, more. Invaluable for dating, identifying vintage items. Also, copyright-free graphics for artists, designers. Co-published with Henry Ford Museum & Greenfield Village. 160pp. 8¼ x 11. 25780-0

HISTORIC COSTUME IN PICTURES, Braun & Schneider. Over 1,450 costumed figures in clearly detailed engravings–from dawn of civilization to end of 19th century. Captions. Many folk costumes. 256pp. 8⅜ x 11¾. 23150-X

STICKLEY CRAFTSMAN FURNITURE CATALOGS, Gustav Stickley and L. & J. G. Stickley. Beautiful, functional furniture in two authentic catalogs from 1910. 594 illustrations, including 277 photos, show settles, rockers, armchairs, reclining chairs, bookcases, desks, tables. 183pp. 6½ x 9¼. 23838-5

AMERICAN LOCOMOTIVES IN HISTORIC PHOTOGRAPHS: 1858 to 1949, Ron Ziel (ed.). A rare collection of 126 meticulously detailed official photographs, called "builder portraits," of American locomotives that majestically chronicle the rise of steam locomotive power in America. Introduction. Detailed captions. xi+ 129pp. 9 x 12. 27393-8

AMERICA'S LIGHTHOUSES: An Illustrated History, Francis Ross Holland, Jr. Delightfully written, profusely illustrated fact-filled survey of over 200 American light-houses since 1716. History, anecdotes, technological advances, more. 240pp. 8 x 10¾. 25576-X

TOWARDS A NEW ARCHITECTURE, Le Corbusier. Pioneering manifesto by founder of "International School." Technical and aesthetic theories, views of industry, economics, relation of form to function, "mass-production split" and much more. Profusely illustrated. 320pp. 6⅛ x 9¼. (Available in U.S. only.) 25023-7

HOW THE OTHER HALF LIVES, Jacob Riis. Famous journalistic record, exposing poverty and degradation of New York slums around 1900, by major social reformer. 100 striking and influential photographs. 233pp. 10 x 7⅞. 22012-5

FRUIT KEY AND TWIG KEY TO TREES AND SHRUBS, William M. Harlow. One of the handiest and most widely used identification aids. Fruit key covers 120 deciduous and evergreen species; twig key 160 deciduous species. Easily used. Over 300 photographs. 126pp. 5⅜ x 8½. 20511-8

COMMON BIRD SONGS, Dr. Donald J. Borror. Songs of 60 most common U.S. birds: robins, sparrows, cardinals, bluejays, finches, more—arranged in order of increasing complexity. Up to 9 variations of songs of each species.
Cassette and manual 99911-4

ORCHIDS AS HOUSE PLANTS, Rebecca Tyson Northen. Grow cattleyas and many other kinds of orchids—in a window, in a case, or under artificial light. 63 illustrations. 148pp. 5⅜ x 8½. 23261-1

MONSTER MAZES, Dave Phillips. Masterful mazes at four levels of difficulty. Avoid deadly perils and evil creatures to find magical treasures. Solutions for all 32 exciting illustrated puzzles. 48pp. 8¼ x 11. 26005-4

MOZART'S DON GIOVANNI (DOVER OPERA LIBRETTO SERIES), Wolfgang Amadeus Mozart. Introduced and translated by Ellen H. Bleiler. Standard Italian libretto, with complete English translation. Convenient and thoroughly portable—an ideal companion for reading along with a recording or the performance itself. Introduction. List of characters. Plot summary. 121pp. 5¼ x 8½. 24944-1

TECHNICAL MANUAL AND DICTIONARY OF CLASSICAL BALLET, Gail Grant. Defines, explains, comments on steps, movements, poses and concepts. 15-page pictorial section. Basic book for student, viewer. 127pp. 5⅜ x 8½. 21843-0

THE CLARINET AND CLARINET PLAYING, David Pino. Lively, comprehensive work features suggestions about technique, musicianship, and musical interpretation, as well as guidelines for teaching, making your own reeds, and preparing for public performance. Includes an intriguing look at clarinet history. "A godsend," *The Clarinet,* Journal of the International Clarinet Society. Appendixes. 7 illus. 320pp. 5⅜ x 8½. 40270-3

HOLLYWOOD GLAMOR PORTRAITS, John Kobal (ed.). 145 photos from 1926-49. Harlow, Gable, Bogart, Bacall; 94 stars in all. Full background on photographers, technical aspects. 160pp. 8⅜ x 11¼. 23352-9

THE ANNOTATED CASEY AT THE BAT: A Collection of Ballads about the Mighty Casey/Third, Revised Edition, Martin Gardner (ed.). Amusing sequels and parodies of one of America's best-loved poems: Casey's Revenge, Why Casey Whiffed, Casey's Sister at the Bat, others. 256pp. 5⅜ x 8½. 28598-7

THE RAVEN AND OTHER FAVORITE POEMS, Edgar Allan Poe. Over 40 of the author's most memorable poems: "The Bells," "Ulalume," "Israfel," "To Helen," "The Conqueror Worm," "Eldorado," "Annabel Lee," many more. Alphabetic lists of titles and first lines. 64pp. 5¾₆ x 8¼. 26685-0

PERSONAL MEMOIRS OF U. S. GRANT, Ulysses Simpson Grant. Intelligent, deeply moving firsthand account of Civil War campaigns, considered by many the finest military memoirs ever written. Includes letters, historic photographs, maps and more. 528pp. 6⅛ x 9¼. 28587-1

ANCIENT EGYPTIAN MATERIALS AND INDUSTRIES, A. Lucas and J. Harris. Fascinating, comprehensive, thoroughly documented text describes this ancient civilization's vast resources and the processes that incorporated them in daily life, including the use of animal products, building materials, cosmetics, perfumes and incense, fibers, glazed ware, glass and its manufacture, materials used in the mummification process, and much more. 544pp. 6⅛ x 9¼. (Available in U.S. only.) 40446-3

RUSSIAN STORIES/RUSSKIE RASSKAZY: A Dual-Language Book, edited by Gleb Struve. Twelve tales by such masters as Chekhov, Tolstoy, Dostoevsky, Pushkin, others. Excellent word-for-word English translations on facing pages, plus teaching and study aids, Russian/English vocabulary, biographical/critical introductions, more. 416pp. 5⅜ x 8½. 26244-8

PHILADELPHIA THEN AND NOW: 60 Sites Photographed in the Past and Present, Kenneth Finkel and Susan Oyama. Rare photographs of City Hall, Logan Square, Independence Hall, Betsy Ross House, other landmarks juxtaposed with contemporary views. Captures changing face of historic city. Introduction. Captions. 128pp. 8¼ x 11. 25790-8

AIA ARCHITECTURAL GUIDE TO NASSAU AND SUFFOLK COUNTIES, LONG ISLAND, The American Institute of Architects, Long Island Chapter, and the Society for the Preservation of Long Island Antiquities. Comprehensive, well-researched and generously illustrated volume brings to life over three centuries of Long Island's great architectural heritage. More than 240 photographs with authoritative, extensively detailed captions. 176pp. 8¼ x 11. 26946-9

NORTH AMERICAN INDIAN LIFE: Customs and Traditions of 23 Tribes, Elsie Clews Parsons (ed.). 27 fictionalized essays by noted anthropologists examine religion, customs, government, additional facets of life among the Winnebago, Crow, Zuni, Eskimo, other tribes. 480pp. 6⅛ x 9¼. 27377-6

FRANK LLOYD WRIGHT'S DANA HOUSE, Donald Hoffmann. Pictorial essay of residential masterpiece with over 160 interior and exterior photos, plans, elevations, sketches and studies. 128pp. 9¼ x 10¾.
29120-0

THE MALE AND FEMALE FIGURE IN MOTION: 60 Classic Photographic Sequences, Eadweard Muybridge. 60 true-action photographs of men and women walking, running, climbing, bending, turning, etc., reproduced from rare 19th-century masterpiece. vi + 121pp. 9 x 12.
24745-7

1001 QUESTIONS ANSWERED ABOUT THE SEASHORE, N. J. Berrill and Jacquelyn Berrill. Queries answered about dolphins, sea snails, sponges, starfish, fishes, shore birds, many others. Covers appearance, breeding, growth, feeding, much more. 305pp. 5¼ x 8¼.
23366-9

ATTRACTING BIRDS TO YOUR YARD, William J. Weber. Easy-to-follow guide offers advice on how to attract the greatest diversity of birds: birdhouses, feeders, water and waterers, much more. 96pp. 5³⁄₁₆ x 8¼.
28927-3

MEDICINAL AND OTHER USES OF NORTH AMERICAN PLANTS: A Historical Survey with Special Reference to the Eastern Indian Tribes, Charlotte Erichsen-Brown. Chronological historical citations document 500 years of usage of plants, trees, shrubs native to eastern Canada, northeastern U.S. Also complete identifying information. 343 illustrations. 544pp. 6½ x 9¼.
25951-X

STORYBOOK MAZES, Dave Phillips. 23 stories and mazes on two-page spreads: Wizard of Oz, Treasure Island, Robin Hood, etc. Solutions. 64pp. 8¼ x 11. 23628-5

AMERICAN NEGRO SONGS: 230 Folk Songs and Spirituals, Religious and Secular, John W. Work. This authoritative study traces the African influences of songs sung and played by black Americans at work, in church, and as entertainment. The author discusses the lyric significance of such songs as "Swing Low, Sweet Chariot," "John Henry," and others and offers the words and music for 230 songs. Bibliography. Index of Song Titles. 272pp. 6½ x 9¼.
40271-1

MOVIE-STAR PORTRAITS OF THE FORTIES, John Kobal (ed.). 163 glamor, studio photos of 106 stars of the 1940s: Rita Hayworth, Ava Gardner, Marlon Brando, Clark Gable, many more. 176pp. 8⅜ x 11¼.
23546-7

BENCHLEY LOST AND FOUND, Robert Benchley. Finest humor from early 30s, about pet peeves, child psychologists, post office and others. Mostly unavailable elsewhere. 73 illustrations by Peter Arno and others. 183pp. 5⅜ x 8½.
22410-4

YEKL and THE IMPORTED BRIDEGROOM AND OTHER STORIES OF YIDDISH NEW YORK, Abraham Cahan. Film Hester Street based on *Yekl* (1896). Novel, other stories among first about Jewish immigrants on N.Y.'s East Side. 240pp. 5⅜ x 8½.
22427-9

SELECTED POEMS, Walt Whitman. Generous sampling from *Leaves of Grass*. Twenty-four poems include "I Hear America Singing," "Song of the Open Road," "I Sing the Body Electric," "When Lilacs Last in the Dooryard Bloom'd," "O Captain! My Captain!"—all reprinted from an authoritative edition. Lists of titles and first lines. 128pp. 5³⁄₁₆ x 8¼.
26878-0

THE BEST TALES OF HOFFMANN, E. T. A. Hoffmann. 10 of Hoffmann's most important stories: "Nutcracker and the King of Mice," "The Golden Flowerpot," etc. 458pp. 5⅜ x 8½. 21793-0

FROM FETISH TO GOD IN ANCIENT EGYPT, E. A. Wallis Budge. Rich detailed survey of Egyptian conception of "God" and gods, magic, cult of animals, Osiris, more. Also, superb English translations of hymns and legends. 240 illustrations. 545pp. 5⅜ x 8½. 25803-3

FRENCH STORIES/CONTES FRANÇAIS: A Dual-Language Book, Wallace Fowlie. Ten stories by French masters, Voltaire to Camus: "Micromegas" by Voltaire; "The Atheist's Mass" by Balzac; "Minuet" by de Maupassant; "The Guest" by Camus, six more. Excellent English translations on facing pages. Also French-English vocabulary list, exercises, more. 352pp. 5⅜ x 8½. 26443-2

CHICAGO AT THE TURN OF THE CENTURY IN PHOTOGRAPHS: 122 Historic Views from the Collections of the Chicago Historical Society, Larry A. Viskochil. Rare large-format prints offer detailed views of City Hall, State Street, the Loop, Hull House, Union Station, many other landmarks, circa 1904-1913. Introduction. Captions. Maps. 144pp. 9⅜ x 12¼. 24656-6

OLD BROOKLYN IN EARLY PHOTOGRAPHS, 1865-1929, William Lee Younger. Luna Park, Gravesend race track, construction of Grand Army Plaza, moving of Hotel Brighton, etc. 157 previously unpublished photographs. 165pp. 8⅞ x 11¾. 23587-4

THE MYTHS OF THE NORTH AMERICAN INDIANS, Lewis Spence. Rich anthology of the myths and legends of the Algonquins, Iroquois, Pawnees and Sioux, prefaced by an extensive historical and ethnological commentary. 36 illustrations. 480pp. 5⅜ x 8½. 25967-6

AN ENCYCLOPEDIA OF BATTLES: Accounts of Over 1,560 Battles from 1479 B.C. to the Present, David Eggenberger. Essential details of every major battle in recorded history from the first battle of Megiddo in 1479 B.C. to Grenada in 1984. List of Battle Maps. New Appendix covering the years 1967-1984. Index. 99 illustrations. 544pp. 6½ x 9¼. 24913-1

SAILING ALONE AROUND THE WORLD, Captain Joshua Slocum. First man to sail around the world, alone, in small boat. One of great feats of seamanship told in delightful manner. 67 illustrations. 294pp. 5⅜ x 8½. 20326-3

ANARCHISM AND OTHER ESSAYS, Emma Goldman. Powerful, penetrating, prophetic essays on direct action, role of minorities, prison reform, puritan hypocrisy, violence, etc. 271pp. 5⅜ x 8½. 22484-8

MYTHS OF THE HINDUS AND BUDDHISTS, Ananda K. Coomaraswamy and Sister Nivedita. Great stories of the epics; deeds of Krishna, Shiva, taken from puranas, Vedas, folk tales; etc. 32 illustrations. 400pp. 5⅜ x 8½. 21759-0

THE TRAUMA OF BIRTH, Otto Rank. Rank's controversial thesis that anxiety neurosis is caused by profound psychological trauma which occurs at birth. 256pp. 5⅜ x 8½. 27974-X

A THEOLOGICO-POLITICAL TREATISE, Benedict Spinoza. Also contains unfinished Political Treatise. Great classic on religious liberty, theory of government on common consent. R. Elwes translation. Total of 421pp. 5⅜ x 8½. 20249-6

MY BONDAGE AND MY FREEDOM, Frederick Douglass. Born a slave, Douglass became outspoken force in antislavery movement. The best of Douglass' autobiographies. Graphic description of slave life. 464pp. 5⅜ x 8½. 22457-0

FOLLOWING THE EQUATOR: A Journey Around the World, Mark Twain. Fascinating humorous account of 1897 voyage to Hawaii, Australia, India, New Zealand, etc. Ironic, bemused reports on peoples, customs, climate, flora and fauna, politics, much more. 197 illustrations. 720pp. 5⅜ x 8½. 26113-1

THE PEOPLE CALLED SHAKERS, Edward D. Andrews. Definitive study of Shakers: origins, beliefs, practices, dances, social organization, furniture and crafts, etc. 33 illustrations. 351pp. 5⅜ x 8½. 21081-2

THE MYTHS OF GREECE AND ROME, H. A. Guerber. A classic of mythology, generously illustrated, long prized for its simple, graphic, accurate retelling of the principal myths of Greece and Rome, and for its commentary on their origins and significance. With 64 illustrations by Michelangelo, Raphael, Titian, Rubens, Canova, Bernini and others. 480pp. 5⅜ x 8½. 27584-1

PSYCHOLOGY OF MUSIC, Carl E. Seashore. Classic work discusses music as a medium from psychological viewpoint. Clear treatment of physical acoustics, auditory apparatus, sound perception, development of musical skills, nature of musical feeling, host of other topics. 88 figures. 408pp. 5⅜ x 8½. 21851-1

THE PHILOSOPHY OF HISTORY, Georg W. Hegel. Great classic of Western thought develops concept that history is not chance but rational process, the evolution of freedom. 457pp. 5⅜ x 8½. 20112-0

THE BOOK OF TEA, Kakuzo Okakura. Minor classic of the Orient: entertaining, charming explanation, interpretation of traditional Japanese culture in terms of tea ceremony. 94pp. 5⅜ x 8½. 20070-1

LIFE IN ANCIENT EGYPT, Adolf Erman. Fullest, most thorough, detailed older account with much not in more recent books, domestic life, religion, magic, medicine, commerce, much more. Many illustrations reproduce tomb paintings, carvings, hieroglyphs, etc. 597pp. 5⅜ x 8½. 22632-8

SUNDIALS, Their Theory and Construction, Albert Waugh. Far and away the best, most thorough coverage of ideas, mathematics concerned, types, construction, adjusting anywhere. Simple, nontechnical treatment allows even children to build several of these dials. Over 100 illustrations. 230pp. 5⅜ x 8½. 22947-5

THEORETICAL HYDRODYNAMICS, L. M. Milne-Thomson. Classic exposition of the mathematical theory of fluid motion, applicable to both hydrodynamics and aerodynamics. Over 600 exercises. 768pp. 6⅛ x 9¼. 68970-0

SONGS OF EXPERIENCE: Facsimile Reproduction with 26 Plates in Full Color, William Blake. 26 full-color plates from a rare 1826 edition. Includes "The Tyger," "London," "Holy Thursday," and other poems. Printed text of poems. 48pp. 5¼ x 7. 24636-1

OLD-TIME VIGNETTES IN FULL COLOR, Carol Belanger Grafton (ed.). Over 390 charming, often sentimental illustrations, selected from archives of Victorian graphics—pretty women posing, children playing, food, flowers, kittens and puppies, smiling cherubs, birds and butterflies, much more. All copyright-free. 48pp. 9¼ x 12¼. 27269-9

PERSPECTIVE FOR ARTISTS, Rex Vicat Cole. Depth, perspective of sky and sea, shadows, much more, not usually covered. 391 diagrams, 81 reproductions of drawings and paintings. 279pp. 5⅜ x 8½.

22487-2

DRAWING THE LIVING FIGURE, Joseph Sheppard. Innovative approach to artistic anatomy focuses on specifics of surface anatomy, rather than muscles and bones. Over 170 drawings of live models in front, back and side views, and in widely varying poses. Accompanying diagrams. 177 illustrations. Introduction. Index. 144pp. 8⅜ x11¼.

26723-7

GOTHIC AND OLD ENGLISH ALPHABETS: 100 Complete Fonts, Dan X. Solo. Add power, elegance to posters, signs, other graphics with 100 stunning copyright-free alphabets: Blackstone, Dolbey, Germania, 97 more—including many lower-case, numerals, punctuation marks. 104pp. 8⅛ x 11.

24695-7

HOW TO DO BEADWORK, Mary White. Fundamental book on craft from simple projects to five-bead chains and woven works. 106 illustrations. 142pp. 5⅞ x 8.

20697-1

THE BOOK OF WOOD CARVING, Charles Marshall Sayers. Finest book for beginners discusses fundamentals and offers 34 designs. "Absolutely first rate . . . well thought out and well executed."–E. J. Tangerman. 118pp. 7¾ x 10⅝.

23654-4

ILLUSTRATED CATALOG OF CIVIL WAR MILITARY GOODS: Union Army Weapons, Insignia, Uniform Accessories, and Other Equipment, Schuyler, Hartley, and Graham. Rare, profusely illustrated 1846 catalog includes Union Army uniform and dress regulations, arms and ammunition, coats, insignia, flags, swords, rifles, etc. 226 illustrations. 160pp. 9 x 12.

24939-5

WOMEN'S FASHIONS OF THE EARLY 1900s: An Unabridged Republication of "New York Fashions, 1909," National Cloak & Suit Co. Rare catalog of mail-order fashions documents women's and children's clothing styles shortly after the turn of the century. Captions offer full descriptions, prices. Invaluable resource for fashion, costume historians. Approximately 725 illustrations. 128pp. 8⅜ x 11¼.

27276-1

THE 1912 AND 1915 GUSTAV STICKLEY FURNITURE CATALOGS, Gustav Stickley. With over 200 detailed illustrations and descriptions, these two catalogs are essential reading and reference materials and identification guides for Stickley furniture. Captions cite materials, dimensions and prices. 112pp. 6½ x 9¼.

26676-1

EARLY AMERICAN LOCOMOTIVES, John H. White, Jr. Finest locomotive engravings from early 19th century: historical (1804–74), main-line (after 1870), special, foreign, etc. 147 plates. 142pp. 11⅜ x 8¼.

22772-3

THE TALL SHIPS OF TODAY IN PHOTOGRAPHS, Frank O. Braynard. Lavishly illustrated tribute to nearly 100 majestic contemporary sailing vessels: Amerigo Vespucci, Clearwater, Constitution, Eagle, Mayflower, Sea Cloud, Victory, many more. Authoritative captions provide statistics, background on each ship. 190 black-and-white photographs and illustrations. Introduction. 128pp. 8⅞ x 11¾.

27163-3

LITTLE BOOK OF EARLY AMERICAN CRAFTS AND TRADES, Peter Stockham (ed.). 1807 children's book explains crafts and trades: baker, hatter, cooper, potter, and many others. 23 copperplate illustrations. 140pp. 4⅝ x 6.   23336-7

VICTORIAN FASHIONS AND COSTUMES FROM HARPER'S BAZAR, 1867–1898, Stella Blum (ed.). Day costumes, evening wear, sports clothes, shoes, hats, other accessories in over 1,000 detailed engravings. 320pp. 9⅜ x 12¼. 22990-4

GUSTAV STICKLEY, THE CRAFTSMAN, Mary Ann Smith. Superb study surveys broad scope of Stickley's achievement, especially in architecture. Design philosophy, rise and fall of the Craftsman empire, descriptions and floor plans for many Craftsman houses, more. 86 black-and-white halftones. 31 line illustrations. Introduction 208pp. 6½ x 9¼.   27210-9

THE LONG ISLAND RAIL ROAD IN EARLY PHOTOGRAPHS, Ron Ziel. Over 220 rare photos, informative text document origin (1844) and development of rail service on Long Island. Vintage views of early trains, locomotives, stations, passengers, crews, much more. Captions. 8⅞ x 11¾.   26301-0

VOYAGE OF THE LIBERDADE, Joshua Slocum. Great 19th-century mariner's thrilling, first-hand account of the wreck of his ship off South America, the 35-foot boat he built from the wreckage, and its remarkable voyage home. 128pp. 5⅜ x 8½.
40022-0

TEN BOOKS ON ARCHITECTURE, Vitruvius. The most important book ever written on architecture. Early Roman aesthetics, technology, classical orders, site selection, all other aspects. Morgan translation. 331pp. 5⅜ x 8½.   20645-9

THE HUMAN FIGURE IN MOTION, Eadweard Muybridge. More than 4,500 stopped-action photos, in action series, showing undraped men, women, children jumping, lying down, throwing, sitting, wrestling, carrying, etc. 390pp. 7⅞ x 10⅝.
20204-6 Clothbd.

TREES OF THE EASTERN AND CENTRAL UNITED STATES AND CANADA, William M. Harlow. Best one-volume guide to 140 trees. Full descriptions, woodlore, range, etc. Over 600 illustrations. Handy size. 288pp. 4½ x 6⅜.   20395-6

SONGS OF WESTERN BIRDS, Dr. Donald J. Borror. Complete song and call repertoire of 60 western species, including flycatchers, juncoes, cactus wrens, many more–includes fully illustrated booklet.   Cassette and manual 99913-0

GROWING AND USING HERBS AND SPICES, Milo Miloradovich. Versatile handbook provides all the information needed for cultivation and use of all the herbs and spices available in North America. 4 illustrations. Index. Glossary. 236pp. 5⅜ x 8½.
25058-X

BIG BOOK OF MAZES AND LABYRINTHS, Walter Shepherd. 50 mazes and labyrinths in all–classical, solid, ripple, and more–in one great volume. Perfect inexpensive puzzler for clever youngsters. Full solutions. 112pp. 8⅛ x 11.   22951-3

PIANO TUNING, J. Cree Fischer. Clearest, best book for beginner, amateur. Simple repairs, raising dropped notes, tuning by easy method of flattened fifths. No previous skills needed. 4 illustrations. 201pp. 5⅜ x 8½.   23267-0

HINTS TO SINGERS, Lillian Nordica. Selecting the right teacher, developing confidence, overcoming stage fright, and many other important skills receive thoughtful discussion in this indispensible guide, written by a world-famous diva of four decades' experience. 96pp. 5⅜ x 8½.   40094-8

THE COMPLETE NONSENSE OF EDWARD LEAR, Edward Lear. All nonsense limericks, zany alphabets, Owl and Pussycat, songs, nonsense botany, etc., illustrated by Lear. Total of 320pp. 5⅜ x 8½. (Available in U.S. only.)   20167-8

VICTORIAN PARLOUR POETRY: An Annotated Anthology, Michael R. Turner. 117 gems by Longfellow, Tennyson, Browning, many lesser-known poets. "The Village Blacksmith," "Curfew Must Not Ring Tonight," "Only a Baby Small," dozens more, often difficult to find elsewhere. Index of poets, titles, first lines. xxiii + 325pp. 5⅜ x 8¼.   27044-0

DUBLINERS, James Joyce. Fifteen stories offer vivid, tightly focused observations of the lives of Dublin's poorer classes. At least one, "The Dead," is considered a masterpiece. Reprinted complete and unabridged from standard edition. 160pp. 5³⁄₁₆ x 8¼.   26870-5

GREAT WEIRD TALES: 14 Stories by Lovecraft, Blackwood, Machen and Others, S. T. Joshi (ed.). 14 spellbinding tales, including "The Sin Eater," by Fiona McLeod, "The Eye Above the Mantel," by Frank Belknap Long, as well as renowned works by R. H. Barlow, Lord Dunsany, Arthur Machen, W. C. Morrow and eight other masters of the genre. 256pp. 5⅜ x 8½. (Available in U.S. only.)   40436-6

THE BOOK OF THE SACRED MAGIC OF ABRAMELIN THE MAGE, translated by S. MacGregor Mathers. Medieval manuscript of ceremonial magic. Basic document in Aleister Crowley, Golden Dawn groups. 268pp. 5⅜ x 8½.   23211-5

NEW RUSSIAN-ENGLISH AND ENGLISH-RUSSIAN DICTIONARY, M. A. O'Brien. This is a remarkably handy Russian dictionary, containing a surprising amount of information, including over 70,000 entries. 366pp. 4½ x 6⅛.   20208-9

HISTORIC HOMES OF THE AMERICAN PRESIDENTS, Second, Revised Edition, Irvin Haas. A traveler's guide to American Presidential homes, most open to the public, depicting and describing homes occupied by every American President from George Washington to George Bush. With visiting hours, admission charges, travel routes. 175 photographs. Index. 160pp. 8¼ x 11.   26751-2

NEW YORK IN THE FORTIES, Andreas Feininger. 162 brilliant photographs by the well-known photographer, formerly with *Life* magazine. Commuters, shoppers, Times Square at night, much else from city at its peak. Captions by John von Hartz. 181pp. 9¼ x 10¾.   23585-8

INDIAN SIGN LANGUAGE, William Tomkins. Over 525 signs developed by Sioux and other tribes. Written instructions and diagrams. Also 290 pictographs. 111pp. 6⅛ x 9¼.   22029-X

ANATOMY: A Complete Guide for Artists, Joseph Sheppard. A master of figure drawing shows artists how to render human anatomy convincingly. Over 460 illustrations. 224pp. 8⅜ x 11¼. 27279-6

MEDIEVAL CALLIGRAPHY: Its History and Technique, Marc Drogin. Spirited history, comprehensive instruction manual covers 13 styles (ca. 4th century through 15th). Excellent photographs; directions for duplicating medieval techniques with modern tools. 224pp. 8⅜ x 11¼. 26142-5

DRIED FLOWERS: How to Prepare Them, Sarah Whitlock and Martha Rankin. Complete instructions on how to use silica gel, meal and borax, perlite aggregate, sand and borax, glycerine and water to create attractive permanent flower arrangements. 12 illustrations. 32pp. 5⅜ x 8½. 21802-3

EASY-TO-MAKE BIRD FEEDERS FOR WOODWORKERS, Scott D. Campbell. Detailed, simple-to-use guide for designing, constructing, caring for and using feeders. Text, illustrations for 12 classic and contemporary designs. 96pp. 5⅜ x 8½. 25847-5

SCOTTISH WONDER TALES FROM MYTH AND LEGEND, Donald A. Mackenzie. 16 lively tales tell of giants rumbling down mountainsides, of a magic wand that turns stone pillars into warriors, of gods and goddesses, evil hags, powerful forces and more. 240pp. 5⅜ x 8½. 29677-6

THE HISTORY OF UNDERCLOTHES, C. Willett Cunnington and Phyllis Cunnington. Fascinating, well-documented survey covering six centuries of English undergarments, enhanced with over 100 illustrations: 12th-century laced-up bodice, footed long drawers (1795), 19th-century bustles, 19th-century corsets for men, Victorian "bust improvers," much more. 272pp. 5⅜ x 8¼. 27124-2

ARTS AND CRAFTS FURNITURE: The Complete Brooks Catalog of 1912, Brooks Manufacturing Co. Photos and detailed descriptions of more than 150 now very collectible furniture designs from the Arts and Crafts movement depict davenports, settees, buffets, desks, tables, chairs, bedsteads, dressers and more, all built of solid, quarter-sawed oak. Invaluable for students and enthusiasts of antiques, Americana and the decorative arts. 80pp. 6½ x 9¼. 27471-3

WILBUR AND ORVILLE: A Biography of the Wright Brothers, Fred Howard. Definitive, crisply written study tells the full story of the brothers' lives and work. A vividly written biography, unparalleled in scope and color, that also captures the spirit of an extraordinary era. 560pp. 6⅛ x 9¼. 40297-5

THE ARTS OF THE SAILOR: Knotting, Splicing and Ropework, Hervey Garrett Smith. Indispensable shipboard reference covers tools, basic knots and useful hitches; handsewing and canvas work, more. Over 100 illustrations. Delightful reading for sea lovers. 256pp. 5⅜ x 8½. 26440-8

FRANK LLOYD WRIGHT'S FALLINGWATER: The House and Its History, Second, Revised Edition, Donald Hoffmann. A total revision—both in text and illustrations—of the standard document on Fallingwater, the boldest, most personal architectural statement of Wright's mature years, updated with valuable new material from the recently opened Frank Lloyd Wright Archives. "Fascinating"–*The New York Times*. 116 illustrations. 128pp. 9¼ x 10¾. 27430-6

PHOTOGRAPHIC SKETCHBOOK OF THE CIVIL WAR, Alexander Gardner. 100 photos taken on field during the Civil War. Famous shots of Manassas Harper's Ferry, Lincoln, Richmond, slave pens, etc. 244pp. 10⅝ x 8¼. 22731-6

FIVE ACRES AND INDEPENDENCE, Maurice G. Kains. Great back-to-the-land classic explains basics of self-sufficient farming. The one book to get. 95 illustrations. 397pp. 5⅜ x 8½. 20974-1

SONGS OF EASTERN BIRDS, Dr. Donald J. Borror. Songs and calls of 60 species most common to eastern U.S.: warblers, woodpeckers, flycatchers, thrushes, larks, many more in high-quality recording. Cassette and manual 99912-2

A MODERN HERBAL, Margaret Grieve. Much the fullest, most exact, most useful compilation of herbal material. Gigantic alphabetical encyclopedia, from aconite to zedoary, gives botanical information, medical properties, folklore, economic uses, much else. Indispensable to serious reader. 161 illustrations. 888pp. 6½ x 9¼. 2-vol. set. (Available in U.S. only.) Vol. I: 22798-7
Vol. II: 22799-5

HIDDEN TREASURE MAZE BOOK, Dave Phillips. Solve 34 challenging mazes accompanied by heroic tales of adventure. Evil dragons, people-eating plants, blood-thirsty giants, many more dangerous adversaries lurk at every twist and turn. 34 mazes, stories, solutions. 48pp. 8¼ x 11. 24566-7

LETTERS OF W. A. MOZART, Wolfgang A. Mozart. Remarkable letters show bawdy wit, humor, imagination, musical insights, contemporary musical world; includes some letters from Leopold Mozart. 276pp. 5⅜ x 8½. 22859-2

BASIC PRINCIPLES OF CLASSICAL BALLET, Agrippina Vaganova. Great Russian theoretician, teacher explains methods for teaching classical ballet. 118 illus-trations. 175pp. 5⅜ x 8½. 22036-2

THE JUMPING FROG, Mark Twain. Revenge edition. The original story of The Celebrated Jumping Frog of Calaveras County, a hapless French translation, and Twain's hilarious "retranslation" from the French. 12 illustrations. 66pp. 5⅜ x 8½. 22686-7

BEST REMEMBERED POEMS, Martin Gardner (ed.). The 126 poems in this superb collection of 19th- and 20th-century British and American verse range from Shelley's "To a Skylark" to the impassioned "Renascence" of Edna St. Vincent Millay and to Edward Lear's whimsical "The Owl and the Pussycat." 224pp. 5⅜ x 8½. 27165-X

COMPLETE SONNETS, William Shakespeare. Over 150 exquisite poems deal with love, friendship, the tyranny of time, beauty's evanescence, death and other themes in language of remarkable power, precision and beauty. Glossary of archaic terms. 80pp. 5³⁄₁₆ x 8¼. 26686-9

THE BATTLES THAT CHANGED HISTORY, Fletcher Pratt. Eminent historian profiles 16 crucial conflicts, ancient to modern, that changed the course of civiliza-tion. 352pp. 5⅜ x 8½. 41129-X

THE WIT AND HUMOR OF OSCAR WILDE, Alvin Redman (ed.). More than 1,000 ripostes, paradoxes, wisecracks: Work is the curse of the drinking classes; I can resist everything except temptation; etc. 258pp. 5⅜ x 8½. 20602-5

SHAKESPEARE LEXICON AND QUOTATION DICTIONARY, Alexander Schmidt. Full definitions, locations, shades of meaning in every word in plays and poems. More than 50,000 exact quotations. 1,485pp. 6½ x 9¼. 2-vol. set.
Vol. 1: 22726-X
Vol. 2: 22727-8

SELECTED POEMS, Emily Dickinson. Over 100 best-known, best-loved poems by one of America's foremost poets, reprinted from authoritative early editions. No comparable edition at this price. Index of first lines. 64pp. 5³⁄₁₆ x 8¼. 26466-1

THE INSIDIOUS DR. FU-MANCHU, Sax Rohmer. The first of the popular mystery series introduces a pair of English detectives to their archnemesis, the diabolical Dr. Fu-Manchu. Flavorful atmosphere, fast-paced action, and colorful characters enliven this classic of the genre. 208pp. 5³⁄₁₆ x 8¼. 29898-1

THE MALLEUS MALEFICARUM OF KRAMER AND SPRENGER, translated by Montague Summers. Full text of most important witchhunter's "bible," used by both Catholics and Protestants. 278pp. 6⅝ x 10. 22802-9

SPANISH STORIES/CUENTOS ESPAÑOLES: A Dual-Language Book, Angel Flores (ed.). Unique format offers 13 great stories in Spanish by Cervantes, Borges, others. Faithful English translations on facing pages. 352pp. 5⅜ x 8½. 25399-6

GARDEN CITY, LONG ISLAND, IN EARLY PHOTOGRAPHS, 1869–1919, Mildred H. Smith. Handsome treasury of 118 vintage pictures, accompanied by carefully researched captions, document the Garden City Hotel fire (1899), the Vanderbilt Cup Race (1908), the first airmail flight departing from the Nassau Boulevard Aerodrome (1911), and much more. 96pp. 8⅞ x 11¾. 40669-5

OLD QUEENS, N.Y., IN EARLY PHOTOGRAPHS, Vincent F. Seyfried and William Asadorian. Over 160 rare photographs of Maspeth, Jamaica, Jackson Heights, and other areas. Vintage views of DeWitt Clinton mansion, 1939 World's Fair and more. Captions. 192pp. 8⅞ x 11. 26358-4

CAPTURED BY THE INDIANS: 15 Firsthand Accounts, 1750-1870, Frederick Drimmer. Astounding true historical accounts of grisly torture, bloody conflicts, relentless pursuits, miraculous escapes and more, by people who lived to tell the tale. 384pp. 5⅜ x 8½. 24901-8

THE WORLD'S GREAT SPEECHES (Fourth Enlarged Edition), Lewis Copeland, Lawrence W. Lamm, and Stephen J. McKenna. Nearly 300 speeches provide public speakers with a wealth of updated quotes and inspiration–from Pericles' funeral oration and William Jennings Bryan's "Cross of Gold Speech" to Malcolm X's powerful words on the Black Revolution and Earl of Spenser's tribute to his sister, Diana, Princess of Wales. 944pp. 5⅜ x 8⅜. 40903-1

THE BOOK OF THE SWORD, Sir Richard F. Burton. Great Victorian scholar/adventurer's eloquent, erudite history of the "queen of weapons"–from prehistory to early Roman Empire. Evolution and development of early swords, variations (sabre, broadsword, cutlass, scimitar, etc.), much more. 336pp. 6⅛ x 9¼. 25434-8

AUTOBIOGRAPHY: The Story of My Experiments with Truth, Mohandas K. Gandhi. Boyhood, legal studies, purification, the growth of the Satyagraha (nonviolent protest) movement. Critical, inspiring work of the man responsible for the freedom of India. 480pp. 5⅜ x 8½. (Available in U.S. only.)   24593-4

CELTIC MYTHS AND LEGENDS, T. W. Rolleston. Masterful retelling of Irish and Welsh stories and tales. Cuchulain, King Arthur, Deirdre, the Grail, many more. First paperback edition. 58 full-page illustrations. 512pp. 5⅜ x 8½.   26507-2

THE PRINCIPLES OF PSYCHOLOGY, William James. Famous long course complete, unabridged. Stream of thought, time perception, memory, experimental methods; great work decades ahead of its time. 94 figures. 1,391pp. 5⅜ x 8½. 2-vol. set.
Vol. I: 20381-6   Vol. II: 20382-4

THE WORLD AS WILL AND REPRESENTATION, Arthur Schopenhauer. Definitive English translation of Schopenhauer's life work, correcting more than 1,000 errors, omissions in earlier translations. Translated by E. F. J. Payne. Total of 1,269pp. 5⅜ x 8½. 2-vol. set.   Vol. 1: 21761-2   Vol. 2: 21762-0

MAGIC AND MYSTERY IN TIBET, Madame Alexandra David-Neel. Experiences among lamas, magicians, sages, sorcerers, Bonpa wizards. A true psychic discovery. 32 illustrations. 321pp. 5⅜ x 8½. (Available in U.S. only.)   22682-4

THE EGYPTIAN BOOK OF THE DEAD, E. A. Wallis Budge. Complete reproduction of Ani's papyrus, finest ever found. Full hieroglyphic text, interlinear transliteration, word-for-word translation, smooth translation. 533pp. 6½ x 9¼.   21866-X

MATHEMATICS FOR THE NONMATHEMATICIAN, Morris Kline. Detailed, college-level treatment of mathematics in cultural and historical context, with numerous exercises. Recommended Reading Lists. Tables. Numerous figures. 641pp. 5⅜ x 8½.   24823-2

PROBABILISTIC METHODS IN THE THEORY OF STRUCTURES, Isaac Elishakoff. Well-written introduction covers the elements of the theory of probability from two or more random variables, the reliability of such multivariable structures, the theory of random function, Monte Carlo methods of treating problems incapable of exact solution, and more. Examples. 502pp. 5⅜ x 8½.   40691-1

THE RIME OF THE ANCIENT MARINER, Gustave Doré, S. T. Coleridge. Doré's finest work; 34 plates capture moods, subtleties of poem. Flawless full-size reproductions printed on facing pages with authoritative text of poem. "Beautiful. Simply beautiful."—*Publisher's Weekly.* 77pp. 9¼ x 12.   22305-1

NORTH AMERICAN INDIAN DESIGNS FOR ARTISTS AND CRAFTSPEOPLE, Eva Wilson. Over 360 authentic copyright-free designs adapted from Navajo blankets, Hopi pottery, Sioux buffalo hides, more. Geometrics, symbolic figures, plant and animal motifs, etc. 128pp. 8⅜ x 11. (Not for sale in the United Kingdom.)   25341-4

SCULPTURE: Principles and Practice, Louis Slobodkin. Step-by-step approach to clay, plaster, metals, stone; classical and modern. 253 drawings, photos. 255pp. 8⅛ x 11.   22960-2

THE INFLUENCE OF SEA POWER UPON HISTORY, 1660–1783, A. T. Mahan. Influential classic of naval history and tactics still used as text in war colleges. First paperback edition. 4 maps. 24 battle plans. 640pp. 5⅜ x 8½.   25509-3

CATALOG OF DOVER BOOKS

THE STORY OF THE TITANIC AS TOLD BY ITS SURVIVORS, Jack Winocour (ed.). What it was really like. Panic, despair, shocking inefficiency, and a little heroism. More thrilling than any fictional account. 26 illustrations. 320pp. 5⅜ x 8½.
20610-6

FAIRY AND FOLK TALES OF THE IRISH PEASANTRY, William Butler Yeats (ed.). Treasury of 64 tales from the twilight world of Celtic myth and legend: "The Soul Cages," "The Kildare Pooka," "King O'Toole and his Goose," many more. Introduction and Notes by W. B. Yeats. 352pp. 5⅜ x 8½.
26941-8

BUDDHIST MAHAYANA TEXTS, E. B. Cowell and others (eds.). Superb, accurate translations of basic documents in Mahayana Buddhism, highly important in history of religions. The Buddha-karita of Asvaghosha, Larger Sukhavativyuha, more. 448pp. 5⅜ x 8½.
25552-2

ONE TWO THREE . . . INFINITY: Facts and Speculations of Science, George Gamow. Great physicist's fascinating, readable overview of contemporary science: number theory, relativity, fourth dimension, entropy, genes, atomic structure, much more. 128 illustrations. Index. 352pp. 5⅜ x 8½.
25664-2

EXPERIMENTATION AND MEASUREMENT, W. J. Youden. Introductory manual explains laws of measurement in simple terms and offers tips for achieving accuracy and minimizing errors. Mathematics of measurement, use of instruments, experimenting with machines. 1994 edition. Foreword. Preface. Introduction. Epilogue. Selected Readings. Glossary. Index. Tables and figures. 128pp. 5⅜ x 8½.   40451-X

DALÍ ON MODERN ART: The Cuckolds of Antiquated Modern Art, Salvador Dalí. Influential painter skewers modern art and its practitioners. Outrageous evaluations of Picasso, Cézanne, Turner, more. 15 renderings of paintings discussed. 44 calligraphic decorations by Dalí. 96pp. 5⅜ x 8½. (Available in U.S. only.)   29220-7

ANTIQUE PLAYING CARDS: A Pictorial History, Henry René D'Allemagne. Over 900 elaborate, decorative images from rare playing cards (14th–20th centuries): Bacchus, death, dancing dogs, hunting scenes, royal coats of arms, players cheating, much more. 96pp. 9¼ x 12¼.
29265-7

MAKING FURNITURE MASTERPIECES: 30 Projects with Measured Drawings, Franklin H. Gottshall. Step-by-step instructions, illustrations for constructing handsome, useful pieces, among them a Sheraton desk, Chippendale chair, Spanish desk, Queen Anne table and a William and Mary dressing mirror. 224pp. 8¼ x 11¼.
29338-6

THE FOSSIL BOOK: A Record of Prehistoric Life, Patricia V. Rich et al. Profusely illustrated definitive guide covers everything from single-celled organisms and dinosaurs to birds and mammals and the interplay between climate and man. Over 1,500 illustrations. 760pp. 7½ x 10⅛.
29371-8

Paperbound unless otherwise indicated. Available at your book dealer, online at **www.doverpublications.com**, or by writing to Dept. GI, Dover Publications, Inc., 31 East 2nd Street, Mineola, NY 11501. For current price information or for free catalogues (please indicate field of interest), write to Dover Publications or log on to **www.doverpublications.com** and see every Dover book in print. Dover publishes more than 500 books each year on science, elementary and advanced mathematics, biology, music, art, literary history, social sciences, and other areas.